Fighting Words

Persuasive Strategies for War and Politics

Richard F. Miller

SB

Savas Beatie

New York and California

Cataloging-in-Publication Data is available from the Library of Congress.

ISBN 978-1-932714-78-4

05 04 03 02 01   5 4 3 2 1
First edition, first printing

SB

Published by
Savas Beatie LLC
521 Fifth Avenue, Suite 1700
New York, NY 10175

Editorial Offices:

Savas Beatie LLC
P.O. Box 4527
El Dorado Hills, CA 95762
Phone: 916-941-6896
(E-mail) editorial@savasbeatie.com

Savas Beatie titles are available at special discounts for bulk purchases in the United States by corporations, institutions, and other organizations. For more details, please contact Special Sales, P.O. Box 4527, El Dorado Hills, CA 95762, or e-mail your inquires or orders to sales@savasbeatie.com, or visit our website at www.savasbeatie.com for additional information.

Contents

Contents (continued)

Contents (continued)

Section Five
Speechlets

Section Six
Three Speeches by President Barack Obama

Contents (continued)

Acknowledgments

My interest in military rhetoric grew over the course of four stints as a journalist embedded with U.S. forces in Iraq and Afghanistan. My thanks are gratefully tendered to the men and women of the USS *Kitty Hawk* (Persian Gulf, 2003), Third Battalion, Eighth Marine Regiment (Fallujah, Iraq, 2005), 3rd Heavy Brigade Combat Team, 4th ID (Baqubah, Iraq, 2006) and most recently in Afghanistan with the 101st Airborne Division (Air Assault), (Paktia Province, FOBs Salerno, Lightning, Boris and Fire Base Shkin, 2008.) As I noted in another forum, this is very much their book. I only took notes.

None of this would have been possible without the support, trust and love of my family. To my wife Alyson, and children Eli, Caroline, and Pesha, I can only offer this expression of love and gratitude, a miserable token in exchange for all that they have given me.

I wish to thank Ellen Ratner of Talk Radio News Service, Inc., for sponsoring these assignments. I am likewise grateful to William M. Fowler, Jr., Distinguished Professor of History at Northeastern University, and a colleague at the New England Quarterly, for his generosity with sources and advice. History cannot be written without libraries or librarians, and my thanks to the staffs at Harvard University's Houghton Library, and of course, the great Widener; thanks, too, to the staff of the Concord (Massachusetts) Free Public Library.

Over the years the house of Savas Beatie has published a string of award-winning, narrative military histories and reference works. Whatever the merits of my book, it is certainly cut from different cloth, and I am grateful to Theodore P. Savas's willingness to lend his firm's imprimatur to this effort. I also wish to thank editor Robert Ayer, whose advice, comments, and corrections helped convert often formless, beat-missing prose into something coherent. Also, my thanks to Sarah Keeney, marketing director at Savas Beatie, for all of her good work in positioning this title for maximum exposure.

I would like to add a few words about the man to whom this book is dedicated, my father, Samuel H. Miller. He was for many years a volunteer speaker-fundraiser for the United Jewish Appeal, raising money for Israel at times when that country's existence was genuinely imperiled. (I have especially vivid memories of his exhortations during the Six Day and Yom Kippur Wars.) Successfully persuading people to give their money may not be as difficult as asking them to give their life, but it is still very difficult.

But there was much more to my father in this connection. For sixty-four years he has worked for the same mid-western real estate company. His job is land acquisition, and during the course of six decades has often represented his company at hundreds of public zoning meetings. His purpose was always the same: to persuade voters or their elected representatives to approve land use changes for company projects. As a boy it was my occasional privilege to accompany him to these meetings.

For good and bad reasons, people often fear change, and these assemblies could be extremely contentious. These were the days before the stultifying hand of political correctness had begun to pinch robust (and often brutal) public expression. To a young boy sitting anonymously among the audience, this unbridled exercise of free speech could be frightening. However, I was always reassured by my father's ability to "read" his audience, empathize with its concerns and speak to its members in their "own" language whether that was the commonsense speech of blue-collar workers or the arcana of zoning experts. Before these meetings, my father would brief me on the projects, the opposition, the politics, and the case that he planned to make. Afterwards, he would discuss how the meeting had gone and why this or that persuasive strategy had failed or succeeded. It is a great blessing to note that as my father prepares to enter his tenth decade of life, he is still called upon to grace a dais and say a few words. To me he will always remain the master of persuasive strategies.

Finally, I wish to thank *Hakadosh Baruch Hu,* who has preserved me to this very moment and has blessed my life with the people and institutions that I have just acknowledged.

Guard your tongue from evil, and your lips from speaking deceit.
Psalm 34:13

To my father, Samuel H. Miller, with love

Introduction

I. Why This Book is Necessary

We live in the Age of Argument. This should not be confused with an Age of Rhetoric, at least of the style that our nineteenth-century forbears would have recognized. Most of that eloquence—along with the time necessary to craft polished sentences and to articulate with perfect diction and in carefully measured cadences—has long since vanished, left behind by rapidly evolving technology and its ubiquitous bequests: hard-pounding, bare-knuckled arguments, sound bites, and, above all, relentless onslaughts of imagery. Today the well of the United States Senate is probably the last place most Americans would look for persuasive argument. If we have no Clays, Websters or Calhouns, it is because we are no longer a willing (or sufficiently educated) audience. Instead, live-casting the disaster *du jour* or "flooding the zone" with images has long since trumped Ciceronian-tempered orators in sheer ability to move the masses. Never until now was a picture—or a video clip—*really* worth a thousand words, simultaneously in a hundred million minds.

Yet no matter how conveyed, most of what we (Americans) bemoan or exploit as hyper-partisanship, cultural warfare, or a nation "sliced" (but only by meme makers) into blue, red or purple states still unfolds in arguments that daily fill newsprint, ether, cyberspace and public squares. The Internet has decentered the mass media and enfranchised millions worldwide in a dynamic that makes Everyman a journalist and editorialist. "Of making many books there is no end," Solomon declared in Ecclesiastes. Today he would have added blogs.[1]

Argument is more than a presidential debate, political blog, newspaper editorial or heated disagreement during Thanksgiving dinner. In fact, all narratives and stories are arguments, and every argument tells a story and contains a narrative. An argument's story is simply an effort to persuade, an attempt to direct action or confirm or change attitudes. Anything that attempts to do that—from the mugger's gun in your face to reading aloud a pointless book report solely to persuade some teacher that the homework was done—is an argument. *It does not have to argue for anything in particular; its mere existence argues for something.* And as long as there are human beings, the existence of anything will argue for something. Even fanatic nihilists extol a beautiful sunset.

When modern advertising is included, arguments are ubiquitous, relentless, aggressive, and, like a dreaded diagnosis, still there in the morning. Our dollars, votes, loyalties, time, and health, our opinions about some elite's gaffe *du jour*, war, peace, and pandemics, are targeted by all comers—including ourselves, each time we silently deliberate some matter.

Why this is so makes interesting questions of historical moment and culture. Western-modeled societies are wealthy; thus, we have abundant resources produced by an economic system whose vitality depends on our abilities to persuade one another to part with resources. Voters elect their governments in most Western-modeled states; influencing these voters is important to many people, from vote-seeking politicians to terrorists seeking to exhaust a nation's will. Our wealth and self-determination have produced historically unprecedented access to education, which has increased literacy. Life expectancies have lengthened, and with them the amount of leisure time available to fill new hours. And certainly one fruit of leisure time is more argument, as life's preoccupations shift from grim struggles over watering holes and hunting grounds to more abstract concerns.

But if arguments are to be found everywhere, and thus reflect the human condition, the reason is to be found in culture, not wealth, power or technology. Since this particular topic is far larger than this book, I will be brief and quote others.

---

1 Ecclesiastes, KJV, 12:12.

'A *culture* . . . refers to a body of socially transmitted information'—the full spectrum of ideas, concepts and skills that is available to us as a society. It includes science and mathematics, carpentry and engineering designs, literature and viticulture, systems of musical notation, advertisements and philosophical theories—in short, the collective product of human activities and thought [italic original].[2]

Cultures are in constant flux (although different cultures flux at different rates). Why cultural changes occur is a topic also beyond this book, so here I will quote Diogenes Laertius paraphrasing Heraclitus and be done with it:

> Change is the road leading upward and the road leading downward; and that the whole world exists according to it.[3]

One reason why Fighting Words *is necessary is that significant cultural change ultimately occurs through argument and persuasion.* Pick any metaphor you like: culture as Coliseum, ideas as gladiators; culture as market place, ideas as products; culture as bordello, ideas as seductresses. The point is that persuasion is one important means by which change occurs, whether by word or deed, at the point of a sword, by avarice, or by more titillating means.

I could rest the case for necessity here. But there are still other reasons why this book is necessary. *Fighting Words* seeks to provide readers with an analytical reference applicable to whatever arguments they are hearing, watching or reading. To do this, I will analyze speeches of a very special kind— battle speeches—and try to draw some general conclusions about how arguments work. But my analysis also extends beyond arguments as models of rhetoric, for how arguments "work" cannot be separated from the fact that they are cultural and historical artifacts pinned to their moments of creation. And yet, while King Solomon declared, "And there is no new thing under the sun," the fact is that Ecclesiastes was new when Solomon wrote it, and his argument about worldly vanity and changelessness changed something, if only by preserving his ideas for later generations.[4]

---

2 Kate Dustin, *The Selfish Meme: A Critical Assessment* (New York: Cambridge University Press, 2005), 2.

3 Diogenes Laertius, *The Lives and Opinions of Eminent Philosophers*, translated by C.D. Yonge (London: George Bell and Sons, 1901), XI.vi, (p. 379).

4 Ecclesiastes, KJV, 1:9.

Thus, despite historical differences, some things about persuading human beings appear to be seamless and timeless. In this spirit, my final chapter will apply some battle speech persuasive strategies to an analysis of three speeches by President Barack Obama: his Inaugural Address, his speech on health care reform to a joint session of Congress, and his eulogy given after the shootings at Fort Hood. My analysis is not uncritical, but my criticisms are limited to matters of rhetorical form and structure, sometimes in an effort to elucidate underlying messages. Thus, partisans of any stripe should be aware that my comments are bereft of all political or policy content. One of the reigning pieties of our age, that the "personal is political," is temporarily suspended between the covers of this book. My interest lies solely in the persuasive strategies that President Obama used to convey his message. I have chosen Obama's speeches over those of, say, Dwight Eisenhower or Andrew Jackson but not because they are historically exceptional speeches. Indeed, with the arguable exception of his Inaugural Address, President Obama's speeches are often unexceptional, marked by an absence of memorable phrases and striking metaphors but replete with rambling narratives (and its first cousin, overlong) as well as surprising inconsistencies in message. Instead, I chose Obama's speeches because they are likely to be more familiar to readers. Thus, choosing Obama was a "persuasive strategy" of my own.

II. Why Battle Speeches?

It is unsurprising that secular history's first detailed account of a battle contains battle speeches. The *Annals of Thutmose* chronicles the story of the May 15, 1479, BCE Battle of Megiddo in which the Egyptians led by Thutmose III battled an alliance of Syrian kings. Establishing (or probably extending) a practice that continues to this day, Thutmose's royal chroniclers recorded their master's words as well as deeds. Thutmose issued pre-battle instructions ("Prepare yourselves; make ready your weapons, for one is to advance to fight with this wretched enemy in the morning") and delivered a midst-of-battle speech: "[F]or it is the capture of a thousand cities, the capture of Megiddo. Capture ye, capture ye, thoroughly!" Without torturing the admittedly spare text, it is clear that Thutmose (or his annalists) embraced several battle speech themes that were probably already hoary by then, but certainly have become so since: dealing with eve-of-battle anxiety, disparaging one's enemy, and exhorting soldiers to fight longer and harder. Both Thutmose III and any given

Commandant of the United States Marine Corps have understood that raising, training, and fighting soldiers requires talking to them.[5]

But there is more to battle speeches than even these practicalities. Few situations rival war's concentration of varieties of human experience. There is *love* (comrades, country, faith, family), *hate* (the enemy), *aggression* (destroying people and property), *revenge* (for enemy misdeeds), *fear* (of one's own death or injury, or of having to kill others), *guilt or shame* (at having taken life, for merely having survived, or at failing in one's duty), *rage* (at the random distribution of death and injury, anonymous death, or the blurred distinctions between combatants and noncombatants), *exhilaration* (at experiencing combat-induced adrenal secretions), *fatigue* (due to prolonged sleeplessness, exposure to the elements, poor nutrition and extreme stress), *and moral numbness* (indifference to the sight of dead bodies, destroyed property, or civilian suffering).

It is to be expected that battle speeches would incorporate these experiences and use them in persuasive strategies meant to motivate listeners to do things that otherwise transgress civilian norms. Speeches from politics, law and commerce can be supremely consequential; but in their ordinary course, few such speeches recruit, train, and exhort their listeners to die—or, to paraphrase George Patton, Jr., to make the other son-of-a-bitch die instead. In short, one reason that battle persuasive strategies are worth studying is that they are *inherently* interesting: birthed in intense drama, their stakes are often high.[6]

Battle speech persuasive strategies must exploit this extraordinary range of human experience with a concision unknown to most other orations or writings. Such concision is necessary: before invasions or battles or while in combat, there is no time for extended speeches. Even for speeches given when combat is not imminent (for example, Post-Battle Speeches), the need to regroup, refresh, or grieve losses still rewards concision. Ample narratives that describe the extremes of human experience are usually reserved for films, feature journalism or novels; battle speeches must also address extremes of experience, but must do it in sentences, not chapters or reels. The result is highly distilled rhetoric.

---

5   Harold Hayden Nelson, *The Battle of Megiddo, A Dissertation Submitted to the Faculty of the Graduate School of Arts and Literature in Candidacy for the Degree of the Doctor of Philosophy* (Chicago: Private Edition, Distributed by the University of Chicago Libraries, 1913), Urk 656 (pages 30-31), Urk 660 (page 45).

6   Martin Blumenson, *Patton: The Man Behind the Legend, 1885-1945* (New York: Quill Press, 1985), 220.

How battle speeches achieve concision is discussed in a later section. What I wish briefly to illustrate here is that concision itself. Consider the density of meaning of a "full-length" battle speech—not, for example, "Remember the Alamo!" but a multi-paragraph narrative intended to convey complex meaning. The situation confronting General Matthew B. Ridgway in Korea in January 1951 required just such a speech. He had assumed command of the troubled U.S. Eighth Army the month before; later, he wrote that "[b]efore Eighth Army could return to the offensive it needed to have its fighting spirit restored, to have pride in itself, to feel confidence in its leadership and have faith in its mission." Ridgway began transforming the army by replacing defeatist, incapable, or exhausted officers; but his task also required re-moralizing the rank and file. And Ridgway believed that one reason why his soldiers were demoralized lay in their confusion about the Korean War's political objectives.[7]

Since the fall of the Berlin Wall it is easy to assume that American soldiers always understood what was at stake in the Cold War, especially during its periodic hot phases. But this was not necessarily true during the Korean War. For many soldiers, that conflict—unwisely labeled from the start "a police action"—had promised short tours and a second-rate enemy; instead, what soldiers found was brutal, relentless combat against a brave and determined enemy entirely unafraid of American uniforms. Moreover, to many Americans Korea itself seemed just as it had been in the hours before June 25, 1950 when the North Koreans had attacked south across the 38th Parallel: an unknown, faraway land that (as some American political leaders had imprudently implied) lay outside of U.S. national interests. It was part of Matthew Ridgway's job to explain to his soldiers why Korea was important, so important that it was worth dying for. In short, it was time for a battle speech.[8]

Entitled "Why We Are Here," Ridgway first converted his experiences being questioned by his troops into Questions from Everyman. "In my brief period of command duty here I have heard from several sources, chiefly from members of combat units, the questions, 'Why are we here?' 'What are we fighting for?'"

---

7 Clay Blair, *The Forgotten War: America in Korea, 1950-1953* (Annapolis: Naval Institute Press, 1987), 571-572, 580-581, 649-650.

8 Blair, *The Forgotten War*, 53-54 (Truman speech, Acheson press conference), 54-55 (Connolly interview).

"The second question [What are we fighting for?] is of much greater significance," Ridgway continued, "and every member of this command is entitled to a full and reasoned answer. Mine follows." He then proceeded to explain why it was necessary for his soldiers to die, kill, endure frostbite, or risk execution as POWs at the hands of North Koreans. Of course, he did not specify these possibilities; there was no need, as the questions had come from combat units, not green soldiers. Bitter experience already had acquainted them with the dark side. Ridgway's answer to Everyman was a model of concise battle rhetoric:

5. To me the issues are clear. It is not a question of this or that Korean town or village. Real estate is, here, incidental. It is not restricted to the issue of freedom for our South Korean Allies, whose fidelity and valor under the severest stresses of battle we recognize; though that freedom is a symbol of the wider issues, and included among them.

6. The real issues are whether the power of Western civilization, as God has permitted it to flower in our beloved lands, shall defy and defeat Communism; whether the rule of men who shoot their prisoners, enslave their citizens, and deride the dignity of man, shall displace the rule of those to whom the individual and his individual rights are sacred; whether we are to survive with God's hand to guide and lead us, or to perish in the dead existence of a Godless world.

7. If these be true, and to me they are, beyond any possibility of challenge, then this has long ceased to be a fight for our Korean Allies and for their potential national survival. It has become, and it continues to be, a fight for our own freedom, and for our own survival, in an honorable, independent national existence.

8. The sacrifices we have made, and those which we shall yet support, are not offered vicariously for others, but in our direct defense.

9. In the final analysis, the issue now joined right here in Korea is whether Communism or individual freedom shall prevail, and, make no mistake, whether the next flight of fear-driven people we have just witnessed across the HAN [River], and continue to witness in other areas shall be checked and defeated overseas or permitted, step by step, to close in on our own homeland and at some future time, however distant, engulf our own loved ones in all its misery and despair.

10. These are the things for which we fight. Never have members of any military command had a greater challenge than we, or a finer opportunity to show ourselves and our people at their best—and thus be an honor to the profession of arms, and a credit to those who bred us.

Ridgway then ordered that these words be distributed to "every single member of his command at the earliest practicable moment." Many historians believe that this speech was an important contribution to re-moralizing the Eighth Army and transforming it into an efficient fighting force.[9]

Here I do not wish to give an extended analysis, but only to make the larger point about battle speech concision and its thematic density. Compared with some other genres of speech, battle speeches present persuasive strategies "in the clear," without having to swim through oceans of verbiage. In a mere 369 words Ridgway successfully appealed to: family, home and hearth, God and country; protecting the values of Western civilization, and individual and collective rights; and (implicitly) the Good Samaritan trope, refocusing his men away from the culturally strange (to Americans) rural peasantry and desolate landscape of Korea toward the larger picture of the enemy's worldwide menace. Astute readers will also detect in Ridgway's speech important themes that would dominate *political* discussion of the Cold War for the next four decades: he referred to the necessity of fighting Communism abroad to avoid having to fight it at home, that even distant wars could be connected to vital interests; and he averred that Communism represented a clash of civilizations, that the struggle against Communism in Korea lay at the heart of U.S. national security.

Contrast this with most political speech. With few exceptions (most prominently, Lincoln's Gettysburg Address), very few political speeches are this thematically dense. In fairness, political speakers usually have the luxury of time to expatiate; audiences of political speeches also have the time in which to consider nuances in language that might have great political significance. Moreover, political speech is generally made in safer, albeit more complex, environments: politics must accommodate numerous constituencies, each of which may "require" some special language (buzzwords, memes, coded phrases); it all adds length to a speech. However, as I will discuss in relation to

---

9   Blair, *The Forgotten War*, 649-650; "Korea, 1951, LtGen Matthew Ridgway: 'Why We Are Here,'"www.milhist.net/whywearehere.html, accessed September 15, 2009.

three of President Barack Obama's important first-year political speeches, the embedded persuasive strategies can be similar to battle speeches.

III. What Is A Battle Speech?

Nothing has changed since I last answered this question in an earlier work: a battle speech "consists of the words, deeds, or words coupled with deeds whose purpose is to recruit, instruct, or exhort soldiers for battles." I added to this that battle speeches also include "the words spoken after a battle whose purpose is to explain why it was fought and what it accomplished, as well as speeches made when an army surrenders or declares victory, or when a commander bids farewell to his soldiers."[10]

My definition of battle speeches is also audience-centric: a battle speech may be given by anyone, but the intended audience must be soldiers, or mostly soldiers (or sailors or marines or coastguardsmen—with apologies to the sister services, I often use "soldier" as shorthand for everyone). Astute readers will see that these criteria exclude many speeches that contain "battle content"—indeed, some of the most memorable battle contents in history. For example, excluded from my definition is Prime Minister Winston Churchill's May 13, 1940, speech to the Parliament ("I have nothing to offer but blood, toil, tears, and sweat") or President Abraham Lincoln's Gettysburg Address ("to that cause for which they gave the last full measure . . . ."). Both of these speeches, while presumably influential on military morale, were in fact intended for civilian audiences. Regrettably, to include every speech with "battle content" would mean overwhelming the number of those actually given exclusively to soldiers, thus losing the uniqueness of "pure" battle speeches, a genre of rhetoric that moves to the beat of its own drummer (pun intended).[11]

However, because *Fighting Words* is really a book about persuasive strategies, I have added an important variation to my definition of battle speeches: Speechlets. These are defined below, but most readers know them as battle cries or war slogans or rallying cries. Some Speechlets, such as "Remember the Alamo!" easily fit the definition of battle speeches. General

---

10 Richard F. Miller, *In Words and Deeds: Battle Speeches in History* (Lebanon, New Hampshire: University Press of New England, 2008), 4-5.

11 *Lend Me Your Ears: Great Speeches in History*, selected and introduced by William Safire (New York: W. W. Norton & Company, 2004), 144-145 (Churchill), 60-61 (Gettysburg Address.)

Sam Houston coined the cry in a longer battle speech given several days before the Battle of San Jacinto; Texians later shouted it as they advanced on Mexican lines.[12]

But many famous Speechlets were not uttered during battles. One of the most brilliant (and concise) military epigrams in American history was Oliver Hazard Perry's "We have met the enemy and they are ours." These words were part of a longer note written to General (later president) William Henry Harrison after the American victory at the Battle of Lake Erie. Some Speechlets, such as John Paul Jones' "I have not yet begun to fight!" did not surface in final form (if these really were his exact words) until forty-five years after the *Bonhomme Richard's* victory over *HMS Serapis*. What these two examples suggest is that a Speechlet's path towards fame and influence is a winding one; that other filters interpose between a Speechlet's utterer and its eventual audience; and, moreover, that the Speechlet's audience itself may consist of more than just soldiers. Indeed, Speechlets are often "cut and pasted" from military communications by politicians, newspaper editors, and other meme-making elites to inspire morale or rationalize a war effort for civilian audiences. Only later are some of these memorable words recycled back to a soldier-audience. Other soldiers in later battles or even later wars may then use some of these Speechlets.[13]

In my earlier writings on battle speeches I was rather fussy about definitions. Why allow Speechlets into this book? The reason is that Speechlets are, from the standpoint of actual language, among the most influential *complex* memes in humanity's repertoire of persuasive strategies. As with "Remember the Alamo!" they contain entire worlds in but a few words, and eventually

---

12 James L. Haley, *Sam Houston* (Norman, Oklahoma: University of Oklahoma Press, 2002), 144.

13 David Curtis Skaggs, *Oliver Hazard Perry: Honor, Courage, and Patriotism in the Early U.S. Navy* (Annapolis: Naval Institute Press, 2006), 117-118; Evan Thomas, *John Paul Jones: Sailor, Hero, Father of the American Navy* (New York: Simon & Schuster, 2003), 192. Each Speechlet has its own path into the meme-stream. Perhaps John Paul Jones' utterance is typical. According to Evans, in Jones' after-action report, he wrote that he had replied "in a most determined negative" to the British demand that he strike his colors; another account then current claimed that Jones declared, "I may sink, but I'll be damned if I strike." Jones himself wrote later (in French) a far less appealing version that Evans translates as "I haven't as yet thought of surrendering, but I am determined to make you ask for quarter." The famous words, "I have not yet begun to fight!" finally entered the meme-stream forty-five years after the battle in an aged crewmember's interview with a Jones biographer.

become larger than the battles or wars that spawned them. They are also evergreen across a wide variety of situations. The Speechlet "I have not yet begun to fight" works in battles, corporate takeovers, football games, divorce proceedings and squabbles with adolescent children. Besides Speechlets, other tools of concision—memes, enthymemes, metonyms and living metonyms—are discussed at greater length below.

IV. When Are Battle Speeches Given?

This is not quite like asking, "Who is buried in Grant's tomb?" Of course, battle speeches *are* given "in connection with" battles. But because I have loosened considerably what, for my purposes, "in connection with" means (recall my earlier claim that battle speeches are those given to "recruit, instruct, or exhort soldiers for battles"), battle speeches include a wide variety of military rhetoric. The best way to approach this subject is to imagine the order in which a hypothetical soldier might encounter these speeches during his wartime experience. Then think of each category as its own subgenre of battle speech, each with its own defining characteristics, or, as I call them, conventions. These categories matter to *Fighting Words* because persuasive strategies in battle (and other) speeches cannot be fully understood without (obviously) referring to the circumstances in which they were given, as well as (less obviously) the rhetorical structure of the speech in which they appear.

The following are battle speeches that a hypothetical soldier might encounter in the tactical cycle of a war:

- *Recruiting Speech*: To persuade him to enlist.
- *Instructional Speech*: To train and instruct him about what he should do in preparation for an invasion or battle.
- *Pre-Invasion Speech*: To ready him to cross some real or imaginary line— a boundary, ocean, river, or frontier—to begin a war or initiate a new phase of an existing war. An actual battle, while perhaps almost certain, is not yet "in view."
- *Pre-Battle Speech*: To ready him for looming combat. The battle is very close; the enemy can be seen or the sounds of battle heard; fighting is not only a certainty, it may be only moments away.
- *Midst-of-Battle Speech*: To exhort or instruct him during a battle.

- *Post-Battle Speeches*: To rationalize the battle's consequences after it is over.
- *Arrival and Departure Speeches*: To mark the assumption or relinquishment of command so as to manage expectations or create a final narrative (Assumption of Command and Farewell Speeches, respectively).[14]

Examples of many of these speeches are used in this book. I will discuss the conventions that shape each category of speech as they appear in later chapters.

Political speeches do resemble some of the battle speeches included in this cycle. Perhaps the closest match is between a president's inaugural address and the Assumption of Command speech. Still, it is important to remember the limits of comparisons between political and battle speeches. Although politicians (among others) often use military metaphors to characterize what they do ("I'm fighting for you") and how they do it ("I'm leading the charge for. . .") or even why they do it ("I've dedicated my life to fighting the good fight"), in truth, in mature democracies political speeches are not battle speeches. Although in the long term the stakes of elections and legislative votes can be high, few audience members are dispatched to kill or to be killed in the name of the minimum wage or taxing capital gains.

However, the *persuasive strategies* of battle speeches and political speeches do bear comparison. One reason is historical: human persuasion long predates the more recent separation of civil and military functions. For example, the person of Alexander the Great united civil and military authority; few listening to the king had the slightest doubt that insufficient responsiveness might result in being killed or conquered. Indeed, no matter how distant from military matters an endeavor may be, the ubiquity of war metaphors to characterize leadership, collective effort, competition, and striving strongly suggest that, at some conceptual level, to lead, to cooperate, to compete, or to strive remains rooted in some historically distant conception of conflict. While this is not an original observation, it may go far in explaining why battle speech and political speech persuasive strategies do share important features.

---

14 Miller, *Words and Deeds*, 85-103 (Recruiting Speech), 104-144 (Instructional Speech), 145-185 (Pre-Invasion Speech), 186-230 (Pre-Battle Speech), 231-275 (Midst-of-Battle Speech), 276-316 (Post-Battle Speech), 317-323 (Assumption of Command Speech), 323-339 (Farewell Speech).

V. How Are Battle Speeches Given?

The question of *what* battle speeches are cannot be separated from *how* battle speeches are given. And the *how* of a battle speech is usually determined by the way it meets the challenges of *dispersion*, *diversity*, and *distraction*. (To readers it also matters because *Fighting Words* finds battle speeches not only in conventional speeches but also in battle cries, banners, printed material, and signal flags.)

Dispersion of soldiers and commanders rarely figures into idealized battle speeches. Since antiquity that ideal has been imagined as a set-piece oration made by an earnest speechmaker to anxious soldiers gathered 'round, or at least in front. Thus Arrian's Alexander the Great stands on a platform at Opis to address his assembled Macedonians; in the film *Patton*, actor George C. Scott, playing General George S. Patton, Jr., faces his soldier-audience as he exhorts them. At least with Patton and *Patton*, art imitated life: while there is no reliable corroboration of what Alexander said at Opis (let alone whether he stood on a platform), there is abundant evidence that *Patton* accurately portrayed the general. Patton's "The Speech," as it was called, was a set-piece oration delivered by him to a soldier-audience assembled for the purpose, often preceded by flags, bands, and sirens. Given Patton's intimate knowledge of military history, this was probably a case of life imitating art. See Chapter Four.[15]

But readers and filmgoers may see certain limitations in this set-piece model. For example, some limits are easily inferred from the opening scenes of the film *Gladiator*, in which actor Russell Crowe, playing Roman general Maximus Decimus Meridius, delivers a variety of exhortations as he walks along his lines of battle. Maximus knows that combat is just moments away, and that it is thus best to address the soldiery as they stand in battle formation, ready for instant action. But there is another, practical reason for Maximus' walkie-talkie. The film accurately depicts the Roman battle lines as quite long, probably too long for Maximus to be heard clearly had he stood at the line's

15 Arrian: *Anabasis of Alexander, Books V-VII*, with an English translation by P.A. Brunt (Cambridge, Massachusetts: Harvard University Press, 1999), VII.8.3 (227). Brunt believes that the speech at Opis was invented by Alexander's later (four hundred years, in the case of Arrian) biographers. See Appendix XXVI generally, but section 6 in particular, 532-533, *Anabasis*; *Patton* (1970); the late Martin Blumenson, editor of the *Patton Papers* and a leading Patton scholar, noted that "George C. Scott's role as the general in the film Patton is a remarkably accurate portrayal of the public figure." Blumenson, *Patton,* 310.

center and delivered a speech. So, the better to be seen and heard by the most troops, Maximus exhorts as he walks, and later as he rides a horse. Perhaps *Gladiator's* director Ridley Scott (or one of his historical consultants) heeded the advice of the Greek, Onasander, who advised his first century CE readers that

> [t]he duty of the general is to ride by the ranks on horseback, show himself to those in danger, praise the brave, threaten the cowardly, encourage the lazy, fill up gaps, transpose a company if necessary, bring aid to the wearied, anticipate the crisis, the hour, and the outcome.[16]

The phenomenon of dispersion is twofold: of the soldiers and of command. Taking Onasander's advice means MBWA—Management By Walking (or sprinting) Around. So Julius Caesar performed a warrior's version of MBWA as he organized to resist an attack: he had "everything to do at once—hoist the flag . . . recall the men from their work on the camp, fetch back those who had gone far afield . . . form the battle line, address the men, and sound the trumpet signal for going into action." But being everywhere at once to manage dispersed soldiers means dispersing command as well. Caesar, Ridley Scott and Onasander are really dealing with both sides of dispersion: that of the battle speechmakers and that of their audiences.[17]

Then as now, there were other solutions to the problem of dispersion. Perhaps the most common was the use of messengers. Here the commander-battle speechmaker convenes a meeting, issues his instructions (Instructional Speech), perhaps a Speechlet, a password, or a prayer, and then orders his immediate audience (field officers or designated messengers) to convey something of what was said to soldiers in the field. In this way most parts of the battle line can be reached simultaneously, thereby enabling complex yet coordinated movements. So the great Roman commander Gaius Marius, who was about to battle the Teutones, wanted to inform his troops about their

---

16 *Gladiator* (2000); *Aeneas Tacitus/Asclepiodotus/Onasander*, with an English translation of *The Illinois Greek Club* (Cambridge, MA: Harvard University Press, 1923), 483-485.

17 Caesar, *The Conquest of Gaul*, translated by S.A. Handford, revised with a new introduction by Jane F. Gardner (London: Penguin Books, 1982), II.20, 67. "MBWA" was popularized by business writers Thomas J. Peters and Robert H. Waterman, in the book *In Search of Excellence: Lessons from America's Best-Run Companies* (New York: Harper Collins Business Essentials, 2004, reprint of 1982), 121-122.

advantages in ground and weaponry. Plutarch informs us that "Marius, sending officers to all parts, commanded his men to stand still and keep their ground," and continues at some length with the details of Marius' message. However, while messengers can repeat much, they cannot do justice to a commander's battle exhortation. And even if some aide-de-camp could faithfully deliver the speech, the result, given by a commander *in absentia*, would likely have only a fraction of the impact of the personally delivered version.[18]

Smoke signals, waved torches, reflecting mirrors, and primitive signal flags could also transmit elementary instructions, but were unable to convey more complex messages, and certainly not full-length battle speeches. However, for the Royal Navy during the Age of Sail, whose sailor-audience was dispersed in separate ships of a fleet, the need was especially pressing for efficient at-sea communications. Signal flag systems of increasing complexity developed throughout the eighteenth century. Perhaps that century's highest evolution of flag signaling came in 1800 when British Admiral Sir Home Popham introduced the Popham Code. Flags bearing geometric patterns, symbols and colors carried pre-designated meanings, ranging from alphabet letters to complete words and even phrases. What matters here is that the system was in place off Trafalgar on October 21, 1805, when Admiral Lord Nelson caused flags communicating the following words and letters to be hoisted aloft on his flagship *HMS Victory*:

"England Expects Every Man Will Do His D-U-T-Y"

Popham's Code had not designated a flag for "duty," which thus had to be spelled out. No matter; Nelson's message numbers among the greatest battle Speechlets in history. A large point here is that to have "heard" the speech one needed to see the flags. But the even larger point is that, for battle speeches, one ignores the medium and looks to the message.[19]

Dispersion is the reason the printing press became so important to the battle speech. Orders, exhortations, rules of engagement, assumption of command and farewell speeches, victory and surrender proclamations, regimental newspapers,

18 Plutarch, *Plutarch's Lives*, edited, notes and preface by Arthur Hugh Clough (New York: The Modern Library, 2001), I: 562-563.

19 Brian Lavery, *Nelson's Navy: The Ships, Men, and Organization, 1793-1815* (Annapolis: Naval Institute Press, 1989), 262-263; Adam Nicolson, *Seize the Fire: Heroism, Duty, and the Battle of Trafalgar* (New York: Harper Collins Publishers, 2005), 128-129.

brigade magazines, and so forth could now be printed on portable presses and distributed to the growing number of subunits that comprised the more complex militaries of modernity—armies, corps, divisions, brigades, task forces, specialists' units, regiments, battalions, platoons, down to individual soldiers. Coupled with telegraphy, and later telephone, teletype, radios, television, CDs, DVDs, NIPR and SIPR, commanders who could no longer mount a platform as at Opis now had other, if occasionally second-best means to deliver battle speeches (and, incidentally, to exercise control over far-flung legions). To take a very historically late example, when Matthew Ridgway issued his "Why We Are Here" battle speech, it was specifically designated as "MEMORANDUM FOR: Corps, Division, Separate Brigade or RCT Commanders, and Commanding General, 2d Logistical Command." In short, Ridgway's great speech was a paper memo, albeit more important than some.[20]

Battle speeches must also cope with *diversity*—the fact that armies, particularly those of alliances, often consist of soldiers who speak different languages, come from different cultures, are loyal to different commanders, and have different ideas about how to wage war. According to Livy, Hannibal's army at Zama was "composed of such men who shared neither language, customs, laws, weapons, dress, appearance, nor even a common reason for serving." Thus, Livy states Hannibal's problem—"the best means of arousing the fighting spirit was no simple matter"—but then offers Hannibal's solution: "[the] hopes and fears, to suit the case, had to be dangled before their eyes."

> [T]he auxiliaries, for instance, were offered their pay not only in cash but increased by a share in the plunder; the fire to kindle the Gauls was their peculiar and ingrained detestation of the Romans; to the Ligurians was displayed the bait of the rich plains of Italy, once they had been brought down from their rugged mountains; Moors and Numidians were scared into courage by the prospect of Masinissa's tyrannical rule, while the Carthaginians were urged to keep before their eyes all they held dear—the walls of their native city [& etc.]

20 "NIPR" and "SIPR" are acronyms for the Department of Defense Internet access systems that permit such communications within the military. NIPR or NIPRNet stands for Nonsecure Internet Protocol Router Network and is for unclassified data. SIPR or SIPRNet is Secure Internet Protocol Router Network and is for classified data; "Korea, 1951, LtGen Matthew Ridgway: "Why We Are Here."

Hannibal addressed only the Carthaginians, while "various national leaders [spoke] to their own countrymen," noted Livy, "mainly through interpreters because of the admixture of foreign troops." It is easy to imagine arrays of motley-garbed legions assembled on some ancient, dusty plain, the air filling with the cacophony of clanging weapons and battle speeches delivered in at least five different languages.[21]

One is tempted to imagine this as a problem of pre-modernity, but it is also a modern problem. Many of *Fighting Words'* battle Speechlets were uttered to very diverse soldier-audiences. The historical record (usually created by the dominant ethnicity) rarely reflects the fact that, at some point, such words were almost certainly translated (and perhaps customized, ala Zama) for the benefit of foreign allies or mercenaries. Many of the wars or campaigns discussed in this book would have involved translating battle speeches into other languages: in particular, Pope Urban II's Call for the First Crusade (which circulated widely throughout a poly-lingual Western Europe); Petraeus' speeches to the Multi-National Forces in Iraq; William the Conqueror's Speechlet "Dex Aie!" (William's so-called "Norman" army contained a large contingent of assorted non-Normans); and even "Remember the Alamo!" At the Battle of San Jacinto, Tejanos serving with Houston shouted "Recuerden el Alamo!" as his Anglo comrades shouted its English counterpart. Likewise, it is estimated that at Trafalgar one-third of British officers and even more sailors were from "Scotland, Wales, Ireland and abroad"—nationalities that for many reasons might not have cheerfully responded to an *England* that expected anything.[22]

The final issue involving the how of battle speeches is *distraction*. Distractions include battle space conditions that impair the composition, delivery, audibility (and, where deeds serve as speech surrogates, the visibility) and eventually, the recall of a speech. Noise, confusion, danger, the focus on personal or unit survival and related tasks (running, crouching, crawling, firing, noise discipline, and so forth) often combine to prevent the delivery of an intelligible instruction or speech. The shout of "Forward!"—or, as Gunnery

---

21 *The War with Hannibal, Books XXI-XXX of The History of Rome from its Foundation,* by Livy, trans. Aubrey De Selincourt, ed. and intro. Betty Radice (London: Penguin Books, 1972), 30.33, 660-661.

22 James W. Pohl, *The Battle of San Jacinto* (U.S.A.: Texas State Hist. Assoc.,1989), 39-40; Nicolson, *Seize the Fire*, 128-129. Recent American experience includes instances in which attempts at joint or integrated operations with host-country forces were complicated because of language problems, particularly in Korea, Vietnam, Iraq, and Afghanistan.

Sergeant Dan Daly memorably exhorted his comrades at Belleau Wood, "Come on, you sons of bitches, do you want to live forever?"—may be as much of an Instructional Speech or Midst-of-Battle exhortation as can be expected during intense combat.[23]

The issue of distraction is severally relevant here. First, increased distraction favors the use of Speechlets, those very short exhortations or instructions with deeply embedded meanings. For example, the "Dex Aie!" (God's Aid!") shouted by William the (shortly-to-be) Conqueror's soldiers at the Battle of Hastings probably combined prayer and battle cry. Normans seeking long-form religious comfort likely had availed themselves of the masses reportedly held the night before; during actual combat, the short-form prayer-cry Dex Aie! would have to suffice.[24]

Distraction also can intrude outside of combat. For example, soldiers are busy before and after battles or invasions. In the hours preceding the ill-fated Dieppe raid on August 19, 1942, the Chief of Combined Operations and Royal family member, Vice Admiral Louis Mountbatten, addressed his soldiers aboard their troop transports. These men, wearing "their oldest, dirtiest battle dress or denims, with oil smears on their cheeks," paused for a few moments amid their more important tasks—"weapons-cleaning and map-reading"—to listen to Mountbatten. The latter spoke briefly, reviewing some important Rules of Engagement and instilling confidence ("I know what it felt like when some admiral who'd been sucking his teeth ashore for months came aboard to tell us how to fight," Mountbatten recalled for them. "I'm not going to tell you how to fight, because you know how"). According to an embedded journalist, Mountbatten spoke, then left, after which men immediately "went back to their weapons and their maps, saying to each other, 'He seems all right.' [The reporter] went back to the fascinating problem of what, or what not, to wear or carry on the raid." In short, battle speeches matter, but perhaps not as much as some speakers imagine.[25]

---

23 *Dictionary of Military and Naval Quotations*, ed. Robert Debs Heinl, Jr. (Annapolis: Naval Institute Press, 1966), 49.

24 *Master Wace, His Chronicle of the Norman Conquest, From the Roman de Rou,* trans. Edgar Taylor (London: William Pickering, 1837), 159.

25   A. B. Austin, *We Landed at Dawn: The Story of the Dieppe Raid* (New York: Harcourt, Brace and Company, 1943), 104-108.

VI. Persuasive Strategies 1.0

Generals, heads of state and the readers of this book all reached a developmental moment, probably as toddlers, when they discovered that their hunger was more efficiently satisfied by uttering the word "More!" rather than by banging a spoon on their high chairs. Here children begin (or precocious children further) their journey into the world of persuasive strategies: they satisfy their needs by exchanging their words for others' deeds. With time, the hypothetical toddler finds, either by inculcation or imitation, that adding the word "Please" produces even more food, and that smilingly tendered; moreover, that by timing the verb "Thanks" strategically (after the adverbial "Please" has produced the goods), yet more smiles appear, and mealtimes become more pleasant (and fruitful) than ever before.

Through these courtesies, the toddler has discovered two important truths. First, words require minimal energy but can quickly produce substances from which all energy comes; thus, words are highly efficient. The toddler has also learned that words invest him with great powers, because now he can manipulate the most powerful, and heretofore mysterious, beings in his life space—adults.

A writer working on a book entitled *Battle Speeches: The Child Is the Mother of the Soldier* might follow our hypothetical toddler through life and observe the occasions when she uses the words "Please" and "Thank you." To appear especially learned, this researcher might classify how these words are used as a specific persuasive appeal; I will call it the Courtesy Appeal. Our learned classifier might then abstract some "conventions" about when and how *and* perhaps even why the Courtesy Appeal is used. Understanding the *when* and *how* are relatively easy matters, and the researcher formulates a rule to explain both:

> The speaker wishing to ingratiate herself with those who have the power to satisfy her needs will bracket her declaration of wishes with socially sanctioned forms of obeisance and gratitude.

The *why* of Courtesy Appeals is trickier; outside of psychology, the best answers are likely to be found in history, that is, what were the historical circumstances that prompted our now-grown toddler to satisfy her wants with a "please" rather than with a pistol?

Battle speechmakers and heads of state alike always have the option of wielding a pistol (or worse) to induce soldiers, citizens and subjects to act. But no matter how brutal these leaders may be, violence is rarely their first option. Whether in battle, in negotiating with law-making assemblies, or in dealing with the citizenry at large, persuasion is far more efficient. The adverbial use of *Please* is rare in battle speeches—other incentives (for example, plunder, glory, duty to one's faith, tribe, nation or comrades) are rather more usual—but various versions of *Thank You* are so common in battle speeches as to merit their own category: the Gratitude Convention.[26] Sometimes a battle speech is just an extended "thank you." After the American Civil War Battle of Williamsburg, General George B. McClellan, one of American history's better battle speechmakers, rode up to one unit and declared,

> Soldiers of the Seventh Maine: I have come to thank you for your bravery and good conduct in the action of yesterday. On this battle-plain you and your comrades arrested the progress of the advancing enemy, and turned the tide of victory in our favor. You have deserved well of your country and your State, and in their gratitude they will not forget to bestow upon you the thanks and praise so justly your due . . . . Soldiers, my words are feeble but from the bottom of my heart I thank you.

Napoleon Bonaparte could be more concise. After the Battle of Jena, he wrote to Marshal Davout, "Inform your corps and your generals of my satisfaction. They have forever acquired a claim on my esteem and my gratitude."[27]

Politician speechmakers also say "Thank you." Gratitude works for them as it does for battle speechmakers—with one important addition, not often found in battle speeches: politicians usually thank audiences merely for having invited them, sometimes for not defenestrating them, and almost always after audience applause. When President Barack Obama spoke at Cairo University to deliver his speech "On A New Beginning," he used the words "thank you" five times: once in response to an audience member who shouted, "Barack Obama, we love

---

26 Miller, *Words and Deeds,* 331-332.

27 *The Rebellion Record: A Diary of American Events*, ed. Frank Moore (New York: Arno Press, reprint 1977), Volume V: 26 ("Poetry and Incidents"), 176 ("General McClellan's Speeches on the Battle-Field"); October 16, 1806, from Weimer, to Marshal Davout, *In the Words of Napoleon: The Emperor Day by Day*, ed. Johnston, with new material by Philip Haythornthwaite (London: Greenhill Books, 2002), 176.

you!" and four times in response to applause. But he also thanked his audience in other ways, about more substantive matters. "As a student of history," the president declared, "I also know civilization's debt to Islam." He then devoted several paragraphs to describing various European and American debts to Islam. Mentioning these "debts" was an embrace of the Gratitude Convention, not unlike McClellan or Napoleon displaying gratitude to units which had helped to deliver a recent victory; the two generals and the president simply sought to trade gratitude for good will. Generals and politicians alike understand that few audiences are alienated by a leader's tendering thanks. After all, "thank you" is just another form of compliment.[28]

I will squeeze the toddler metaphor one last time for a more complex example of a persuasive strategy. Probably quite soon after mastering "please" the toddler discovers that simply prefixing that word to a request is no guarantee of satisfaction. The parent-audience might be unwilling to dole out "third" helpings, or perhaps what the toddler wants is non-nutritious or even harmful. (Many readers of a certain age have observed, perhaps while in supermarkets, very young children who, meeting parental resistance to their demands, repeat the word "Please!" each time more loudly and insistently, but without effect. A *failed* persuasive strategy, this.)

But our toddler, now aging, now accessing an increasing range of emotions and experience (and imitable mentors), will, by some intuitive use of elementary psychology, not be denied. For example, if, after seeing a sibling being given some candy, he may ask for the same; should he be refused, he might shout at his parent, "You love her more than me!" This can be an especially potent persuasive strategy, and our learned researcher, observing its efficacy, might well label it Appeal to Shame, or, in its more modern twist, Appeal to Guilt. The child may not be able to explain why the approach works, but our researcher should know: the parent-audience subscribes to a standard (that the researcher might label the "Always Treat Your Children Equally Convention"); the child has intuited how to exploit the cleavage between the standards that his parents profess and their current behavior. If successful, the child will have created

---

28 Barack H. Obama, ""A New Beginning," June 4, 2009, www.whitehouse.gov/the
_press_office/remarks-by-the-president-at-cairo-university-6-04-09. Accessed September
29, 2009. (Hereafter, "Cairo Speech.") Mentioning these debts also amounted to the
politician's equivalent of the Comrade Convention, in which the speaker attempts to
identify with his audience using such markers as race, religion, culture, history, and so
forth. For Comrade Convention, see Miller, *Words and Deeds*, 234-235.

guilty tensions within the parent that can only be relieved by handing over the candy.

Gods as well as men use the same persuasive strategy. When Homer's Poseidon made a battle speech to rally the Greeks in front of Troy, he eschewed his divine powers in favor of words. "Greeks, shame on you, young warriors!" he shouted. "You are the very men on whose bravery I had relied to save our ships." Some millennia later during the American Civil War, the Tenth Massachusetts' Battery's Private David R. Stowell sought to rally comrades fleeing through his lines. "Shame on you, boys! Will you leave the old Tenth Battery to fight it out alone?" Like the aging toddler, both god and man were exploiting the cleavage between professed principles and deeds: a soldier's (strongly masculinized) duty to be brave and to fight versus his deed of fleeing combat.[29]

Appeals to Shame/Guilt are also frequently employed from the political podium. On September 9, 2009, President Obama addressed a joint session of Congress on the subject of health care reform. The first part of his speech was arguably one long Appeal to Shame, of which the following paragraph is representative:

> We are the only democracy—the only advanced democracy on Earth—the only wealthy nation—that allows such hardship [that is, financial ruin for uninsured or underinsured Americans] for millions of its people. There are now more than 30 million American citizens who cannot get coverage. In just a two-year period, one in every three Americans goes without health care coverage at some point. And every day, 14,000 Americans lose their coverage. In other words, it can happen to anyone.

Obama's Appeal to Shame implicitly asserted a principle that he believed his audience professed: health care is a right that inheres in American citizenship. This principle is quite different from the gendered idea of combat courage asserted by Poseidon and Private Stowell, but is exploited in exactly the same way. The president drew attention to the cleavage between the professed principle and the current practice. The objective is to shame his audience into acting, and his technique is exhortatory: to stimulate tensions of shame and guilt

---

29 Homer, *The Iliad*, trans. E.V. Rieu, rev. Peter Jones and D.C.H. Rieu (London: Penguin Books, 2003), 219; John D. Billings, *The History of the Tenth Massachusetts Battery of Light Artillery in the War of Rebellion, 1862-1865* (Boston: 1909), 359.

inside his listeners that can be relieved only by passing the measure that he seeks.[30]

VII. Persuasive Strategies 2.0

What is the most efficient way for speakers to appeal to shame, gratitude, or any of the other appeals that appear in this book? The answer—concision—results from two factors: a shortage of time and the audience's limited attention span. Battle speechmakers typically have very little time in which to speak. Politicians usually have more time, but both soldier and solon must confront an audience's limited attention span. (Whether pitching soldiers or voters, it is always wise to remember the apocryphal preacher's observation that "No soul was saved after the first twenty minutes of the sermon.")[31]

The most important time-saving device available to battle or political speechmakers is simply to make a demand. Julius Caesar, in one Post-Battle Speech, criticized his men for having made an impulsive charge, and then insisted: "I want obedience and self-restraint from my soldiers, just as much as courage in the face of danger." But readers should note that there is also an appeal lurking behind this seemingly straightforward demand: the word "soldier" is the fulcrum between two points: "obedience" and "self-restraint" on one side and "courage" and "face of danger" on the other. Caesar made a direct appeal, but as his persuasive vehicle he was using (and unbundling) the *meme* of "soldier." In other words, Caesar may well have been—one cannot know for

---

30 Barack H. Obama, "Remarks by the President to a Joint Session of Congress on Health Care," September 9, 2009, www.whitehouse.gov/the_press_office/remarks-by-the-president-to-a-joint-session-of-congress-on-health-care/. Accessed September 10, 2009.

31 Although often attributed to Mark Twain (and countless others), the line about limited time and saving souls seems to be of unknown origin. Two important points: first, within physiological limits, attention spans may be culturally determined. Excepting the well known speech-a-thons of certain modern-era dictators (whose audiences were presumably captive), attention spans appear to lengthen as one recedes in history. While Edward Everett had the misfortune of delivering a long speech (approximately two hours) at Gettysburg compared with Lincoln's very short (and great) one, the former's address was still listened to—and lauded—by many. Garry Wills, *Lincoln at Gettysburg: The Words That Remade America,* (New York: Simon & Schuster, 1992), 34. The other issue is comfort. It is one thing to sit in some Parliament's leather chair, breathing temperature-controlled air, with discrete access to sanitary facilities, and listen to speakers drone. It is another matter entirely, say, to stand wearing 50 to 100 pounds of equipment in 100-degree heat and have to listen to speakers drone. Here, KISS has two meanings: Keep It Simple, Stupid, and Keep It Short [and] Sweet.

sure—reminding his men of something they already knew: that proper soldiering combines self-discipline *and* courage. Or possibly (although unlikely) it may be that Caesar was creating a completely new meme for the word "soldier": redefining it to include the quality of self-discipline as well as courage. In either case, the next time Caesar shouted, "Act like soldiers!" there would be no need to list a soldier's desired traits; the word "soldier" would say it all.

Here I will explain my use of five concepts that appear throughout this book: *meme, Speechlet, enthymeme, metonym* and *living metonym*. Each of these words represents a different way of embedding multiple meanings in words or phrases. They are concision's very soul, and attempt to accomplish the following:

Reduce speech length; amplify and concentrate the power of appeals by leveraging into the speech *what the audience already knows*.

Simultaneously, audiences will leverage into their preexisting understanding what they already know (or think they know) about the speaker or his subject.

All speeches are negotiation: the speaker seeks something from the audience and the audience has expectations of the speaker. While the audience may appear as motionless as figures in an oil painting, on a purely cognitive level, active negotiation takes place. The use of memes, Speechlets, enthymemes, and metonyms are what facilitate this negotiation process.

Memes can combine to transform speakers into what I call "living metonyms:" here, the speaker's *very person* becomes emblematic of the institution or cause that he champions.

Memes and Speechlets

In his 1976 book *The Selfish Gene*, scientist Richard Dawkins introduced the word "meme" (from the Greek *mimema*, or "something imitated") to describe what he called "a unit of cultural transmission." Dawkins, a neo-Darwinist, believed that "Darwinism is too big a theory to be confined to the narrow context of the gene;" thus, he hypothesized that culture too is transmitted generationally and evolves through some cultural version of natural selection. Memes, like genes, replicate in living things. Of course, Dawkins was comparing memes and genes only analogically: unlike genes, which are tangible, memes are merely abstractions, of which he gave examples: "tunes, ideas, catch-phrases, clothes fashions, ways of making pots or of building arches." Dawkins described how he imagined memes work:

> Just as genes propagate themselves in the gene pool by leaping from body to body via sperms or eggs, so memes propagate themselves in the meme pool by leaping from brain to brain via a process which, in the broad sense can be called imitation. If a scientist hears, or reads about, a good idea, he passes it on to his colleagues and students. He mentions it in articles and his lectures. If the idea catches on, it can be said to propagate itself, spreading from brain to brain.[32]

My use of the word "meme" begins not with how they spread but with what they contain, and I extend the meme-gene analogy only this far: as genes contain a special sequence of DNA, so memes contain a sequence of embedded ideas. Yet my analogy justifiably can be blurred: one can choose whatever metaphor one likes to describe, for example, how Julius Caesar's meme of "soldier" included obedience and self-restraint as well as courage. Were these three ideas "embedded," "contained," "associated," "attached" or "connected" with the word, "soldier?" Pick what you please, I do not care. What matters to *Fighting Words* is that when Caesar's soldier-audience heard him utter the word "soldier," at some level they also heard, believed, or felt "obedience," "self-restraint" and "courage."

Compactness matters to battle, political or any other category of speech. Why should speakers waste time, clutter their narratives, and weaken their emotive wind by having to extensively define matters that the audience has already defined? It is so much more efficient (and intimidating) to snap, "Act like soldiers!" than it would be to say, "Act like soldiers, by which I mean, add obedience and self-restraint to your existing qualities of courage and willingness to face danger!"

What is true for one-word memes becomes truer for *complex memes*. These are several words that, when joined together, produce a sum of meaning that exceeds its parts by several orders of magnitude. In both battle and political speeches I call one variety of these complex memes *Speechlets*. In this sense, speeches are only extruded Speechlets. For example, consider the Speechlet

---

32 Richard Dawkins, *The Selfish Gene* (New York: Oxford University Press, 2006), 190-192.

"Remember the Alamo!" It is on anyone's short list of the most famous utterances in American military history. It also originates what I call the "Remembrance Meme" series of Speechlets, several of which also number among very famous military sayings:

Remember the Alamo! (Battle of San Jacinto, 1836);

Remember Fort Sumter! (*Casus belli*, Civil War, 1861);

Remember Fort Pillow! (Massacre of surrendered black federal soldiers, 1864);

Remember the Maine! (*Casus belli*, Spanish-American War, 1898);

Remember Pearl Harbor! (*Casus Belli*, World War II);

Remember Wake Island! (Determined resistance of the "Alamo of the Pacific" against Japanese invasion, 1941);

Remember 9-11! (*Casus Belli*, Global War on Terror, 2001).

(Anyone seeking evidence that Dawkins' "catch phrases" transmit across generations need only consult this list.)

Consider the multiple and profound meanings embedded in these Remembrance Speechlets. First, "Remember" is meant to be synonymous with feelings and acts of revenge; these revenge-acts can only be accomplished by going (or continuing) to war. Second, "Remember" is also a vestibule to an entire chamber of historical narrative about the reasons why revenge is necessary. Third, that revenge narrative is contained in the noun(s) Alamo, Fort Sumter, Fort Pillow, *Maine*, Pearl Harbor, Wake Island, and 9-11. Out of context, the words merely refer to three forts, one port, a ship, an island and a date; but in context, each implies something of enormous importance, as contained in the following one-size-fits-all formula:

Enemy injustice: a sneak attack or barbaric massacre

+

Inflicted on peaceable victim, or abider of the rules of civilized warfare

=

Victim's righteous fury; and,
Uniting of victim's population, expressed as
An act or intensification of war

How enormous were the contributions made by these Speechlets? Remembering the Alamo steeled Sam Houston's men on the plains of San Jacinto, produced a retaliatory massacre of Santa Anna's soldiers, and helped achieve Texas independence; remembering Fort Sumter helped fill Northern recruiting offices in 1861 (as did remembering Wake Island and 9-11 for their respective conflicts); remembering the Fort Pillow massacre helped stiffen Northern morale in the war's final year, and in some places complicated attempts by individual Confederate attempts to surrender; remembering the *USS Maine's* destruction in Havana Harbor gave Americans a pro-war meme that helped propel the Spanish-American War from the editorial pages to San Juan Hill; remembering Pearl Harbor probably had the most influence of any battle meme of twentieth-century America—not only did it fit neatly into the Remembrance Meme template, but advanced communications technology assured that it would be reinforced throughout World War II by compelling audio-visuals: radio broadcasts, President Roosevelt's request for a declaration of war, photographs and film of the actual attack, a famous film re-enactment, and other feature film references.[33]

That three words of the Remembrance Meme are sufficiently influential on a population's willingness to kill, be killed, produce goods and be taxed to help enable large-scale, organized violence suggests that concise meaning is to Speechlets what matter is to black holes—quite dense, and with a powerful gravity.

Like Professor Dawkins, *Fighting Words* is also concerned with how memes spread. However, my ambitions are pygmean compared with his much grander visions of inter-generational transmissions and cultural evolution. Specifically, because I emphasize the importance of a speaker's existing reputational memes to how a soldier-audience responds to a speech, it is very important to establish as precisely as possible what those memes were and from

---

33 Safire, *Lend Me Your Ears*, 156-158; War date movies include *Pearl Harbor: Now It Can Be Shown* (1942); *Avenge December 7* (1942), *December 7* (1943). Films, both shorts and features, in which Pearl Harbor is referenced make a very long list indeed.

whence they came. With Ulysses S. Grant, George S. Patton, Jr., Oliver Hazard Perry, and David Petraeus, I attempt to do this by linking the speechmaker and the speech with media-propagated memes and evidence from the contemporary reactions of soldiers and journalists. My evidence is news stories, diaries, letters, and memoirs. (Far less inference is required to establish memes for modern figures than for those of the distant past, such as Pope Urban II's use of the Cross meme in his Call for the First Crusade.)

Here I wish to emphasize another departure from Dawkins' biology-based metaphor of meme transmission and selection. I prefer using the business model of manufacture-and-distribution to explain how memes spread. Thus, there are meme makers, wholesalers, and retailers, each with varying degrees of originality and/or mimicry. Memes are indispensable to any political process grounded in soliciting votes; they are also indispensable to battle speeches, where time is short.

In politics, the larger the voting base, the more indispensable memes become as vehicles of persuasion. Here the meme-makers include politicians, their consultants and speechwriters, screenwriters, advertisers, and academics. Next, memes are wholesaled into various "meme-streams" by reliable epigones: print and broadcast journalists seeking increased attention and market share by writing to curry favor with factions, pander to readers or create controversy; opinion columnists; cable talking heads; politicians lower on the pecking order; and so forth. "Meme-stream" describes any network of reliable dissemination: in militaries, the "chain of command" is a meme-stream; in politics, wide meme-streams may be (pejoratively) described, for example, as "the liberal mainstream media" or "a vast right-wing conspiracy;" narrower meme-streams might be subscription lists for *Foreign Affairs* magazine or the National Rifle Association's *American Rifleman*. The final step in the distribution process depends on whether the meme will "play in Peoria," or, to use the journalists' metaphor, whether it "has legs." This means that it must, and appears to, first, express some potentially compelling narrative, and, second, does it "smartly" so as to increase the velocity of distribution; think here of captions ("Watergate," "Travelgate," fitting gloves acquitting), songs (national anthem), or slogans ("Marines make no better friend or no worse enemy"). Here the meme goes retail: it is insinuated into the vernacular as a claimed representation of some reality.

For an example of a political meme, consider this passage from President Obama's health care speech: "When I spoke here last winter, this nation was facing the worst economic crisis since the Great Depression." The president did not create the meme "the Great Depression;" it has been in common use since the 1930s. But merely mentioning "the Great Depression" allows him to incorporate all of its associations—most famously, stock market crashes, high unemployment, breadlines, and bank holidays—without having to be specific about whether the current economic environment is "like" that of the 1930s or somehow different, and, if the latter, why and how it may be different. This is not criticism of the president—he was delivering a persuasive speech, not a disquisition on economic history. Here I wish only to emphasize that for speechmakers historical analogies are efficient, in that they carry powerful memes (and may themselves be memes); historical analogies are often intended for retail, prime time. Here, think "Munich," "Vietnam," or "another 9-11."[34]

The case for how memes are distributed is perfectly illustrated by Ulysses S. Grant and the meme of "unconditional surrender." The words were Grant's, contained in a longer note to Confederate General Simon Buckner demanding the surrender of Fort Donelson:

No terms except an unconditional and immediate surrender can be accepted. I propose to move immediately upon your works.[35]

Grant may have authored the words, but he cannot be credited with creating the meme. That achievement belongs to the meme-makers, of which there were chiefly two: the first was some now-forgotten wag, probably in the federal ranks, who converted Grant's first two initials—"U" and "S"—into "Unconditional Surrender," thus creating the enduring moniker-cum-meme "Unconditional Surrender" Grant. The second were Northern newspapers, who cut the phrase "unconditional surrender" from Grant's note and pasted it onto the public consciousness in articles and editorials.[36]

In this case, meme wholesalers were those civilians who linked the words "unconditional surrender" with Grant and then incorporated them into political orations, after-dinner toasts, patriotic groups' public resolutions, and so forth.

34 Obama, Health Care Speech.

35 U.S. Grant, *Personal Memoirs of U.S. Grant, In Two Volumes* (New York: Charles L. Webster & Company, 1885), I: 311.

36 Bruce Catton, *Grant Moves South* (Boston: Little, Brown and Company, 1988), 181; see for example, *Brooklyn Eagle*, Feb. 18, 1862, "The Rebellion," *New York Times,* February 19, 1862; Benjamin Franklin Cooling, *Forts Henry and Donelson: The Key to the Confederate Heartland* (Knoxville, TN: The University of Tennessee Press, 1989), 245.

The retailers, as I will discuss in Chapter One, were ordinary soldiers who recycled the meme up and down the chain of command, as well as soldiers and civilians who ping-ponged the meme back and forth in letters to and from home. As I discuss in Chapter Thirteen the meme "unconditional surrender" was destined to join other, related memes that together formed Grant's bulldog reputation; this was to have important consequences later in the war. The larger point for battle or political speeches is that their influence cannot be understood without analyzing how the audience was prepared to receive the speaker. When it comes to understanding speechifying, there is nothing analogous to a "Death of the Author" doctrine. Quite the contrary: no matter the speechwriter, the speechmaker is almost always the speech.[37]

Speechlets and their memes also have political analogues. The 2008 presidential election produced several such battling Speechlets: "Country First" (McCain/Palin) versus "Yes We Can" and "Change We Can Believe In" (Obama/Biden.) "Country First" was an obvious appeal to patriotism; but it likely had two deeper meanings: the first was its patent connection with ticket-topper John McCain, whose Vietnam War service and five-and-a-half-year ordeal as a POW of the North Vietnamese had been long established as its own patriotic and "personal journey" meme. But there was a still deeper meaning: "Country First" also means "Self Second," and probably was meant to appeal to those "values voters" who believed that America was led by self-serving politicians and awash in a narcissistic, hedonistic culture. As with Grant, monikers are also political meme vehicles. McCain's moniker "Maverick" was used during the campaign to summarize his public persona of independence and integrity.

Enthymeme

One rhetorical device that is indispensable to concision in both battle and political speeches (and also serves as the mainspring of Speechlets) is the enthymeme. Aristotle, who first described enthymemes, called them "rhetorical syllogisms," by which he meant that they resembled a special form of argument—the syllogism—but with one or more of the premises missing.

---

37 "Death of the Author" is a literary doctrine that holds that creations must be considered entirely on their own terms and separate from the intent, design or biography of the creator. The doctrine was formulated by French literary theorist Roland Barthes and translated into English in *Aspen*, Numbers 5+6, Fall-Winter 1967, Roaring Fork Press.

"[The] enthymeme," Aristotle declared, "[may be] deduced from fewer premises, often from fewer than the regular syllogism; for if any one of these [that is, missing premise(s)] is well known, there is no need to mention it, *for the hearer can add it himself.*" [Italics added] The enthymeme, then, is an almost-autonomic form of discourse within a community that is already united in common understandings; this obviously includes language, but also other ideas: history, religion, culture, unit loyalty, political ideologies, and many other values.[38]

Here is an example of a syllogism:

First Premise: A United States' naval vessel should never surrender.

Second Premise: The *USS Chesapeake* is a United States' naval vessel.

Conclusion: Therefore, the *USS Chesapeake* should never surrender.

Now here is the Speechlet that this syllogism was extruded from:

"Don't give up the ship!"

This Speechlet saw double service during the War of 1812. It was first reportedly uttered by the mortally wounded Captain James Lawrence just before his ship, the *USS Chesapeake*, surrendered to the British in June 1813. Once retailed by the newspapers, Lawrence's "last words" (Lawrence having survived his wound for some days, it is unlikely that they actually were his last words) became an instant meme. Attesting to the meme's popularity (and the fact that it was a meme), four months later it was reused by Oliver Hazard Perry at the Battle of Lake Erie. Both uses will be discussed in more detail in Chapter Thirteen. For now, I would like to use this example to illustrate several points about how enthymemes work.

By comparing the syllogism and the Speechlet readers can see for themselves that substantial information about the United States Navy was required to make "Don't give up the ship!" intelligible to its first audience of sailors. Aristotle declared that the enthymeme "must neither be drawn from too

---

38 Aristotle, *Art of Rhetoric*, translated by John Henry Freese, (Cambridge, Massachusetts: Harvard University Press, 2000), I.ii.8, I.ii.13.

far back nor should it include all steps of an argument." In battle circumstances, neither speakers nor audiences have time to dwell overlong on explicated meaning; to do so at any time, Aristotle observes, would mean that a speech's "length causes obscurity" or the speech would "waste . . . words, because it states much that is obvious." Without the enthymeme, Captain Lawrence would have had to explain at length *why* the *USS Chesapeake* should not be surrendered; indeed, had his crew somehow consisted of clerks who had never been to sea and knew nothing of ships or naval warfare, Lawrence might well have had to provide this lengthy exposition, either before the battle or at the time—an improbability, given that when the Speechlet was uttered Lawrence was already *hors de combat* and the British were boarding his ship.[39]

Of course, Lawrence spoke not to clerks but to sailors, many widely experienced—and that is the point. The enthymeme, whether used in Speechlets or speeches, taps into what the audience knows. And every man-jack aboard the *Chesapeake* was already familiar with their captain's premises; thus, Lawrence could "rush" to his conclusion. The enthymeme is a piece of persuasion whose "evidence" (missing premises) is already established with the soldier/sailor/voting-audience.

The second common use of enthymemes in military and political speeches is one which *gives the premises but invites the audience to provide the conclusion.* Speechmakers have different motives for doing this, but the technique allows a speaker to lead an audience with what to an outsider at first might appear to be mere wind, but on closer inspection may have great significance for the soldier-audience. Consider this excerpt from a battle speech by Napoleon Bonaparte to his Grand Armee:

> Soldiers! The second Polish war has begun. The first ended at Friedland and Tilsit. At Tilsit, Russia swore eternal alliance with France and war on England. Today, she breaks her oaths! She refuses to give any explanation for her strange conduct unless the French eagles retire beyond the Rhine, thus leaving our allies at her mercy.
>
> Russia is swept along by her fate! Let her destiny be accomplished. Have we degenerated? Are we no longer the soldiers of Austerlitz? Russia gives us the

---

39 Aristotle, *Art of Rhetoric*, II.xxii.1-3.

choice between dishonor and war. Our choice cannot be in doubt. Let us march forward, then! Let us cross the Niemen, let us carry the war into her territory![40]

In the first paragraph, Napoleon gives his army a formal rationale for fighting Russia, an erstwhile ally. His given premises are first, that Russia had an alliance with France; second, that Russia betrayed this alliance; third, that Russia now behaves like the unprincipled betrayer that it is by asking France to betray her own allies; but the fourth premise is enthymematic and unstated: that France, unlike Russia, does not betray her allies.

But are these the real reasons that Napoleon gives the Grand Armee to fight Russia? Perhaps these sufficed for some soldiers; but one suspects that Napoleon's real persuasive argument was made in the second paragraph. Diplomatic and legal cases for war will not always suffice to stir souls, and Napoleon chose an entirely different argument to convince the army to cross the Niemen River. Enter the audience-baiting enthymeme.

He began with two so-called rhetorical questions: "Have we degenerated?" and "Are we no longer the soldiers of Austerlitz?" Rhetorical questions are not genuine questions—they are unstated (and thus enthymematic) premises designed to bait listeners into hoped-for conclusions. Napoleon's words properly should be understood as declarations, not questions: "*You have degenerated* in your skill and courage;" and because you lack these, "*You are not* the army that won at Austerlitz." Obviously, his soldiers were invited to deny these premises by asserting their opposites. And the only way that soldiers could prove the opposites would be by crossing the Niemen River. That was Napoleon's conclusion—but he left it the Grand Armee-audience to prove!

Invented dichotomies are also enthymematic. They enable the speechmaker to control the argument by defining choices, and thus available premises. The effect of this is to leave listeners with limited, but usually unstated, conclusions. For example, President Barack Obama's Inaugural Address posed various choices:

> *On this day, we gather because we have chosen hope over fear, unity of purpose over conflict and discord.*" [But some may have gathered for other reasons, which might have varied from witnessing the historic inauguration of America's first African-American president to selling trinkets to tourists.]

40 *The Mind of Napoleon: A Selection from His Written and Spoken Words*, ed. and trans. J. Christopher Herold (New York: Columbia University Press, 1955), 199-200.

The question that we ask today is not whether our government is too big or too small, but whether it works . . . ." [Some may believe that government's size is the question; others believe that government's size is not a question at all; while still others believe that the important questions about government are unrelated to its size.]

As for our common defense, we reject as false the choice between our safety and our ideals." [For some, the choice is in fact between safety and ideals; others may already be satisfied with the common defense; while still others may believe that the common defense is best served by purposes beyond safety or ideals, such as changing American foreign policy or intensifying attacks on enemies.][41]

Metonyms and Living Metonyms

Some speakers occupy positions or have reputations that make them, as individuals, their own persuasive argument, all without having to utter a word. As noted above, Pope Urban II and George S. Patton, Jr., were in this category: *who* they were and even *how* they appeared was a significant part of their persuasive strategy. Most of us may be familiar with living metonyms through what I call "platform people." When politicians or generals speak, they may share a platform with well-known but otherwise silent figures: other soldiers, civilian superiors, celebrities, or prominent leaders of different constituencies. The purpose of these visible, silent yet respiring props is to endorse whatever speech or act is being performed onstage, which they do simply by appearing with the speaker. The not-coincidental language used to report these living props' appearances might be, for example, "The President signed the bill today, and present was Jane Doe *representing* the Association." Indeed, one could easily substitute the word "symbolizing" for "representing." In ordinary conversation most people refer to living metonyms as "living symbols," as in, for example, statements that Martin Luther King and Mahatma Gandhi were living symbols of non-violent change.

To grasp what kind of symbol "living metonyms" are, I must briefly turn to metonyms. Metonyms are a subset of metaphors. Metaphors operate by associating two ideas to create a third idea. In *Rhetoric*, Aristotle offered an example of metaphor by quoting Pericles, who "said that the youth that had perished during the war had disappeared from [Athens] as if the year had lost its

---

41 Barack H. Obama, "Inaugural Address," January 20, 2009, www.whitehouse.gov/blog/inaugural-address/. Accessed September 29, 2009.

springtime." Two familiar ideas—a lost spring and the death of the young—are associated to create a third idea: losing the young is like a disruption of nature's cycle. What makes metaphors work for any speech is their efficiency. Pericles was spared from having to define terms or expatiate at length on why losing the young before the old is unnatural.[42]

Whereas a metaphor normally associates two unrelated things (lost youth and lost springtimes), metonyms usually associate a part of a thing with its whole. I think of it as associating two ideas that are already connected in some pre-existing relationship.

My favorite example of metonym is from the true crime cable series *City Confidential*. Each episode narrated the story of a murder and described how the killer and victim were connected to the larger community. When the talented (and lamentably late) voice-over of actor Paul Winfield described how each community reacted to the crime and trial, he usually declared something like, "Austin was shocked by news of the murder" or "Aspen was terrified that a killer might be loose." Needless to say, whatever their considerable merits, Austin and Aspen are bloodless municipalities, not sentient beings, and thus cannot be "shocked" or "terrified" by anything. But in such usages viewers understand exactly what Winfield meant: the cities "Austin" and "Aspen" are used to represent a subset of their residents who meet the following criteria: they work or reside within or near the municipal boundary; they have been paying attention to and have opinions about the case; and those opinions are the ones attributed by Winfield. By virtue of work or residency, these subsets all have pre-existing connections with Austin and Aspen. In sum, "Austin" and "Aspen" are metonyms for the local community that was paying attention to events after the crime.[43]

Presidents and emperors alike often use metonymy. In a Pre-Battle Speech before Borodino, Napoleon proclaimed:

---

42 Aristotle, *Art of Rhetoric*, III.x.7. My phrasing of metaphor as two unrelated ideas to create a third idea was taken from the useful Richard A. Lanham, *A Handlist of Rhetorical Terms, Second Edition,* (Berkeley: University of California Press, 1991), 100-101.

43 *City Confidential*, television series, 103 episodes, 1999-2006.

Do what you did at Austerlitz, at Friedland, at Vitebsk, at Smolensk, and let posterity point with pride to your conduct on this day: let people say of you: 'He was at that great battle fought under the walls of Moscow!'[44]

As with *City Confidential*, Napoleon's use of a string of cities to represent battles is more efficient than having to include the words "on the battlefield in the vicinity of . . . " before mentioning each town. Similarly, President Obama's Inaugural Address frequently used the word "America" metonymically, of which this excerpt is typical: "[F]rom the grandest capitals to the small village where my father was born, know that America is a friend of each nation . . . ."

But how did Pope Urban II "work" as a living metonym, and what has this to do with battle speeches? Understanding speakers metonymically is just an attempt to capture the totality of what an audience "saw" as it viewed and heard a speaker. In the case of Pope Urban II, this means not only placing oneself in the field in Clermont, France, looking up at the platform, the papal throne, and the tall, handsome, bearded figure of the Pope, garbed in his formal vestments, delivering his call for the First Crusade. True, this in itself must have been a once-in-a-lifetime experience for many in that crowd. But beyond such sights, what else did the audience "see"?

What they likely "saw" was more than a man. First, the Pope was the avatar of an otherwise bloodless but hierarchical abstraction: the Church of Rome. He was Heaven's infallible representative on earth, who had (in theory) authority over all matters relating to the Church. Of even greater importance to Urban's Call for the First Crusade, he also had the custody of the Church's defining symbols, especially the Cross, and the authority to interpret their symbolism. By the late eleventh century, most western Europeans had some contact with that Church through its cardinals, bishops, monsignors, priests, monasteries and nunneries, or with church buildings. For these reasons (and not just the sights themselves), for many pious Catholics seeing and hearing the Pope was less a sight than a vision; for many, perhaps, "seeing" the pope was the closest they might ever come to having a transcendent religious experience in this world.

The point of understanding Pope Urban II as a *living* metonym is to try to grasp something of the audience's immediate experiencing of the speaker and his words. Where supported by evidence, recreating historical events is always helped by descriptions of such things as weather, topography, and personalities;

---

44 *In the Words of Napoleon*, 247.

these matters likewise help in re-imagining battle speeches. But by themselves they are insufficient to explain a speech's impact. Speeches use symbols—words, dress, setting and props—but the most important symbol is the speaker. Thus, understanding battle speechmakers as metonyms forces one to probe not just the *conventional* historical details such as biography, but to ask what the speaker represented *in full* to his audience. For Urban II's speech, his personal biography, the preceding events of his papacy, and historians' more abstract findings regarding life in late eleventh-century Western Europe are by themselves insufficient to explain the wild enthusiasm with which his audience responded.

VIII. Were Battle Speeches Even Given?

Fighting Words references numerous battle speeches and Speechlets. How many were really a speaker's *ipsissima verba* ["the very words"]? How many were something else, perhaps an historian's fabrication, a "docu-dramatic" recreation, or a half-remembered fragment conveyed by secondary sources years, or even centuries, after the speech? Generally speaking, the older the speech, the less certain anyone can be that it was actually made, or, if made, was made in the words, at the time, or even by the speechmaker claimed by some later text. Chronicler bias, lost original sources, lack of corroborating evidence, and improbable historical, stylistic or philological details have, since antiquity, led historians to question the veracity of many battle speeches.[45]

---

45 A recent debate that combines high learning and entertaining reading may be followed in the exchange between classicists Mogens Herman Hansen and W. Kendrick Pritchett. Mogens Herman Hansen questioned not just the veracity of most ancient battle speeches, but whether anything more than a "harangue" was ever given; the speeches themselves were largely historians' fabrications. – Mogens Herman Hansen, "The Battle Exhortation in Ancient Historiography: Fact or Fiction?" *Historia: Journal of Ancient History* 42 (1993), Heft 2, 163, 172, 179. Pritchett responded in "The General's Exhortation in Greek Warfare," *Essays in Greek History* (Amsterdam: J. C. Gieben, 1994), 27-109 and *Ancient Greek Battle Speeches and a Palfrey* (Amsterdam: J.C. Gieben, 2002), 1-80. While not claiming that ancient battle speeches were the speaker's *ipsissima verba,* Pritchett argued that there is a high likelihood that many did present the essence or some reconstruction of what was actually said. Various historians entered the fray, generally against Hansen. See C.T.H.R. Erhardt, "Speeches before Battle?" *Historia: Journal of Ancient History* 44 (1995), Heft 1, 120-121; Michael Clark, "Did Thucydides Invent the Battle Exhortation?" *Historia: Journal of Ancient History* 44 (1995), Heft 3, 375-376. Jon R. Stone, *Latin for the Illiterarti: Excorcising the Ghosts of a Dead Language,* (New York: Routledge, 1996), 50.

This is a question I have reviewed in earlier writings. Most of the scholarly debate has raged over the speeches of antiquity; for example, the speeches contained in Herodotus, Thucydides, Xenophon and Arrian. I have argued that while this issue is of obvious concern to classicists and interesting to others, it is less urgent for battle speech historians. As centuries passed it began to matter less whether, say, Alexander the Great actually spoke at the Hyphasis River, or spoke as Arrian claimed, than it did that subsequent ages *believed* that Alexander had spoken as Arrian claimed. Either way, for later generations his supposed speech was available to serve as one paradigm for what to do or not do to quell a mutiny. Thus it is irrelevant that some scholars question whether the Hyphasis River was even the eastern terminus of Alexander's empire, an important outcome from Alexander's speech at the river. (See Chapter Six.)[46]

What I wish to highlight are the issues of veracity for more recent battle speeches. The existence of modern means of recordation—the availability (in print and electronic form) of public records, official and secondary histories, media accounts, memoirs, letters, diaries and so forth—has narrowed considerably the scope of these questions. For example, there are at least four contemporary printed versions of Patton's "The Speech," which differ only in small details; and both Ridgway's Memorandum and Grant's demand for the "unconditional surrender" of Fort Donelson are part of the army's official record. In these cases, the question is about the influence such speeches had on soldier-audiences or their wider historical significance.[47]

Yet some rather famous remarks remain subject to what I call the Liberty Valance Problem. Readers familiar with John Ford's classic film *The Man Who Shot Liberty Valance* (1962) may recall the exchange between Randall Stoddard and newspaperman Maxwell Scott. Stoddard had built a successful political career on a foundation of having shot and killed the notorious bully Liberty

---

46 My own summary of this issue may be found in *Words and Deeds*, 12-20. Therein I argued, first, as above, that whether or not certain speeches were actually given, later centuries accepted them as given, and thus they became models for historians and battle speechmakers; second, that whatever was said, both the nature of ancient battlefield deployments and realities of ancient combat provided both the opportunity and the moral necessity for exhortatory battle speeches. Admittedly, this is inference and not proof, but noteworthy here is the fact that many of these speeches were written by historians who were themselves soldiers, including some with first-hand experience of the wars they narrated. A list would include Xenophon, Caesar, Josephus, Arrian, Thucydides, Sallust, and Polybius (if one counts the latter's close relationship with the Scipio family.)

47 For versions of "The Speech," see Chapter Four, footnote 2.

Valance; years later Scott learned the truth about who had really shot Valance. Stoddard was worried.

Stoddard: You're not going to use the story, Mr. Scott?

Scott: No sir. This is the West, sir. When the legend becomes the fact, print the legend.[48]

Of course, there is no residency requirement for printing legends as facts. As I will discuss, such Speechlets as "Don't fire until you see the whites of their eyes!" and the first iteration of "Don't give up the ship!" had aspects of legend that were too compelling not to use as facts, even for many historians who should have known better. For the "Don't fire" Speechlet, the question is twofold: was the remark ever made, and if so by whom? For "Don't give up the ship!" the question is slightly different: it is well attested that Captain Lawrence said *something* like "Don't give up the ship!" but his exact words are uncertain. However, that mattered little when, four months later at the Battle of Lake Erie, Oliver Hazard Perry, aboard his flagship *Lawrence*, raised the fighting banner bearing the "final" Speechlet. Nor do I believe it would matter if by some magic of anachronism a tape recording surfaced of Captain Lawrence's exact words. The influence of memes, speeches and Speechlets does not depend upon historical "proof;" it requires only that they have "legs."[49]

Fighting Words explores this issue of "legs," from the standpoint of *why* these Speechlets evolved as they did. But what I wish to emphasize here are the reasons why even modern Speechlets and battle speeches may not be entirely trustworthy. First, the problem of dispersion may produce different versions of the same speech. This was the case with Patton's "The Speech," which he delivered from memory many times in many places to recently arrived Third Army units throughout southern England. But the principal questions that revolve around *ipsissima verba* are those of distraction—combat itself can impair memory—and time—which (as readers of a certain age will attest) can transform even recent memory into fiction.

And there may be other reasons. Consider two recollections of one speech from the American Civil War. At the Battle of Balls Bluff, fought in Virginia in 1861, Colonel Winfield Scott Featherston, commanding the Seventeenth Mississippi, ordered his infantry to make what would be the final assault on the

---

48 *The Man Who Shot Liberty Valance*, (1962).

49 See Chapters Thirteen and Fourteen.

federal line. Featherston wrote later that "[m]y next order to them was "forward Mississippians, & drive them into the Potomac or into eternity."

Stirring stuff. But Mississippi Private William Meshack Abernathy remembered Featherston stirring with even more vigor: "Mississippians, forward, charge, drive the Damn Yankees into the Potomac or Hell!"

What accounts for the differences in recollections? One is tempted to blame (and often would be correct in doing so) the impairments caused by the distractions of combat or the passage of time. But years later Private Abernathy recalled:

> After the war Featherstone [sic] got religion and somehow modified that order. "I never said it," he says, "that way." But whenever he was talking with an old Seventeenth man he always winked, and all I can say is, I hope the Recording Angel got the revised version.[50]

Occasionally, history can be far more interesting than what actually happened.

---

50 I am indebted for this delightful anecdote to James A. Morgan III's fine study of the Battle of Ball's Bluff, *A Little Short of Boats: The Fights at Ball's Bluff and Edwards Ferry, October 21-22, 1861: A History and Tour Guide* (Ft. Mitchell, Kentucky: Ironclad Publishing, 2004), 161-162.

Section One

The Speaker Is the Speech

My theory is that an army commander does what is necessary to accomplish his mission, and that nearly eighty percent of his mission is to arouse morale in his men.

— General George S. Patton, Jr.[1]

What does it mean to say that the speaker *is* the speech? Aristotle observed in *Rhetoric* that the speaker's identity may be as persuasive as his speech:

> [I]t is not the case, as some writers of rhetorical treatises lay down in their "Art" that the worth of the orator in no way contributes to his power of persuasion. On the contrary, moral character . . . constitutes the most effective means of proof.[2]

Thus the commonsense point that a speaker with good "moral character" is more likely to persuade an audience than one with an unknown or a suspect character. The implication is clear: an audience may fuse a speaker's moral character with the credibility of his words. But exactly how does a speaker's moral character "fuse" with his speech? And what is meant by "moral character"? Obviously, a speaker's reputation for honesty and personal integrity matters. But "moral character" can mean something else: a form of energy that has less to do with honesty or personal integrity, but everything to do with a

---

1 George S. Patton, Jr., *War As I Knew It* (Boston: Houghton Mifflin Company, 1995), "Earning My Pay," X: 374.

2 Aristotle, *Art of Rhetoric*, I, ii, 5.

reputation for success—or failure. Reputations bearing on moral character include a speaker's perceived history of being efficient or incompetent, lucky or jinxed, and for achieving victory or defeat, or profits or losses. For speechmakers these forms of moral character rest in the audience's belief that, in the past, whatever the speaker predicted or promised actually came true. How this "moral character" differs from simple morals is best illustrated by noting the many persuasive speeches made by known charlatans, lawbreakers, liars, and those who dissemble for a living.

The process of how a battle speechmaker's "moral character" fuses with his words is the subject of this section. The first example highlights the importance of reputation, and is explored in American military history's great "wordless speech": the nighttime ride of Ulysses S. Grant on May 7, 1864. Next considered is Pope Urban II's call for the First Crusade, and specifically how he used his unique relationship with the most powerful symbol of his age—the Cross—to imbue it with new meanings. Finally considered is General George Washington's Newburgh Address in which he prevented a mutiny among his officers. The Newburgh Address unites the themes of reputation and symbols by illustrating how one skilled speaker combined them into a powerful persuasive strategy that avoided a disaster.

Chapter One

The Meme Becomes the Man:
Grant in the Wilderness

[To] MAJOR-GENERAL MEADE.
Commanding A.P.

Make all preparations during the day for a night march to take position at
Spottsylvania C.H. with one army corps, at Todd's Tavern with one, and another
near the intersection of the Piney Branch and Spottsylvania road with the road
from Alsop's to Old Court House.

...All vehicles should be got out of hearing of the enemy before the troops move, and
then move off quietly.

[Signed]
U.S. GRANT
Lieut.-General.

— Excerpt from Grant's orders for the Army of the Potomac for the night of May 7,
1864

Soon after dark. . . . With my staff and a small escort of cavalry I preceded the
troops. Meade with his staff accompanied me. The greatest enthusiasm was
manifested by Hancock's men as we passed by. No doubt it was inspired by the fact
that the movement was south. It indicated to them that they had passed through the

"beginning of the end" in the battle just fought. The cheering was so lusty that the enemy must have taken it for a night attack.[1]

— Grant's recollection of the night of May 7, 1864

I. Historical Background

Since the Federals' main eastern army was first driven off the field at the Battle of First Manassas in July 1861, it had grown accustomed to failed offensives that were invariably followed by retreats: the Peninsula Campaign and the battles of Second Manassas, Fredericksburg, Chancellorsville and Mine Run had all fit this pattern; even the victories at Antietam and Gettysburg were followed by weak pursuits of the enemy. Some historians have detected a larger, attitudinal pattern: the Federal army would first fight bravely to a draw or a loss, and then, commanders demoralized, withdraw from the field. Now, after two days of indescribable savagery in Virginia's Wilderness, not far from the earlier scenes of bloodlettings at Chancellorsville and Fredericksburg, many bluecoats braced behind their battered entrenchments and expected the old pattern would repeat. They awaited the order to withdraw north across the Rapidan River.[2]

But on the evening of May 7, 1864, the Army of the Potomac underwent a remarkable change. That night federal soldiers beheld their supreme commander, Ulysses S. Grant, silently riding "at an easy jingling trot" in a southerly direction just behind the main battle line along the Brock Road. It was enough to convince thousands of exhausted bluecoats that this war, now entering its fourth year, was about to take a new and decisive turn.[3]

1   U.S. Grant, *Personal Memoirs of U.S. Grant*, (New York: Da Capo Press, Inc, 1982), 411. War of the Rebellion. *Official Records of the Union and Confederate Armies in the War of Rebellion*, Series 4, 128 vols., (Washington D.C: Government Printing Office, 1894-1922), hereafter *OR*, Series I, Volume 36, pt. 2, 481.

2   For an account of the Army of the Potomac's defeatism, see Michael C. C. Adams, *Our Masters the Rebels: A Speculation on Union Military Failure in the East, 1861-1865* (Cambridge, Massachusetts: Harvard University Press, 1978).

3   Bruce Catton, *A Stillness at Appomattox* (New York: Washington Square Press, 1958), 105; see also James McPherson, *Battle Cry of Freedom: The Civil War Era,* (New York: Ballantine Books, 1989), 728.

II. The "Wordless" Speech

Notwithstanding the darkness of the night, the form of the commander was recognized, and word was passed rapidly along that the chief who had led them through the mazes of the Wilderness was again moving forward with his horse's head turned toward Richmond. Troops know but little about what is going on in a large army, except the occurrences which take place in their immediate vicinity; but this night ride of the general-in-chief told plainly the story of success, and gave each man to understand that the cry was to be 'On to Richmond!' .... Wild cheers echoed through the forest, and glad shouts of triumph rent the air. Men swung their hats, tossed up their arms, and pressed forward to within touch of their chief, clapping their hands, and speaking to him with the familiarity of comrades.

— Eyewitness Horace Porter, staff officer to Lieutenant General Ulysses Grant, May 7, 1864[4]

III. Parsing the "Speech"

Why did this sight of the silent Grant energize his army? Grant never intended that his personal movement that evening should signify anything; indeed, he regretted his soldiers' enthusiasm. "This is most unfortunate," he complained to Porter after hearing the cheers. "The sound will reach the ears of the enemy, and I fear it may reveal our movement."[5]

The answer to this question lies in what Grant's soldier-audience already believed about him; the sight of Grant riding south only confirmed what it "knew." Thus, the general's silent act was the equivalent of a brilliantly worded, passionately delivered exhortation, because knowledge of Grant's (to use Aristotle's phrase) "moral character" had long been insinuated into the army's collective mind, a process that began in 1861. These bits of information—memes—created the profile of a man who the soldiers now believed was able to lead them south despite a bloody battle. To his soldiers, Grant was simply acting according to a type that had been amply "proved" by newspaper articles, campfire conversations, letters, public proclamations, and politicians' speeches. All Grant had to do in order to re-moralize his army was

---

4   General Horace Porter, *Campaigning with Grant* (New York: Da Capo Press, Inc., 1986), 78-79.

5   Porter, *Campaigning with Grant*, 79.

act in a way consistent with his reputational memes. The neologism "meme" may have been coined in 1976; but it describes a process of diffusing knowledge that has roots in the beginning of human time. And nothing better illustrates memes' power than does the nighttime ride of General Grant.

What memes defined Grant in the spring of 1864? Perhaps the clearest meme summary appeared in a May 1863 *New York Times'* editorial published a full five weeks before Grant's pivotal capture of Vicksburg and almost a year before the Battle of the Wilderness. The editorialist observed that the Civil War was "strewed with faded and ruined military reputations"; by contrast, he noted that Grant's renown "[had] been steadily gaining from the outset." The *Times* thought this unusual not just because Grant was young ("but a man of forty at the commencement of the war") but also because "when he took command at Cairo [Illinois in 1861] he was not much known and attracted little attention." What especially impressed the writer was that "Gen. Grant, though perhaps possessed of no great military genius, yet combines qualities which, in such a war as this, are even better calculated to insure success, and which scarcely any of his brother Generals have exhibited in complete combination."[6]

The *Times* proceeded to list five of these qualities: "*First*, he has absolute singleness of purpose. . . . [W]ithout a thought about . . . political advantage; without a look either toward Washington for favor, or toward home for popularity. *Second*, his Spartan simplicity of character, his abstemiousness, his readiness to share any privation with his soldiers, his impartial justice, his strict discipline and his personal fearlessness. . . . *Third*, his modesty. . . . *Fourth*. . . . his sound judgment and sterling sense." [Italics original]

But it was Grant's fifth quality that really impressed the writer:

> [He] has, what tells more than all else, a most extraordinary combination of energy and persistence. In these two moral elements, he probably has not his equal. Nothing daunts him, nothing discourages him. There is nothing he does not dare to undertake, there is nothing he can bear to give up. In that one great point at least, he is a perfect counterpart of the Napoleon who said that the word 'impossible' was not in his vocabulary. Thus indomitable resolution and perseverance is that element which, of all others, contributes most to make up the master-spirit in war. It is Grant's preeminence in this that has done most to give him preeminence in everything [Italics in original]

---

6 "Gen. Grant and His Splendid Success at Vicksburgh," *New York Times,* May 28, 1863.

The *Times'* observations derived from some very specific reporting about Grant's earlier victories. These reports soon became stock perceptions about him, repeated endlessly in articles and speeches and by word of mouth. This process of meme diffusion was assisted by the era's structure of news distribution: most small newspapers could not afford to field reporters, and so simply reprinted verbatim (sometimes without attribution) stories carried by their larger newspaper brethren. By May 1863 some contemporaries still adhered to Grant's pre-war memes of hard luck and alcoholism, while others believed that Shiloh, a victory, was nevertheless tainted by charges of Grant's incompetence and alcoholism. But the vast majority of Northern (and more than a few Southern) newspaper readers, if asked to list Grant's achievements, might have produced the following list: a minor victory at Belmont (November 1861); two great victories with the capture of Forts Henry and Donelson (February 1862); a bloody, near-miss of a victory at Shiloh (April 1862); the May 1863 capture of Mississippi's state capital at Jackson; and, finally, the against-all-odds investment of Vicksburg. Of almost equal importance is that if asked, these same readers would probably have expressed general agreement about the makeup of Grant's "moral character."

What was Grant's "moral character?" It is worth briefly discussing one of Grant's early victories because it provided the most fundamental meme conveyer of them all, in use at least since the time of Homer: the epithet. Of particular importance to Grant memes was that this, his most famous epithet, was a perfectly shaped vessel that could hold his other moral qualities.

The morning of February 16, 1862, found Grant and his army besieging the Confederate works at Fort Donelson, located on the Cumberland River. In the pre-dawn hours Grant was handed a note from General Simon B. Buckner, an old friend and now his rebel adversary. Buckner commanded the besieged fort and was requesting that Grant agree to appoint commissioners to discuss terms of surrender; accordingly, he asked for an armistice.

But Grant would have none it. He replied in a note that contained the words that would follow him for the rest of his life. (It also set a popular standard for victory that would shadow every future American war.):

No terms except an unconditional and immediate surrender can be accepted. I propose to move immediately upon your works.

By coincidence, Grant's initials were U.S., and his soldiers, from respect and affection, immediately nicknamed him "Unconditional Surrender" Grant.

Fifteen months later the *Times* concluded its May 1863 editorial, "U.S. GRANT—or, as his soldiers style him, Unconditional Surrender Grant—has given the Confederacy blows such as no other arm has dealt and, if he is let alone, as we trust he will be, he will in due time bring the whole concern to the dust." Grant's epithet implied pure determination and decisiveness. "Unconditional Surrender" appeared repeatedly in stories about Grant. And what it had come to connote by the time of the May 1863 editorial now in May 1864 filled Grant's exhausted soldiers' thoughts as they awaited his decision about which way the Army of the Potomac would move after yet one more bloody battle in Virginia.[7]

What were his soldiers' thoughts? Between March, 1864 (when Grant assumed command of all Federal armies) and the night of May 7, many soldiers expressed the same views as the *Times'* editorialist. No claim is made here that those soldiers read the *Times'* piece; indeed, the *Times* is cited only as a contemporary reflection of Grant's memes; other than pushing distribution, it likely added little to already-established ideas about Grant. And these ideas were well established by May 1863; significantly, several of Grant's greatest victories—the final surrender of Vicksburg and the relief of Chattanooga and the victory at Lookout Mountain—still lay in the future.

Consider this montage of Eastern soldiers' views of Grant in the weeks and months preceding the Battle of the Wilderness. Private Simon B. Cummins of the 151st New York Infantry wrote to his father on March 23: "We expect to see hard fighting this summer.... Gen Grant is a going to take command of his army himself.... The old Gen says take Richmond and the war is over and I believe it." Major Henry L. Abbott of the 20th Massachusetts Infantry wrote to his mother on April 4, "From what I can learn, I feel pretty sure that we shall be victorious at last. I have no idea that Grant is a genius. In fact, I am very sure that he is not. But still if he has only as much shrewdness & character as he is supposed to have, with the immense resources which he can command, I feel that it is pretty safe." Private Wilbur Fisk of the 2nd Vermont Infantry, who also doubled as a correspondent for his hometown newspaper *The Green Mountain Freeman*, declared in a letter published on April 7 that "It seems to be the prevailing opinion here in the army, that we are at last to have a campaign that will for once

---

7   Grant, *Personal Memoirs*, 158-159; *New York Times* editorial, "Gen. Grant and His Splendid Success at Vicksburgh," May 28, 1863. Later wartime appearances of the Donelson meme are too numerous to list, but for one especially prominent example, see "Grant's First Proposition and His Last," *New York Times*, May 13, 1864.

be really 'short, sharp, and decisive,' and I will add, victorious. Great confidence is felt in the plans that General Grant will adopt." On April 18 Grant reviewed the corps to which Sergeant John F.L. Hartwell's 124th New York Infantry belonged, and the sergeant wrote in his diary, "The Hero of Vicksburg is a fine looking man. He took no pains to show off." Just before crossing the Rapidan River into the Wilderness, one of the Carter brothers wrote in a letter, "Every soldier I saw is in high spirits, and I never saw such confidence in success manifested. General Grant's operations produce no partisan feeling, and that fills all hearts with hope. All are in good spirits and '*confident of success.*'" [Italics original] Finally, Elisha Hunt Rhodes of the 2nd Rhode Island Infantry, writing on May 7 but presumably before Grant's nighttime ride, already knew, based on Grant's reputation, what direction the army would take: "We have entrenched ourselves the best we can with logs and earth and are awaiting events. If we were under any other General except General Grant, I should expect a retreat, but Grant is not that kind of soldier, and we feel that we can trust him." Years later, Corporal James Donnelly of the 20th Massachusetts reflected on Grant in the Wilderness. "I never had a doubt that General Grant would lead us on to final victory," he recalled. "A great many thought it was another fall back across the Rapidan [but] now we had a Commander that didn't believe in falling back."[8]

---

8   Melvin Jones, ed., *Give God the Glory: Memoirs of a Civil War Soldier* (Grand Rapids, Michigan: Paris Press, 1979), "Dear Father," March 23, 1864, 53-54; edited by Robert Garth Scott, ed., *Fallen Leaves: The Civil War Letters of Major Henry Livermore Abbott*, (Kent, Ohio: Kent State University Press, 1991), "My Dear Mother, April 4, 1864," 242; Emil & Ruth Rosenblatt, eds., *Hard Marching Every Day: The Civil War Letters of Private Wilbur Fisk, 1861-1865*, (Lawrence, Kansas: University Press of Kansas, 1992), letter of April 7, 1864, 206; Anne Hartwell Britton and Thomas J. Reed, eds., *To My Beloved Wife and Boy at Home: The Letters and Diaries of Orderly Sergeant John F. L. Hartwell* (Cranbury, New Jersey: Associated University Presses, 1997), "Diary Entry. Monday 18 April 1864," 219; Robert Goldwaite Carter, ed., *Four Brothers in Blue: A Story of the Great Civil War from Bull Run to Appomattox* (Norman, Oklahoma: University of Oklahoma Press, 1999), 390; Robert Hunt Rhodes, ed., *All for the Union: The Civil War Diary and Letters of Elisha Hunt Rhodes* (New York: Orion Books, 1985), diary entry for 7 May 1864, 146; "Written by James Donnelly, Late Corporal Co. D, 20th Massachusetts, to Capt. Robbins, from N.Y.C., August 10, 1897," MOLLUS Collection, Houghton Library, Harvard University.

Immediate Result

Northern soldier Private Frank Wilkerson almost certainly spoke for a majority of the Army of the Potomac. "Instantly, all of us heard a sigh of relief," he recalled after seeing Grant. "Our spirits rose." Historian Bruce Catton offered an army-wide perspective: The soldiers, he wrote, "had had their fill of desperate fighting, and this pitiless little man was leading them into nothing except more fighting, and probably there would be no end to it, but at least he was not leading them back in sullen acceptance of defeat, and somewhere many miles ahead, there would be victory for those who lived to see it."[9]

Grant rode south and never turned back. Many battles have turning points; but Grant's nighttime ride was a turning point two-fer: it signaled both a dramatic change in the Army of the Potomac's psychology, and confirmed for the balance of the war that policy had changed. Hereafter, the Federal army would wage a relentless, aggressive war.

Legacy

Grant's nighttime ride epitomized his taciturn style of command. In fact, saying little and doing much became one of two basic styles of American military command—the opposite being illustrated by the more extroverted figure of George S. Patton, Jr. (See Chapter Four.) Grant's famous economy with words and deeds created a standard to which later civilian and battle speechmakers adhered and which admiring publics expected. Seen in this light, Dewey's laconic order from the *USS Olympia's* bridge ("You may fire when ready, Gridley") or even President Theodore Roosevelt's proverb ("Speak softly and carry a big stick; you will go far") conform neatly with what the public expected from leaders perceived as decisive. And they expected such epigrams because Grant had long since created the American warrior's template: less is more.

---

9   As quoted in Gordon C. Rhea, *The Battles for Spotsylvania Court House and the Road to Yellow Tavern, May 7-12, 1864* (Baton Rouge: Louisiana State University Press, 1997), 39; Bruce Catton, *A Stillness at Appomattox,* 105.

Leadership Principle

Grant's ride illustrates several points that apply universally to speakers on any topic. First, so influential is reputation that a speaker's "speech" may be made without uttering a word. These reputational memes matter because they can shortcut—or cut short—a speaker's credibility. In Grant's case, reputation was so powerful that no exhortatory command, "Southward, Ho!" was necessary—his deed literally became word, the whole of which was entirely imputed by his soldier "audience." His ride south might have meant many things, not all of which would have signified "On to Richmond!"

Second, speakers must be conscious of their memes because these aggregate into reputation, and thus become Aristotle's "moral character." The Leadership Principle here is to understand that in most cases audiences bring with them some notion of the speaker, and the cause or institution he represents, and thus have already applied a premium or a discount to what they will, or think they will, hear. Successful speakers must master complete and utterly candid self-awareness of how they, their cause, or their institution is perceived by the audiences they seek to persuade. What they do with this awareness becomes the foundation of their persuasive strategy.

Persuasive Strategy

Vegetius's classic military manual *De Re Militari* offers this advice to readers (who have included Roman Emperors, kings of medieval Europe, and a good many commanders since): "It is necessary to know the sentiments of the soldiers on the day of an engagement. Their confidence or apprehensions are easily discovered by their looks, their words, their actions and their motions." This articulates the essence of knowing one's audience—the men from whom the commander is likely to be asking a great deal. It is also the empathy that every speaker must have not just with the audience as an abstraction, but also (where possible) the knowledge of individuals composing that audience. [10]

---

10   *The Military Institutions of the Romans (De Re Militari)*, by Flavius Vegetius Renatus, translated from the Latin by Lieutenant John Clark, *Roots of Strategy: The Five Greatest Military Classics of All Time*, ed. Brig. Gen. Thomas R. Phillips, U.S. Army (Mechanicsburg, Pennsylvania: Stackpole Books, 1985), Book III, "The Sentiments of Troops Should Be Determined Before Battle," 152.

But Vegetius' prescription is incomplete because it fails to incorporate "meme analysis." Nerves on the eve of battle may be influenced by memes that soldiers absorbed months earlier. And not all memes relate to *personal* reputation. Some may be stereotypes; but not all stereotypes are invidious. For example, Grant was acutely aware that his status as a "westerner" made him a type about which many easterners had ambivalent feelings. On one hand, westerners were admired as "natural men," a somewhat advanced white American Protestant version of Alexander Pope's "noble savages"; at the same time, easterners could despise their western cousins for their frontier twangs and lack of polish. Grant's natural taciturnity already disposed him to embody the positive western memes in order to create an appealing character—say little, do much—that easily conformed to the backwoods types that many easterners believed westerners to be.

Grant was also deeply conscious of his predecessors' memes—in particular, the way they were remembered by the soldiery. Irwin McDowell's reputation had been sullied after the loss at First Bull Run by charges of incompetence and disloyalty; George B. McClellan's memes were a mixture of filial devotion but also social pretensions, indecision and partisanship; Ambrose Burnside's reputation combined bad luck and well-meaning incompetence; Joseph Hooker, flamboyance, political scheming and indecision at the crux of combat; McClellan, Burnside, and Hooker were recalled as men who promised too much; George G. Meade's generalship was recalled as too conservative, and Meade himself perhaps unlucky; but all of Grant's predecessors delivered too little. Speakers must correlate their messages with their memes. On the night of May 7, 1864, federal soldiers may have had doubts, but somehow they *expected* Grant to advance. The sight of his actually doing so was in accordance with his reputation, and thus could be accepted in the form of a wordless speech. Fortunately for the fate of the United States, Grant's memes closely paralleled the man.

Should readers assume that Grant was *no more* than an inkblot to which his soldiers imputed some meaning of their own? The short answer is, no. Grant's influence must be assessed holistically. To his men that May evening, Grant was much more than some aggregation of reputational memes. First, he held a superior rank in that most hierarchical institution—the army—that was defined by symbols of authority: uniforms, insignia, and a number of special practices such as salutes, special music, and armed escorts. And within this same institution, he held the historically unusual rank of lieutenant general, the first incumbent since George Washington, and thus was able to borrow some of his predecessor's luster. The army to which Grant belonged commanded its soldiers' loyalty, as did the government and nation that it served. But army, government, and nation are abstractions, and however one unbundles what they "stood for" in May 1864, they surely cloaked Grant with even more credibility than was already conferred by the nickname "Unconditional Surrender." Indeed, the cloaking credibility of institutions and access to its symbol system (for example, the Stars and Stripes or the historical link to George Washington) can not only compensate for a speaker's personal deficits, but may tower above the speaker in importance. Thus the expression, "I respect the office, not the occupant." In such cases the speaker remains the speech, but the speaker is only a mouthpiece for the institution he represents.

In human society two most powerful wielders of symbols are nation-states and religions. When these combine in common cause, the power of symbols can subsume a speaker in ways that transform him into a symbol incarnate. How this process works and the importance of institutional symbols to Leadership Principles and Persuasive Strategies is nowhere better illustrated than with Pope Urban II's November 1095 Call for the First Crusade.

Chapter Two

Living Symbols:
Pope Urban II Calls for the First Crusade

I. Historical Background

Pope Urban II's Call for the First Crusade ranks among the most influential battle speeches in history. The Call was really a summons to war, or what I call a Recruiting Speech. Its persuasive force rested on two pillars. The first was the speaker. Urban II was St. Peter's representative in this world, and as such his words were invested with unique, Heaven-sanctioned authority; that authority included the power to grant or withhold eternal life. Second, inseparable from his papal authority yet even larger in meaning, was the Cross, Christianity's most revered symbol that antedated even the papacy.

Pope Urban II convened the Council of Clermont in France on November 18, 1095. The pope and 310 distinguished prelates were cloistered for nine days in the Church Notre-Dame du Port where the holy assembly decided ecclesiastical controversies, judged lawsuits and managed routine Church business. But on November 27 word circulated that the pope wished to convene "a public session to make a great announcement." As the church was too small to accommodate the large gathering, a platform was erected in a nearby field, on which was placed the papal throne. Presumably appearing in full papal garb, the fifty-three year old Urban rose to deliver his speech. Described as by one historian as, "tall, with a handsome, bearded face, courteously mannered and persuasive in his speech," to his audience Urban II would have incarnated (as much as a human being can) the abstractions of Church, State, and the Triune God; all this, and the power to unlock heaven's gates. In sum, Pope Urban II was as close to a "living metonym" as Western society could ever produce. And now the time had arrived to reverse recent Muslim conquests in the Levant, take back Jerusalem, and re-Christianize the Holy Land.[1]

II. The Speech

We want you to know what sad cause has brought us to your land and what emergency of yours and of all the faithful it is that has brought us here. Disturbing news has emerged from Jerusalem and the city of Constantinople and is now constantly at the forefront of our mind: namely that the race of Persians [Muslims], a foreign people and a people rejected by God...has invaded the lands of those Christians, depopulated them by slaughter and plunder and arson, kidnapped some of the Christians and carried them off to their own lands and put others to a wretched death, and has either overthrown the churches of God or turned them over to the rituals of their own religion. They throw down the altars after soiling them with their own filth, circumcise Christians and pour the resulting blood either on the altars or into the baptismal vessels. . . . And most especially let the Holy Sepulchre of Our Lord the Redeemer move you—in the power as it is of foul races—and the holy places now abused and sacrilegiously defiled by their filthy practices. Oh most valiant soldiers and descendents of various ancestors, do not fall short of, but be inspired by, the courage of your forefathers. . . . Do not be held back by any possession or concern for your family. . . . Set out on the road to the Holy Sepulchre, deliver that land from a wicked race and take it yourselves—the land which was given by God to the sons of Israel, as Scripture says a land flowing with milk and honey. . . . Jerusalem is the navel of the earth. It is a land more fruitful than any other, almost another Earthly Paradise. Our Redeemer dignified it with his arrival, adorned it with his words, consecrated it through his Passion, redeemed it by his death and glorified it with his burial. . . . So seize on this road to obtain the remission of your sins, sure in the indestructible glory of the Heavenly Kingdom.

— Excerpts from Pope Urban II's Call for the First Crusade, November 27, 1095 (Robert the Monk's version)[2]

---

1   August C. Krey, *The First Crusade: The Accounts of Eyewitnesses and Participants*, (Princeton, New Jersey: Princeton University Press, 1921), excerpt from Fulcher of Chartres, 26; Steven Runciman, *A History of the Crusades, Volume I: The First Crusade and the Foundation of the Kingdom of Jerusalem* (Great Britain: The Folio Society, 1994), 89, 83. The description of Urban is Mr. Runciman's.

2   Robert the Monk's *History of the First Crusade* (*Historia Iherosolimitana*), translated and edited by Carol Sweetenham (Burlington, Vermont: Ashgate Publishing, 2005), 79-81.

III. Parsing the Speech

No parsing of Urban's Call can be made without understanding its structure as a Recruiting Speech, a type of battle speech with its own conventions and appeals. The Call very much conforms to its type. First, it uses the Staging convention: seeking to attract and inspire the largest possible audience, the Call was publicly announced, a special place was designated for the gathering, and a platform built on which the Papal throne was mounted. Staging heightens drama and typically runs in direct proportion to the importance of the speaker: important speakers require impressive staging. In 1095 there were few speakers as important as Pope Urban II, and even fewer speeches as dramatic as his Call for the First Crusade.[3]

A second vital organ of the Recruiting Speech is the Family Appeal convention. The Recruiting Speech is different from most battle speeches because its audience includes few soldiers; instead, listeners are mostly potential recruits and perhaps important family members (what some moderns might call "decision-makers"): parents, wives, siblings, and extended family. Even if no family members are actually present, they weigh on most recruits' minds. Putting aside purely filial and romantic considerations, there is this: in more primitive societies, military-aged males are often indispensable to families' economies, which is to say, their survival—as sole or contributing breadwinners, caregivers or protectors. Indeed, even modern militaries continue to recruit using Family Appeals. Since Urban's day, the reasons offered families to part with their younglings have changed—but not the need to make the case.[4]

Besides Robert the Monk's account, there are two other versions of Urban II's Call that have strong claims to being eyewitness accounts: those of Fulcher of Chartres and Baldric of Dol. The fourth, by Guibert of Nogent, was probably based on eyewitness accounts. Each of the four was written between five and thirteen years after the speech; thus, there are substantial differences between versions, and, perhaps not surprisingly, each auditor remembered things about the speech that likely held some special ethnic or theological interest. Each version may also have included some retrospective constructions about what the Pope should have said given subsequent events. Understandably, scholars have spilled considerable ink in efforts to reconcile these versions. I have selected Robert the Monk's version because it offers the most complete account of Urban's important follow-on speech.

3   These conventions and appeals may be found in, Miller, *In Words and Deeds*, 85-87.

4   Modern militaries' recruiting appeals often contain arguments meant to persuade families about enlistment's benefits for children: vocational training, increased confidence, and so forth. For an example of the modern Family Appeal that stresses recruit benefits, see www.parents.marines.com/page/personal-growth.jsp. Accessed July 19, 2009.

And Urban's Call addresses family concerns. He uses the most persuasive means he had—the authority of the Gospel. "If affection for your children and parents and spouse holds you back," he admonished in a passage unexcerpted above, "remember what our Lord says in the Gospel …." The Pope then constructs a single meaning by joining two sentences from the Gospel of Matthew: "*he that loveth father or mother more than me is not worthy of me*" (Matthew 10:37) with "*And everyone that hath forsaken houses, or brethren, or sisters, or father, or mother, or wife, or children, or lands, for my name's sake, shall receive an hundredfold, and shall inherit everlasting life.*" (Matthew 19:29.) [Robert's Italics original]

Here Urban's appeal is a work of double-edged persuasion aimed at two audiences. First, the potential recruit is offered shame in exchange for any hesitation to answer the Call; those who love parents more than God are unworthy of His grace. Second, families are urged to let the recruit go. After all, what mother would deny her son, what wife her husband, what sister her brother, an opportunity for "*everlasting life?*"

Ipso facto, Urban's Call embraced the Recruiting Speech convention of Speechmaker Identity: he was the pope, and had no need to demonstrate anything beyond his holy office. But his Speechmaker Identity differed from the usual situation in which the recruiter must overcome audience concerns about the potential hazards of military life. Recruiters usually do this by "proving" that they have the experience and competence to manage men in camp and on campaign. Here, recruiters generally fall into two categories. First are recruiters who by insignias, medals or sidearms self-identify as successful (and surviving) veterans. Second are speechmakers who may have no military experience but can tap deep reservoirs of local or national prestige to persuade people to enlist. Pope Urban II was obviously in this class, but with a significant twist, unavailable to secular leaders of a later age: the pope was able to leapfrog the risks of camp and campaign by simply declaring absolution for Crusaders in the event of death from any cause.

The most numerous of the Call's vital organs are its Appeals. Why would a young man wish to leave home for the deadly hazards of military adventure? Some personal reasons—such as a desire for adventure, or to escape boredom or some unpleasant domestic situation—are probably eternal verities for enlistments, but are also difficult to document. Yet the reasons why Pope Urban II thought men should go—or at least what he believed would persuade them to go—are easily documented because they are the heart of the Call.

The Pope's Appeals fall broadly into two categories. First, there are the rewards of this world. "So set out on the road to the Holy Sepulchre [Jerusalem], deliver the land from a wicked race and take it yourselves," Urban pleads, "the land which was given by God to the sons of Israel, as Scripture says, *a land flowing with milk and honey.*" [Italics original] This not-very-subtle appeal to material rewards is of ancient pedigree, although often expressed more directly, as a chance for recruits to enrich themselves by plunder and pillage. After all, "wicked" enemies deserve to lose their goods as well as their lives. But when Urban couches his appeal in Biblical terms by referring to the Hebrew Bible and the Book of Joshua, he cleverly sacralizes plunder. God had ordered the Israelites to cross the Jordan, eliminate its occupants, and settle the land. Now Urban, presumably channeling divine will, implicitly asks eleventh-century Franks and others to do the same. Thus, plunder, an activity that since ancient times was usually permitted by more secular customs of war, is now given religious sanction. It certainly helped that the Israelites' "land flowing with milk and honey" was the same land that Urban now proposed be retaken.[5]

Urban employs other Appeals of "this world," including the pride of family honor ("Oh most valiant soldiers and descendents of various ancestors, do not fall short of, but be inspired by, the courage of your forefathers") as well as atrocity stories, an ever-reliable battle speech Appeal which generally serves as a predicate for vengeance—although not that of Heaven. "They throw down the altars after soiling them with their own filth," the Pope angrily declared, "circumcise Christians and pour the resulting blood either on the altars or into the baptismal vessels." Recruits usually bank the anger stoked by such tales for later withdrawal.

In the second category of appeals are those that were of even greater importance to many in this audience: the rewards of the next world. "So seize on this road to obtain remission of your sins," the Pope exhorted, "sure in the indestructible glory of the Heavenly Kingdom." In short, Crusaders could expect absolution in exchange for making the armed pilgrimage. In Urban's time and place, this was powerful stuff—to which he would return with even greater force only moments later.

When the Pope had finished—or thought he had finished—Robert the Monk reports that the audience was "so moved that they united as one and

---

5   The phrase "A land flowing with milk and honey," can be found in Exodus, 3:8, 17 and 33:3, Vulgate.

shouted 'God wills it! God wills it!'" And so moved was Urban by their enthusiasm that he continued speaking, delivering what was in effect a second speech that concluded with some very specific instructions for making the crusade. "When the venerable Pope heard this [acclaim]," Robert reports, "he raised his eyes to Heaven, thanked God, and, gesturing with his hand for silence, said:

> Had the Lord God not been in your minds, you would not have spoken with one voice; certainly the voices were many but the thought behind them was one. So let that cry be a warcry for you in battle because it came from God. When you mass together to attack the enemy, this cry sent by God will be the cry of all—God wills it! God wills it!' [6]

And here was born the principal Speechlet of the First Crusade: "God wills it!" or, in Latin, "Deus Volt." The words would pass many a Crusader's taut lips from Europe to the gates of Jerusalem.

But there was more, and it was here that Urban demonstrated not only cleverness—plunder justified by biblical references showed that—but brilliance. The Pope continued speaking, now presumably extempore. First, he established rules for who should *not* make the crusade to Jerusalem: "the old, the simple-minded or those unsuited to battle;" next, women were prohibited unless escorted by "husband, brother or other legitimate guarantor"; finally, clergy could not go without the specific permission of their bishop. But it was in Urban's final instruction where he used his ultimate symbol—the Cross—in a way that literally sewed the Cross and the Crusader together:

> Anyone who has a mind to undertake this holy pilgrimage, and enters into that bargain with God, and devotes himself as a living sacrifice, holy and acceptable, shall wear the sign of the Cross on his forehead or his chest. And conversely anyone who seeks to turn back having taken the vow shall place the cross on his back between his shoulders. Such men will bring to pass through this double symbolism

---

6 Robert the Monk, 81. For an analysis of appeals typical in medieval battle speeches, several of which appear in Pope Urban II's Call, see John R. E. Bliese, "Rhetoric and Morale: A Study of Battle Orations from the Central Middle Ages," *Journal of Medieval History*, 15 (1989).

what God himself orders in the Gospel: *he that taketh not his cross, and followeth after me, is not worthy of me*. [Italics original][7]

Whether by design or afterthought, Pope Urban II had just created a unit insignia for God's Army. It was a literal badge of sanctity, righteousness, prestige and self-sacrifice in a society that supremely valued both the symbol and its contents. But as military historians also know, the effect of such symbols—Roman eagles, General Joseph Hooker's corps badges, national colors, crosses, crescents, Death Heads, or Red Stars—can be powerful enhancements to morale, stimulants to bravery, and metonyms for which men will kill or be killed. The Crusader army that eventually formed from the disparate groups marching toward Italy or Constantinople was drawn from every quarter of Western and Central Europe. They spoke many languages and had different customs, ethnic and feudal loyalties. While some may have enlisted for plunder, adventure or power, they all shared at least lip service to the same religion. Through tens of thousands of sewn Crosses, Urban had a found a way in this world to provide the unity many once believed existed only in the next.

Immediate Result

When the Council of Clermont dispersed, prelates, noblemen and ordinary folk spread the Call in sermons, feudal levies, and word of mouth throughout Western Christendom. Within one year, several bodies of armed pilgrims were on the road toward Jerusalem. Within four years, Jerusalem was taken.

Assessing immediate results would have to include the audience's reaction to Urban's command to "take the cross." Overwhelming contemporary evidence makes clear that Urban's transformation of "taking the Cross" from a subjective state of belief into a physical act—that is, sewing the Cross onto one's tunic—became wildly popular. Most principal sources for the First Crusade affirm this. "How many of various ages and abilities and stations in life took crosses and committed themselves to pilgrimage to the Holy Sepulchre! " gushed Robert the Monk. Fulcher of Chartres, present at Clermont as well as the First Crusade, wrote:

---

7   Robert the Monk, 82; Sweetenham identifies the italicized quotation with the Gospels of Matthew 10:38 and Luke 14:27.

Oh, how fitting and how pleasing to us all to see those crosses, beautiful, whether of silk, or of woven gold, or of any kind of cloth, which these pilgrims, by order of Pope Urban, sewed on the shoulders of their mantles, or cassocks, or tunics, once they had made the vow to go. It was indeed proper that soldiers of God who prepared to fight for His honor should be signed and fortified by this fitting emblem of victory; and since they thus marked themselves with this symbol under the acknowledgment of faith, finally they very truly obtained the Cross of which they carried the symbol. They adopted the sign that they might follow the reality of the sign.[8]

The actual recruiting experience of Bohemond, Duke of Apulia, one of the First Crusade's principal commanders, directly linked his efforts to Urban's command. In preparation for his Recruiting Speech, Bohemond ordered two robes cut into strips and sewn into crosses. "If you want to match your words with your actions," Bohemond challenged his audience, "let each of you take one of these crosses; accepting a cross shall be taken as a promise to set out on pilgrimage." Robert the Monk noted the sequel: "So many surged forward to take crosses that there were not enough for all those wanting them." [9]

Legacy

There are two aspects of the Call's legacy. The first is its success in accomplishing Urban's immediate aims. Tens of thousands of Europeans (sometimes accompanied by entire families) were persuaded to sell their possessions, leave home, and embark on the perilous road to Jerusalem. Exact numbers, which would have to include camp followers and other non-combatants, are unknown. Modern estimates (not including camp followers) place the total number of Peter the Hermit's popular crusade at 20,000, while the more disciplined commands led by experienced soldiers are estimated at 30,000 infantry and between 4,000 and 4,500 cavalry.[10]

---

8 Robert the Monk, 83; August C. Krey, *The First Crusade: The Accounts of Eyewitnesses,* Fulcher of Chartres, 29.

9 Robert the Monk, 92.

10 Estimates drawn from Runciman, *The First Crusade*, "Appendix II: The Numerical Strength of the Crusaders," 278-281.

For battle speech historians, the second legacy of Urban's Call is that it established something of a template for future crusades: a formal Call exhorting collective action and made to (to use an anachronism) a "multinational" audience. Here one must distinguish between crusades whose goal was the Holy Land and those limited to European conquest or conversion; between 1095 and 1291 at least nine "Holy Land" crusades were mounted. All were preceded by various calls, sometimes at the behest of clerics, other times by secular leaders with self-proclaimed religious motives.

Leadership Principle

The Call's success can be partly attributed to Urban's leadership; he understood well both his times and environment. Urban's world was low-literacy, dangerously traveled, and with difficult and haphazard communications. Yet for the Call to succeed it needed a wide distribution, and ready acceptance even in his absence—he did not extensively take the road and use the Call as a stump speech. First, Urban accomplished this by using well-known Biblical imagery and quotations. The "land of milk and honey" and the Gospel of Matthew are not only easily remembered, but were also textually accessible to most churches and convents in Europe, where they were further disseminated by sermon (a distinct meme-stream.) Thus also Urban's insightful use of the Cross, by which he essentially "exported" his speech onto the garb of every crusader. In exchange, the wearer could wordlessly boast of embodying the Christian virtues as defined in the Call: he was a deliverer of the Holy Sepulcher from pagan defilement, a potential martyr, a courageous fighter of the Lord's wars. Urban's understanding of his times compelled him to transcend his immediate audience at Clermont to reach the many thousands who, while not there, were just as important to his plans as the high prelates and medieval lords who were present.

Persuasive Strategy

Recruiting Speech conventions and appeals—Staging, Speechmaker Identity, Family and other Appeals—exist to enhance persuasion. Given the Pope's enormous authority, his personal embrace of these Recruiting Speech conventions added to the Call's persuasive power.

But Urban also gave his Call something quite different. He not only expanded the Cross's meaning—it now offered absolution for holy war and armed pilgrimage as well as sanctioning plunder—but transformed it from a collective, perhaps distant symbol (for some) to an individually-possessed thing, thus allowing all those acting in its name to literally attach it to themselves. This symbol, which in its most dramatic forms had been confined to churches, cathedrals, and the bejeweled adornments of prelates, could now be seen on the tunics and cloaks of any man who took the Cross to Jerusalem.

For modern speechmakers, expanding the meaning of existing symbols as well as transforming symbols from the purely figurative to the physical has acquired increasing importance. Politicians, clerics, soldiers and corporate executives all have privileged access to systems of symbols, such as hoary national flags, revered religious signs, symbols or rituals, unit insignias or corporate logos. Each day bears witness to this process, most commonly in the political arena. Whenever a politician wishes to introduce a new policy or wage new wars, a majestic background of Old Glory, a bust of Abraham Lincoln, speaking platforms crowded with soldiers, police officers, doctors or schoolteachers are attempts to take a symbol with commonly held associations—for example, the national flag—and add whatever change the politician is proposing. Individuals are also induced to join this transformation process by converting previously figurative, distant or collective symbols into personal statements by the use of lapel flag pins, auto bumper stickers, or necks graced with religious symbols. In modern societies the tendency of different meme-streams to merge is also pervasive. For example, philanthropies have taken the once exclusively political "yellow ribbon" changed its color and expanded its meaning as a fundraising-awareness tool to fight certain diseases; commercially, on Presidents' Day, few Americans can escape the sight of Old Glory waving proudly on car dealer lots throughout the country, establishing a direct link between Washington, Lincoln, and Chevrolet.

The messages have changed, but Urban's persuasive strategy lives on.

Sometimes speakers lack either ready access to symbol systems, or find the systems that they can access to be inadequate for their present needs. Thus they face a challenge: how to create new symbols? Urban answered this question by enlarging the meaning of the existing symbol of the Cross. George Washington had a different approach. He imbued an ordinary object with profound symbolic significance. In so doing, in one of the most pivotal battle speeches of the American Revolution, General George Washington helped quell a mutiny with an ordinary pair of spectacles.

Chapter Three

George Washington Quells
the Newburgh Mutiny

I. Historical Background

The October 1781 Franco-American victory at Yorktown ended the military phase of the American Revolution. After the battle, Washington marched his army to New Windsor, New York, from where it would keep a wary eye on its erstwhile British enemy in New York City. But the army soon became more concerned with the American Congress in Philadelphia than Englishmen in New York. By March 1783 many months had passed since Washington's army had been paid; worse, looming peace brought more anxiety: the likelihood of discharge for men, many of whom had sacrificed health and comfort during the seven-year war, and all of whom had incurred an opportunity cost beyond measure—while they had devoted their 20s or 30s to perfecting the arts of war, their non-serving peers at home had continued to practice the trades of peace. To some soldiers, the prospect of discharge brought apprehensions not only of lost status but also real fears of beggary.[1]

The only recompense for service like this was a fair government pension. And years earlier, Congress had seemed to respond, especially for officers: in

---

1 Richard H. Kohn, "The Inside History of the Newburgh Conspiracy: America and the Coup d'Etat," *The William and Mary Quarterly: A Magazine of Early American History*, Third Series, Number 2, Vol. XXVII, 189-190.

1780 the legislature had pledged pensions. But this pledge had not been redeemed by legislation, and some soldiers were beginning to understand the ancient and brutal calculus of power: once dissolved, the army would lose all leverage to obtain its due; indeed, some soldiers now claimed that a perfidious Congress intended to evade its pension promises by just such a dissolution. But a few soldiers reasoned that as long as the army remained intact, it would have other options, one of which might include marching on Philadelphia and spearing a pension bill on the points of their bayonets.[2]

Stoking the army's anxieties was a handful of civilians. The weak Confederation was reliant on sometimes-recalcitrant states for revenue; as the fledgling government sought to establish credit and struggled to pay its current debts, enacting—let alone funding—pension legislation was hardly a priority. But some in Philadelphia sought to use the army's winter of discontent (1782/83) to lobby for a better system of government finance. Just as the army cared less for sturdy finances than that the Congress redeem its pension pledges, these politicians cared little about pensions per se; they had a larger agenda.

In December 1782, with George Washington's tacit blessing, army officers had sent Congress a petition reminding that body of its promise and requesting pension relief; it was generally respectful, but contained some ominous language. "Our distresses are now brought to a point. We have borne all that men can bear—our property is exhausted—our private resources are at an end, and our friends are wearied out and disgusted with our incessant applications," the petitioners pleaded. "The uneasiness of the soldiers, for want of pay, is great and dangerous; any further experiments on their patience may have fatal effects." Only a fool would not have seen the implied threat.[3]

But still nothing was done. By March 1783, after a winter of forced inactivity and intensifying anxiety stirred by the expectation that every ship from Europe might bring news of a rife-rumored peace treaty, a few discontented officers decided that it was time to act. On March 10 an

---

2   Kohn, "Inside History," 189-190.

3   Louis Clinton Hatch, *The Administration of the American Revolutionary Army* (New York: Longmans, Green, and Co., 1904), 162-163; *Journals of the Continental Congress, 1774-1789*, Worthington Ford, et al, Volume XXIV: 1783, January 1-August 29 (1922: GPO), Paper No. VII, 290-293; Kohn, "The Inside Story," 194.

anonymous letter[4] circulated within the New Windsor encampment that implicitly criticized Washington's "moderation and longer forbearance"; indeed, the letter invited worse. It recommended that if the army was ordered to disband, it "should retire to some unsettled country, smile in [its] turn, and 'mock when their fear cometh on.'" The language only appeared vague—this was an unmistakable invitation to mutiny and one that held a promise of worse to follow. The same day a second anonymous notice appeared calling for a meeting "of the general and field officers" to convene the next day (March 11) in order "to consider . . . what measures (if any) should be adopted to obtain that redress of grievances which they seem to have solicited in vain." A letter containing mutinous sentiments was bad enough. But this anonymous summons, not cleared through Washington's headquarters, threatened to make the word a deed.[5]

In response, Washington decided to buy time, and made his purchase shrewdly. First, he did not cancel the conspirator's call for a meeting, but only rescheduled it—for noon, March 15. Next, he did not attempt to counter the anonymous letter's accusations, but merely condemned its lack of good military procedure: "The reputation and true interest of the army requires [my] disapprobation of such disorderly proceedings." But in what would prove perhaps his wisest decision, Washington implied that he would not attend the meeting. Instead, General Horatio Gates, a man Washington strongly suspected of belonging to the mutinous cabal, would chair the gathering. Gates had thus far remained in the conspiracy's shadows; Washington would now pin accountability on him for the meeting's results.[6]

Thus at noon on March 15 an estimated three hundred Continental Army officers crowded into a building known as the Temple and took seats on its long

---

4   The anonymous writer was John Armstrong, Jr., an aide de camp to General Horatio Gates. Seventeen years old when he joined the Continental Army in 1775, Armstrong served throughout the war on several generals' staffs. After the war he was elected several times to the United States Senate, and later served as ambassador to France and as Secretary of War for part of the War of 1812. Appletons' *Cyclopaedia of American Biography*, edited by James Grant Wilson and John Fiske, (New York: D. Appleton and Company, 1887), Volume I of VI, 92.

5   Kohn, "The Inside History," 201, 206-207; *Journals of Continental Congress*, Paper VIII, Enclosure No. 1, 294-295.

6   *Journals of the Continental Congress*, Paper VIII, Enclosure No. 3, "General Orders, Tuesday, March 11, 1783," 297-298.

wooden benches. Eyewitness accounts suggest that the mood was somber. Many thought they were there to make some new, if lamentable contribution to the history of their nascent country.

But suddenly and without prior warning, the tall figure of General George Washington entered the room; if army protocol was followed, the entire assembly would have stood at attention in his presence. But whatever the protocol, the mood suddenly had changed. Twenty-nine year old Bostonian Major Samuel Shaw had been with Washington from Dorchester Heights to Yorktown. He was also standing with his comrades in the Temple. "Every eye was fixed upon the illustrious man," he wrote, "and attention to the beloved General held the assembly mute." The revered Washington "appeared, not at the head of his troops, but as it were in opposition to them and for a dreadful moment the interests of the army and its General seemed to be in competition!" Indeed they were in competition; and it was this tension that Washington came to relieve.

It was now Washington's turn to speak. After apologizing to his "brother officers" for appearing unannounced, he took the lectern.[7]

II. The Speech

Gentlemen,

By an anonymous summons, an attempt has been made to convene you together—how inconsistent with the rules of propriety!—how unmilitary!—and how subversive of all order and discipline—let the good sense of the Army decide.

In the moment of this summons, another anonymous production was sent into circulation; addressed more to the feelings of passions, than to the reason & judgment of the Army. . . . the Author of the Address, should have had more charity, than to mark for Suspicion, the Man who should recommend moderation and longer forbearance.

---

7 *Journals of the Continental Congress*, Volume XXIV, Paper No. VIII. (No. 1), 294-295 and (No. 3), General Orders, Thursday, March 11, 1783, 297-298. "The meeting of the officers was in itself exceedingly respectable, the matters they were called to deliberate upon were of the most serious nature. . . " *The Journals of Major Samuel Shaw, The First American Consul at Canton*, edited by Josiah Quincy (Boston: Wm. Crosby and H.P. Nichols, 1847), 103; George Bancroft, *History of the Formation of the Constitution of the United States of America* (New York: D. Appleton and Company, 1889), I: 96.

. . . . If my conduct heretofore, has not evinced to you, that I have been a faithful friend to the Army, my declaration of it at this time wd. be equally unavailing & improper. But as I was among the first who embarked in the cause of our common Country—As I have never left your side one moment, but when called from you, on public duty—As I have been the constant companion & witness of your Distresses, and not among the last to feel, & acknowledge your merits—As I have ever considered my own Military reputation as inseperably connected with that of an Army—As my Heart has ever expanded with Joy, when I have heard its praises—and my indignation has arisen, when the mouth of detraction has opened against it—it can scarcely be supposed, at this late stage of the War, that I am indifferent to its interests. . . .

But—how are [pensions] *to be promoted? The way is plain, says the anonymous Addresser—If War continues, remove into the unsettled Country—there establish yourselves, and leave an ungrateful Country to defend itself—But who are they to defend?—Our Wives, our Children, our Farms, and other property which we leave behind us. . . . This dreadful alternative, of either deserting our Country in the extremest hour of her distress, or turning our Arms against it, (which is the apparent object, unless Congress can be compelled into instant compliance) has something so shocking in it, that humanity revolts at the idea. My God! What can this writer have in view by recommending such measures?*

. . . Why then should we distrust [Congress]—*and in consequence of that distrust, adopt measures, which may cast a shade over that glory which, has been so justly acquired; and tarnish the reputation of an Army which is celebrated thro' all Europe for its fortitude and Patriotism?*

By thus determining—& thus acting [that is, if you follow my advice], *you will pursue the plain & direct road to the attainment of your wishes. . . .—You will give one more distinguished proof of unexampled patriotism & patient virtue, rising superior to the pressure of the most complicated sufferings;—And you will, by the dignity of your Conduct, afford occasion for Posterity to say, when speaking of the glorious example you have exhibited to Mankind, "had this day been wanting, the World has never seen the last stage of perfection to which human nature is capable of attaining."* [Spelling and punctuation as in original]

G. Washington

—Excerpts from George Washington's Newburgh Address, March 15, 1783[8]

---

8 *George Washington's Newburgh Address: A Massachusetts Historical Society Picture Book*, Foreword by Bernhard Knollenberg (Massachusetts Historical Society, 1966), no

III. Parsing the Speech

Washington's speech turned on four basic themes, common to battle speeches but not necessarily effective for every battle speechmaker. The first three were the Appeals to Shame, Comradeship, and, most importantly, Stakes—this latter being the technique by which Washington persuaded his men that they had more to lose through mutinying than by waiting for Congress to act. The fourth Appeal was Guilt, and ranks among the most difficult to successfully make. Few battle speechmakers have the personal standing with a soldier-audience to provoke this feeling. But it is the Appeal of Guilt (close cousin of Shame) that distinguished the Newburgh Address as one of the most dramatic battle speeches in American history.[9]

Shame works as a two-step. First, the speechmaker must refer to some value shared with the soldier-audience that he then seeks to portray as having been violated. (Remember the Introduction's toddler.) Next, the speechmaker must assert *his* personal authority to hold the soldier-audience *morally* accountable for the violation. As a result if experiencing *shame*, the speaker hopes that the audience next will feel *guilt*.

Washington opened his speech by appealing to his men's sense of Shame. For a moment, he was the "father" who had come to admonish his adult children. However, what was critical to Washington's ability to peacefully resolve the threat of mutiny was the standard to which he held his audience. First, the men were not explicitly blamed for attending the meeting; rather, it was the "anonymous summons" which was denounced. Most importantly, throughout his speech Washington refused to denounce the summons, summoner, or his men in terms of moral evil, character deficiencies, or the crime of mutiny. Instead, his objection was exclusively on *military* grounds. The men were to feel ashamed because, as an exasperated Washington declared:

> how inconsistent with the rules of propriety!—how unmilitary! and how subversive of all order and discipline. . . .

page numbers. This publication also includes an excellent facsimile of the original Address, now in the collection of the Massachusetts Historical Society.

9 Miller, *Words and Deeds*, 179-180 (Shame); 234-235 (Comradeship); 187-188 (Stakes); Appeal to Guilt is discussed here for the first time.

The grounds matter because men who behave inconsistently with "propriety" or are "unmilitary" or are "subversive of all [military] order and discipline" can be rehabilitated. But men who are evil or felons or suffer from irremediable personal defects may not be redeemable. And in closing this paragraph, Washington signaled his men that in his view they were redeemable: "let the good sense of the Army decide," he declared. Underpinning this was Shame—the "good sense" appealed to by Washington is that which informed his men's consciences: the tension was between their awareness of the wrong that they had done and the "good sense" that Washington claimed they possessed. It was Shame that arose in the tense space between these two sensibilities.

Of course, Washington was taking no chances. He did not allow the army's "good sense" to decide; rather, he provided a definition of "good sense" by judiciously criticizing the anonymous letter that had preceded the summons. That writer, who had identified himself only as a "Fellow Soldier," almost certainly sat somewhere on the benches; moreover, Washington could not know how many sitting nearby already had been persuaded by the writer. For his part, Washington had elected moral and personal suasion over legal measures—the latter being a path Washington knew well, having in the past executed men for mutiny.[10]

First, Washington used sarcasm to address both the personal slight as well as to diminish the anonymous writer: "[The] Author of the Address, should have had more charity than to mark for Suspicion, the Man who should recommend moderation and longer forbearance." By transforming the writer's criticism of "moderation and longer forbearance" into a virtue, Washington drew an important contrast: his qualities versus the qualities he implied about his critic: the writer (whose insistence on anonymity had diminished his credibility) was immoderate and lacked patience. These are rarely winning qualities in an argument the terms of which (as set by Washington) will be decided on the basis of "good sense" and not a firing squad.

Washington later returned to the writer's substantive arguments. But first, he felt compelled to restate his own credentials. Throughout the Newburgh Address, Washington frequently shifted, like many battle speechmakers before and since, between the roles of "father"—always inherent in the male hierarchy of military command—and that of "brother"—a family metaphor that is

10 *Journals of the Continental Congress*, Paper VIII, Enclosure No. 2, 295-297.

produced not by hierarchy but by battle's *shared experience*. (Readers will remember that when entering the Temple, Washington apologized to his "brother officers.")

In matters of persuasion, comrade-as-brother—included under what I call the Comrade Convention—is generally the more effective approach: it allows higher-ranking speakers to step out of their command roles and bridge with their soldier-audiences what may be profound differences in rank, social class, race, or religion. And Washington certainly differed from his audience in several important ways: he was a Virginian, a large landowning plantation aristocrat and slaveholder, born into the Anglican Church (although notably non-sectarian as an adult), and an esteemed general. His soldier-audience was (at Newburgh) chiefly New England men, the descendents of Puritans, now Congregationalists or Presbyterians, drawn from the ranks of small farmers, merchants, craftsmen, and professionals.

Given Washington's great prestige then and later, these concerns might strike today's reader as superfluous. But Washington apparently did not think so, because in his speech he was at great pains to re-establish these shared bonds. He now gave evidence that he was indeed their brother, their comrade. And membership in this family was open only to those who had forsaken their homes to risk their lives from disease, starvation, frostbite or a lead ball in defense of the Revolution. This was his Appeal to the Comrade convention.

"If my conduct heretofore," Washington reminded his men, "has not evinced to you, that I have been a faithful friend to this Army, my declaration of it at this time wd. be equally unavailing and improper"—but not so improper that Washington avoided mentioning it. Washington proceeded to detail why he was both a father and a brother, a commander and a comrade. He was "among the first who embarked in the cause of our common Country." He had "never left [their] side one moment, but when called . . . on public duty." He had been "the constant companion & witness of your Distresses, and not among the last to feel, & acknowledge your merits." Comradeship is about identification: Washington's army life had been their lives, his reputation their reputations; their angers, frustrations, joys and indignations had been his feelings as well. Thus, he concluded, "*It can scarcely be supposed*, at this late stage of the War, that I am indifferent to [your] interests." [Italics original] And after having listed these shared traits, Washington introduced a second source of Shame: the tension between how his men regarded him—as a brother comrade—and how they had treated him: as a man "indifferent" to their interests.

Father, brother-comrade, and a man of reason, Washington now proceeded to demolish the writer's main argument. Here Shame returned. If the men "remove into the unsettled Country" they were abandoning not only their duty as soldiers but also their more intimate duties as husbands and fathers, as well as the duty to work the farms that support them. If soldiering was synonymous with doing one's duty, there were few defaults as serious as this, including the abhorrent prospect Washington next raised: "either deserting our Country in the extremest hour of her distress, or turning our Arms against it." And Washington's next statement shocked his men by emphasizing the Shame they should feel at even entertaining these thoughts. "My God!" he exclaimed. "What can this writer have in view by recommending such measures?" In a word, the letter's advice was not only foolish but shameful—the first fruits of immoderation.

Despite the anonymous writer's toxic recommendations, Washington had attempted to truthfully, indeed eloquently, address his soldier-audience's real grievances. These were not to be denied simply by deprecating the writer's anonymity (at one point implying that he might be a British agent) or showing that the writer's proposed solutions were foolish. But the heart of the matter still beat loudly: How should Washington address what his men resented most, that Congress had failed to redeem its pension promises? And what of his men's greatest fear, that as a result of this failure, and in the face of the army's imminent dissolution, they faced the prospect of reduced status and perhaps poverty itself?

Washington's answer was to "prove" that his men had far more to lose from mutiny than by a failure to obtain pensions. Since the soldier-audience's lives were never in question—Washington specifically had eschewed threats—the men would have to be given a Stake in something besides Congress' pension bill. And here Washington offered a convincing emotional swap: he would exchange his officers' fears of societal scorn and poverty for the incomparable riches of a grateful posterity as well as the envy of peers. These Stakes had already been earned by battlefield success, and thus were perfections already in hand—but to fully realize their Stake, all his officers had to do was avoid besmirching it with mutiny.

Washington immediately described this Stake in terms that overwhelmed even the distrust that men felt in Congress. "Why then should we distrust [Congress]?" he asked:

—and in consequence of that distrust, adopt measures, which may cast a shade over that glory which, has been so justly acquired; and tarnish the reputation of an Army which is celebrated thro' all Europe, for its fortitude and Patriotism?

Congress may or may not be trustworthy, but men could trust this: under his officers' leadership the Continental Army had achieved "glory...justly acquired" and an "Army celebrated thro' all Europe." And doing right would also be doing well. By avoiding mutiny, they will "pursue the plain & direct road to the attainment of [their] wishes." But even here Washington suggested that what the men would receive in exchange for not mutinying was far more valuable even than pensions. Indeed, the Stakes were nothing less than the very reason they fought the Revolution:

> And you will, by the dignity of your Conduct, afford occasion for Posterity to say, when speaking of the glorious example you have exhibited to Mankind, 'had this day been wanting, the World has never seen the last stage of perfection to which human nature is capable of attaining.'

Amidst the anxiety and confusion, Washington had offered clarity.

There remained one final act that many men would remember as their most intimate moment with Washington. Before his officers could react to his speech, Washington prepared to read a letter from Joseph Jones, Congressman from Virginia and a personal friend. As Major Shaw remembered it, Washington announced that Jones' letter would be a "corroborating testimony of the good disposition of that body towards the army."

And so Washington read one paragraph—and then stopped. During this "short pause," Shaw wrote, Washington "took out his spectacles, and begged the indulgence of his audience while he put them on." It was at this moment—and recollections differed as to the exact words—that Washington, who had never worn glasses before in public, adjusted his spectacles, and observed to none and to all: "I have grown gray in your service, and now find myself growing blind."[11]

What happened next may top the list of America's most sentimental official moments. "There was something so natural, so unaffected in this appeal, as

---

11 *Journals of Major Samuel Shaw*, 104. Bancroft offers a slightly different version of what Washington said, Bancroft, History, 98.

rendered it superior to the most studied oratory," wrote Shaw. "[I]t forced its way to the heart, and you might see sensibility moisten every eye." Scarred veterans of many battles and cruel winters wept openly.

When Washington finished reading Jones' letter he walked out of the Temple, leaving a probably nonplussed Horatio Gates as chair. By likely prearrangement, he also left a handful of loyalists to work the audience to help conclude the meeting with favorable written resolutions. And Washington would not be disappointed. Among these was a declaration that "the officers of the American army view with abhorrence and reject with disdain the infamous propositions contained in the late anonymous address to them."

The resolution passed unanimously.[12]

Immediate Result

The audience's immediate reaction after the speech was overwhelmingly positive. Major General Philip Schuyler wrote that "The whole assembly was in tears at the conclusion of his address." After the meeting, Schuyler shared a coach with General Henry Knox, but "in absolute silence, because of the solemn impression on our minds." Schuyler also believed that "posterity will repeat the closing words of his Excellency's address"—and he then went on to quote them. The Newburgh Address had become one more meme in George Washington's already-established renown. Washington had demolished the mutiny.[13]

Legacy

Washington aide Lieutenant David Humphreys wrote shortly afterward what would be the final judgment on the Newburgh Address:

It was a proud day for the Army & ought not to be forgotten in the Annals of America. . . . Those who have seen General Washington at the head of our Army on the day of Battle & in the most awful & glorious attitude to which a human

---

12 Readers wishing further information about the Newburgh Conspiracy should consult Richard H. Kohn, whose article is cited above and whose book, *Eagle and Sword: The Federalists and the Creation of the Military Establishment in America, 1783-1802* (New York: The Free Press, 1975), 17-39, also treats this episode. These two studies provide much of the basis of this narrative.

13 Schuyler quoted in Hatch, 175.

character can ever aspire, think he appeared unshakably greater on a late occasion than ever he did before. . . . The whole transaction ought to be *known*. It will do honour to the Army, it will do honour to the Country, it will do honour to human Nature. [Italic original]

Humphreys' hope was realized, and the speech did indeed become known. With Washington, American's foremost military chief and first president, setting the example, Newburgh's permanent legacy would be an American military entirely subordinate to civilian control.[14]

Leadership Principle

Washington transcended matters of legality and even army discipline to empathize with his audience's stated and unstated concerns. But his greatest act of leadership was how he invoked Guilt by mixing his personal prestige with the blood and suffering of the Revolution, and in the process transformed an ordinary pair of spectacles into a profound symbol of loss, comradeship, and the bittersweets of a victory that had been achieved at enormous personal cost. If a symbol was to be used, it would have to be a personal one that was as intimate as the occasion.

In this sense, Washington's Newburgh Address is best understood not so much as a principle (civil-military relations) or even a tactic (how to avoid a mutiny); rather, it was a highly personalized negotiation between a beloved commander and the men who had followed him through many trials, as well as the imagined "presence" of comrades who had followed him to their deaths. Washington had summoned them both with just a pair of spectacles.

Persuasive Strategy

Washington's speech combined two elements emphasized in this section: personal reputation and the use of symbols. Moreover, his deft use of Appeals—Shame, Comradeship, and Stakes—were excellent psychological preparation for the persuasive strategies that followed: Guilt and Remission.

---

14 *The Life and Times of David Humphreys, Soldier—Statesman—Poet*, by Frank Landon Humphreys (New York: G.P. Putnam's Sons, 1917), I: 269-270.

Washington's use of Guilt was especially prominent when he withdrew his spectacles. "I have grown gray in *your* service," he declared—for you, my comrades, and not for scheming politicians; for you, my children and brothers, and not for some abstraction. The guilt invoked here was most likely that which belonged to soldiers who had betrayed him and the army (or were contemplating such a betrayal) and soldiers that had merely survived the war when others did not. In some minds, Washington, his spectacles, his dimmed vision and lost years at war (contrasted with seven might-have-been years at Mount Vernon, surrounded by family, enjoying comforts and pursuing his livelihood) had become metonymic for the loss and suffering of the soldier-audience and that of their comrades who had perished along the way; likewise, many in the audience may have experienced a surge of guilt at the prospect of betraying Washington, this living metonym for their army and their cause, and in whose weakened eyesight the hardships of campaign and battle were suddenly and painfully discernable. The emotional conflict was more than many men could stand.

And yet there was even more to Washington's persuasive strategy. Concealed within the Newburgh Address' structure is a narrative that confronted sin and stoked guilt, but also offers remission. (The Temple doubled as a church, and thus, this same narrative had, through prayer and chaplain sermons, doubtless been re-enacted within its walls many times before.) Sins of betrayal—of Washington, the Army, the cause, dead comrades, wives and children—must have created unbearable tension, the product of the "competition" that Major Shaw described when Washington first entered the hall. But the general offered relief. If his officers would only take his suggestions—to show more patience, to have more trust in Congress and greater confidence in Washington's efforts to lobby Philadelphia for pensions—Shaw and his comrades would be relieved of their guilt, redeemed, and forgiven. Instead of Heaven and eternal life, Washington could offer only Posterity, Mankind, and the World; but it was enough. The Newburgh Address can be seen as a thinly veiled religious cycle of sin, renunciation, penitence, and forgiveness.

Was Washington's Newburgh Address the spontaneous expression of a commander wounded by his comrades' disloyalty, ingratitude, and lack of trust? Or was Washington's speech something designed, a species of performance art by a skilled leader deliberately using a surprise appearance, emotionally manipulative speech and carefully withdrawn spectacles? There is little evidence to support the idea that Washington and his cronies unrolled the event and pulled out the props according to some plan. Even still, historians have had their doubts. "I am convinced," wrote Richard Kohn, "that the whole affair was managed by Washington and his confidants." General Knox, perhaps the officer closest to Washington, wrote the following day to Secretary of War Benjamin Lincoln, and summarized the affair. "The General's address," he beamed, "is a masterful performance."[15]

The question is of more than passing interest here. As we turn to the next section—Battle Speechmakers and Their Audiences—the issue of how and why speakers manipulate their audiences comes to the fore.

---

15 John, "Inside Story," 211, footnote 7. General Henry Knox to Benjamin Lincoln, March 16, 1783, Knox Papers, Microfilm Reel 6A, New York Historical Society. I wish to express my deep gratitude to Dr. William Fowler of Northeastern University for sharing this source.

Section Two

Speechmakers and Their Audiences

The dissimulation of the general consists of the important art of hiding his thoughts. He should be constantly on the stage and should appear most tranquil when he is most occupied, for the whole army speculates on his looks, on his gestures, and on his mood. If he is seen to be more thoughtful than customary, the officers will believe he is incubating some project of consequence. If his manner is uneasy, they believe that affairs are going badly, and they often imagine worse than the truth. . . . It is necessary, therefore, that the personal conduct of the general should be so well reasoned that his dissimulation will be so profound that no one can ever penetrate it.

— Frederick the Great, "Talents That a General Must Have, Ruses, Stratagems of War, Spies," *The Instruction of Frederick the Great for His Generals, 1747*[1]

This section will examine battle speechmaking as a species of performance art. Frederick the Great's famous instructions concede this: the commander is constantly on the stage; and I would add that he is never more so than when delivering a battle speech. Combined with Vegetius' advice that a commander must know "the sentiments of the soldiers" through "their looks, their words, their actions and their motions," the speaker must simultaneously maintain two levels of awareness. The first is to "read" his soldier-audience, especially how it is "reading" him as he speaks; and the second is to coordinate this awareness with "dissimulation": stylizing his message for the soldier-audience, that is, making it convincing, reassuring, or provocative—no matter what the speaker's

---

1 "The Instruction of Frederick the Great for His Generals, 1747," translated by Brig. Gen. Thomas R. Phillips, contained in *Roots of Strategy*, 346-347.

true feelings. Like stage actors, battle speechmakers are performers. For that matter, so are politicians.[2]

But there is an important difference between commanders and stage actors. Few believed that Kenneth Branagh was the real Henry V in the film *Henry V*; yet every soldier listening to the four leaders discussed in this section—George S. Patton, Jr., Sam Houston, "Deaf" Smith, and Alexander the Great—knew that the speaker was exactly who and what he claimed to be. The subject of this chapter is to explore how each accomplished—or in Alexander's case, failed to accomplish—the persuasive trick of dissimulation.

Here it might be helpful to think of Patton as the veteran actor; Houston, a director, and Alexander the Great as a once fine actor who had forgotten how to play an audience.

---

2 *Roots of Strategy*, Vegetius, *De Re Militari*, 152.

Chapter Four

Patton Maintains his Memes: Thespian in Uniform

I. Historical Background

In May and early June 1944 Major General George S. Patton, Jr., made the rounds of Third Army units in England that had just arrived from the United States. The purpose of these visits was to introduce himself to his men, many of whom were without combat experience and knew Patton only by reputation. Patton had a stump speech that he delivered to each soldier-audience; many of his biographers might agree that he had devoted a lifetime to its perfection. Patton scholars refer to it as "The Speech," and it gained national prominence in the film *Patton*, whose opening scene had actor George C. Scott deliver a truncated and bowdlerized version. Less-censored versions exist, although some historians believe that no surviving account captures the rich veins of profanity that marbled the original.[1]

---

1   Many biographers devote attention to The Speech. See Carlos D'Este, *Patton: A Genius for War* (New York: Harper Perennial, 1995), 601-605; Roger H. Nye, *The Patton Mind: The Professional Development of an Extraordinary Leader* (New York: Avery Publishing, 1993), 142; Martin Blumenson, *Patton: The Man Behind the Legend, 1885-1945* (New York: William Morrow, 1985), 220-221; Charles M. Province, *The Unknown Patton* (New York: Bonanza Books, 1983), 26-37.

II. The Speech

Men, this stuff you heard about Americans wanting to stay out of this war and not wanting to fight, is a lot of bull shit. Traditionally, Americans love to fight. All real Americans love the sting of battle. When you were kids you all admired the champion marble player, the fastest runner, the big league ball players, the toughest boxers. The American loves a winner and cannot tolerate a loser. Americans despise cowards. Americans play to win all the time. I wouldn't give a hoot for a man who lost and laughed. That's why Americans have never lost and will never lose a war—for the very thought of losing is hateful to an American.

You are not all going to die. Only two percent of you here, in a major battle would die. Death must not be feared. Every man is frightened at first in battle. If he says he isn't he is a God damned liar. Some men are cowards, yes, but they fight just the same or get the hell scared out of them watching men who do fight and who are just as scared as they. The real hero is the man who fights even though he is scared. Some get over their fright in a few minutes under fire, some take hours, for some it takes days. The real man never lets his fear of death over-power his honor, his duty to his country and his innate manhood. All through your career of Army life, you men have bitched about what you call this chicken shit drilling. That is all for one reason, instant obedience to orders and it creates instant alertness. I don't give a damn for a man who is not always on his toes. You men are veterans or you wouldn't be here. You are ready. A man to continue breathing must be alert at all times. If not, sometimes, some German son of a bitch will sneak up behind him and beat him to death with a sack full of shit.

There are 400 neatly marked graves somewhere in Sicily. All because one man went to sleep on his job. But they are all German graves for we caught the bastards asleep before they knew it.

An army is a team; lives, sleeps, eats and fights as a team. The individual heroic stuff is a lot of crap. The billious bastard who wrote that kind of stuff for the Saturday Evening Post didn't know anymore about real battle than he did about fucking.

We have the finest food, the finest equipment, best spirited men in the world. Why, by God, I actually pity those sons of bitches we are going up against—by God, I do.

My men don't surrender. I don't want to hear of a soldier under my command getting captured unless he is hit. Even if you are, you can still fight back. This is not bull shit either. The kind of man I want is like a Lieutenant in Libia, who with a lugar against his chest, jerked his helmet off, swept the gun aside with the other hand and busted hell out of the Boche with the helmet. Then he jumped on the bum and went out and killed another German. By this time the man had a bullet through his chest. That is the man for us.

All real heroes are not story book combat fighters either. Every man in the army plays a vital part. Every little job is essential to the whole scheme…. Every man, every department, every unit, is important to the vast scheme of things. The ordnance men are needed to supply the guns, the QM to bring up the food and the clothes for us, for where we are going, there isn't a hell of a lot for us to steal. . . . Even the chaplain is important, for if we get killed and he isn't there to bury us, we would all go to hell. Each man must think for not only himself, but think of his buddy fighting beside him. We don't want yellow cowards in this army, to go back to the States after the war and breed more like them. The brave men will breed brave men.

Don't forget, you don't know I'm here at all. No words of the fact are to be mentioned in any letter. The world is not supposed to know what the hell they did to me. I'm not supposed to be commanding this Army. I'm not supposed to be in England. Let the first bastards to find out be the God damn Germans. Some day, I want them to rise up on their hind legs and howl, Jesus Christ! It's the God damn Third Army and that son of [a] bitch Patton again.

We want to get the hell over there. We want to get over there and clean the God damn thing up. Then we'll have to take a little jaunt against the purple pissing Japanese and clean their nest out before the Marines get all the credit.

Sure we all want to get home. We want this thing over with, but you can't win war laying down. The quickest way to get it over is to go get the bastards. The quicker they are whipped, the quicker we go home. The shortest way home is through Berlin. There is one thing you will be able to say when you go home. You may thank God for it, thank God that at least thirty years from now, when you are sitting around the fireside with your brat on your knee, and he asks you what you did in the Great War II, you don't have to say, 'I shoveled shit [in Louisiana]'

—Excerpts from Maj. Gen. George S. Patton, Jr.'s, speech to XII Corps, probably given on May 31, 1944, at Camp Brewdley, located near Stourport, England[2]

---

2   Grammar and spelling as in original. There exist at least four different written versions of The Speech. The version used is taken from the pamphlet, "Speech of General George S. Patton, Jr. to His Third Army on the eve of The Normandy Invasion," edited by C. E. Dornbusch (Cornwall, N.Y.: Hope Farm Press, 1963). Other versions will be found in Martin Blumenson, *The Patton Papers, 1940-1945* (Boston: Houghton Mifflin, 1974), II: 457-58; "A General Talks To His Army," the Patton File, archives, Virginia Military Institute in Lexington Virginia; Province, *Unknown Patton*, 30-37. There are considerable differences between the versions. Dornbusch, the great bibliographer of American Civil War military histories, explicated the scholarly process through which he passed his version of The Speech before publication; for that reason alone I have used his speech. However, Patton delivered The Speech repeatedly, and every other version was as likely to have been delivered on one occasion or another. Of the four versions, Dornbusch's alone omits the concluding words "in Louisiana." I included it because it was too good an ending to forego.

III. Parsing the Speech

Although The Speech was made repeatedly in the days leading up to D-Day, it was not a Pre-Invasion Speech. Patton's Third Army was secretly ferried to France in the weeks after the first Normandy invasion. The Speech is actually an Assumption of Command Speech—but with an asterisk. Third Army would not be formally activated until August 1, and Patton's presence in England was still secret. Patton could thus dispense with several conventions of the Assumption of Command genre, especially establishing his Authority and Acknowledging Predecessors. Instead, he focused on the two conventions that were The Speech's real object: Staging and Managing Expectations.[3]

Patton sought to manage his soldier-audience's expectations of him as their commander, themselves as combatants, and to introduce his own fighting style—that if anything, his own warrior memes had been understated by rumors and media accounts. He accomplished this by three rhetorical strokes. First, he explained something to his men about themselves; next, he explained something about war itself; finally (and most importantly), he explained more than just something about himself. Regarding these self-revelations, Patton had long been the reigning, if self-appointed, army expert in combining the medium—his staging, props, mode of introduction, personal appearance, language, and humor; in other words, his very self—with his message. In short, like speakers in the last section, *he* was the message.

In "teaching" his men about themselves, The Speech opened with two ideas. First, he implied the existence of a phantom pacifist ("this stuff you heard about Americans wanting to stay out of this war and not wanting to fight") who had misled some soldiers into believing that Americans disdained fighting; but Patton wanted to prove that the pacifist was wrong. If soldiers ever doubted that "The American loves a winner and cannot tolerate a loser," they had only to remember that as children the athletes they admired were those who had competed and won; thus, his green soldier-audience had also been competitors, albeit vicarious ones: "you all admired the champion marble player, the fastest runner, the big league ball players, the toughest boxer." Patton, a former Olympic contender and lifetime athlete, thus "proved" that the looming combat

---

3 D'Este, *A Genius for War*, 613; Blumenson, *Patton*, 216, 229. Assumption of Command Speeches are characterized by the Conventions of Authority, Acknowledge Predecessors, and Managing Expectations, Miller, *In Words and Deeds*, 317-323.

was only a higher-staked extension of something his men had always valued, and thus also reflected who they really were. Prominent athletes became Patton's bridge to his soldiers, over which he marched the warlike values he now demanded that they embrace.[4]

But resting matters on an implied sports-as-war analogy only trivialized war, and for Patton war was not trivial. A veteran of three conflicts, he had personally killed men and had walked corpse-strewn battlefields. He had experienced fear in combat and revulsion in its aftermath. Thus, it was predictable that The Speech would address a first-time combatant's greatest worry: death. Here, Patton refined the ancient psychological strategy probably being self-applied by many in his soldier-audience: denial.[5]

"You are not all going to die," Patton declared. "Only two percent of you here, in a major battle would die." Patton's persuasive strategy was brutally simple: a "scientific" statistic was intended to soothe men's anxieties about *their* dying. Two percent—only two chances out of a hundred—must have struck many as manageable. Of course, Patton omitted the more comprehensive arithmetic: what happened over a series of battles, or that front-line units could experience mortality far in excess of two percent. Nevertheless, "two percent" is a time-honored strategy for affirming denial's foundational principle: "It won't happen to me."

The Speech also sought to build confidence. In part, this meant reducing anxiety by connecting individuals to the larger group—everyone shared the same fears. "Every man is frightened at first in battle," Patton declared. "If he says he isn't he is a God damned liar." Patton added that there was nothing unmanly about being afraid. Indeed, even a frightened man could fight: "The real hero is the man who fights even though he is scared." And feeling cowardly was also normal. ("Some men are cowards, yes but they fight just the same or get

---

4 Athletics as War is an ancient concept, found in Biblical, Greco-Roman, and early Christian literature. Athletics mattered to Patton. He competed in the 1912 Olympics in Stockholm, Sweden. D'Este, *Genius for War*, 130-136. Patton was also a lifetime—and, often to his physical detriment, a very aggressive—horseman and polo player.

5 Patton served in Pershing's Punitive Expedition (1916-1917), World War I and World War II. Patton shot at least three Villistas during the gunfight at San Maguelita—which biographer D'Este compares with the "infamous shootout at the OK Corral." D'Este, *Genius for War*, 172-175. In addition, Patton *may* have killed one of his own men for failing to advance during battle in World War I; see D'Este, 257. Blumenson, *Patton,* 184, D'Este, 259 (fear in combat); D'Este, 237 (repelled by sights of mass death on battlefield).

the hell scared out of them watching men who do fight and who are just as scared as they.") What mattered was what a man did while he was afraid.

Patton wanted to convey to his men a sense of control in an environment that threatened a complete loss of self-control. "The real man never lets his fear of death over-power his honor, his duty to his country and his innate manhood." In essence, Patton offered each man a menu of self-control memes—respect of self and comrades (honor), and/or patriotism (duty to his country); he then he gender-wrapped these by appealing to his soldiers' "innate manhood." In 1944 few would argue that duty, honor, and country were masculine virtues—"innate manhood."

Patton also built confidence by stock references to his team's advantages in food ("the finest"), equipment ("the finest") and morale: "[we have the] best spirited men in the world." Indeed, he cleverly turned the tensions generated by fear and the need to maintain self-discipline into an advantage: "I don't give a damn for a man who is not always on his toes."

After he interpreted for his men their emotional states and highlighted their fighting advantages, Patton next turned to the nature of the war. He began with the enemy. "A man to continue breathing must be alert at all times," he cleverly warned. "If not, sometimes, some German son of a bitch will sneak up behind him and beat him to death with a sack full of shit." The enemy was insidious, but Patton's real concern was the state of American alertness. What made this clever was that one's alertness was within each man's control. A man could not control the random artillery shell; but he could control himself.

With the "400 graves in Sicily" anecdote came a tension-cracking humorous reversal. Few soldiers probably expected the conclusion: "But they are all German graves," Patton said, "for we caught the bastards asleep before they knew it." In other words, the enemy both erred and died like other human beings. Here Patton shrewdly diminished the enemy by *humanizing* rather than dehumanizing him. This may have been necessary because the Germans had a better—that is, more "military"—reputation among the soldiery. (Nazi propaganda touting the *Wehrmacht's* successes during the Blitzkrieg had been successful in planting memes of "invincibility.") In another anecdote—that of the "Lieutenant in Libia" [sic]—who, enemy gun to his chest notwithstanding, took his own helmet, killed him with it, and then, "despite having a bullet in his chest," killed another German—Patton conveyed war's desperate nature, restated the enemy's vulnerability, and implied an important "moral": war was survivable.

Indeed, the impression he sought to make was that war was survivable because it was mostly a collective effort. "The army is a team; lives, eats and fights as a team." But Patton did not articulate this as an abstraction. Instead, he reduced teamwork to any two men: "each man must think for not only himself, but think of his buddy fighting beside him." It was Patton's style to lavish recognition on subordinates and important non-combatants, and he was notorious for generously awarding medals and sharing credit for success. Predictably, The Speech praised non-combatants. Here Patton (disingenuously) dismissed the "individual heroic stuff" as "a lot of crap." This assertion allowed Patton to emphasize that his army was more than just lines of advancing tanks and riflemen. In North Africa and Sicily, Patton had proved that he was a master pursuer; but this also entailed mastering logistics; thus, many Third Army men would not be personally killing any Germans. "All real heroes are not story book combat fighters either," Patton reminded his soldier-audience. Those who supply guns, ammunition, food and clothing all perform jobs that were just as "essential to the whole scheme."[6]

But an extrovert such as Patton could not long dissimulate about his own core values. "My men don't surrender," he warned. "I don't want to hear of a soldier under my command getting captured unless he is hit. Even if you are, you can still fight back. This is not bull shit either." This warning approached a "no surrender" rule, which is among the most extreme a commander can issue. Someone who was determined to fight until he died or was severely wounded *was* something like a "story book combat fighter," a character whose importance Patton had just moments earlier (and doubtless with less sincerity) valued as equivalent to the critical work of non-combatants.

Patton closed The Speech by suggesting a rationale for why the war was worth its cost in blood and treasure. This was Patton's view of war's legacy; significantly, he said nothing about protecting democracy, liberating Europe and defeating Nazi evil. Instead, he appealed to soldiers' personal posterity:

---

6 "Decorations are for the purpose of raising the fighting morale of troops," he instructed his officers on March 6, 1944; he enjoyed decorating subordinates and sharing credit for Third Army successes. See General George S. Patton, *War As I Knew It* (New York: Houghton Mifflin, 1995), 402; Patton commanded the Western Task Force of Torch. Those landings, the subsequent campaign and the invasion of Sicily are discussed at length in D'Este, *Genius for War*, 417-441 (organizing Torch and subsequent landings); 460-487 (Tunisian Campaign); 491-532 (Sicily).

There is one thing you will be able to say when you go home. You may thank God for it, thank God that at least thirty years from now, when you are sitting around the fireside with your brat on your knee, and he asks you what you did in the Great War II, you don't have to say, "I shoveled shit [in Louisiana.]"

Here Patton may have remembered Shakespeare's King Henry V's "Band of Brothers" speech: "Old men forget; yet all shall be forgot/But he'll remember with advantages/What feats he did that day. Then shall our names/Familiar in his mouth as household words . . . /Be in their flowing cups freshly rememb'red/This story shall the good man teach his son." By Patton's lights, fighting in war—almost any war—was its own reward, a self-defining vindication of "honor, duty to country, innate manhood." Not every Patton peer felt this way, and readers might compare The Speech with Dwight D. Eisenhower's D-Day Pre-Invasion Speech. There the Supreme Allied Commander had spoken of a "Great Crusade" for the "elimination of Nazi tyranny over the oppressed peoples of Europe," and of "free men…marching together in Victory" and had mentioned God by requesting his blessing, instead of invoking the deity in a blasphemous oath.[7]

The Speech cannot be fully understood without mentioning its two larger aspects. First were Patton's extensive references to cowardice. He twice elaborated on the word "coward," most strikingly when he declared "We don't want yellow cowards in this army to go back to the States after the war and breed more like them." The Speech's soldier-audience certainly knew that while visiting hospitals in Sicily the previous summer, Patton had nearly destroyed his career when he slapped two (in his view) "cowards" whom he believed were malingering. (While many of Third Army's men were still training stateside, these incidents were the subject of withering high-profile media and prominent politicians' criticism.) A more-timid, less-astute manipulator of personal memes might have avoided any mention of cowards.[8]

7   William Shakespeare, "King Henry V," edited by Andrew Gurr, *The New Cambridge Shakespeare* (Cambridge, Great Britain: Cambridge University Press, 1995), Act IV, Scene 3, v. 49-56; Dwight D. Eisenhower, "Soldiers, Sailors and Airmen of the Allied Expeditionary Force!" original leaflet in author's possession.

8   Accounts of the slapping incidents and their aftermath can be found in Blumenson, *Patton,* 209-216; D'Este, *Genius for War,* 533-567; Robert H. Patton, *The Pattons,* (Washington, DC: Brassey's Inc., 2004), 262-264; *New York Times,* November 24 and 25, 1943, December 14 and 16, 1943.

Why did Patton believe it was advantageous to raise this issue now, even if obliquely? The answer is that the slapping memes likely had different meanings for soldiers facing battle than for distant civilians dosed on domestic propaganda that obscured the brutality of the war being waged by "our boys." First, the slappings were just extensions of Patton's existing warrior memes. Patton gambled that soldiers might value a commander with a reputation for efficiency, professionalism and victory, even if it meant (as Patton declared in The Speech) that "[t]he shortest way home is through Berlin," (thus implying more casualties.) Some soldiers might indulge a brutal commander if his behavior could be rationalized as in the army's best interests. And some soldiers may not have seen Patton's behavior as brutal at all: slapping malingerers might have transgressed the written rules, but might have been privately applauded by those forced to do the duty of such "comrades" or who had contempt for their unmanly behavior. In sum, Patton's use of "coward"—"yellow cowards" in one passage—was probably intended to summon the slapping memes as a benefit—and for some soldiers, a forewarning—of his special fighting and command style.[9]

The Speech's second larger aspect was embodied in the soldier-audience's reaction to Patton's remark that the Germans would panic when they realized that they faced not only the Third Army but "that son-of-[a]-bitch Patton." (Here one Speech historian noted that the men "roared approval and cheered delightedly.") If Ambrose Bierce's definition of applause is "the echo of a platitude," then roared approval and cheering must have been a deeply felt affirmation of something already known. So who was "that son-of-a-bitch Patton" who provoked such cheering?[10]

The "son-a-bitch Patton" had been aggressively marketing himself to the world well before his successes at the 1912 Stockholm Olympics. Four years later he garnered national headlines for a shootout during the 1916-1917 Punitive Expedition into Mexico. During World War I he earned more national headlines for his exploits leading the 1st Tank Brigade at the Saint-Mihiel

---

9 Patton's views about malingering were summarized in the posthumous publication of his memoirs, *War As I Knew It*, 362: "I am convinced that, in justice to other men, soldiers who go to sleep on post, who go absent for an unreasonable time during combat, who shirk in battle, should be executed."

10 "A General Talks to His Army," Patton File, VMI Archives; Ambrose Bierce, *The Unabridged Devil's Dictionary*, edited by David E. Schultz and S.J. Joshi (Athens, Georgia: University of Georgia Press, 2001), 16.

salient and during the Meuse-Argonne Offensive. He had shown exceptional courage, was severely wounded, and later highly decorated.[11]

These incidents occurred before many in his soldier-audience had been born. However, while publicly dormant (except within the army), these memes were vigorously revived with the approach of World War II. By the time the Japanese attacked Pearl Harbor a generic newsreader already would have been very familiar with Patton's exploits during several highly-publicized, pre-war training exercises. But no newspaper article could compete with the July 7, 1941, cover of *Life Magazine*. Readers saw a color picture of Gen. George S. Patton standing in a tank turret, war face fixed, steely eyes intently looking ahead. For a new generation, Patton the warrior was reborn. *That* was the "son-of-a-bitch," an equal to any of Hitler's polished Prussians, who gave green soldiers such confidence.[12]

There remains to discuss only Patton's "wordless text" that accompanied The Speech. Here Patton carefully correlated his personal memes with his physical appearance, costume and staging and props. Third Army staffer Colonel Robert S. Allen left this description of Patton as he delivered a different address around the same period that he was giving The Speech:

> He was attired in a superbly tailored, form fitting, brass buttoned battle jacket, studded with four rows of campaign ribbons and decorations, pink whipcord riding breeches, and gleaming high topped cavalry boots with spurs. Around his waist was a hand-tooled, wide leather belt with a large, embossed, shiny brass buckle. In his hand was a long riding crop; on his shoulders, shirt collar, and helmet, fifteen large stars.

11 Sample newspaper coverage for the Stockholm Olympics can be found in the *Los Angeles Times*, August 7, 1912 ("ONLY SWEDS [sic] BEAT PATTON"); for the Mexican shootout see *New York Times*, May 23, 1916 ("CARDENAS'S FAMILY SAW HIM DIE AT BAY; Shot Four Times, Villa Captain Fought Before Mother, Wife, and Daughter. DRAMATIC FIGHT at Ranch: Lieut. Patton and Ten Men Killed Three Bandits."); for World War I see *New York Times*, October 22, 1918 ("TANK CORPS LEADER WOUNDED IN FRANCE[.] Maj. G.S. Patton, Who Helped Organize That Branch, Hurt In Air Fighting [sic]").

12 "'Panzer' Division Will Enter Manoeuvres For the First Such Field Test in Our History," *New York Times*, May 25, 1941; "Blue Army Patrols Fight Off 'Invaders,'" *New York Times*, June 4, 1941; "Big Armored Unit Ready to Attack in First Such Army Manoeuvre," *New York Times*, May 16, 1941; *Life Magazine*, July 7, 1941.

Here personal appearance reinforced the message of the need for unrelenting discipline. First, Patton's message emphasized the importance of obedience to authority, because "instant obedience to orders...creates instant alertness." Then came self-discipline—thus, The Speech's forewarnings about cowardice. And there was no better advertisement for these disciplinary memes than the perfectly fitted uniform and brightly polished accoutrements. Patton's decorations reinforced the idea that war was survivable (the "two percent" reference) and war's honors desirable because of a grateful posterity ("[Y]ou don't have to say, 'I shoveled shit [in Louisiana]).'" The bemedaled Patton incarnated war's survivability and its glory.[13]

Moreover Patton's cavalry attire—as irrelevant to his function as the ivory grips on his pistols—nevertheless served to reinforce the meme of bold, aggressive leadership by using some very special props: riding crop, boots, trousers, and spurs. Indeed, for Americans these props had a special resonance likely drawn from a shared historical legacy that celebrated the mounted man: there were cowboys and gunfighters, and for most of the soldier-audience, films about cowboys and gunfighters; there was J.E.B. Stuart and George Armstrong Custer, and Roosevelt's Rough Riders.

His attire might have been flawless. But it was by what that attire represented that Patton "proved" that he was no martinet; quite the contrary, he was the rider and the outrider, the cavalryman and the scout, seducing with war's historical romance yet promising a thrill of danger. It was hardbitten and glorious and brilliantly exploited uniquely American memes.[14]

Immediate Result

The Speech alternately spellbound, thrilled, and fascinated Patton's soldier-audience, absorbed them in the celebrity of Patton, a man who had

---

13 Colonel Robert S. Allen, *Lucky Forward: The History of Patton's Third U.S. Army* (New York: Vanguard Press, 1947), 18; D'Este, *Genius for War*, 478.

14 Having come up through army cavalry (and early distinguishing himself militarily by redesigning the official army cavalry sword), George Patton was probably first among equals in his romance of horse soldiery. And there were personal ties to the mounted service. Patton's father and grandfather had attended J.E.B. Stuart's wake, and the Grey Ghost John Mosby was a frequent visitor to Patton's boyhood home. Patton, *Personal History*, 56; Blumenson, *Patton*, 30 (Mosby.) For Patton's numerous Confederate connections, see Ashley Halsey, "Ancestral Gray Cloud Over Patton," *American History Illustrated*, March 1984, 42-48.

become a living metonym for warfare itself. Reacting to The Speech, one soldier—almost certainly speaking for the majority of his comrades—wrote home as follows:

> [When] General Patton walked out on the little terrace, three steps above us…the surprise was no less exciting than it was official. Most of us had never seen him in the flesh, and when the drum, ruffles, and bugles sounded the General's march, we stood transfixed upon his appearance. Not one square inch of flesh [of everyone there was] not covered with goose pimples. It was one of the greatest thrills I shall ever know. You stood at rigid attention . . . that towering figure impeccably attired froze you in place and electrified the air. . . . He talked on to us for half an hour, literally hypnotizing us with his incomparable, if profane eloquence. When he had finished, you felt as if you had been given a supercharge from some divine source. Here was a man for whom you would go to hell and back.

Some took exception to Patton's behavior, mostly those who were offended by his profanity and blasphemy. But most accounts of men's reaction to The Speech described them as "roaring . . . clapping and howling delightfully . . . cheering delightfully . . . laughing." In fact, the whole experience was one that inspired "many a barracks [sic] about the Old Man's choice of phrases."[15]

Legacy

The Speech helped establish Patton, the extroverted fire breather, as an opposing model of command to that of the taciturn Ulysses Grant. But part of Patton's battle speech legacy that has assumed increasing importance since World War II is a speechmaker's legal responsibility for his words. Patton himself was confronted with this issue after the invasion of Sicily. Following a battle for the Biscari Airfield on July 14, 1943, GIs murdered nearly seventy Axis prisoners of war. Two men were tried for the crime, and both claimed a "Patton defense," that is, that the general, in a Pre-Invasion Speech, had authorized the atrocities. One defendant insisted that Patton's speech included the command that "[i]f you[r] company officers in leading your men against the enemy finds him shooting at you and, when you get within two hundred yards of

---

15 This "young soldier" is quoted in Blumenson, *Patton*, 220. These descriptive phrases were taken from "A General Talks To His Army," from the VMI archives; I have altered the verb tenses for narrative purposes.

him and he wishes to surrender, oh no! That bastard will die!" (In fact, Patton was vehemently opposed to maltreating prisoners and had no record of authorizing any prisoner abuses.) However, whatever Patton's intentions, his hyperbole might be misconstrued by weak, less-disciplined or pathologically violent men. Although investigated, Patton was never charged in the Biscari Massacres, and historians remain divided over his responsibility.

However, since Patton's time, international treaties now impose far greater responsibility for a commander's words and deeds implicated in war crimes. Patton may enjoy a unique legacy as a battle speechmaker in part because in today's battlefield environment, the presence of more restrictive rules and the presence of international media mean Patton imitators risk being charged with inciting, or even ordering, the commission of war crimes.[16]

Leadership Principle

In early 1945, Patton wrote to his son about leadership. "I have it," he declared, "but I'll be damned if I can define it." In fact, he defined it often in letters of instruction to his officers and in his posthumously published memoirs. It might be summarized in four words: boldness, aggression, personal execution, and "visible personality." "Visible personality" seemed to subsume the rest, and The Speech embodied the whole concept. Patton's grandson Robert defined visible personality: "On the tank training ground outside Langres, on a hill under fire at Cheppy [in World War I France], on a polo field, at a cocktail party, around the dinner table at home, Georgie was compulsively driven to emote, dazzle, dominate—in short, to exhibit personality in everything he did."[17]

Persuasive Strategy

How and why did The Speech work as Patton's "visible personality?" First, The Speech stands as one of the best-known examples of a near-perfect correlation between personal appearance, props and message in support of a

---

16 As quoted in D'Este, *Genius for War*, 754. For a closer examination of Patton's role, see James J. Weingartner, "Massacre at Biscari: An American War Crime," *The Historian: A Journal of History*, Vol. LII, No. 1, November 1989, 24-39.

17 D'Este, *Genius for War*, 699; Patton, *Family History,* 196.

speaker's existing memes. Patton knew his own warrior reputation, and made certain that everything he wore and said during The Speech supported it. Patton also evinced the two most important levels of awareness noted previously: first, knowing the mind of his soldier-audience; and second, in response to this, dissimulating to achieve The Speech's objectives.

What were The Speech's objectives? Patton's soldier-audience was drawn from a bourgeois society steeped in commercial, religious, and democratic values. It was also a society with a longstanding antimilitary bias. The Speech helped to prepare them for a war in which they must kill with malice aforethought, destroy property, become numb to the deaths of friends, foes, and suffering civilians, and voluntarily place themselves in lethal combat—a situation against which for many every natural instinct rebelled. Patton's first persuasive technique was to sell himself as a successful leader who, by survival and discipline, could shorten the war by producing victories. By implication, he reintroduced his men to the ancient calculus of decisiveness: higher casualties in the short-term might mean fewer casualties over time.

The Speech continued the process (presumably begun in boot camp) of "reprocessing" civilian norms. Patton's repeated use of profanity, blatant sexual imagery and blasphemy violated what, in 1944, were rigid taboos against using such language in public spaces. Patton swore and cursed enemies ("God damned liar," "purple pissing Japanese"); he amused ("The billious [sic] bastard who wrote that stuff for the Saturday Evening Post didn't know anymore about real battle than he did about fucking," or "shoveling shit in Louisiana"), and even self-effaced ("that son-of-[a]-bitch Patton again.") The point was to subtly delegitimize concepts and institutions that might impede his soldier-audience's inurement to the war they had to fight.

The Speech persuaded because it resolved the inherent contradictions between citizen-armies and that war. First, Patton's appearance and his words both insisted on militaristic discipline, obedience, and self-control—virtues not necessarily inherent in civilian life. But The Speech insisted upon those virtues on behalf of two things devoutly wished by every ex-civilian-now-soldier: personal survival and quick victory. Patton's personal appearance and words also suggested that there was order in war, an activity that to the soldier-audience might threaten only chaos and the loss of personal control.

And here lies The Speech's persuasive trick: Patton offered a temporary remittance of his citizen-soldiers' civilian values. In their place, he gave official blessing to other values, some summarized by the training slogan of the day

("Kill Or Get Killed"), and still other values based on fear or emulation of those comrades who could transform that slogan into reality. This began with Patton himself, and The Speech offered dispensation. It worked because in the timeless negotiation between battle speechmakers and soldiers facing battle, dispensation was exactly what the audience wanted—and needed. [18]

---

18 D'Este, *Genius for War*, 745; *Kill or Get Killed: A Manual of Hand to Hand Fighting*, by (then) Major Rex Applegate (Harrisburg, Pennsylvania: Military Service Publishing Co., 1943) It remains in print.

Chapter Five

The Directors: Sam Houston (and "Deaf" Smith) at San Jacinto

I. Historical Background

The Battle of San Jacinto, although fought between numerically small forces, was as decisive in its outcome as the battles of Cannae, Agincourt or Austerlitz. In some eighteen minutes, the Texian victory conclusively decided Texas' fate: the Mexican President, General Don Antonio Lopez de Santa Anna y Perez de Lebron (better known as Santa Anna, or the self-styled "Napoleon of the West") fled and his routed army was slaughtered or captured.[1] Santa Anna would be apprehended the next day, and brought before Texian General Sam Houston, who, although painfully wounded and propped up against a tree, was still able to dictate surrender terms. These were soon accepted; shortly thereafter, Texas ceased to be Mexican territory and became an independent republic. In 1845, it would be the twentieth-eighth state admitted to the United States.[2]

---

1 "Texian" rather than "Texan" is used throughout this chapter but not because I take pleasure in sending readers to dictionaries; rather, the words mean different things. A "Texian" refers to those who emigrated to what is now the State of Texas while it still belonged to Mexico.

2 My narrative of the Battle of San Jacinto relies on four accounts: James L. Haley, *Sam Houston* (Norman, Oklahoma: University of Oklahoma Press, 2002); James W. Pohl, The Battle of San Jacinto (Texas State Historical Association, 1989); Stephen L. Moore, *Eighteen Minutes: The Battle of San Jacinto and the Texas Independence Campaign* (New

The story of the San Jacinto Campaign and its climactic battle has been called the "Texas Iliad." Like Homer's epic, Texas' story of independence was filled with massacres and miracles, heroes, villains and the deeds of outsized characters. But as is often the case, the ballad only imperfectly mirrors the campaign's actual history. For battle speech historians, one accurate part of that story was the birth of the seminal Speechlet "Remember the Alamo!" That Speechlet and its legacy were discussed in the Introduction. This chapter will instead explore an obscure speech shouted by Sam Houston's scout, confidant and surrogate speechifyer Erastus "Deaf" Smith just moments before the Texian Army fired on the Mexican camp. It illustrated the battle-speechmaker-as-trickster (with Sam Houston directing) and provides a case study as to why some speechmakers may be tempted to deceive their own soldiers.[3]

The meaning of short battle speeches cannot be understood without context. And the context (but not necessarily the speech) for "Deaf" Smith's cry—"Vince's Bridge is down! Fight for your lives! Vince's Bridge is down!"—is well attested: many soldiers who might have heard Smith's cry disliked and, worse, distrusted their own commander, Sam Houston. That distrust was mutual. Houston's relationship with his army was among the worst in American military history, perhaps exceeded only by that between Andrew Jackson and his militia at the Battle of Horseshoe Bend—the same battle in which Sam Houston received his baptism of fire.[4]

As a young man, Houston had spent almost five years in the United States Army, and while there developed a regular's disdain for volunteer militia. But there was far more to Houston's attitude than institutional prejudice. Horseshoe Bend, Houston's defining military experience until San Jacinto, had been fought

York: Republic of Texas Press, 2004), whose time-line-in-in-the-title I have accepted per above; Frank X. Tolbert, *The Day of San Jacinto* (New York: The Pemberton Press, 1959).

3   Stephen L. Hardin, *Texian Iliad: A Military History of the Texas Revolution, 1835-1836* (Austin: University of Texas Press, 1996).

4   Marquis James, *The Raven: A Biography of Sam Houston* (Indianapolis: The Bobbs-Merrill Company, 1929), 251; besides James, many but not all historians cite the Smith speech. These include Alfred M. Williams, *Sam Houston and the War of Independence in Texas* (Boston: Houghton Mifflin, 1893), 200; Tolbert, *Day of San Jacinto*, 142; M. K. Wisehart, *Sam Houston: American Giant* (Washington: Robert B. Luce, 1962), 239; Cleburne Huston, *Deaf Smith: Incredible Texas Spy* (Waco, Texas: Texian Press, 1973), 86; two recent books that do not mention the speech are Pohl, *Battle of San Jacinto*, and Moore, *Eighteen Minutes*. Unless otherwise noted, all details about Jackson's Creek Campaign are from Henry Adams, *History of the United States of America During the Administrations of James Madison* (New York: Library of America, 1989), 782-801.

against empowered Creek tribes during the War of 1812. A combined force of friendly Indians, United States Regulars and civilian militia comprised General Andrew Jackson's strike force, sent to suppress the Creek insurgency. During the campaign that culminated in the Battle of Horseshoe Bend, Jackson's greatest problems came not from hostile Indians but from his own militia. The iron-willed Jackson repeatedly confronted these querulous frontier units, and much of the story preceding the battle was a relentless drama of desertions, mutiny, arrests, and finally a "warning" execution intended to discourage further militia disobedience. Worse, when the long-sought battle came, it was Jackson's resourceful Indian allies and the regular U.S. army that achieved the victory; citizen militia, for all their trouble, had proven of little worth. During the battle, Houston had sustained a groin wound that would never properly heal. Twenty-two years later, besides that pain, Houston apparently continued to cherish the larger "lesson" of Horseshoe Bend: that volunteer militia was untrustworthy. And the story of "Deaf" Smith's cry is really the story of this distrust.[5]

In what must have seemed a dreary repetition of history, in the five months after Houston had been appointed Major General of the Army of the Republic of Texas, some senior officers and many in the ranks had been disobedient, insubordinate and mutinous. Camp letter writers had secretly denounced him to Texas' fledgling provisional government, while other "comrades" schemed to replace him as commander. However lamentable their conduct, these malcontents had their reasons: until capped by the victory at San Jacinto, Houston's management of the campaign had not gone well. Indeed, his San Jacinto Campaign offered a nineteenth century preview of French Prime Minister Georges Clemenceau's twentieth century observation that "War is a series of catastrophes that results in a victory."[6]

Much of the fault lay with Sam Houston himself. Despite his deserved reputation as a brilliant orator, while in command he was surprisingly

---

5 Dixon and Louis Wiltz Kemp, *The Heroes of San Jacinto* (Houston, Texas: The Anson Jones Press, 1932), "Houston, Samuel," 37-40

6 Houston was elected commander-in-chief of Texas' Regular Army on November 12, 1835; he assumed field command on March 11, 1836. Tolbert, *The Day of San Jacinto*, 35, 45; 85-86 (scheming for Houston's job); Moore, *Eighteen Minutes*, 216-217, 137-138 (disobedience, mutiny); 191-192 (camp letter writer). *The MacMillan Dictionary of Political Quotations*, ed. Louis D. Eigen and Jonathan Paul Seigal, (New York: MacMillan, 1993), 689.

uncommunicative: as a general, he proved a far better strategist and tactician than morale builder. Worse, his secretiveness was combined with his wise choice of a Fabian strategy in response to the advance of Santa Anna's forces. Houston initially faced overwhelming Mexican superiority before he had had the opportunity to concentrate or even train his own army. Fearing to fight before he was ready, Houston chose to preserve his army, so instead he withdrew—often over the protest (and occasional mutiny) of his own troops, who were zealous to avenge the Alamo's fall and Goliad's massacre. Having adopted the same strategy as its namesake (the great Roman general Fabius Maximus) had over two millennia earlier, Houston would now suffer the same criticism: he was accused of lacking the moral and physical courage to command. These charges were also accompanied by intense lobbying for his removal.[7]

Complicating matters was the fact that Houston had personal flaws probably not shared with Fabius. He was a notorious alcoholic not destined for enduring sobriety until his second marriage many years later. (Or perhaps it would count as his third such union; Houston had married a Cherokee woman before moving to Texas.) His first marriage, to the daughter of a prominent Tennessee family, had mysteriously dissolved within days of the nuptials. Fearing scandal, he abruptly resigned as Tennessee's governor (where some thought him heir-apparent to Andrew Jackson) and decamped for the Cherokee Nation. While there he became a Cherokee citizen, took an Indian wife (joined by tribal ritual), and, by one account, dressed in native garb and refused to speak English. Meanwhile, his drinking worsened.[8]

The larger point is that this period of scandal and self-exile had become part of Houston's "mystique" even before he engaged in a practice so widespread that contemporaries had initials for it: "G.T.T.," or Gone To Texas. But it was precisely this sort of mystery that gave his Texian civilian superiors so much anxiety: before receiving command, Houston was forced to sign a vow containing respectfully oblique but unmistakable promises to avoid alcohol. Moreover, Houston's extensive—and loving—relationships within the

---

7 Livy, *The War With Hannibal, Books XXI-XXX of The History of Rome from its Foundation*, trans. Aubrey De Selincourt, ed. and intro. Betty Radice (London: Penguin Books, 1972), 107-108. Once Houston began falling back he was criticized from all quarters until the battle itself. For one example, see Moore, *Eighteen Minutes*, 189.

8 The period of Houston's disastrous first marriage, self-exile and worsening alcoholism is covered in Haley, *Sam Houston*, 51-80.

Cherokee Nation also provided malcontented soldiers with complaints. Many referred to him as "the God damned old Cherokee blackguard."[9]

Predictably, reports soon emerged that Houston, if he had not resumed his bad habits, had acquired some new and perhaps more dangerous ones. Major James Perry, a member of Houston's own staff, complained on April 9 that although Houston had "entirely discontinued the use of ardent Spirits" his poor management of the army was "some say from the effect of opium," which for Perry explained Houston's "condition between sleeping and walking which amounts nearly to a constant state of insanity."[10]

This discontent grew as Houston's retreat lengthened. For example, after withdrawing across the Colorado River, one of Houston's captains recalled that "[h]ere there was a strong desire on the part of a large portion of the army to attack [the pursuing Mexicans]…and a considerable murmuring was heard at the commander-in-chief's refusal to gratify this desire." Words soon threatened to become deeds. Another participant recalled that "[m]any of us declared it was necessary to have a better leader [than Houston], and that, if he could do no better, we would elect someone better fitted to command." When rumors flew that such a change was imminent (even naming one of Houston's subordinates as a successor), "Houston…at once caused notices to be written and stuck on trees with wooden pegs to the effect that the first man who should beat for volunteers, should be court-martialed and shot." While Houston insisted that this "mutiny and sedition" was limited to his officers, the truth was otherwise. A sergeant recalled that he and his company were solicited to mutiny by one prominent officer. "[The officer] was assured by both our officers and our men [that] he could rely on their cooperation," the sergeant wrote. "There was no injunction of secrecy—and Gen'l Houston could not have been ignorant of what was in agitation." Sedition, mutiny, and threats of executions would become another stock, but accurate, subplot of the Texas Iliad.[11]

The context for "Deaf" Smith's cry must also include something about the character of the militia that Houston commanded, and which he was also

---

9 Haley, *Sam Houston*, 116, 99; Tolbert, *Day at San Jacinto*, 85.

10 Moore, *Eighteen Minutes*, 192. The accusations of opium use were false.

11 Eugene C. Barker, "The San Jacinto Campaign," *The Quarterly of the Texas Historical Association*, Volume IV, No. 4, April 1901, "Kuykendall's Recollections of the Campaign," 302; "Labadie's Account of the Campaign," 309; "R. J. Calder's Recollections of the Campaign," 334.

expected to recruit, march and train while simultaneously engaging Santa Anna. This Army of Texas embodied every vice (and virtue) of raw citizen armies: its members were enthusiastic; undisciplined; unschooled in tactics, strategy or tradition. Moreover, they were highly individualistic in that peculiarly American way: contemptuous of discipline and suspicious of officers. They understood military service as contractual, with obedience contingent on (among other things) the leader performing to their expectations. Because Houston's command decisions, style, and real intentions during his long retreats were even then (and have been since) controversial, most historians agree that he had disappointed the expectations of many of his men. The militia attitudes that Houston distrusted contributed to the militia's distrust of him.[12]

Contributing to these bad relations was the fact that Houston's San Jacinto army was also unstable. During the campaign leading up to the battle, its numbers and unit composition constantly fluctuated. This had the effect of further weakening the already-shaky cohesion between Houston and his soldier-audience. Houston began the San Jacinto campaign with 374 men; by mid-March, the number was 420 men, net of desertions; a few days later, the army numbered over 500; by March 21, it had grown to 810; by March 26 it had grown to perhaps 1,400. But within one week, this force had fallen to somewhere between 750 and 800 men; at San Jacinto, the numbers had risen to 930 men. And this only hints at the considerable turnover *within* units; thus, absolute numbers fail to convey the full measure of personnel fluctuations. The larger point is that this situation further weakened cohesion and added to the distrust between Houston and his soldier-audience.[13]

Yet another factor also contributing to the mistrust was the short time that most soldiers had actually resided in Texas: Houston himself belonged to the 51% who had lived there for less than five years; 17% had been in the self-proclaimed nation less than one year. Houston may have wondered

---

12 Stephen L. Hardin, in *Texas Iliad*, characterizes the different views of Houston's leadership: "Two distinct images of Houston emerge. One is of a timid man, who schemed to avoid combat until his troops literally forced him into action. The other is of a stalwart hero in the Kipling mold, a confident man who kept his head while petty and presumptuous subordinates were losing theirs. Neither view is entirely true nor entirely false. Since Houston was careful not to reveal certain aspects of himself, there will always be an air of mystery surrounding the man," 208.

13 Moore, *Eighteen Minutes*, 75, 100, 116, 139, 147, 295. Typical of nineteenth-century American armies, the actual number of men cannot be precisely determined.

whether, at the critical moment, such men would fight for a Texas that many hardly knew. Houston may have remembered that the Horseshoe Bend campaign had been fought in the United States' thirty-eighth year of independence, and militia desertions had nearly prevented Jackson from marching at all: would Texians' loyalty to their far more embryonic government prove just as weak?

There were also other reasons that Houston's doubts may have related to his early experience against the Creeks. First, his units' identities were based on loyalty to their recruiters, men who were later elected as company officers; to Houston they owed him almost nothing but *legal* compliance. Houston's army was also plagued by desertion, to Houston always an indicator of morale. Both of these problems had also been prominent issues during Houston's own experience at Horseshoe Bend.[14]

Not surprisingly, "Deaf" Smith's ride was not the first time that Houston had used trickery and deceit to manage soldiers and his civilian superiors. This included the outright lie. For example, as Houston's men deserted, he lied to his civilian superiors about morale. And to his men, he lied often. Some lies embraced the heart of Frederick the Great's advice on dissimulation. When news of the Alamo's destruction arrived, Houston believed it true, although, in order to prevent panic, he publicly pretended otherwise. To instill confidence, he sometimes brazenly exaggerated the strength of his forces. And when one Peter Kerr arrived in camp bearing news of the Goliad Massacre, Houston branded him a spy, although he probably knew the information was accurate; likewise, on the morning of the battle of San Jacinto itself, as Santa Anna's army was reinforced by the clearly visible arrival of some 400 Mexicans under General Martin Perecto de Cos, Houston declared it "a sham, and no reinforcement."[15]

But what men remembered most about Houston's trickery were the *ruses de guerre*. For example, although no field commanders were ever

---

14 Paul D. Lack, *The Texas Revolutionary Experience: A Political and Social History, 1835-1836* (College Station: Texas A&M University Press, 1992), 127.

15 Sam Houston to Thomas Rusk, March 23, 1836, 380-381; Houston to Rusk, April 4, 1836, 395-396; Houston to David Thomas, April 14, 1836, 410-411, all in *The Writings of Sam Houston, 1813-1863*, edited by Amelia W. Williams and Eugene C. Barker (Austin, Texas: University of Texas Press, 1940), Volume I; *Texas Almanac, 1857-1873, A Compendium of Texas History* (1859), compiled by James M. Day, (Waco: Texian Press, 1967), "Reinforcements to the Enemy," 161.

court-martialed for mutinous behavior, two enlisted men were; one was charged with desertion and mutiny, the other with disobeying orders and desertion. Both were found guilty and sentenced to a firing squad. For Houston, this was the opportunity for what a later age would call "a teachable moment," albeit one with rather high stakes. One of the two men was actually "taken to his grave and the whole army paraded to witness the execution of the sentence;" at the climactic moment, Houston pardoned the man, using the opportunity to issue a stern order reciting the evils of desertion and the importance of obedience. Significantly, one of Houston's ruses—jointly perpetrated with "Deaf" Smith (in an eerie foreshadowing of the rigged speech at the Battle of San Jacinto)—had the trusted scout gallop up to the camp and announce that "a large body of Mexicans [were] just around a point of timber, and that they were marching on us." Houston immediately shouted, "To Arms! To arms! The enemy is upon us!" As an infantryman eyewitness recalled, "Houston had arranged this false alarm to see if he could depend on the volunteers; he had all the time been afraid of them in a close place." The "them" that frightened Houston were his own men.[16]

Finally, Houston was confronted with outright disobedience and even mutiny at the senior command level. An instance of the first occurred after he had ordered Lieutenant Colonel James W. Fannin to abandon his position at Goliad and retreat to Guadalupe Victoria. But Fannin had hesitated for days. On March 19-20, Fannin fought against, lost to and properly surrendered to Mexican forces at the Battle of Coleto. Although accepted as prisoners, Fannin and his men were massacred one week later on Palm Sunday, on the direct orders of Santa Anna. Another case occurred within the precincts of Houston's own army. Two company captains had simply refused orders to retreat across the Brazos River. Rather than risk a demoralizing showdown—one Houston

---

16 The executions episodes are covered in Moore, *Eighteen Minutes*, 158-161; the "near death" experience of the condemned will be found in Kuykendall, "Recollections of the Campaign," *The Quarterly of the Texas State Historical Association*, Volume IV, Number 4, April 1901, 301; the "To Arms!" episode is from "Recollections of S.F. Sparks," *The Quarterly of the Texas State Historical Association*, Volume XII, Number 1, July 1908, 69. See also Cleburne Huston, *Deaf Smith: Incredible Texas Spy* (Waco, Texas: Texian Press, 1973), 71.

might have lost—he ordered both officers to remain in defensive positions on the river, essentially acquiescing to the mutineers' demands.[17]

For all of these reasons, until the afternoon of the Battle of San Jacinto the campaign revealed a disturbing mix of distrust, disobedience, and failures of communications, principally by Houston to his soldiery. For Houston's part, he had listened for weeks to campfire bravado; now that the army faced the real enemy across San Jacinto's field, Houston must have wondered if his soldiers' ardor had begun to cool. Whatever doubts he had were only amplified by the council of war convened that morning.

Once assembled Houston immediately put a question to his chief subordinates, whose members also included his civilian superior, Texas Secretary of War Thomas J. Rusk: "Shall we attack the enemy in position, or receive their attack on ours?" The majority together with the Secretary voted against an attack. Rusk spoke for the "no" voters: "to attack veteran troops with raw militia is a thing unheard of," he declared. "[T]o charge upon the enemy, without bayonets, in an open prairie, had never been known; our situation is strong; in it we can whip all Mexico." In short, Rusk argued that Houston should remain in his defenses and await Santa Anna's attack.

Houston's only formal response to this vote—"two to one in favor of waiting"—was to adjourn the meeting without issuing an order to attack. He left no record of his thoughts at that moment. Perhaps he felt dispirited and burdened by the loneliness of command; perhaps he felt ambivalent about what to do. However, given his history and considering what he did in fact do, it was more probable that he looked around and saw that the ghosts of Horseshoe Bend had returned.[18]

II. The Speech

Vince's Bridge is down! Fight for your lives! Vince's Bridge is down!

—Erastus ("Deaf") Smith, April 21, 1836[19]

---

17 Houston to Fannin, March 11, 1836, *The Papers of the Texas Revolution*, edited by John H. Jenkins (Austin, Texas: Presidial Press, 1973), V: 51-52; Moore, *Eighteen Minutes*, 216-217, 137-138.

18 Moore, *Eighteen Minutes*, 301-303.

19 Marquis James, *The Raven*, 251.

III. Parsing the Speech

How should one parse a twelve-word speech that is not a Speechlet? There is nothing of embedded narrative here. The words were directed to a Texian soldier-audience and were meant as a literal warning ("Vince's Bridge is down!") Or was it a threat ("Fight for your lives!")? Was it a ROE ("Fight for your lives!"), urging a special ferocity against an already-hated foe? And—whether it was a warning, threat, ROE, general exhortation, or all of the foregoing, what purpose was served by having Houston "preconcert" with Smith—as some historians believe happened—the latter's dramatic ride along the Texian battle line? These twelve words can only be parsed by considering their probable—highly probable in my view—purpose.[20]

Thus, the words summon context, and the context becomes the speech. Houston's personal history and the mutually poor relations with his soldierly already have been discussed. For more context, I will turn to specific events that happened immediately before and after the council of war.

First, a few factoids about Vince's Bridge. Built from wood, it spanned an estuary of the Buffalo Bayou and was located some eight miles west of the battlefield on the Harrisonburg Road. While Vince's Bridge was not the only line of retreat, it was the shortest and, because it joined Harrisonburg Road, the easiest; a wet spring season had filled nearby swamps and swollen otherwise-fordable bayous and rivers. If one knew nothing about Houston's relationship with his army, the first reason for cutting Vince's Bridge was that it would also cut Santa Anna's best line of retreat. If this was Houston's sole motivation, then logically, he should have directed "Deaf" Smith to make his cry in Spanish (which the scout spoke) towards the Mexican line; or, if massacre was Houston's motive (not likely given his later efforts to halt such indiscriminate killing after the battle), why order Smith to make any announcement at all?[21]

But the sequence of events leading up to Houston's final order to destroy Vince's Bridge suggests that he intended to use Smith's announcement not to facilitate the massacre of Mexicans, but rather, to spur Texians to make the charge. (Whether Houston was correct in doubting his men's mettle is a separate question from what he believed about their morale.)

20 Tolbert, *Day of San Jacinto*, 142.

21 Pohl, *Battle of San Jacinto*, 32.

First, *before* the council of war, Houston (at least by his own account) procured two axes, and privately ordered Smith to "select a companion in whom he had unbounded confidence;" furthermore, Houston ordered Smith "not to leave the camp that day without orders; that [Smith] would be wanted." At this point, Houston apparently did not tell Smith what his mission might be. But one can infer that Houston already had the mission in mind. More of a stretch, but still a quite reasonable inference was that Houston meant to attend the council of war, take the temperature of his command, and then make a decision—not about destroying Vince's Bridge (as noted, there were sound military reasons for doing so), but rather, whether or not to instruct "Deaf" Smith to stage a highly dramatic announcement of that fact after the deed was done and as his men were advancing towards the Mexican camp. The question is, why?

After his *entre nous* with Smith, Houston convened the council, listened to the objections, and took the vote. Immediately afterwards he sent for Smith (who meanwhile had recruited a companion—ultimately, he would enlist an entire squad). It was here that Houston must have explained both the objective of destroying Vince's Bridge *and* ordered Smith to stage his high profile announcement afterwards; what is certain (by Houston's account) is that he handed his scouts the axes and gave this ambiguous order: "You will be speedy if you return in time for the scenes that are to be enacted here." Some historians believe that one of those "scenes" was to be "Deaf" Smith's ride along the line, ordered by Houston sometime before Smith departed or at the very latest, immediately after his return. Neither Houston nor Smith (who died the next year) ever admitted that his orders included the trick.

What was the trick? A *ruse de guerre* to be sure, but one applied to comrades, not the enemy. Houston, unsure of his men's willingness to fight, wanted to strengthen their steel, and his means was Smith's announcement. Although most historians believe that the Texians wanted to fight, at the time, Houston probably had doubts. So he ordered Smith to make his announcement at a critical moment. It was a paradoxical, and uncomplimentary, appeal to some presumed Texian cowardice: if your ideals, hatred of enemy, loyalty to the state, love of comrades, or loyalty to your commander fail to motivate you to attack, then the desire to save yourselves just might.

The closest Houston ever came to acknowledging that Smith's ride-along-the-line might have been intended to motivate his own men came twenty-three years later in a speech to the United States Senate. Houston was defending himself against an accusation that the destruction of Vince's Bridge was *not* his idea:

[Cutting the bridge] was announced to the army for the first time; for the idea that the bridge would be cut down was never thought of by any one but [me], until [I] ordered it to be done, and then only known to Smith and his comrade. *Vince's bridge was to be destroyed, for it cut off all means of escape for either army. There was no alternative but victory or death.* [Italics added][22]

Houston had an indispensable ally who unwittingly lent credibility to Smith's cry: Santa Anna—or, more precisely, his policy of "No Quarter." Perhaps Houston failed to recognize the depth of his men's feelings, but many of his Texians were indeed hell-bent on massacre, a desire to revenge the Alamo and Goliad. The war, never a matter between professional armies, had become personal as Texians mourned-via-musket friends and relations brutally liquidated by Santa Anna. Houston may have been counting on his men's fear of Santa Anna (versus their desire for revenge) and probably hoped that Smith's speech would be seen as a grim reminder that against such a foe it really was "Victory or Death." Houston, through Smith, was determined to exploit his own act (cutting the bridge), but then use the fear of Santa Anna to "interpret" its meaning.

There was no lie in declaring that Vince's Bridge was "down"; in fact, Smith had destroyed enough of the span to render it unusable. The trick lay in the use to which Houston put that fact. And it was better (and more believable) to have the announcement come from the respected Smith than the despised Houston.

Immediate Result

Almost 175 years have passed since San Jacinto was fought, and at this distance it is impossible to attribute how much any terror created by Smith's shouts factored into the robustness of the Texians' charge. It must be remembered that the time elapsed from Smith's ride to the first contact with the enemy was probably only moments; memories no doubt were lost in the excitement of battle.

---

22 *The Writings of Sam Houston, 1813-1863*, edited by Amelia Williams and Eugene C. Barker (Austin, Texas: University of Texas Press, 1940), Volume V, "A Refutation of Calumnies Produced and Circulated Against His Character as Commander-in-Chief of the Army of Texas, February 28, 1859;" IV, 320.

But whatever the mix of fear and hate, self-preservation and revenge the fighters internalized, the charge was indeed robust, and the Texians quickly overwhelmed Santa Anna's poorly deployed defensive line. And whatever Smith's true influence, the battle cry that men would prefer to enshrine was "Remember the Alamo!" It spoke better to history, not only to justify the tit-for-tat massacre of Mexican soldiers at San Jacinto but also to cast Texian motives in a better light: for it is always better to be remembered as fighting from the love of one's comrades rather than a fear of losing one's own life.

Legacy

The notable legacy of "Deaf" Smith's speech had less to do with the speech itself—it was barely remembered after the battle—but rather how it manifested Houston's attitudes towards his men. The regulars' prejudice against militia was a standing feature of nineteenth-century American warfare and forms part of the history of every conflict from the War of 1812 into the twentieth century. But managing volunteers did not necessarily call for tricks and ruses. Approaches such as stern-but-fair discipline and persuasive strategies for building confidence in leadership would prove (and still prove) far more effective. And arguably, at least some of the bitterness that arose between the veterans after the Battle of San Jacinto (which surpassed in intensity the usual postwar disputes among veterans) was attributable to the mistrust sown by Houston during the campaign.

Leadership Principle

Houston certainly integrated "dissimulation" into his command style. But Frederick the Great's advice was intended to use dissimulation in order to *conceal* negatives; Houston frequently lied to conceal negatives; but through "Deaf" Smith, Houston's dissimulation was used to *create* a negative—fear. This dissimulation was itself the product of negative feelings between himself and his men. For example, years later Houston evidenced some of these negative feelings when he gave his reasons why he kept his counsel during the march:

> [I] was the only one of the officers who had ever witnessed an array of hostile armies, or been in a general battle; and it is not probable that [I] would surrender [my] opinions to those on whom no responsibility rested. If victorious, the victory

would take the name of the place, if it were a defeat it would bear the name of the General, but not that of his subalterns![23]

"All warfare is based on deception," the (perhaps mythic) sixth century BCE Chinese manual writer Sun Tzu famously declared, a refrain thoroughly seconded by commanders ever since. But Sun Tzu's deceptions were usually intended for the enemy: feints, disinformation, sabotage and so forth. Less often acknowledged is the trickery some battle speechmakers use to deceive their own men.[24]

Persuasive Strategy

Included in Houston's considerable array of talents was his ability to play the role of trickster. Clearly, his lack of candor and the ruses he felt necessary to employ grew from a mutual lack of confidence between him and his soldier-audience. Given his perspective, Houston had many reasons to doubt his army's discipline: their lack of military experience, their insubordination and mutinous behavior, and probably the absence of any army-wide cohesion. But what Houston may have misread was that their desire for revenge would provide an effective substitute, at least in a short fight, for the attributes that a former regular might believe were necessary for an army to be capable of victory.

Trickery is always a risky persuasive strategy, and never more so than when applied to one's own soldiers. There is evidence that Houston's tricks sometimes failed; for example, after the Kerr episode, there were those who saw it as a ruse, and therefore believed the information about the Goliad Massacre; likewise, most who heard Houston's foolish attempts to deny the plain sight of Santa Anna's reinforcements at San Jacinto disregarded his words. Such clumsy attempts at disinformation could only further diminish Houston's standing within his command. It was fortunate that the battle of San Jacinto essentially concluded the campaign, because by then Houston had exhausted his already-limited credits with this army. It is unlikely that he would have been able to continue as commander had another hard march, battle, or campaign been required.

---

23 Moore, *Eighteen Minutes*, 221.

24 Sun Tzu, *The Art of War*, translated by Lionel Giles (El Paso, Texas: El Paso Norte Press, 2005), 117.

Significantly, there were many veterans of San Jacinto who believed that Houston's severe ankle wound was really the result of being "fragged" by some dissatisfied soldier. This was false, but that so many could believe that Houston would market his wound as heroic while knowing that it had been inflicted by one of his own soldiers indicates how badly Houston was distrusted by some of his men. Of course, Houston repaid the compliment—by sending "Deaf" Smith on an errand better suited for an army of imbeciles than the serious, if undisciplined, army that he actually commanded.[25]

25 Moore, *Eighteen Minutes*, 417.

Chapter Six

Failing Performer: Alexander the Great at the Hyphasis River

I. Historical Background

By the summer of 326 BCE Alexander the Great and his army had reached the west bank of the Hyphasis River[1] in western India. Since leaving Macedonia eight years earlier, his army had marched some 11,250 miles. Behind him was an uneasy empire stretching from northern Libya to western India: a patchwork of regions assembled by shrewd political maneuver, intimidation or outright conquest. Now (July?—depending upon the historian), Alexander assembled either his entire "multinational" army (Curtius' version) or just his Macedonian "regimental commanders" (Arrian's version) for the purpose of exhorting his men to cross the Hyphasis River and continue his relentless campaign of conquest.[2]

---

1 Known today as the Beas River.

2 Robin Lane Fox, *Alexander the Great* (New York: Penguin Books, 2004), 369; Peter Green, *Alexander of Macedon, 356-323 B.C: A Historical Biography* (Los Angeles: University of California Press, 1991), for chronology see "Table of Dates," xxxiii-xxxvii; Arrian, *Anabasis*, V.25.2. *Quintus Curtius,* with an English translation by John C. Rolfe (Cambridge, Massachusetts: Harvard University Press, 1946), Vol. II, *History of Alexander*, IX.ii.12. The two most detailed versions of this event (sometimes called the Mutiny at the Hyphasis) consulted frequently by historians are those of Arrian and Curtius. Arrian's version has become the most popular of the ancient Alexander biographers,

Ancient writers disagree about what Alexander said and to whom he spoke, but all concur about *why* he spoke. Arrian wrote that

> the Macedonians' spirits were flagging by now, as they saw the king taking on one hard and dangerous task after another; meetings took place in the camp among men who complained of their own plight—they were the most moderate kind—or who flatly denied that they would follow Alexander's leadership any farther. When Alexander heard of this before indiscipline and despair grew worse among the troops, he summoned [them] and addressed them....

Curtius used Alexander's own thoughts to depict a reluctant army "grown old in battle and in camp" that had become "sated and loaded with booty" and "would prefer to enjoy what they had obtained rather than wear themselves out by acquiring more." But even in Curtius' account what was emphasized was not the weight of the men's booty but the depth of their destitution:

> Look upon these bodies drained of blood, pierced by so many wounds, rotted by so many scars. Already our weapons are dull, already our armour is giving out. Clad in Persian dress, because that of our own country cannot be brought to us, we have degenerated into foreign ways. How many of us have a cuirass? Who has a horse? Bid it be asked how many are attended by their own slaves, what each man has left from his booty. Victors over all, we lack everything.

Most modern Alexander biographers have melded these reports into a composite picture of an army's summer of discontent. Alexander was about to ask his exhausted Macedonians to cross just one river too many.[3]

Arrian and Curtius, Alexander's two most important ancient biographers, preserved, rewrote or perhaps invented Alexander's speech as something like a dialogue between the king and a member of his soldier-audience, Coenus, son-in-law of Parmenio, the great general who had served Alexander's father and later Alexander himself. Coenus was in his own right one of Alexander's

---

perhaps because the scholarly consensus agrees with P.A. Brunt's assessment that "Arrian unquestionably provides us with the best evidence we have for Alexander. . . ." "Introduction," *Anabasis*, xvi.

3   Arrian, *Anabasis*, V.25.2; Curtius, *History*, IX.ii.10. See also *Diodorus of Sicily*, with an English translation by C. Bradford Welles (Cambridge, Massachusetts: Harvard University Press, 1963), Book XVII.94. Treatment of Hyphasis in Green, *Alexander of Macedon*, 402-411; Fox, *Alexander the Great*, 368-370.

most trusted officers; he had successfully led cavalry columns and infantry phalanxes on critical missions and to important victories. Disease would soon take Coenus; perhaps already ill, he may have felt he had little to lose. But in the eyes of the army, especially its Macedonian component, Coenus wore a cloak of authority that no battle could bestow: he belonged to the old guard, linked to Parmenio and to Alexander's father, King Philip.[4]

When Coenus spoke ("plucked up his courage," according to Arrian) he may have first removed his helmet ("customary as a gesture of respect," according to Curtius). But whatever Coenus' personal affectations, he proceeded to tactfully, respectfully, but candidly state his comrades' case against crossing the river—and thus, against continuing the conquests. Alexander's exhortation and Coenus' response illustrated first, a famous historical example of disconnection between a battle speechmaker and his soldier-audience; but this dialogue also illustrated a famous remedy—albeit one not satisfactory to one of the parties.[5]

II. The Speech

I observe that you, Macedonians and allies, are not following me into dangers any longer with your old spirit. I have summoned you together, either to persuade you to go forward, or to be persuaded by you to turn back. If indeed you have any fault to find with the exertions you have hitherto endured, and with me as your leader, there is no object in my speaking further. [Here Alexander offers a lengthy list of his conquests]. . . . [Thus] *why do you hesitate to add the Hyphasis and the peoples beyond the Hyphasis to this Macedonian empire of ours? Do you fear lest other barbarians may yet withstand your approach?*

For my part I set no limit to exertions for a man of noble spirit, save that the exertions of themselves should lead to deeds of prowess. Yet if any one longs to hear what will be the limit to the actual fighting, he should understand that there remains no great stretch of land before us up to the river Ganges and the eastern sea. This sea, I assure you, will prove to be joined to the Hyrcanian sea.... And it will be for me to show Macedonians and allies alike that the Indian gulf [Arabian Sea] *forms*

---

4   Coenus, son of Polemacrates, was Macedonian and also Parmenio's son-in-law. Parmenio had been a key lieutenant of both Alexander and Philip until the former had him executed for treason, likely on a trumped-up charge. For examples of Coenus' importance, see Green, *Alexander of Macedon*, 342, 200, 325-326, 359-360, 366; for Coenus' reply to Alexander, see Arrian, *Anabasis*, V.27.

5   Arrian, *Anabasis*, V.27.1; Curtius, *History*, IX.iii.3.

but one stretch of water with the Persian gulf, and the Hyrcanian Sea with the Indian gulf. From the Persian gulf our fleet shall sail round to Libya, as far as the Pillars of Heracles [Straits of Gibraltar]*; from the Pillars all the interior of Libya then becomes ours in its entirety, and the boundaries of our Empire here are becoming those which God set for the whole continent.*

But if we flinch now, there will be many warlike races left behind on the far side of the Hyphasis up to the Eastern Sea, and many too stretching from these to the Hyrcanian Sea to the north, and the Scythian tribes not far from these, so there is reason to fear that if we turn back, even our present possessions, which are not held securely, may be stirred to revolt by those who are not yet under our control. Then our numerous exertions will indeed be profitless, or we shall have to start again with fresh exertions and dangers. But you must persevere, Macedonians and allies. Exertions and dangers are the price of deeds of prowess, and it is sweet for men to live bravely, and die leaving behind them immortal renown.

. . . Let it be your task to add what yet remains of Asia to the possessions already won, a small conquest in comparison. For that matter what great or noble success could we ourselves have achieved, had we sat still in Macedonia and thought it enough to guard our own home without effort, merely keeping in check the Thracians on our borders or Illyrians or Triballians, or those Greeks too, who were not well disposed to us?

Now if the exertions and dangers had been yours, and I had personally escaped them, while issuing commands as your leader, it would not have been unreasonable for you to have grown weary in spirit before me, when you alone were taking part in the exertions, while the prizes they procured went to others; but as it is, we undergo the exertions in common, our share in the dangers is equal, and the prizes are open to all alike. For the land is yours; it is you who are its satraps; the greater part of the treasure is now coming to you, and, when we overrun all Asia, then by Heaven I will not merely satisfy you, but will surpass the utmost hope of good things each man has, I will send all who desire to go home back to their own country or will myself lead them back, while those who remain behind I shall make the envy of those who depart.

After Alexander had spoken these words or in this sense, for a long time, there was silence; no one either dared to oppose the King on the spur of the moment, or was yet willing to agree. In this interval Alexander often invited any who wished to speak, if he really held opposite views to those he had expressed himself; yet even so silence reigned long, and only after some time Coenus, Polemacrates' son, plucked up his courage and spoke thus . . . .

—Excerpts from Alexander the Great's Speech before the Hyphasis (Beas) River, urging his men to cross and continue his conquests.[6]

III. Parsing the Speech

Both Alexander and Coenus implicitly conceded to each other the authority that successful battle speechmakers always require. However, the issue here was not authority, but rather each speaker's *credibility* with the soldier-audience. True persuasion requires credibility—which, speakers sometimes forget, is not always congruent with authority. Alexander must persuade his army to follow him across the river; and it must be genuinely voluntary, for—despite his status as an absolute monarch with divine antecedents—he knew that a reluctant army would have been useless in meeting hardship; and—if the past was prologue—there would be hardships. Likewise, Coenus could only persuade, for his audience was but one man, and that was Alexander, and his burden was to persuade him not to cross the Hyphasis. Instead, Coenus argued that the army must return home.

To best parse one of the most unsuccessful battle speeches in military history, it is imperative to analyze Alexander's arguments (which were presented in one speech) alongside Coenus' response, which followed Alexander's speech. Whatever is lost in segmenting Alexander's remarks is gained in understanding the reasons why he made his specific appeals, the reasons why his soldier-audience rejected them, as well as two larger issues: the dire results of a speaker's disconnection from his soldier-audience, and at least one way—the Macedonian way—of remedying that disconnect.

Alexander first dispensed with absolutism in favor of comradely persuasion. "I have summoned together, either to persuade you to go forward or to be persuaded by you to turn back," he declared. He thus initiated a discourse among (for a temporary period) rough equals; while his deeds later proved that Alexander was being somewhat disingenuous, his words remained democratic throughout his speech. "If indeed you have any fault to find with the exertions you have hitherto endured, and with me as your leader," he continued, "there is no object in my speaking further." He attempted to reestablish credibility (presumably lost in his army's current state of exhaustion) by reciting "our"—as in us-as-comrades—resumé of conquests. He hoped to remind his men what he

6 Arrian, *Anabasis*, V, 25-26.

and they—as comrades—had accomplished. "If, however, it is through these exertions that Ionia is now in our hands...."—and here Alexander provided an astonishing list of peoples subjugated, lands conquered and waters and deserts crossed. But this resume was no more than an intangible prop for his real questions: "[W]hy do you hesitate to add the Hyphasis and the peoples beyond the Hyphasis to this Macedonian empire of ours?" (One can imagine his emphasis on the word "hesitate.") And next, "Do you fear lest other barbarians may yet withstand your approach?" (Again, one can imagine his emphasizing the word "fear.") In his opening argument, Alexander's persuasive strategy was twofold: to reclaim credibility by emphasizing the success of "our" resume, as well as to challenge his men's fortitude.[7]

When Coenus later responded to Alexander, it was very likely with the soldiers' consent, and perhaps at their behest. According to Arrian, the soldiers had already met privately to mull their discontents. But even if the soldiers had not asked Coenus to speak, they apparently acquiesced by respectful silence when he did speak. Thus, Coenus appeared to speak with a credibility that Alexander had lost. But the Mutiny on the Hyphasis was not about democratic rights, and Coenus remained a loyal subject, knowing that he was being granted only a temporary dispensation to speak freely. "Seeing that you, Sire, do not yourself desire to lead the Macedonians as a dictator, but say that you will lead them by persuasion, and that, if they persuade you, you will not coerce them, I shall speak not on behalf of those here present [only the officers, by Arrian's account, but the entire army in Curtius' version]," Coenus began, "but on behalf of the majority in the army." Coenus knew that he had to be very careful. Of late, Alexander had become increasingly unstable; today's dispensation would not necessarily prevent tomorrow's retribution. Thus, in an unexcerpted passage, Coenus reassured Alexander that his men are "zealous to serve you in every way."[8]

Yet Coenus also coupled his flattery with an ambiguous threat, and thereby gave weight to his response that Alexander would do well to heed: he must be heard, for his message will be "most conducive to safety for the future." In context, a discerning ear might understand what "safety" meant: retreat from the Hyphasis now, or risk a full-blown mutiny later. Having made the point, Coenus hurried to match his résumé with that of his king. "My age entitles me not to

---

7   Arrian, *Anabasis*, V.25.3-6.

8   Arrian, *Anabasis*, V.27.2.

conceal the views I think best and so does the superior rank you have granted me," Coenus reminded Alexander, "and the unhesitating daring I have shown up to now in exertions and dangers." Of course, when Coenus mentioned his age, he was subtly reminding Alexander that he was a genuine member of the Old Guard, one of the few bridges that remained between the great Philip of Macedon and his greater son, Alexander.[9]

Returning to Alexander's speech, the king's next appeal—explorer's bragging rights—was curious given that it ran counter to what often motivated ancient warriors: plunder, land, and slaves (incentives that Alexander mentioned later). "And it will be for me to show Macedonians and allies alike that the Indian gulf [the Arabian Sea] forms but one stretch of water with the Persian gulf, and the Hyrcanian Sea [Caspian Sea] with the Indian gulf," he boasted. For Alexander knew it would have been an easy matter for his fleet to sail round to Libya and as far as modern-day Gibraltar. King Alexander, descendant of gods, assured his men that "the boundaries of the Empire here are becoming [that is, will become] those which God set for the whole continent [that is, the entire earth]."

The close reader of Arrian is suddenly struck by a painful disconnect. The exhausted, ill-equipped, battle-scarred, homesick and weather-beaten army was essentially being told to press on, effectively in the service of Aristotle, Alexander's former tutor from whom the king had learned most of his theories about geography. How could Alexander, one of the most successful military leaders in history, have assumed that such an appeal would work for men in such poor physical and spiritual condition? Alexander's contemporaries believed that he was driven by *pothos*, a Greek word meaning a "longing for things not yet within reach, for the unknown, far distant [and] unattained." So consumed was Alexander by his own *pothos* that he assumed his men were likewise obsessed. As he stood on the west bank of the Hyphasis, Alexander looked east and imagined that he would be the first to reach the great Eastern Ocean whose waves lapped all the shores on earth.[10]

9 Arrian, *Anabasis*, V.25.2 and Curtius, *History*, IX, ii10 (Macedonians' unwillingness to follow). All references to Coenus' reply will be found in Arrian, *Anabasis*, V.27.1-9.

10 As quoted in Green, *Alexander of Macedon*, 128. Green states that *pothos* "is so used of no other person in the ancient world." Green's discussion of Alexander, Aristotle and geography can be found on 403-404. See also Fox, *Alexander the Great*, 363-364.

But when Coenus responded, he made clear that the army was not so consumed. Coenus was necessarily obeisant and respectful, and praised his sovereign for the "successes achieved by you" that were "numerous and splendid;" nevertheless, he inverted Alexander's argument. Because of the very successes that Alexander had achieved, "I think it more in our interest to set some limit to exertions and dangers." Coenus then appealed to Alexander to look, not to distant vistas across the Hyphasis, but to his rear; and indeed, no further ahead than under his very nose: "[The] Macedonians' forces have lost part of their number in battle," Coenus began,

> others have been invalided from wounds, and left behind in different parts of Asia; but most have died of sickness, and of all that host [that left Macedonia eight years before] few survive, and even they no longer enjoy their bodily strength while their spirit is far more wearied out. One and all, they long to see their parents, if they are still alive, their wives and children and indeed their own homeland.

In sum, old Coenus argued, enough was enough. It was long past time to go home.[11]

Returning again to Alexander's speech, the king next appealed to the practical needs of his empire. Its rear and borders were insecure. "But if we flinch now, there will be many warlike races left behind on the far side of the Hyphasis"—by which Alexander meant the unconquered lands to his front—and "many too stretching from these to the Hyrcanian Sea to the north and the Scythian tribes not far from these"—by which he meant his empire's northern border. Alexander now argued *his* only conclusion: "So there is reason to fear that if we turn back, even our present possessions, which are not held securely, may be stirred to revolt by those who are not yet under our control." He thus presented his men with the conqueror's paradox: that security only came from the constant insecurity of perpetual war. To "flinch now" might risk wasting the past eight long battle-and siege-filled years ("our numerous exertions") that would prove "profitless" and thereby compel the army "to start again with fresh exertions and dangers."

And it was here that Alexander mixed his call to secure the empire with a celebration of the "deeds of prowess" that were his special obsession: glory and the undying name. "[It] is sweet for men to live bravely, and die leaving behind

11 Arrian, *Anabasis*, V.27.5-6.

them immortal renown," he declared, and filled these passages with allusions to the exploits of Heracles, son of Zeus and Alcmene, and one of the claimed progenitors of Alexander's family. Alexander obviously assumed that, like him, his men also (or still) followed the cult of glory. In what may have been a foolish remark (as it could only intensify the soldier-audience's homesickness) Alexander suggested that their lives before the conquests were barely worth living. "[W]hat great or noble success could we ourselves have achieved, had we sat still in Macedonia and thought it enough to guard our own home without effort, merely keeping in check the Thracians on our borders or Illyrians or Triballians, or those Greeks too, who were not well disposed towards us?" The answer may have seemed self-evident to Alexander; perhaps it was once just as clear to his men; but it was no longer so.[12]

Alexander saved his most potent appeals for last. His first argument was his well-known personal leadership in battle. He often led from the front, sometimes dangerously far in advance of any support: reckless, yes, feckless even; but such leadership had bound him to his men, and was perhaps the greatest such bond in military literature. These bonds were the common property of every soldier, and Alexander sought to exploit his share in them:

> Now if the exertions and dangers had been yours, and I had personally escaped them, while issuing commands as your leader, it would not have been unreasonable for you to have grown weary in spirit before me when you alone were taking part in the exertions, while the prizes they procured went to others; but as it is, we undergo the exertions in common, our share in the dangers is equal and the prizes are open to all alike.[13]

Here was the bond of shared hardship. But carefully woven into the talk of shared dangers and common exertions was that of the prospect of riches for crossing the Hyphasis. While no amount of money would have persuaded Alexander not to cross the river, he certainly believed that some amount of money would persuade his men to do so. "For the land is yours," Alexander said

---

12 Olympus, Alexander's mother, claimed descent from Achilles; her father reportedly believed that his ancestors included Helen of Troy. Fox, *Alexander the Great*, 44. Phillip II, Alexander's father, included Zeus among his ancestors, *ibid.*, 30.

13 The connection between personal leadership and ancient Greek battle is made by Victor Davis Hanson, *The Western Way of War: Infantry Battle in Classical Greece* (Berkeley: University of California Press, 1989), see Chapter 9, "A Soldier's General," 116.

in introducing this final appeal, "[and] it is you who are its satraps." He then elaborated for those perhaps too weary to grasp the point:

> [T]he greater part of the treasure is now coming to you, and, when we overrun all Asia, then by Heaven I will not merely satisfy you, but will surpass the utmost hope of good things each man has, I will send all who desire to go home back to their own country or will myself lead them back, while those who remain behind I shall make the envy of those who depart.

One can imagine Alexander's men believing at least half of this. The king always had been generous with rewards and bribes. But what his men probably did not believe was that crossing the Hyphasis would ever get them home. They had marched with Alexander for eight years; each step eastbound was towards unknown lands containing thoroughly believed terrors; each step was another yard further from Macedonia. And it was now up to Coenus to convince Alexander to do that which, for him, came quite unnaturally: reverse course. [14]

Coenus had already used the army's suffering and homesickness as a reason to return home. But he knew that for Alexander the pain of others would never be sufficient to induce him to withdraw. Although Coenus reminded Alexander that he too shared some of that pain ("But if it please you, return in person to your own country, look on your own mother, [and] settle the affairs of the Greeks..."), he also knew that some other reason was needed—a reason that Alexander could not ignore. Indeed, it may have been the only reason that Alexander would take seriously:

> It is not for you now to be a leader of unwilling troops. For you will no longer find men meeting dangers as they once did, when it is not by their own choice that they engage in conflicts.

And here Coenus' earlier vague reference to "safety for the future" must have struck Alexander with the full force of an imperative: retreat from this river or face, if not outright mutiny, then a sullen, unmotivated army that would neither advance your boundless ambitions nor protect your swollen empire. As a practical general whose tactics usually reflected reality, Alexander just might understand this.

---

14 For instances of Alexander's apparent generosity towards his men, see Arrian, *Anabasis,* VII.5. (debt forgiveness); VII.12.1 (severance pay).

Yet Alexander was a human being swollen with a titan's ambition, and lately had become unstable; Coenus did not end with a threat, however skillfully buried. He realized that Alexander needed hope to nurture his dreams, and Coenus concluded by giving him a future that brimmed with new worlds to conquer. All Alexander had to do was return home and recruit "other Macedonians, other Greeks, young men in place of old, men who are fresh and not worn out, who will have no immediate fear of war, having no experience of it, and whose warlike ardour will be excited by their hopes of the future." But to fully realize this second expedition, Alexander's army must first return home with all its booty, so that prospective recruits "will follow you with all the more enthusiasm, because they see the partners in your earlier exertions and dangers returned to their own lands and raised from poverty to riches and from obscurity to high renown."

Immediate Result

Alexander lost the argument. By Arrian's account, Coenus' speech was greeted by an "uproar among the audience and that many even shed tears, still further proof that their minds did not go with further dangers and what they wanted was to return home, and of the joy with which they would hail a retreat." Alexander turned back, and the Hyphasis River forever marked his empire's eastern frontier.[15]

Legacy

Alexander's battle speeches have bequeathed two perpetually relevant legacies through the millennia. The first was that the study of Alexander's speeches would be essential to the study of the man; given the few primary sources, Alexander's words—or versions of his words—are still parsed by scholars as part of, in biographer Robin Lane Fox's phrase, "the search for Alexander."[16]

The second legacy of Alexander's battle speeches were their contributions, not just to a "Western way of war"—aggressive, command-driven, often total and annihilating—but also to the way in which commanders *spoke* to soldiers

15 Arrian, *Anabasis*, V.28.1.

16 Fox, *Alexander the Great*, 27-28.

about war: Alexander's speeches helped establish battle speech paradigms (such as the Comrade Convention) that continue to influence battle rhetoric. And the speeches of Alexander and Coenus affirmed another of Alexander's legacies—his unique relationship with his army. Alexander's personal leadership and his relationship with his soldiers created paradigms for each that have been the envy for Western armies ever since. Alexander was deeply influenced by the comradely ideals of Homer, especially Achilles (from whom Alexander also claimed descent) and his Myrmidons. And these ideals allowed for occasions of rough equality even between common soldiers and a king who was descended from gods, an absolute monarch and a man whose final years were increasingly fraught with probable alcoholism and erratic, often unpredictable violent outbursts. Changing technology and modes of troop deployment eventually rendered Alexander's tactics obsolete; but the comradely ideal would live on.[17]

Leadership Principle

The leadership Alexander displayed at the Hyphasis River was paradoxical. First there was Alexander's failure to empathize with his soldier-audience so as to be able to "read" their condition of exhaustion and homesickness. Alexander and his Macedonians had been slowly parting ways for some time. In the eyes of many soldiers, he had already transformed himself from Macedonian royal to Oriental despot, adopting hated Persian modes of dress and ritual; and worse, he accepted Persians as soldiers and generals as well as appointing them to senior positions in civil administration. Historians have argued about the real depth and necessity of these changes, but for Macedonians who had been recruited by Alexander in part to take revenge for Xerxes' Persian invasion of Greece the century before, even token assimilation was too much. Coupled with

---

17 Hanson describes the "most prominent element of Western military prowess" as "the preference for decisive infantry battle through shock and direct assault;" I have added the other elements to the "Western way of war." Hanson, *The Western Way of War*, xxiii. For structural and thematic continuities in battle speeches, see Miller, *In Words and Deeds*, 7-8, 20-26; Fox, *Alexander the Great*, 59-62. Green is often critical of his subject, and describes his personal deterioration generally, 324-325; his growing mistrust of his own troops, 347; the murder of Cleitus, 361-366, and other references to his advancing degeneration, 443, 453, 459.

Alexander's deteriorating personal behavior, by the time the Hyphasis was reached, the army had become alienated from Alexander.[18]

Yet, there was also a remedial mechanism in Alexander's style of leadership: space was granted for discussion and dissent, albeit at carefully specified times and places. Arrian observed that after presenting his views, "Alexander often invited [to speak] any who wished to speak, if he really held opposite views to those he had expressed himself." Coenus still had to "pluck...up his courage" to speak; nevertheless, by long custom, Alexander had established a time for doing so. And even after Hyphasis he honored it—there is no real evidence that Coenus or those applauding him met the fates often assigned to those who incurred royal displeasure in ancient Macedonia: death. Indeed, two centuries after these events, the Greek historian Polybius described this established practice of open discussion known as the *isegoria*, "the equal right to speak freely that Macedonians have always enjoyed in addressing the king."[19]

Persuasive Strategy

Alexander's persuasive strategy failed because he made false assumptions about his soldier-audience. Eight long years of hard campaigning had changed both Alexander and his men, but in different ways. His soldiers had dwindled in numbers and were exhausted in energy, while Alexander's ambitions had blossomed from the conquest of Persia to that of the world. Alexander's failed persuasive strategy at the Hyphasis revealed the consequences of a battle speechmaker's failure to know his audience. It was a case of the performer having misread his audience: Alexander assumed that the old script that had called for glory, riches and new discoveries, was still current; however, his men

---

18 Alexander's transgressive behavior by which he alienated his Macedonian cohort is usually referred to as his "Orientalization," and is a trope for biographers. See Green, *Alexander of Macedon*, 333-336 and Fox, who takes a softer line on Alexander's orientalizing tendencies, 272, Philotas conspiracy, 288, and the *proskynesis* controversy, 320-328. Fox describes Alexander's transgressiveness as his "two veils to life," that is, his attempts to assimilate Greek/Macedonian and Persian cultures, 319.

19 This despite Alexander's drunken murder of Clitus, himself intoxicated (and a man who had saved his life in battle) for insolent remarks at a dinner – Arrian, *Anabasis*, IV.8; however, it reveals why Coenus now approached Alexander with considerable trepidation – Polybius quoted indirectly in "Introduction," Arrian, *Anabasis*, xliv-xlv.

were in a far less aggressive mood, their withered ambitions matched by a longing for home.

Interestingly, while Alexander campaigned in Asia, his former tutor Aristotle was classifying rhetoric into *The Art of Rhetoric*, a work whose strategic advice assumes throughout that the speaker knows his audience. "[T]he speaker should endeavor to guess how his hearers formed their preconceived opinions," Aristotle wrote, "and what they are, and then express himself in regard to them." As one scholar has observed of Aristotle's advice in *Rhetoric*, carefully structured appeals, their timing and placement in the argument are by themselves insufficient to persuade. The speaker "must be able to decide without hesitation to which class of mind his hearers belong and then seize the opportune moment for the employment of each kind of discourse." Thus, battle speakers must always know what Alexander had forgotten: the true mind of their soldier-audience.[20]

---

20 Aristotle, *Rhetoric*, II.xxi.15-16; "Analysis," xxvi; *Rhetoric* is believed to have been written sometime between 335 and 322 BCE; xxv.

Section Three

The Surge: Three Battle Speeches
by General David H. Petraeus

This section considers three battle speeches by General David H. Petraeus made during the Surge, a phase of the Iraq War that began shortly before he assumed command in January 2007 and continued after his September 2008 departure. The Surge was an American incarnation of long-standing principles of counterinsurgency warfare (COIN). It culminated years of study and combat experience by hundreds of soldiers and imaginative civilians. Petraeus and others had overseen the distillation of this experience into formal doctrine. Their work attained its final written form in Field Manual No. 3-24, better known as *Counterinsurgency*.[1]

For students of battle speeches, perhaps the most salient feature of both *Counterinsurgency* and the Surge was the great extent to which they were

---

1 Field Manual No. 3-24, *Counterinsurgency* (Washington: Headquarters, Department of the Army, 2006). Future historians with better access to primary sources will ultimately argue the question of credit for the Surge. At present, there is no reason to argue with journalist and historian Thomas Ricks' observation that General Petraeus was the Surge's "adoptive parent" and "the public face of the troop buildup," while it was his lieutenant, General Ray Odierno, "who was the surge's true father." – Thomas E. Ricks, "The Dissenter Who Changed the War," *The Washington Post,* February 9, 2009.

products of persuasion. For the Surge to work, at least five important audiences needed convincing. First were ordinary Iraqi civilians who had to be persuaded that after four years of lawlessness, the Coalition was now genuinely committed to enforcing security. Next, those insurgents deemed "reconcilable" (unaffiliated with Al Qaeda and other hard-liners) had to be persuaded—or paid off to believe that they had a future in the new Iraq. The Shi'a-dominated Iraqi government of Prime Minister Nouri al-Maliki had to be persuaded to support the Surge. The American people and their elected representatives had to be persuaded that this change in tactics and strategy, requiring an additional 30,000 troops, would produce results. Finally, Coalition troops (and especially their commanders) had to be persuaded—reeducated—to shift from the failing tactical mode of "kill, capture and withdraw" to COIN's insistence on the "Clear, Control and Retain" doctrine: now troops were to live in key neighborhoods, ingratiate themselves with civilians, help restore municipal services, and persuade "reconcilable" insurgents into neutrality or alliance, while simultaneously seeking to kill or capture irreconcilable insurgents.[2]

Chapter Seven considers Petraeus' Assumption of Command speech, in which he managed expectations about the new policies, tactics and strategy, and offered a new, plural definition of both the enemy—now enemies—and what constituted success. Chapter Eight discusses the Midst-of-Battle Speech, in which Petraeus confronted an issue that had almost derailed Coalition efforts: the abuse of Iraqi detainees by Coalition members. Chapter Nine considers Petraeus' Farewell Speech, in which he sought to establish a "final" narrative of the Surge and his leadership. Readers should note that various reputational memes, factoids, and policy statements preceding these speeches were available in advance online, thus informing (and preparing) Petraeus' soldier-audience about the points he sought to make.

---

2   The best current account of how *Counterinsurgency* was written can be found in Ricks, *The Gamble: General David Petraeus and the American Mlitary Adventure in Iraq, 2006-2008* (New York: The Penguin Press, 2009), 24-31.

Chapter Seven

General David H. Petraeus Assumes Command

I. Historical Background

The history that led to Petraeus' Assumption of Command speech (AOC) was also a history of the type of speech that he gave. As readers will recall from Patton's The Speech, the key to the AOC speech is Managing Expectations. But with Petraeus, the expectations to be managed had less to do with him than with the new policy he came to implement: the Surge. And so Petraeus' speech answered the policy questions that AOC speeches have always tried to answer: Will things change, and if so, how? The best way to understand how Petraeus presented change is to examine his memes and the speech for signals of *continuity* or *discontinuity* with past Coalition policies.

Continuity is easy. The speaker professes loyalty to his predecessor's policies and pledges that he will continue them. But discontinuity is more difficult, especially under the circumstances in which it often occurs: re-moralizing a defeated army, fixing serious problems, or radically changing tactics or strategies. A good example of both continuity and discontinuity is found in the case of young Publius Cornelius Scipio (the future Africanus) who, during the Second Punic War, had assumed command of a defeated Roman Army in Spain. In his AOC speech, he expressed gratitude to his soldiers for their past loyalty (continuity), but then quickly shifted to discontinuities:

> [By] God's blessing, the object before us is not to stay in Spain ourselves but to push the Carthaginians out of it—not to stand in front of the Ebro and keep the

enemy from crossing it, but to cross it ourselves and take the initiative on the other side. . . . Come my veterans, take with you across the Ebro a new army and a new commander; taken into territory you have so often trod, fighting like the brave men you are.

The discontinuity Scipio signaled here was that the army would now take the initiative and win battles. And 2,217 years later, David Petraeus wanted to do the same. However, unlike the simpler situation confronting Scipio, Petraeus' task required persuading two armies, two governments and two peoples that the ends were attainable. Deeds, not words, are what ultimately matter in a successful counterinsurgency; but the effort must begin with words.[1]

When considering modern, media-enveloped commanders such as Petraeus, it is more useful to explore the speaker's existing memes—that is, the "history" of his reputation. By January 2007 what might Petraeus' soldier-audience have been led to expect from their new commander?

Petraeus' pre-Surge memes came early in the war. In a repetition of *Life Magazine's* July 1941 cover of George S. Patton, Jr., in July 2004 *Newsweek* featured Petraeus on its cover. He was photographed standing on sandy brown desert and wearing full ballistic gear; he dominated the foreground while a Blackhawk helicopter waited behind. "CAN THIS MAN SAVE IRAQ?" was the cover question. (The "saving" it then hoped Petraeus would accomplish was the training of an Iraqi army.) Linda Robinson, in her recent book, *Tell Me How This Ends: General David Petraeus and the Search for a Way Out of Iraq*, writes that Petraeus struck "a Patton-like pose." Her comparison was perhaps more apt than she knew.[2]

But beyond glossy covers, Petraeus' memes circulated everywhere, from his official online biography to information disseminated in books and media. Fifty-four years old when he assumed command of the Multi-National Force-Iraq, he was a 1974 West Point graduate, and—in a factoid that echoed repeatedly in the years before his AOC speech—had received both his masters and doctoral degrees in international relations from Princeton University. (This unconventional background helped establish personal memes of discontinuity.)

---

1 Livy, *The War with Hannibal*, Books XXI-XXX of *The History of Rome from its Foundation*, trans. Aubrey De Selincourt, ed. and intro. Betty Radice (London: Penguin Books, 1972), 409-411.

2 Linda Robinson, *Tell Me How This Ends: General David Petraeus and the Search for a Way Out of Iraq,* (New York: Public Affairs, 2008), 76.

A survey of twenty-four major media pre-Surge articles about Petraeus found eleven making reference to his Princeton credentials. These included such epithets as "warrior-soldier," "soldier-scholar," and "premier intellectual." In 2004 a reader would have learned from one article that Petraeus was "one of the Army's most highly regarded generals;" from another, that he was "a celebrated American field commander;" and finally, that he was "one of the Army's most highly regarded officers." In 2005, he was described as "one of the most fascinating people in the United States Army." "He's one of the Army's most pre-eminent thinkers," *Washington Post* reporter Rick Atkinson was quoted in a 2006 article. (Also an historian and author, Atkinson first introduced Petraeus to a national audience in his book *In the Company of Soldiers: A Chronicle of Combat*.)[3]

3   The articles were: Michael Gordon, "The Struggle of Iraq: Reconstruction; 101st Airborne Scores Success in Northern Iraq, *New York Times,* September 4, 2003; Lucian K. Truscott IV, "A Million Miles From the Green Zone to the Front Lines," *New York Times,* December 7, 2003; Eric Schmitt and Thom Shanker, "The Struggle for Iraq: The Military; Training Skills of U.S. General Sought After Poor Performance by Some Iraqi Forces," *New York Times,* April 15, 2004; Dexter Filkins, "The Reach of War: The Military; Biggest Task for U.S. General Is Training Iraqis to Fight Iraqis," *New York Times,* June 27, 2004; Rod Norland, "Iraq's Repairman," *Newsweek Magazine,* July 5, 2005; Eric Schmitt, "Effort to Train New Iraqi Army Is Facing Delays," *New York Times,* September 20, 2004; Richard A. Oppel, Jr., et al, "U.S. Officials Say Iraq's Forces Founder Under Rebel Assaults," *New York Times,* November 30, 2004; Julian E. Barnes, "An Open Mind For A New Army," *U.S. News and World Report,* October 21, 2005; David H. Petraeus, "Learning Counter-insurgency: Observations from Soldiering in Iraq," *Military Review,* January- February 2006; Michael R. Gordon, "Military Hones a New Strategy on Insurgency," *New York Times,* October 5, 2006; Wesley Morgan, "Our Man in Iraq: Petraeus GS '87 grooms new officer corps in bid to rebuild army," *The Daily Princetonian,* October 26, 2006; Gordon and Shanker, "Bush to Name a New General to Oversee Iraq," *New York Times,* January 5, 2007; Tom Bowman, "Leader of the Fabled 101st to Command in Iraq," *NPR,* January 5, 2007; Michael Gordon, "A New Commander, in Step With the White House on Iraq," *New York Times,* January 6, 2007; Rick Atkinson, "Iraq Will Be Petraeus's Knot to Untie," *Washington Post,* January 7, 2007; Wesley Morgan, "Petraeus takes reins in Iraq," *The Daily Princetonian,* January 10, 2007; Michael R. Gordon, "Bid to Secure Baghdad Relies on Troops and Iraqi Leaders," *New York Times,* January 11, 2007; David E. Sanger, "Bush Adds Troops in Bid to Secure Iraq," *New York Times,* January 11, 2007; Wesley Morgan, "Petraeus faces tough road in Iraq," *The Daily Princetonian,* January 12, 2007; Rachel Dry, "Petraeus on Vietnam's Legacy," *Washington Post,* January 14, 2007; Michael R. Gordon, "In Baghdad, Pressing to Meet, With Iraqi Help, Pentagon's Own Standard for Force Levels," *New York Times,* January 19, 2007; "General Petraeus's Opening Statement," *New York Times,* January 23, 2007; Michael R. Gordon, "General Says New Strategy in Iraq Can Work Over Time," *New York Times,* January 24, 2007; Carl Hulse, et al, "The Struggle for Iraq; In Senate, Allies Of Bush Attempt To Halt Iraq Vote," *New York Times,* January 31, 2007; Rick Atkinson, *In the Company of Soldiers: A Chronicle of Combat* (New York: Henry Holt and Company, 2005).

But Petraeus' memes included more than just widely-touted claims of smarts. Thirteen of 24 articles stressed that Petraeus was innovative. Four articles stressed his expertise in COIN warfare; seven articles highlighted his successes while commanding the 101st Airborne earlier in the war. Yet Petraeus' memes were mixed. The military as well as the public and politicians were divided over the Surge's wisdom. Unsurprisingly, then, 13 articles—the same number as praised Petraeus' innovativeness—had also quoted critics. These included some who were unhappy with "Petraeus' penchant for self-promotion and PR" and others who had purely professional doubts about whether the "Surge" would work.[4]

The most important contributor to Petraeus' discontinuity message was his January 2007 U.S. Senate confirmation hearings. Expected to be controversial (the Democrats had just taken control of the Senate), the hearings were given wide publicity. Like *Counterinsurgency*, transcripts of the hearings (and videos) were available online. First, Petraeus told Senators (and simultaneously prepped his would-be soldier-audience) that Coalition strategy would be changing— from enemies-centric to population-centric. As he explained:

> The primacy of population in the capital will mean a greater focus on that task, particularly on the most threatened neighborhoods. This will, of course, require that our unit commanders and their Iraqi counterparts develop a detailed appreciation of the areas in which they will operate recognizing that they may face a combination of Sunni insurgents, international terrorists, sectarian militias and violent criminals.

But it was how the tactics would change that really mattered to his soldiers:

> Together with Iraq forces, a persistent presence in these neighborhoods will be essential.

No soldier had to be told what this meant. But if any soldier somehow failed to grasp Petraeus' meaning when he declared that "undoubtedly there will be

---

4 "Iraq's Repairman," *Newsweek Magazine*, July 5, 2005, summarizes personal criticisms also found in other articles reviewed. A thoroughly professional (and creatively presented) treatment of the Surge (done in the context of Bush's January 10, 2007, speech announcing the new policy) can be found in Anthony H. Cordesman's "Bush's Iraq Plan, Between the Lines," *New York Times*, January 11, 2007. Link: www.nytimes.com/2007/ 01/11/opinion/ 2007111_bushspeech_graphic.html. Accessed 24 June 2009.

tough days," there was no misunderstanding President George W. Bush when, two weeks earlier in a televised address to the nation, he had warned that "[e]ven if our new strategy works exactly as planned, deadly acts of violence will continue—and we must expect more Iraqi and American casualties."[5]

Thus was Petraeus' soldier-audience prepared for the AOC speech by a combination of his efforts and those of the media.

II. The Speech

February 10, 2007

To the Soldiers, Sailors, Airmen, Marines, and Civilians of Multi-National Force-Iraq:

We serve in Iraq at a critical time. The war here will soon enter its fifth year. A decisive moment approaches. Shoulder-to-shoulder with our Iraqi comrades, we will conduct a pivotal campaign to improve security for the Iraqi people. The stakes could not be higher.

Our task is crucial. Security is essential for Iraq to build its future. Only with security can the Iraqi government come to grips with the tough issues it confronts and develop the capacity to serve its citizens. The hopes of the Iraqi people and coalition countries are with us.

The enemies of Iraq will shrink at no act, however barbaric. They will do all that they can to shake the confidence of the people and to convince the world that this effort is doomed. We must not underestimate them.

Together with our Iraqi partners, we must defeat those who oppose the new Iraq. We cannot allow mass murderers to hold the initiative. We must strike them relentlessly. We and our Iraqi partners must set the terms of the struggle, not our enemies. And together we must prevail.

The way ahead will not be easy. There will be difficult times in the months to come. But hard is not hopeless, and we must remain steadfast in our effort to help improve security for the Iraqi people. I am confident that each of you will fight with skill and courage, and that you will remain loyal to your comrades-in-arms and to the values our nations hold so dear.

---

5   General Petraeus's Opening Statement," *New York Times*, January 23, 2007; George W. Bush, "President's Address to the Nation, 10 January 2007," www.georgewbush-whitehouse.archives.gov/news/releases/2007/01/print/20070110-7.html. Accessed June 23, 2009.

In the end, Iraqis will decide the outcome of this struggle. Our task is to help them gain the time they need to save their country. To do that, many of us will live and fight alongside them. Together, we will face down the terrorists, insurgents, and criminals who slaughter the innocent. Success will require discipline, fortitude, and initiative—qualities that you have in abundance.

I appreciate your sacrifices and those of your families. Now, more than ever, your commitment to service and your skill can make the difference between victory and defeat in a very tough mission.

It is an honor to soldier again with the members of the Multi-National Force-Iraq. I know that where you serve in this undertaking you will give your all. In turn, I pledge my commitment to your mission and every effort to achieve success as we help the Iraqis chart a course to a brighter future.

Godspeed to each of you and to our Iraqi comrades in this crucial endeavor.

David H. Petraeus
General, United States Army
Commanding

—Assumption of Command Speech by General David Petraeus.[6]

III. Parsing the Speech

Petraeus' AOC speech spent few words on exposition. In part I believe that this was because he assumed, probably correctly, that his soldier-audience was already familiar with the online manual *Counterinsurgency*, together with his recent public statements; this assumption of familiarity was important for the soldier-audience to fully understand the AOC speech. Petraeus' speech also offered no bombast and reserved its exhortations for the end. His prose throughout the speech was spare, and this starkness heightened its dramatic effect. Earlier, Petraeus had testified to the Senate that Iraq's situation was "dire;" for him, direness and wordiness were mutually exclusive: hyperbole or prolixity would only sap the drama. "We serve in Iraq at a critical time," Petraeus began, "The war here will soon enter its fifth year."

6   "Petraeus Addresses Coalition, Iraqi Partners," February 10, 2007, MNF-Iraq.com. The official document is available from www.mnf-iraq.com/index.php?option=com_content &task=view&id=9830&itemid=128. Accessed on June 22, 2009.

A decisive moment approaches. Shoulder-to-shoulder with our Iraqi comrades, we will conduct a pivotal campaign to improve security for the Iraqi people. The stakes could not be higher.

This opening paragraph set the tone for the rest of the speech. Three mutually-supporting themes dominated. First was the sense of urgency, and Petraeus' words certainly raised the temperature: A *decisive* moment approaches—a *pivotal* campaign—The *stakes* could not be higher—Our task is *crucial*—*Now* more than *ever*—the *difference* between *victory* and *defeat* in a *very tough mission*. [Italics added] Placed throughout the speech, these words seized attention by shaking complacency and stirring anxiety. They implicitly drew a contrast between *how the war had been fought and how the war will now be fought*. In short, these words established *discontinuity*.[7]

In his first sentence Petraeus subtly introduced a topic that he used to support urgency and discontinuity—the history of the war. The arguments for a new policy cannot be made persuasively without some reference to why the old policy had failed. And some history was necessary to make this argument. But a candid discussion of the war's history meant criticizing civilian superiors (the Bush administration), previous commanders (colleagues), and the Iraq government (whose goodwill remained necessary for success.) Furthermore, making these criticisms might have transgressed civil-military boundaries and produced controversy in circumstances that required unity.

So how did Petraeus introduce history to make his case for discontinuity? Succinctly; his second sentence did the trick: "The war here will soon enter its fifth year." No further explanations were necessary. The Iraq War had lasted longer than America's involvement in World Wars I and II and the Korean War. Perhaps these historical analogies were questionable; all wars are different. But in the three months before this speech, prominent opinion media had extensively retailed "the Iraq war has been longer than" meme. Thus, merely by noting the length of the war enabled Petraeus to incorporate these still-circulating memes into his speech without having to provide details. No politician needed singling out; also unnecessary were divisive arguments about where the fault lay for failure; likewise, no predecessors needed disparaging, nor were Iraqi allies

---

7 See Miller, *Words and Deeds*, 174, in which the Urgency Convention is defined. This is an appeal normally used in Defenders' Speeches to enlist support against invaders. In the Urgency Convention a "speech's voice or tone must convey . . . urgency and anxiety in support of a fearful earnestness about prospects."

denounced (at least on Iraqi soil) for corruption or sectarianism. The "longer than" meme included all of these; Petraeus simply summoned the meme and allowed his soldier-audience to interpret for themselves why the war had lasted so long yet had produced so little progress.[8]

Petraeus' third theme was diminished expectations. He had articulated this during his Senate confirmation hearing. "I would like to offer a word on expectations," he explained—and then listed various factors intended to deflate expectations: the Surge would take time to learn about urban neighborhoods, to plan, to understand Iraqi partners, and to implement improved security. (Like Grant, Petraeus was acutely aware that events had not been kind to politicians and generals who had previously underestimated the war's complications.) Here Petraeus used his Senate testimony to prep the public and his soldier-audience to diminish their expectations.

Petraeus' AOC speech resembled his confirmation statement to the Senate—surely an effort at message consistency. To Senators, Petraeus filled "the Surge" meme with new content: the phrase, "the way ahead" was used five times in his confirmation speech and once in his AOC speech; indeed, "the way ahead" became a Speechlet—one that probably piggybacked on the title of the recently-released and widely-publicized Iraq Study Group report entitled *A Way Forward—A New Approach*. Balancing fear and optimism but avoiding traditional military "can-do," Petraeus explained to both Senators and soldiers that "hard is not hopeless." Both speeches also used the anxiety stirrer, "The stakes could not be higher." The word security (or "secured") mentioned as a goal appeared six times in his confirmation statement and four times in the AOC speech.[9]

---

8 For an example of the "larger than" meme,, see Ari Berman, "Iraq>World War II," The Notion, blog in the *Nation Magazine*, August 18, 2006, www.thenation.com/blogs/notion/113486; Frank Rich, "Has He Started Talking to the Walls," *New York Times*, December 3, 2006; "Interview with Maj. General Robert Scales," *All Things Considered, NPR*, November 27, 2006, www.npr.org/ templates/story/story.php?storyid=6545249. Accessed June 24, 2009; "The war in Iraq and World War II have now both lasted three years, eight months and seven days. Veterans nostalgically recall the Good War as a time of unity on the homefront, shared sacrifice and national purpose. And Iraq? Not so much," contributions by Tom Brokaw, Bob Dole, Michael Gambone, Frank Lautenberg, Rick Atkinson, D'ann Campbell, John Dingell, Howard Zinn, Edward W. Wood, Jr., Henry Hyde, David Hoogland Noon, Ted Stevens, *Washington Post*, November 26, 2006.

9 Iraq Study Group Report: *A Way Forward—A New Approach* (New York: Vintage Press, 2006).

As part of diminishing expectations, Petraeus was also careful in how he described the enemy—singular became plural. The administration's focus on Al Qaeda now had disappeared. Instead he explained to the Senate that the adversaries were "insurgents, international terrorists, sectarian militias, regional [meddlers], violent criminals, government dysfunction and corruption." But Petraeus' AOC speech was not a mere précis of his much-longer Senate confirmation statement. In his AOC speech the list of adversaries changed: now they were "terrorists, insurgents, and criminals" as well as "mass murderers." These changes were not happenstance. When speaking to a mixed Iraqi-Coalition audience, Petraeus probably thought it unwise to demonize Iraq "government dysfunction and corruption"—no matter how true.

What was the new policy that the AOC speech's urgency, history, and diminished expectations sought to promote? Petraeus declared its objectives in his first paragraph: "Shoulder-to-shoulder with our Iraqi comrades, we will conduct a pivotal campaign to improve security for the Iraqi people." First, it is important to note what he did *not* say about the Surge, especially given the rhetorical themes that had characterized many speeches during the four preceding years. Absent from the AOC speech were exhortations about democracy, liberation or free elections; instead, the Surge was simply about security. In the course of diminishing expectations, Petraeus made clear that achieving this will be hard; but compared with trying to make Baghdad into a Topeka-on-the-Tigris, reasonable levels of security were possible: "hard is not hopeless."

Why did Petraeus make security a priority instead of, for example, continuing his predecessor General George Casey's policy of speedily "standing up" Iraqi forces so that Coalition forces could "stand down?" (This slogan became its own meme during the pre-Surge period.) The AOC speech offered several answers. "Security is essential for Iraq to build its future," Petraeus declared. "Only with security can the *Iraqi government* come to grips with the tough issues it confronts and develop the capacity to serve its citizens." [Italics added] In short, Petraeus provided his soldier-audience with the new policy's rationale: the Surge would produce security; security produces time; hopefully, Iraqis will use the time to "come to grips" with their own "tough issues" in order to "serve [their] citizens." Several paragraphs later Petraeus was more explicit: "Our task is to help [Iraqis] gain the time they need to save their country." As discussed below, "serv[ing] [Iraq's] citizens" was a critical Surge objective. By serving Iraqi citizens, Petraeus did not mean organizing a Baghdad PTA; instead, given Iraq's appalling living conditions, he meant only to help provide Iraqis with clean water, public sanitation, electricity, and safe marketplaces. Few in the soldier-audience who had experience in-country needed specifics about what the Iraq government's "tough issues" also included: sectarian violence, corruption and incompetence. [10]

This is the reason why Petraeus' AOC speech mentioned security five times. Here Petraeus linked *Counterinsurgency's* more detailed program with the short AOC speech. It was likely that he assumed *Counterinsurgency* was already familiar to many in the soldier-audience. For the manual too declared that success requires security: "The cornerstone of any COIN effort is establishing security for the civilian populace." How so? "Without a secure environment," the manual asserted, "no permanent reforms can be implemented and disorder spreads." Thus security served an important purpose, indeed, *Counterinsurgency's* bedrock doctrine: "[t]o establish legitimacy" of the host nation—in this case, the Iraqi government. Indeed, the manual declared that "Legitimacy Is the Main Objective." And this objective was also the AOC speech's main burden. [11]

Petraeus' shift from "enemy" to "enemies" has already been noted. But the AOC speech offers more: it also declared what these enemies wanted. There were no descriptions of menacing world caliphates or enemy hatred of American freedoms. Instead, Petraeus offered his soldiers this: "[The enemy] will do all that they can to shake the confidence of the people and to convince the world that this effort is doomed." The enemy's objectives then were limited, and involved psychology and local politics; the battleground was the Iraqi people's perceptions. Thus implied was symmetry between Coalition and its enemies' objectives: because these enemies had more modest objectives (compared with those stated earlier by some Coalition leaders), so Coalition objectives, while daunting, were more modest as well. The new objectives also had the added virtue of being more realistic. This is why Petraeus added to his previous enemies list, including "terrorists," the categories of "insurgents" and "criminals": criminals and insurgents usually seek local, not worldwide

---

10 Ricks' *Gamble* includes two Appendices that contrast Casey's transition strategy with Odierno's first application of COIN principles. See Appendices B and C, 337-338.

11 *Counterinsurgency*, 1-2; 1-113; 1-31; 1-116; 4-16; 5-116; in this section, soldier-readers would have learned that there were "six possible indicators of legitimacy," the first of which was "The ability to provide security for the populace." Petraeus' speech gave a clear reason for providing security: so the Iraq government could "develop the capacity to serve its citizens."

advantages; while both may use terror, terror is only a tactic and not a political vision. In this sense, Petraeus diminished the enemy from being a threat to world order to being a more limited threat to Iraqi order.

Thus, while the Coalition will help, it was local (Iraqi) forces that had to defeat enemies who sought only local advantages. Petraeus emphasized joint efforts throughout his AOC speech. "Shoulder-to-shoulder with our Iraqi comrades," "Together with our Iraqi partners," "We and our Iraqi partners must set the terms of the struggle, "together we must prevail," and finally, this: "In the end, Iraqis will decide the outcome of this struggle." All that would happen between now and "in the end" is that Coalition forces would adopt strategies to forestall a defeat of the Iraq government. This would give that government an opportunity to establish its legitimacy with its own citizens.

And one of those strategies still required Coalition soldiers to engage in dangerous combat operations. "We cannot allow mass murderers to hold the initiative," Petraeus declared. "We must strike them relentlessly." He expressed his confidence that Coalition forces will "fight with skill and courage;" implementing the new strategy now required that "many of us will live and fight alongside [Iraqis.]" The enemies can be "face[d] down." Here Petraeus included some confidence-building flattery that is a stock feature of many battle speeches: "Success will require discipline, fortitude, and initiative—qualities that you have in abundance." (This was Petraeus' major exhortation in his concisely-written speech.)

The word "face" was also one of the most arresting—and revealing—metaphors in the speech. Introducing the image of "face" suddenly transformed the doctrine of "Hold" into what it really was: a narrowing of distance not only between Coalition forces and civilians but also with the enemy. That enemy had heretofore been largely without a face, present only at the end of a remotely triggered IED, or as anonymous suicide bombers blown to even-more-anonymous bits. Here Petraeus implied a fact and made a promise: Like other Iraqis, the faceless enemy also lived in neighborhoods; now Petraeus promised that his army will live among them, to perhaps meet them and do to them that which these enemies had been unwilling to do to his soldiers: "face [them] down." As a metaphor, "face" worked not only to emphasize the new policy's closeness to civilians and enemies (for one must be close to recognize a face), but also appeals to an ancient warrior tradition that it is more honorable to "face" one's foe. And if the foes will not show their faces, then they must be forced to do so.

Having elected candor, Petraeus now indicated hardships and increased casualties: "The way ahead will not be easy. There will be difficult times in the months ahead." Any soldier unable to decode this phraseology would be confronted by less-subtle evidence very soon.[12]

In his AOC speech Petraeus departed in other ways from battle speeches given earlier in the war, which sometimes rested their cases on the enemies' evilness or its dislike of American values. While Petraeus did note the enemy's barbarism, he also summarized a basic premise of *Counterinsurgency*: "[These enemies] will do all that they can," he told his AOC soldier-audience, "to shake the confidence of the people and to convince the world that this effort is doomed." Here Petraeus made clear that the enemies' objective was not to publicly decapitate prisoners for decapitation's sake, or to detonate car bombs in marketplaces simply to sate blood lust; quite the contrary: given its objectives, the enemy was adopting rational means to demonstrate that the Iraq government and its allies were too weak to provide basic security. To survive, citizens would have to submit to the insurgency. When Petraeus' speech admonished his soldier-audience that "[w]e must not underestimate them," it was a reminder that underestimation was not only a matter of complacency about ambushes or IEDs, or that Iraqis murdering each other was somehow "normal;" it also meant constantly working to understand that the enemies were not crazed but smart, adaptive, and constantly adjusting means to ends.[13]

But in order to understand the enemies, counterinsurgents must first understand the elements of the new battlefield: civilians, their security needs, grievances, and neighborhoods. In his speech Petraeus told his soldier-audience that in order to "help [Iraqis] gain the time they need to save their country," the Coalition would have to adopt new tactics. Then Petraeus introduced the key discontinuity that distinguished the new tactics from the old: "To do that [to buy Iraqis time], many of us will live and fight alongside them."

Here such words as "face" (discussed above) became metaphors to establish the discontinuity. For several years before this, Coalition forces had been concentrated in some fifty Forward Operating Bases (FOBs) around Iraq,

---

12 See Truth Speech, in Miller, *Words and Deeds*, 170.

13 *Counterinsurgency*, 1-8, 1-9. An example of an Iraq War battle speech that emphasizes enemy evil (enemy being still understood in the singular) can be found in Gary Livingston, *Fallujah, With Honor: First Battalion, Eighth Marine's Role in Operation Phantom Fury* (Topsail Beach, North Carolina: Caisson Press, 2006), 256.

constantly patrolling but generally returning to base afterwards. The effect was not only to establish a garrison mentality among the soldiers, but also to cut them off from the war's real battleground—the civilian population. Thus, while Coalition forces won virtually every skirmish against insurgents—that is, they successfully "cleared" them from the battle space—by later returning to their FOBs they then failed to "hold" the areas just cleared; thus COIN's third strategic pillar—"to build"—became impossible. Put simply, when the Coalition regularly abandoned the field (villages, towns, cities), the insurgents immediately returned; they then proceeded to implement their own criminal, ethnic, or religious agendas, "killing" government and Coalition public services as well as cooperative Iraqis. But as Petraeus' soldier-audience knew from reading *Counterinsurgency*, to "[c]oncentrate military forces in large bases for protection" had been labeled an "Unsuccessful practice." Petraeus did not have to mention his predecessors' failed garrison strategy—it was something his soldier-audience already knew from time in-country or had read for themselves in the COIN manual.[14]

Immediate Result

It is difficult to gauge how a widely-dispersed soldier-audience reacts to a written battle speech. Unlike Patton's The Speech, there was no physically concentrated audience to cheer, be stony-faced, or hiss. Also making assessment difficult was that soldiers' diaries, letters, memoirs, emails, oral histories and many official assessments are not public or may not yet exist. What has been reported is that during 2007 army morale improved dramatically. As one soldier declared, "I understand the surge and I believe in the surge. I went into Fallajuh three times and I could never understand why we kept having to retake things." Improving morale occurred despite the sharp rise in Coalition casualties during the Surge's early months.[15]

---

14 *Counterinsurgency*, "Clear-Hold-Build" will be found in 5.51 and after; Table 1-1: "Successful and unsuccessful counterinsurgency operational practices."

15 Ricks, *The Gamble*, 240-241.

Legacy

Historian J. E. Lendon observes in *Soldiers and Ghosts* that for ancient Greeks, "Homer was the mirror into which Greek warriors looked to see themselves." Except for a brief, quickly forgotten period of counterinsurgency around the Vietnam War, American soldiers also had a mirror in which "to see themselves"—and the reflected image was that of a conventional warrior whose origins lay in World War II and had been reinforced by over half a century of the Cold War. In this image wars were won by mechanized assaults and by defeating conventional counterparts. Perhaps Petraeus' greatest legacy as embodied in his AOC speech, was to create a new reflection, in which the warrior used narrative, population-centric tactics, political strategies and deeds that were consistent with the message to support these as the means of victory. The strongest battalions still mattered; but now, what those battalions did would change. As redesigned by Petraeus, Ray Odierno, and their colleagues, COIN became America's best response to its first "postmodern" war.[16]

Leadership Principle

According to *Counterinsurgency*, "Victory is achieved when the populace consents to the government's legitimacy and stops actively and passively supporting the insurgency." In short, the struggle's end would not be marked by white flags or surrender ceremonies; indeed, few human endeavors can compete with the end of insurgencies in fulfilling T.S. Eliot's final lines from "The Hollow Men": "*This is the way the world ends/Not with a bang but a whimper.*" And it was David Petraeus' leadership skills that re-moralized an army to accept a definition of victory that was built of monthly casualty metrics, number of neighborhood shops reopened, liters of clean water pumped, and the like.[17]

Petraeus taught his forces to relearn the war they were actually fighting versus the war they had once been told they were fighting; that what was once thought right (for example, obsessive concern with force protection, large-scale sweeps and detentions) actually may have been wrong—troops segregated from

---

16 J. E. Lendon, *Soldiers & Ghosts: A History of Battle in Classical Antiquity* (New Haven: Yale University Press, 2005), 124; the phrase "postmodern" was first applied to the war in Robinson, *Tell Me How This Ends*, 344.

17 *Counterinsurgency*, 1-14; "The Hollow Men," T.S. Eliot, *Poems: 1909-1925* (London: The Faber Library No. 4, 2007), 123-128.

the population cannot understand the real battlefield, and large-scale sweeps and detentions probably created more enemies than they detected. Victories now consisted of: regular garbage collection; keeping bridges open so ordinary Iraqis could commute to work; and reworking the electric power grid.

Thus Petraeus' great leadership insight was that waging this kind of war required an "information operation" that simultaneously persuaded not just Iraqis but Coalition forces as well, reshaping their expectations about what could be accomplished, and re-schooling both about what the war really was and how it had to be fought. Petraeus had simply applied an ancient insight in a new way: armies had always wanted victories; for his army, Petraeus redefined what victory meant, and then helped his soldiers to attain it.[18]

Persuasive Strategy

Petraeus' AOC speech intentionally heightened drama ("critical . . . pivotal . . . The stakes could not be higher") in an effort to insert some new thinking at the climax: the importance of security for civilians; that the struggle really belonged to the Iraqis; and that "many of us will live and fight alongside them." None of this would have been comprehensible in a 437- word speech unless the soldier-audience had had access to other persuasive texts, beginning with the Internet-available *Counterinsurgency* as well as his confirmation testimony. Logically, all battle speeches (or any speech) requires advance context for full comprehension. This speech is an example of a new breed: required context that is specific enough to be retrieved with a web address.

Petraeus also relied on Speechlets whose meanings he attempted to fill out with the longer arguments of *Counterinsurgency*. In particular, two of his Speechlets entered the media-military information slipstream: "The way ahead will not be easy" and "Hard is not hopeless." If these seem less thrilling than "Don't fire 'til you see the whites of their eyes," they were nonetheless entirely appropriate for the war Petraeus had to fight: a slog of persuasion and dueling perceptions, not a battle of firing lines.

---

18 Information Operations (IO) is central to *Counterinsurgency*. For example, see 1-97, 5-19 to 5-34, especially the summary found in Table 5-1.

Chapter Eight

Midst-of-Battle Speech: Petraeus as Therapist-in-Chief

I. Historical Background:

In his February 2007, AOC speech Petraeus had expressed the hope that his soldier-audience would "remain loyal to [their] comrades-in-arms and to the values our nations hold so dear." Loyalty to comrades refers to the ancient band of soldier-brotherhood; whereas loyalty to "the values our nations hold so dear" is a far more complex appeal. The values Petraeus referred to here were embodied in the Coalition's commitment to obey its own regulations, members' national laws, and international conventions that required the humane treatment of civilians, especially detainees, and their property. That there might be a *contradiction* between loyalty to comrades and to a nation's values was something that Petraeus probably preferred not to address in his AOC speech.

Three years previously the revelations of detainee abuse at Abu Ghraib prison, accompanied by lurid photographs of hooded, tortured, and sexually-abused prisoners, had for many transformed the Iraq War from one of liberation into a brutal occupation. Overnight the Coalition's presence seemed to conform to the earlier examples of detainee abuse by France in Algeria, Great Britain in Northern Ireland and the U.S. in Vietnam. And history strongly suggested that such abuse could be disastrous for aspiring counterinsurgency campaigns. *Counterinsurgency*, written in the wake of the Abu Ghraib revelations, insisted that "Security Under the Rule of Law is Essential." The manual defined abuse and explained why it was so corrosive to the war effort. As was true with so much of COIN doctrine, the issue here was also legitimacy:

> Illegitimate actions are those involving the use of power without authority—whether committed by government officials, security forces or counterinsurgents. Such actions include unjustified or excessive use of force, unlawful detentions, torture, and punishment without trial. Efforts to build a legitimate government through illegitimate actions are self-defeating, even against insurgents who conceal themselves amid non-combatants and flout the law.[1]

Given this, and mindful of the damage that even one highly-publicized war crime might inflict on the entire COIN effort, Petraeus must have been dismayed to read the report by the Mental Health Advisory Team (MHAT) IV. Mental health professionals had surveyed U.S. soldiers and Marines who were or had been based in Iraq during the summer of 2006. The MHAT IV findings included such factoids as that only 40% of Marines and 55% of soldiers answered "yes" to the following question: "I would report a unit member for injuring or killing an innocent noncombatant." This reluctance to "rat-out" comrades was the newspaper headline. But the complete report delved far deeper into soldiers' psychological states, and Petraeus understood that he faced a genuine mental health crisis, one rooted in war generally but also aggravated by factors specific to the Iraq War. Like much else about COIN strategy, easing this crisis lay in education and changing attitudes—in short, persuasion.[2]

---

1   Thomas E. Ricks, *Fiasco: The American Military Adventure in Iraq* (New York: The Penguin Press, 2006), 197-200, 290-293, especially 378-380; the Abu Ghraib story was first reported by CBS's *60 Minutes II* on April 28, 2004 – that sufficed for images; the first print narrative appeared almost simultaneously in Seymour M. Hersh's "Torture at Abu Ghraib: American soldiers brutalized Iraqis. How far does the responsibility go?" *The New Yorker,* May 10, 2004, www.newyorker.com/archive/2004/05/10/040510fa_Fact. Accessed August 20, 2009.

2   Reuters, "Not All Troops Would Report Abuse, Study Says," *New York Times,* May 5, 2007; Benedict Carey, "Stress on Troops Adds to U.S. Hurdles in Iraq," *New York Times,* May 6, 2007; Final Report, Mental Health Advisory Team (MHAT) IV, Operation Iraqi Freedom 05-07, Office of the Surgeon Genera, Multinational Force-Iraq and Office of The Surgeon General, United States Army Medical Command, November 17, 2006 (hereafter "MHAT IV"), 36-37, Figure 17.3. See "Charts to accompany the testimony of GEN David H. Petraeus," *Report to Congress on the Situation in Iraq, by Commander David H. Petraeus, 10-11 September 2007.* http://foreignaffairs.house.gov/110/pet091007.pdf. Accessed August 20, 2009; MHAT IV.

But the time available to make these changes was almost non-existent. (The report was publically released on May 4, 2007; when Petraeus first learned of it is unclear.) By deploying forces throughout Baghdad neighborhoods, the Surge had already *increased* contact between soldiers and civilians. As predicted by both President Bush and Petraeus, the Surge had become very hazardous. Although by May Iraqi civilian deaths, ethno-sectarian violence, and high-profile attacks had declined significantly from their December peaks, attacks against soldiers had risen substantially, and were about to peak the following month. Based on the survey's findings, which connected a variety of combat and deployment stressors to a failure to observe battlefield ethics, a crisis loomed. To Petraeus, it was time for a battle speech.

This chapter explores how Petraeus' speech rendered a 44-page technical report containing 27 graphs and 7 tables comprehensible to his soldier-audience. It is also about how Petraeus took his soldier-audience in a direction that for many was new and, in some ways almost as frightening as the war they faced "outside the wire."[3]

II. The Speech

Soldiers, Sailors, Airmen, Marines, and Coast Guardsmen serving in Multi-National Force Iraq:

Our values and the laws governing warfare teach us to respect human dignity, maintain our integrity, and do what is right. Adherence to our values distinguishes us from our enemy. This fight depends on securing the population, which must understand that we—not our enemies—occupy the moral high ground. This strategy has shown results in recent months. Al Qaeda's indiscriminate attacks, for example, have finally started to turn a substantial proportion of the Iraqi population against it.

In view of this, I was concerned by the results of a recently released survey conducted last fall in Iraq that revealed an apparent unwillingness on the part of some US personnel to report illegal actions taken by fellow members of their units. The study also indicated that a small percentage of those surveyed may have

---

3 See "Charts to accompany the testimony of GEN David H. Petraeus," *Report to Congress on the Situation in Iraq, by Commander David H. Petraeus, 10-11 September 2007.* http://foreignaffairs.house.gov/110/pet091007.pdf. Accessed August 20, 2009; MHAT IV.

mistreated noncombatants. This survey should spur reflection on our conduct in combat.

I fully appreciate the emotions that one experiences in Iraq. I also know firsthand the bonds between members of the "brotherhood of the close fight." Seeing a fellow trooper killed by a barbaric enemy can spark frustration, anger, and desire for immediate revenge. As hard as it might be, however, we must not let these emotions lead us—or our comrades in arms—to commit hasty, illegal actions. In the event that we witness or hear of such actions, we must not let our bonds prevent us from speaking up.

*   *   *

We are, indeed, warriors. We train to kill our enemies. We are engaged in combat, we must pursue the enemy relentlessly, and we must be violent at times. What sets us apart from our enemies in this fight, however, is how we behave. In everything we do, we must observe the standards and values that dictate that we treat noncombatants and detainees with dignity and respect. While we are warriors, we are also human beings. Stress caused by lengthy deployments and combat is not a sign of weakness; it is a sign that we are human. If you feel such stress, do not hesitate to talk to your chain of command, your chaplain, or a medical expert.

We should use the survey results to renew our commitment to the values and standards that make us who we are and spur re-examination of these issues. Leaders, in particular, need to discuss these issues with their troopers—and, as always, they need to set the right example and strive to ensure proper conduct. We should never underestimate the importance of good leadership and the difference it can make.

Thanks for what you continue to do. It is an honor to serve with each of you.

—Excerpts from Midst-of-Battle Speech by General David H. Petraeus, May 10, 2007[4]

4 www.centcom.mil/images/petraeusarchives/08-%2010%20may%202007%20%20gen %20petraeus%20letter%20about%20values.pdf. Accessed April 10, 2008. Readers should note that when describing his adversaries in this speech, Petraeus mostly uses the word "enemy" rather than the "enemies" of his AOC speech. There was no attempt to redefine the adversaries here so the change is probably without significance. However, my narrative in this chapter conforms to Petreaus' usage in this speech.

III. Parsing the Speech

Petraeus established the pattern for his speech in the first paragraph, where he alternated appeals to idealism and expedience. Indeed, he argued that the two are linked: his soldiers will do well by doing right, because in COIN operations, right was necessary for well. And here he described what is right. "Our values and laws governing warfare teach us to respect human dignity, maintain our integrity and do what is right," he declared. "Adherence to our values distinguishes us from our enemy." Of course, his definition of right suited his purpose of preventing war crimes against civilians. Soldiers were asked to do that which made them morally superior to their enemies: to respect human dignity; to maintain (presumably by moral means) individual and unit integrity; and—the all-purpose enthymematic injunction—to always "do what is right."

From this appeal Petraeus next concluded that right produces well. Doing the right thing "has shown results in recent months," and he cited as his example that "Al Qaeda's indiscriminate attacks . . . have finally started to turn a substantial proportion of the Iraqi population against it." And indeed, what was termed "High Profile Attacks"—the mass casualties caused by explosives concealed in cars or on persons—had by May steeply declined after spiking in March. Petraeus' example of Al Qaeda was chosen cleverly. His intent was not chauvinistic (as in, we are inherently superior to them), but rather to "prove" that the way in which the soldier-audience is superior—in its "respect for human dignity"—had also resulted in measurable improvements in the battle space: fewer High Profile Attacks. Implicit here was an appeal to soldiers' self-interest: by following Petraeus' approach to reducing High Profile Attacks *in general*, soldiers might eventually reduce such attacks aimed *at them*.[5]

It was in this linkage between the right and the expedient that Petraeus first discussed MHAT IV's findings. In the second paragraph, the lecture that opened this speech now gave way to something else: a situation report. The SitRep Convention is characteristic of speeches such as this one; Midst-of-Battle speeches pivot on sitreps, for they usually contain the reason for the speech as well as suggestions about going forward. (The sitrep usually incorporates a new fact or development that requires the battle speechmaker to inform or exhort his soldier-audience.) This particular sitrep was about the MHAT IV report. (As

---

5 "High Profile Attacks," Charts, *Report to Congress on the Situation in Iraq, by Commander David H. Petraeus, 10-11 September 2007.*

jargon rarely serves understanding, Petraeus omitted the official acronym MHAT IV and simply refers to it as "the survey" or "the study.")[6]

Embedded in the study's lengthy text, charts and tables were many important, interrelated findings. For example, the report found that soldiers/Marines who "handled dead bodies or human remains" were more likely than others to have "Insulted/cursed noncombatants in their presence," "Damaged/destroyed Iraqi property when it was not necessary," or worse, "Physically hit/kicked noncombatants when it was not necessary." But Petraeus initially focused on two other important findings (which also headlined the news stories); and he began to translate the survey's conclusions from dry statistical findings into remarkably intimate discourse. Here is the sitrep portion of this Midst-of-Battle speech:

> I was concerned by the results of a recently released survey conducted last fall in Iraq that revealed an apparent unwillingness on the part of some US personnel to report illegal actions taken by fellow members of their units. The study also indicated that a small percentage of those surveyed may have mistreated combatants.[7]

Petraeus' concerns were prompted by these particular MHAT IV findings: while a small number of Soldiers/Marines (4% and 7% respectively) reported using violence against noncombatants or detainees, a much larger number (45% and 60% respectively) declared that they would not report comrades who engaged in such abuse. This situation could be disastrous for the COIN operation: small numbers of emotionally unbalanced or criminally inclined abusers, enabled by the silence of near half their comrades, might go far in alienating Iraqis from the COIN effort as well as giving adversaries immense propaganda advantages—and all before the chain of command would know about the abuses. This was arguably the heart of Abu Ghraib: a handful of miscreants misbehaved, while a far larger number of observers knew about the abuses but remained silent.[8]

---

6   Miller, *Words and Deeds*, 232.

7   MHAT IV, see Figure 22b, page 40 and Figure 23b, page 41 (human remains).

8   MHAT IV, Figure 17, page 36 (reported using violence); Figure 18, page 37; figures are derived from the inverse percentages of those who said that they *would* report violations – these were 40% and 55%, respectively.

Here the speech reached a climax. Having introduced these disclosures, Petraeus reacted to them. And how he reacted shaped the rest of his speech. His choices here were many. He could have applied the same reactions that had followed Abu Ghraib and speak of the military's shame and tarnished reputation; he could have dilated on the moral weakness and criminality of abusers and those who might shield them by their silence; and, as the sequel to Abu Ghraib had demonstrated, he might also have threatened harsh discipline and remind his soldier-audience that lengthy prison terms awaited those who abused noncombatants.

But instead, with one word, Petraeus takes an unexpected and revealing turn. "This survey should spur *reflection* on our conduct in combat," he concluded in the pivotal passage. [Italic added] By some lights, calling for reflection about "our conduct in combat" might seem to trivialize an enormous wrongdoing: the abuse of noncombatants is a serious crime, its perpetrators are criminals, and most cases of abuse probably do not exist in the grays of difficult judgment calls; thus, on one level, someone might wonder what there is to reflect about. Yet while nothing in the MHAT IV survey challenged the criminality of abusive behavior, it did have its own theory of causation—one that Petraeus now embraced. This theory held that, viewed statistically, abuse may have derived from non-criminal factors—mainly, the incidences of psychological stress. And although the report does not explicitly say so, clearly these stressors stemmed from both the nature of the Iraq War and its management.

The study analyzed these stressors by surveying the "Behavioral Health Status" of participants. Status was determined by measuring morale, depression, anxiety, acute stress (PTSD), anger, marital concerns, suicide, and battlefield ethics. The survey then looked to factors that might mitigate mental health issues ("Protective Factors"), such as NCO and officer leadership, training, unit cohesion, the availability of R&R, and mid-tour leaves. Finally, it crossed these categories with "Risk Factors," several of which were inherent in earlier political/military decisions made in managing the war: combat exposure, deployment concerns, branch of service, multiple deployments, and deployment length. The report detected important connections between these factors. For example, soldiers who screened as "angry" or who suffered from clinically-significant anxiety, depression, or PTSD were twice as likely as others to violate battlefield ethics.[9]

Since Petraeus understood that the causes of abuse were largely psychological, easing the crisis meant using what psychological tools he had available. His challenge was twofold: first, he had to identify in a comprehensible way those risk factors that his soldier-audience faced that might predispose members to commit acts of abuse. But to succeed with even this, Petraeus also needed to help his soldiers overcome one stubborn and costly reality identified in the MHAT IV survey: fewer than half of soldiers who screened positive for mental health problems sought counseling. The survey even had a name for it—"Psychological Stigma"—and the reasons for it suggested that the shade of George Patton (of the slapping incidents) still stalked the battle lines. Soldiers rejected counseling because they were afraid of being treated differently by comrades, or being seen as weak, or were fearful that it might damage their careers. Some just mistrusted counselors. For Petraeus' speech to work, he must banish Patton's ghost once and for all.[10]

First, he invoked the Comrade Convention in an effort to *redefine* the moral contract between comrades. For commanders using this convention, a fixture of Midst-of-Battle Speeches, "the preferred tone is not of demand, orders, or threats, but rather the simple appeal of one soldier to another." And here Petraeus spent his considerable moral authority as a veteran—he had served in Bosnia, led the 101st Airborne in the initial invasion and early occupation of Iraq, and did another tour training Iraqi forces. "I . . . know firsthand the bonds between members of the 'brotherhood of the close fight,'" he reminded his soldier-audience. In his next sentence he attempted to empathize, and used a therapist's language to access his soldier-audience's emotional selves: "Seeing a fellow trooper killed by a barbaric enemy can spark *anger*, *frustration*, and *desire* for *immediate revenge*." [Italics added][11]

Petraeus recognized that to report a comrade is "hard"; but again, using the language of therapy, he urged that "we must not let our emotions lead us—or our

---

9   MHAT IV, Figures 20, 21, 22a, 22b, 23a, 23b, and accompanying narrative materials, 37-42.

10 The survey also found "organizational barriers" obstructing recruits' access to counseling: a lack of free time, leaders discouraging treatment, difficulty accessing the location of mental health services, and their unavailability.

11 Miller, *Words and Deeds*, 234-235.

comrades in arms—to commit hasty, illegal actions." Significantly, Petraeus avoided stigmatizing these actions in morally judgmental terms: they are "hasty [and] illegal" and are motivated by "emotions"—not by evil or moral weakness. This probably recognized the fact that while a very small number of soldiers/Marines actually had committed such acts, a far larger number had probably fantasized about committing them. The point, as would become clear two paragraphs later, was not to further stigmatize soldiers in emotional crisis, but to channel them toward treatment.

Thus, in claiming the comrade's mantle, Petraeus sought to slip into the shoes (while adding his prestige as commander) of the 55% of soldiers and 40% of Marines—a not-inconsiderable number—who *would* report abuse of civilians or detainees. The Leadership Principle here was clear: build on one's strengths.

As Patton's The Speech illustrated, self-control is an evergreen meme in battle speeches. But its meaning has changed. Until recently, self-control meant controlling one's fears when in battle. Indeed, part of the traditional preparation for battle sought to overcome fear by encouraging soldiers to feel anger toward their enemies; the battle speech often played its part by retailing atrocity stories or stoking feelings of revenge for fallen comrades, or making defiant calls to defend home and hearth (recall General Ridgway's speech). But Petraeus now urged a different type (for soldiers) of self-control: controlling not fear, but rather the rage which may result from combat or lengthy deployments. Using "we" as both Comrade convention and anaphora, Petraeus confronted this reality:

> We are, indeed, warriors. We train to kill our enemies. We are engaged in combat, we must pursue the enemy relentlessly, and we must be violent at times.

But "we" must also know when to exercise self-control over our violence—and that violence must halt at the firewall of the "standards and values that dictate that we treat noncombatants and detainees with dignity and respect." And it was here that Petraeus made a shift that exorcised forever Patton's shade as an expert on battle stress: "While we are warriors, we are also human beings."

As a matter of policy, warriors had been "outed" as human beings at least since World War I, when doctors and soldiers alike confronted the psychological and physiological effects of "shell shock." But older notions continued to linger with remarkable persistence, as evidenced by the MHAT IV survey's findings of "psychological stigma." And it was this stigma that

Petraeus deemed the real enemy, because it acted to separate potentially-needy patients from caregivers. Soldiers can be disciplined; moral miscreants can be judged; criminals can be imprisoned. But understood in psychological terms, stressed men and women can only be treated. With this understanding, Petraeus, using the ancient Leadership Principle that a good commander will share his soldiers' hardships, again used "we"—only now, "we" signaled that Petraeus was more Freud than Patton; generals were also human beings, and the continual use of "we" implied that they may be as susceptible as privates to the emotional experience of this war:

> Stress caused by lengthy deployments and combat is not a sign of weakness; it is a sign that *we are human*. If you feel such stress, do not hesitate to talk to your chain of command, your chaplain, or a medical expert. [Italics added] [12]

Petraeus' earlier call for "reflection" was now fully fleshed. He was calling for soldiers to think seriously about their psychic burdens, and decide if they should seek counseling. He next asked that "Leaders, in particular, need to discuss these issues with their troopers—and as always, they need to set the right example to ensure proper conduct." Here Petraeus struck directly at one of the survey's findings: that a percentage of NCOs and officers had actually discouraged soldiers from seeking help. (Patton's ghost?) As senior commander, Petraeus was offering official remission for what had always been technically permissible but perhaps in practice, deplored: that soldiers could seek psychological counseling if they felt the need. Moreover, he was also not-so-subtly asking his NCOs and officers to engage in the same self-assessment as their charges.

Soldiers who showed signs of emotional stress could always be *ordered* into counseling. But Petraeus sought to forestall the abuse of civilians and detainees, so waiting until soldiers' psychic angst resulted in overt acts would be too late; the goal was prevention. In terms of effective treatment, this required that soldiers identify themselves as candidates for treatment, receive support from their leaders, and then agree to counseling. To accomplish these things Petraeus had to change attitudes throughout his command, and move soldiers in directions that many were obviously reluctant to go.

---

12 Eric T. Dean, Jr., *Shook Over Hell: Post-Traumatic Stress, Vietnam, and the Civil War* (Cambridge, Massachusetts: Harvard University Press, 1997), 29-34.

Immediate Result

The impact of Petraeus' speech on army mental health issues can only be measured by subsequent increases in requests or referrals for treatment, or the findings of some future survey about attitudinal changes toward seeking treatment. This information is not yet publicly available. Likewise, there is no available data whether there were any increases in peer reporting of battlefield ethics violations. Also not yet available for exploring either issue is the more inferential evidence of letters, diaries or memoirs that may eventually help illuminate the speech's impact on individuals or units. All that can be said is that during Petraeus' nineteen-month tenure, there were no more Abu Ghraib-like scandals—as far as is publicly known.

Legacy

Men who "malingered" had once been slapped by Patton and shown disdain by peers; however, if Petraeus' spoken injunctions held, soldiers who voluntarily limited their exposure to in-theater stressors or removed themselves entirely from combat would now be seen as praiseworthy: in the gasoline-filled fishbowl of counterinsurgency, it is far better to do no harm than to "tough it out" at the risk of the entire mission.

While the MHAT IV survey received brief attention and Petraeus' speech almost none, the changes he called for were no small matter. First, he attempted to further alter the ancient warrior code that refused to recognize as *hors de combat* any wound short of severe physical injury. Second, he sought to "amend" the comrades' contract to include, as a higher duty than even brotherhood, the obligation to report abuse, even if that compromised a combat buddy.

Leadership Principle

Petraeus embodied several important leadership principles. The first was insight: he grasped that for this war, Abu Ghraib-like incidents were potentially more destructive than the faceless insurgents setting mortar tubes and IEDs. Here the timing of the MHAT IV survey (ordered by his predecessor, General George W. Casey) was serendipitous because it gave Petreaus a good reason (at a critical time) to publicly discuss how to effectively deal with some important causes of the abuse of civilians. The second principle involved placing the problem in its proper proportion: because he understood its gravity, Petraeus made it the subject of a personal battle speech. (He could have chosen other courses of action—for example, he might have quietly referred it to army medicine to handle.) But Petraeus recognized that the survey's recommendations required major shifts in long-entrenched attitudes, and he obviously believed that this in turn required the expenditure of his personal credibility.

The way in which he spent that credibility embodied another important leadership principle. By choosing to make a battle speech that embraced the "we," Petraeus drew from the most valuable account he owned—the appeal to comradeship. He threw his considerable personal status as leader in favor of the attitudinal shift, and thereby legitimized the difficult acts of self-assessment, seeking psychological counseling or reporting comrades for violations of battlefield ethics. If the commanding general publically encouraged mental health counseling and the reporting of ethical violations, it would become far more difficult for those down the chain of command to do otherwise.

Persuasive Strategy

Appeals to comradeship dominated Petraeus' persuasive strategy. But in trying to change attitudes or difficult behaviors, the use of comradeship can be risky: speakers who invoke the communitarian "we" had better be perceived as an actual community member, that is, to have borne all of the "expenses" of membership; otherwise, the "we" invites ridicule. Fortunately for Petraeus, his membership had been firmly established by an already-memetic biography: shot in the chest during a training accident, suffering a serious spinal injury from a parachute jump gone bad, service in Bosnia, a third-time deployer in Iraq, and the man who commanded the 101st Airborne in combat and during the early occupation. Like many effective commanders before him, Petraeus also enjoyed the reputation of talking to his soldiers, and being everywhere at once, in and out of hostile fire. Petraeus' "*we*" was a genuinely credible "us."[13]

One key to the speech's coherence was Petraeus' balanced language. His voice did not forfeit the tone of commander, but was not that of the

---

13 Petraeus' biography may be found in both Atkinson, *In the Company of Soldiers*, 33-38; and online at www.centcom.mil/en/fact-sheets/biography-gen.-david-h.-petraeus.html. accessed August 16, 2009.

disciplinarian, either. Rather, in language it was the voice of therapy: "reflection . . . emotions . . . frustration . . . anger...desire . . . how we behave . . . stress . . . weakness . . . we are human . . . feel . . . do not hesitate to talk . . . need to discuss these issues."

The goal was to encourage soldiers to talk—horizontally among comrades and vertically in the chain of command. And the most efficient way to address the problem was to encourage soldiers suffering from dangerous levels of stress to self-identify.

Chapter Nine

Petraeus Bids Farewell: The Final Narrative

I. Historical Background

On July 10, 2008, the United States Senate voted 95 to 2 to confirm General Petraeus as commander of the United States Central Command (CENTCOM). This was a promotion. CENTCOM is by far the most kinetic of the six regional commands through which the American military conducts operations around the globe. Within its area of operations lie twenty countries, encompassing two wars (Iraq and Afghanistan); southwest Asia and the Middle East; important allies such as Kuwait, Jordan and Saudi Arabia; as well as countries that border areas of active combat, notably Pakistan, Iran, Syria and Yemen. The Senate's near-unanimous confirmation vote, which included most Democrats and all Republicans who initially had opposed the Surge, was another affirmation that Petraeus had (for the time being) succeeded.[1]

The metrics, which had always dominated discussion of the Surge's progress, partially told the story. By the first week in August 2008 security incidents—which included attacks employing IEDs, mines, grenades, mortars, rockets, and surface-to-air weapons; and in the form of sniper attacks and ambushes—had fallen to their lowest level since 2004. Civilian deaths from

---

1   David M. Herszenhorn, "Petraeus Gets Confirmation For New Post From Senate," *New York Times*, July 11, 2008; information about CENTCOM may found at www.centcom.mil /en/countries/aor/. Accessed August 16, 2009.

ethno-sectarian violence (mostly Shiite versus Sunni) barely registered on official charts. The discovery and destruction of weapons and ammunition caches—which depend on considerable civilian cooperation—had skyrocketed from 1,833 in all of 2004 to 6,326 for just the first seven months of 2008. Detainees had been reduced by five thousand since October 2007; by July 2008 the Coalition claimed a recidivism rate of less than one percent.[2]

But neither metrics nor Surge tactics revealed the whole story, and to evaluate Petraeus' Farewell Speech, a brief summary is necessary. First, Petraeus had been lucky in his timing. By 2007, Shiite militia had already rendered many Baghdad neighborhoods "Sunni-*rein*." Later that year, radical cleric and Mahdi Army leader Muqtada al-Sadr, representing the largest anti-government force, had declared a ceasefire. In the months before that, tribal leadership in the Sunni-dominated Anbar Province had begun to cooperate with Coalition forces to expel Al Qaeda-Iraq. This led directly to the creation of the Coalition-subsidized Sons of Iraq. These were often former insurgents who were now organized and given responsibility for security in their own neighborhoods. Add the much lower profiled "surge" of 100,000 Iraqi forces in sensitive areas and continuing progress in rebuilding Iraq's economy, and the summary is more complete.[3]

Future historians will probably debate how many of these conditions were luck and how many grew from the Surge's improved security. (It may be difficult to improve upon Helmuth von Moltke's apothem that "Luck in the long run is given only to the efficient.") However that may be, the results were clear. *New York Times* journalist Dexter Filkins had been based in Iraq for the war's first years, then returned in September 2008 after a two-year absence. The

---

2 Researching final metrics for the Surge should begin with Gen. David H. Petraeus, "Iraq: Building on Progress," *Army*, October 2008, 109-123; Thomas E. Ricks, "The Dissenter Who Changed the War," *Washington Post*, February 8, 2008; Thomas E. Ricks, "A Military Tactician's Political Gamble," *Washington Post*, February 9, 2008; "Charts to accompany the testimony of GEN David H. Petraeus, 8-9 April 2008, http://www.mnf-Iraq.com/images/stories/Press_briefings/2008/april/080408_petraeus_handout.pdf; "General Petraeus' Testimony to the Senate Armed Service Committee," April 8-9, 2008, www.mnf-iraq.com/images/stories/press_briefings/2008/april /080408_petraeus_testimony.pdf; Dexter Filkins, "Exiting Iraq, Petraeus Says Gains Are Fragile," *New York Times*, August 21, 2008.

3 This summary was condensed from Ricks' *The Gamble* and his February 8 and 9 *Washington Post* articles cited above.

situation was summarized by his article's title, published six days after Petraeus made his Farewell Speech: "Back in Iraq, Jarred by the Calm."[4]

II. The Speech

Soldiers, Sailors, Marines, Coast Guardsmen, and Civilians of Multi-National Force-Iraq:

It has been the greatest of privileges to have been your commander for the past 19 months. During that time, we and our civilian and Iraqi partners have been engaged in an exceedingly complex, difficult, and important task. And in the face of numerous challenges, we and our partners have helped bring new hope to a country that was besieged by extremists and engulfed in sectarian violence.

When I took command of Multi-National Force-Iraq in February 2007, I noted that the situation in Iraq was hard but not hopeless. You have proven that assessment to be correct. Indeed, your great work, sacrifice, courage and skill have helped to reverse a downward spiral towards civil war and to wrest the initiative from the enemies of the new Iraq.

Together, Iraqi and Coalition Forces have faced determined, adaptable, and barbaric enemies. You and our Iraqi partners have taken the fight to them, and you have taken away their sanctuaries and safe havens. You have helped secure the Iraqi people and have enabled and capitalized on their rejection of extremism. You have also supported the Iraqi Security Forces as they have grown in number and capability and as they have increasingly shouldered more of the responsibility for security in their country.

You have not just secured the Iraqi people, you have served them, as well. By helping establish local governance, supporting reconstruction efforts, assisting with the revitalization of local business, fostering local reconciliation, and conducting a host of other non-kinetic activities, you have contributed significantly to the communities in which you have operated. Indeed, you have been builders and diplomats as well as guardians and warriors.

Your accomplishments have, in fact, been the stuff of history. Each of you should be proud of what has been achieved and of the contributions you continue to make. Although our tasks in Iraq are far from complete and hard work and tough fights lie ahead, you have helped bring about remarkable improvements.

---

4 *Dictionary of Military and Naval Quotations*, 177; Dexter Filkins, "Back in Iraq, Jarred by the Calm," *New York Times*, September 21, 2008.

Your new commander is precisely the right man for the job. General Ray Odierno played a central role in the progress achieved during the surge. He brings tremendous skill, experience, and understanding as he returns to Iraq for a third tour and takes the helm of MNF-I just seven months after relinquishing command of Multi-National Corps—Iraq. I have total confidence in him, and will do all that I can as the commander of Central Command to help him, MNF-I, and our Iraqi partners to achieve the important goals that we all share for the new Iraq.

Thank you for your magnificent work here in the "Land of the Two Rivers." And thank you for your sacrifices—and for those of your families—during this crucial phase of Operation Iraqi Freedom. I am honored to have soldiered with you in this critical endeavor.

Thank you!

With great respect and best wishes.

—General David H. Petraeus' Farewell Speech, September 15, 2008[5]

III. Parsing the Speech

What were Petraeus' goals for his Farewell Speech? First, much is explained by simply recognizing the Farewell Speech as a humane form of expression between a battle speechmaker and his comrades-in-arms. It is a bittersweet leave-taking, a recounting of achievements, losses, and future hopes. That Petraeus' Farewell Speech shares most of the rhetorical attributes of its genre may be less a reflection of conscious design than the fact that these speeches' narrative structures are drawn from common human emotional experiences that transcend epochs and cultures. Taking leave always has been difficult and always in the same way.

Like other military Farewell Speeches, Petraeus' is a close cousin of the Post-Battle Speech and shares many of its attributes. Indeed, readers will find that appeals and narrative conventions move easily between these two battle speech genres, for the simple reason that Farewell Speeches often include narratives of battles fought during the speaker's tenure. And the most basic of these shared attributes are the stories that speechmakers seek to impose on a

---

5 General David H. Petraeus, www.mnf-iraq.com/images/CGs_messages/080915_gen _petraeus_final_letter_to_troops.pdf. Accessed August 20, 2009.

just-concluded battle or the incidents that occurred during his tenure. As is also common to both Farewell and Post-Battle Speeches, Petraeus' speech tells his story using special narrative conventions whose functions are exhortatory, although in different ways. He uses the Triumphal History Convention to describe success; the Gratitude Convention credits his soldier-audience for that success; while the Legacy Convention emphasizes the success' enduring aspects. Remembering the Fallen helps gel cohesion by recalling the cost of that success; and the Preparedness Convention reminds his soldier-audience that the battle is not over, the war continues and that another commander is replacing him.[6]

The story told by Petraeus' Farewell Speech is meant as a history, but should not be confused with historical writing, any more than a eulogy pretends at balanced biography. Most notable in what it omits, Petraeus' historical summary is a carefully-edited version of the "true history" of his tenure. For example, he omits the fact that by the time he assumed command, many Baghdad Sunni neighborhoods were already ethnically cleansed by Shiite militia (thus already reducing ethno-sectarian violence); likewise, Muqtada al-Sadr's ceasefire is unmentioned, as are the beneficial effects of recently-rising oil prices on Iraq's economy. Yet there is nothing sinister in these omissions. By focusing almost exclusively on his soldier-audience and the military institutions to which it belongs, the Farewell Speech's broad exhortatory purposes are best fulfilled.

As is always the case, the persuasive power of speech rests with the speaker, his story, and how the story is told. Petraeus opens by using Gratitude and Triumphal History to tell his story. "It has been the greatest of privileges to have been your commander these past 19 months," he begins (Gratitude).

> During that time, we and our civilian and Iraqi partners have been engaged in an exceedingly complex, difficult, and important task. And in the face of numerous challenges, we and our partners have helped to bring new hope to a country that was besieged by extremists and engulfed in sectarian violence.

Petraeus' 19-month history is thus bracketed by "extremists and...sectarian violence" at the beginning and "new hope" to Iraq at the end (Triumph). From

---

6   More detail about these conventions may be found in Miller, *Words and Deeds,* 324 (Farewell Speeches, Gratitude), 327-328 (Triumphal History), 300-311 (Legacy), 283-288 (Remembering the Fallen), 282 (Preparedness).

the first, Petraeus thus declares that he will give his soldier-audience a history of what fell between these events that marked his tenure.

His version of that history is straightforward, as battle speech histories invariably are. He arrived at a time of violence and chaos to face a "determined, adaptable, and barbaric enemy." But his soldier-audience, by their "great work, sacrifice, courage and skill" succeeded in "revers[ing] the downward spiral." Cooperating with the Iraq Security Forces (ISF), they "have taken the fight to" the enemies and removed "their sanctuaries and safe havens." They have also supported the ISF, which has now "grown in number and capability" as well as willingness to assume "more responsibility for security in their country." But as COIN doctrine seeks, the soldier-audience, "by supporting local governance, supporting reconstruction efforts, assisting with the revitalization of local businesses" and other such "non-kinetic activities," have become the very model of counterinsurgents: "[Y]ou have been builders and diplomats as well as guardians and warriors." And of course, Petraeus' history has an ending, at least for that moment: "You have helped secure the Iraqi people and have enabled, and capitalized on, their rejection of extremism."[7]

He continually alternates between Gratitude and Triumphal History Conventions throughout the speech. "Hard but not hopeless" was the Speechlet by which Petraeus entered this fight; twice in this speech he emphasizes that what hope (Triumph) now exists is attributable to his soldier-audience's "great work, sacrifice, courage, and skill" (Gratitude) "[which] have helped reverse a downward spiral toward civil war and to wrest the initiative from the enemies of the new Iraq" (Triumph).

Petraeus offers a unit historical narrative of the joint Coalition-ISF effort. Battle speeches invariably draw on one or several of four historical narratives: unit, religious, social or political. For Petraeus, the unit historical narrative is very important: cooperation between the Coalition and the ISF, as well as improving the latter's capabilities, were a large part of his mission. And Petraeus celebrates both the cooperation and the improvements in several passages emphasizing Triumph. "You and our Iraqi partners have taken the fight to them.... You have helped secure the Iraqi people... You have also supported the Iraq Security Forces as they have grown in number and capability...." His

---

7   Petraeus is describing the ideal COIN warrior, and the phrases are taken from FM3-24. See "Host-Nation Civil Authorities," 2-36 ("diplomats [as well as] warriors"); "Forward" ("nation builders as well as warriors").

phrasing is skillful because each praise (Gratitude) is also about their achievements (Triumph).[8]

Farewell Speeches often confront the fact that wars kill and maim soldiers and civilians, destroy property and displace the innocent. As was noted in the preceding chapter, this destruction, especially death, also produces enormous psychological harm—anger, but also grief and guilt. Because this suffering is not doled out according to deservedness, the importance of rationalization becomes paramount in sustaining morale. Petraeus, like many Post-Battle and Farewell speechmakers before him, remembers the Fallen, and thereby assures his soldier-audience that the Surge's gains were worth the costs:

> The progress achieved has been hard earned. There have been many tough days along the way, and we have suffered tragic losses. Indeed, nothing in Iraq has been anything but hard. But you have been more than equal to every task.

What distinguishes Petraeus' commemoration of the Fallen ("tragic losses") from similar treatment by others is found in his next sentence: "Indeed, nothing in Iraq has been anything but hard." Understood in the full light of the war's troubled history, this statement seems tinged with bitterness. How might his soldier-audience have defined the enthymematic use of "hard?" After all, the Iraq War's casualties were to that point a fraction of those from the world wars, Korea or Vietnam; moreover, deployed soldiers' standards of living would have struck their previously-uniformed fathers and grandfathers with disbelief.

Certainly the Iraq War's length had made it "hard." But I think Petraeus' comment also understands "hard" in other ways: hard, because so many political and military misjudgments were made in the war's planning and execution, and because it was the soldier-audience—present, injured, stateside and the remembered dead—who paid for and ultimately had to rectify those mistakes. The war was hard because so many well-aired controversies at home contributed to soldiers' doubts during multiple and extended deployments. Finally, it was hard because the Iraqis themselves were so ambivalent about the war and the soldier-audience's presence: soldiers were simultaneously liberators and hated occupiers; welcomed for deposing Saddam, but a national reproach that Iraqis were themselves unable to do this; welcomed as harbingers of political rights and economic prosperity, but threats to traditional religious and tribal values.

---

8 Miller, *Words and Deeds*, "The History in Battle Speeches," 27-64.

Iraqis yearned for the security soldiers provided, yet simultaneously wanted these soldiers to leave their country. In short, Petraeus' "hard" is a highly-personalized usage among soldiers sharing combat experience from the same war; to define it would have invited controversy from far outside the circle of the soldier-audience. But there is no need to define it—Petraeus' listeners/readers almost certainly understood exactly what he meant.

Having commemorated the Fallen, Petraeus transitions to Legacy. In the aftermath of battles, wars, and combat commands, just glorying in triumphs is not enough. The blood spilled is usually far more than a cup of praise can hold. What has been achieved must be recast in larger terms, sometimes spanning worlds or reaching to the heavens, but invariably linking the soldier-audience with future generations. This perspective is the Legacy convention, and should the soldier-audience ever come to idealize their experiences, it is the Legacy Convention that will likely influence how they interpret the war's meanings. Petraeus had already described what his soldiers accomplished, and his use of Gratitude and Triumphal History often implied Legacy: forces that rebuild countries, save communities and train national armies and police are likely to leave important legacies. But it is the "H" word—history—that battle speechmakers usually use to confer legacy, and Petraeus obliged:

> Your accomplishments have, in fact, been the stuff of history. Each of you should
> be proud of what has been achieved and of the contribution you continue to make.

Legacy is important to modern battle speechmakers representing a secular government. Such authorities, in or out of uniform, are usually unable to invest with religion an achievement's meaning. But if Petraeus cannot invoke eternity to elevate his soldiers' achievements, he can use the next best thing: human memory, "the stuff of history," the scribblings of present and future chroniclers whose business it is to create records of great deeds for the enrichment of future generations. In short, the true audience for his soldiers' deeds is far larger than grateful (or even ungrateful) fellow citizens, politicians and Iraqis, larger too than just their own comrades: the Legacy audience, which will presumably become more grateful over time, will include all the descendants of the world, as long as records are kept. It is history and not God that will assure that

And Crispin Crispian shall ne'er go by
From this day to the ending of the world
But we in it shall be remembered.[9]

Unlike the Farewell Speeches of Washington and Robert E. Lee, Petraeus' speech is not given at the end of a war. In this sense it also resembles a Post-Battle Speech, given after a battle but before the larger conflict is over. Petraeus acknowledges this by using the Preparedness Convention—his soldier-audience's achievements represent only a phase in the larger struggle, and they must be prepared for the struggle to continue. There can be no resting on laurels. Petraeus acknowledges this in his Legacy: "Although our tasks in Iraq are far from complete and hard work and tough fights lie ahead, you have helped bring about remarkable improvements."

Readers will recall from this section's first chapter that Assumption of Command speeches seek to answer the key question of continuity/discontinuity: will the new commander bring change, and if so, what kind of change? In his Farewell Speech's final point, Petraeus transfers both the torch and his prestige to his successor, General Ray Odierno. And the emphasis here is on continuity. "Your new commander is precisely the right man for the job," he begins, and concludes with his blessing: "I have total confidence in him, and I will do all that I can as the commander of Central Command to help him, MNF-I, and our Iraqi partners to achieve *the important goals that we all share for the new Iraq.*" [Italics added] This is a flexible form of continuity—Odierno shares the same goals, Petraeus will be his superior, but nothing is said about what means Odierno may adopt to suit his own management style or changed conditions on the ground. In short, Petraeus has not committed his successor to any particular set of tactics.

This Farewell Speech was distributed in Coalition facilities throughout the Iraq theatre. Petraeus clearly wanted his soldier-audience to actually read the printed copies, for in the official version's lower right hand corner, across from Petraeus' facsimile signature, are the double underlined, handwritten words, "Thank you!" These words are an unexpected human touch on an otherwise anodyne-looking army document.

The very next day, General Ray Odierno would make his own Assumption of Command speech—and the cycle of command was ready to repeat.

---

9 Shakespeare, *Henry V*, Act IV, Scene III, 57-59.

Immediate Result

There is not enough available information to gauge soldier-audience reaction to Petraeus' Farewell Speech. For the previous chapter's speech, reaction might be quantifiable by examining the number of post-speech counseling visits or peer reporting of ethical violations; of course, no similar metrics can ever be available to assess reactions to a Farewell Speech. A good historical archive may take fifty to one hundred years to ripen, and soldiers' reactions to this speech will have to be inferred from their diaries, letters, and memoirs.

Legacy

Perhaps the most important legacy of Petraeus' Farewell Speech is that he chose to continue a distinguished line of Farewell Speeches that began with George Washington. The Father of his Country actually gave two notable Farewells (to his army by proclamation and personally to his officers at Fraunces Tavern); other notable Farewells were made by George McClellan, Robert E. Lee and Douglas MacArthur.[10]

Petraeus' continuation of the tradition was exactly that—continuity. He offered new wine in a much older bottle. While America had not fought a COIN war on this scale since Vietnam (and thus, some of the Farewell Speech's content was new, at least to this generation), in finalizing a narrative for his tenure Petraeus used forms that were already well established as part of the Farewell and Post-Battle Speech genre.

---

10 Stanley Weintraub, *George Washington's Christmas Farewell: A Mount Vernon Homecoming* (New York: Free Press, 2003), 85-86, (Fraunces Tavern); "Papers of George Washington," http://gwpapers.virginia.edu/documents/revolution/farewell. Accessed on August 22, 2009; George B. McClellan, "To the Army of the Potomac, November 7 1862," *The Civil War Papers of George B. McClellan: Selected Correspondence, 1860-1865,* edited by Stephen W. Sears (New York: Da Capo Press, 1989), 520-521; Robert E. Lee, "General Order No. 9, April 10, 1865," *OR*, Series I, Volume 46, Part III, page 744; Douglas MacArthur, "Old Soldiers Never Die," *Lend Me Your Ears: Great Speeches in History*, edited and introduction by William Safire (New York: W.W. Norton & Co., 1992), 425-431.

Leadership Principle

Nothing required Petraeus to make a Farewell Speech. Thus, the first leadership principle evidenced here is that he chose to make one at all. The Farewell Speech represents a leader's decision to fashion a narrative of his own tenure; Petraeus was unwilling to leave the contemporary narrative solely to others. And later historians of the Surge will likely incorporate this speech as one more piece of evidence in their assessments.

The second leadership principle, further discussed below, is that Petraeus did not make himself or his relationship with his soldier-audience the center of his Farewell Speech. What was accomplished during the Surge was to their credit, not his; and what they did was done not for him, but for the mission. He credits himself with only one thing—a prediction: "When I took command of Multi-National Force-Iraq in February 2007, I noted that the situation in Iraq was hard but not hopeless." But he credited the successful fulfillment of the condition entirely to his soldiers: "You have proven that assessment to be correct."

The resulting speech, entirely soldier-audience-centered, is presumably better for morale than its opposite: Farewell Speeches that are speaker rather than audience-focused (see below). The word "I" appears only six times in Petraeus' Farewell Speech, four of which are in sentences praising or supporting others.

Persuasive Strategy

In contrast to Petraeus' speech on battlefield ethics, where his underlying persuasive tool was comradeship, here his chief persuasive tool is gratitude toward the soldier-audience. Indeed, the comradely "we" and "our" is used only nine times in this speech; but "you" and "your" rate twenty-three mentions.

However, unlike the gratitude often found in speeches by a Napoleon or McClellan, which was highly personal—they depicted their soldiers as performing well because of some unique relationship they had with them—the gratitude Petraeus summons is not personal to him. While he does express his personal satisfaction for his soldiers' efforts—the handwritten "Thank you!"—Petraeus largely submerges his own identity in favor of what his soldiers have accomplished for the mission ("our tasks in Iraq"), the country of Iraq ("new hope to the country") and the Iraqi people ("you have served them"). Speaking personally, Petraeus enjoys only "the greatest of privileges" to have commanded them, as he professes in his humble close: "I am honored to have soldiered with you in this critical endeavor."[11]

Readers may wonder why Petraeus omits any grateful expression on behalf of soldiers' countries. This was in part a solution to the problem of the diversity described in the Introduction: his soldier-audience came from many countries, and nothing would be more off-putting than to mention one country at the expense of others, or more cluttering of the narrative than to recite the list of contributing powers. Referring to the "Multi-National Force-Iraq" or "MNF-I" did the trick.

Persuasion and style are inseparable. And Petraeus, an admirer of Ulysses S. Grant, seems to have adopted the latter's style of written communication. As one of Grant's contemporaries observed, "There is one striking feature about Grant's orders: no matter how hurriedly he may write them on the field, no one ever has the slightest doubt as to their meaning, or ever has to read them over a second time to understand them." Petraeus too is plain spoken, and his reputation as the army's premier intellectual does not impede his ability to communicate with all soldiers. And he does so without a trace of condescension or paternalism.[12]

11 McClellan's Farewell Speech cited above is replete with paternal family metaphor. For an even more extreme example, see Napoleon's "Farewell to the Guard," April 20, 1814, *In the Words of Napoleon,* 302.

12 Porter, quoting Meade's chief of Staff, *Campaigning with Grant,* 241.

Section Four

Failure

This section will explore the reasons why some battle speeches fail. Readers will recall Alexander the Great's failed speech at the Hyphasis River. It failed for the most fundamental reason: Alexander's inability to empathize with his men. Consumed with *pothos*, he had lost the capacity to "read" his exhausted, homesick troops. This failure to empathize, even temporarily, with the soldier-audience, or at the very least take seriously its concerns, is probably the most common reason for battle speech failure.

But it is not the only reason. Chapter Ten will consider a speechmaker's failure to control himself and, by extension, his speech's contents. The example used is that of American Civil War General John Pope's disastrous AOC speech to his army. It failed because, by temperament, Pope was blind to how his boasts and presumably "motivational insults" were likely to be heard by his soldier-audience; moreover, by Pope's own admission, he foolishly allowed some highly-partisan passages to be written by civilian superiors whose interests may have been other than giving a sound and badly-needed exhortatory speech. These passages were not only political, they were also bad politics: Pope's criticisms deepened existing fault lines that ran through Northern society and his soldier-audience. Thus, while Pope sought tactical discontinuity—to help reverse the fortunes of the admittedly demoralized units that comprised his newly-formed command—what he provoked instead was further political and regional division. Here the *mechanics of failure* will be closely examined: the reasons why, in a particular time and place, a speech can go terribly awry.

Chapter Eleven will consider other reasons why battle speeches commonly fail. The first of these deals with speeches containing incorrect factual assertions whose erroneousness is well known to the soldier-audience. The failure here is not a lack of empathy with the audience, but rather the denial or omission of commonly-known *facts*, or a speaker's failure to match his *assumptions* with realities well known to his audience. A second reason for battle speech (or any speech) failure is closely related to the failure to match assertions with facts: the inappropriate, overblown or inapplicable use of historical analogies. Scolds who are quick to repeat George Santayana's well-worn observation that "[t]hose who cannot remember the past are condemned to repeat it" usually fail to mention its two assumptions: first, that someone's recollections of the past bear an actual resemblance to it, and second, that his grasp of present reality is sufficiently strong—and relevant—to enable a valid comparison.

Both flaws are present in the example used here: General Walton H. Walker's notorious "Stand or Die" speech made to American forces during the early, desperate fighting after the North Koreans first crossed the 38th Parallel. This chapter demonstrates that successful, distinguished commanders also can make failed battle speeches. General Walker had compiled a fine combat record as a tank commander under George Patton during World War II. His generalship in Korea, while controversial, had critical successes. But even good generals can give bad battle speeches.

Chapter Twelve reaches outside strictly rhetorical analyses to examine speeches that fail because their contents produce clearly foreseeable and profoundly self-destructive results. Two linked examples are used here: the notorious Commissar Order originating from Adolf Hitler's Headquarters in 1941, and the notes taken by an audience member of the speech Hitler gave that inspired the measure. The Commissar Order that was eventually issued by Field Marshal Wilhelm Keitel authorized the outright murder of certain Soviet prisoners of war. These policies, besides forming a part of the most monstrous criminal enterprise of the last century, ultimately boomeranged and contributed to the destruction of the original battle speechmakers, their soldier-audience, the military and regime to which it belonged.

I include this example to suggest that a purely rhetorical, content-free analysis of battle speeches sometimes may be insufficient to judge their success or failure; in rare instances, certainly justified here, content must be examined and a question raised: even if a speech "worked" with its soldier-audience, can it, should it, still be deemed a success?

Chapter Ten

John Pope and the Failure to Transcend Self

I. Historical Background

On June 26, 1862, Abraham Lincoln appointed forty-year-old Major General John Pope to lead the newly organized Army of Virginia, created by consolidating federal forces based around the Shenandoah Valley. Pope's promotion continued Lincoln's pattern for selecting eastern army commanders: the successor, buoyed by some recent military triumph (no matter how inapplicable in circumstance or in scope to his new position) was contrasted with his predecessor, who was invariably blighted by military failure, bad political odor or temperamental shortcomings.[1]

To the Lincoln administration, John Pope shone in most columns. Just months earlier, Pope, commanding 8,000 men, had captured New Madrid, Mississippi, and nearby Island No. 10, thus opening the Mississippi River almost to Memphis. Shortly afterward, he distinguished himself as a fast-moving, aggressive commander in General Henry Halleck's otherwise painfully slow advance on Corinth, Mississippi. Socially, Pope was a well-connected, preeminently western man: his father had helped organize the

---

1 *OR*, Series I, Volume 12, Part III, 434-435, "A. Lincoln, Telegraphed to Banks, Fremont, and McDowell," June 26, 1862. Consistent with this pattern, each new commander of the Army of the Potomac was thought to have the specific virtues missing in his predecessor. Pope would thus remedy what many in the Lincoln administration believed was McClellan's lack of combat aggressiveness, disloyalty and political ambition.

State of Illinois and later became a Federal judge (and a man Lincoln knew well from his own days riding the circuit courts.) Pope's uncle had been a Senator from Kentucky and his father-in-law was a wealthy Republican Congressman from Ohio. Politically, Pope was a rarity for an antebellum West Point graduate: he was not only a Republican but also an early proponent of hard war against the South. By contrast, George B. McClellan, the commander whom Lincoln hoped Pope would eventually replace, was a Democrat, a proponent of soft war, and, most recently, the general who many believed had squandered time, treasure and blood in a fruitless campaign on Virginia's Peninsula. Secretary of the Navy Gideon Welles, an astute inside chronicler of the Lincoln administration, believed that there was more to Pope's appointment than just a contrast with McClellan. He declared that Pope had been brought to Washington "as much . . . to humiliate McClellan as to serve the country." Of course, this was not the only, or probably not even the major reason for Pope's appointment; but Welles' comment reveals that the Lincoln administration could have its own feet of clay.[2]

Two aspects of Pope's failed AOC speech deserve comment. First, Pope was correct in wanting to give some kind of tough, exhortatory speech to his soldier-audience. Some of his units were demoralized, having been led by poor commanders who had repeatedly suffered defeat at the hands Thomas "Stonewall" Jackson, among the Confederacy's most able generals. If Pope was to succeed, he needed to stress *discontinuity in command, tactics, and esprit*.[3]

But unlike the later General Petraeus, Pope seemed temperamentally unable to introduce the required discontinuities without also widening sharp divisions in command loyalties and political ideologies, as well as (unwisely) challenging soldier identity. When McClellan organized the eastern armies, he had also given them a proud unit historical narrative. Eastern soldiers certainly had

---

2 Ezra Warner, *Generals in Blue: Lives of the Union Commanders* (Baton Rouge: Louisiana State University Press, 1999), 376-377; Appleton's *Cyclopaedia*, V: 68-69; Peter Cozzens, *General John Pope: A Life for the Nation* (Chicago: University of Illinois Press, 2000), 26; *Diary of Gideon Welles, Secretary of the Navy Under Lincoln and Johnson, with an Introduction by John T. Morse, Jr., Volume I: 1861—March 30, 1864*, (Boston: Houston Mifflin Company, 1911), I: 221.

3 Pope assessed well over half of his consolidated force (Fremont and Bank's 23,000 soldiers) as "much demoralized and broken down, and unfit for active service for the present." Pope rated Irwin McDowell's 19,000 men as "by far the best, and in fact, the only reliable portion of my command." – John Pope to George McClellan, July 4, 1862, *OR*, Series I, Volume 11, Part III, 295-296.

experienced their share of reverses; nonetheless, by the summer of 1862 defeat had not erased this original proud narrative; if anything, it had been sustained by battle. They now understood themselves as a fully-veteranized and brave if somewhat pessimistic and long-suffering, force. Pope's AOC speech foolishly attacked the positive aspects of this narrative, and might have failed for that reason alone.[4]

But there was far more involved with Pope's failed speech. The fault lines that divided the North were many but included differences by region (east versus west and north versus loyal border states) as well as social and political factors of class, ethnicity and ideology. It is probably more useful to divide Northern society circa mid-1862 into proponents of hard war versus soft war rather than into Democrats and Republicans. At their extremes these two schools of war also encompassed opposing views of slavery (abolition versus toleration), society (destroying versus retaining the Southern planter class), military policy (for example, whether or not to arm African Americans), and, of course, tactical (whether to lay on Southern civilians "the hard hand of war"). Here John Pope and George McClellan became symbols for opposing views.[5]

And certain to further widen these fault lines was John Pope's character. Many contemporaries, especially his army peers, thought him vain, boastful, insubordinate, dishonest, and abusive to subordinates; he handled command stress poorly; he shared many westerners' contempt for the eastern army; and he deeply disliked George McClellan and his military circle. But far worse than these prejudices was John Pope's lack of restraint in proclaiming them. Sometimes John Pope was unable to keep his mouth shut.

Later Pope would claim that the anti-McClellan passages of his speech were written at the insistence of Secretary of War Edwin M. Stanton and Secretary of the Treasury Salmon P. Chase. Whatever the case, they clearly mirrored Pope's own deeply-held beliefs—and in venting these, Pope was foreshadowing other personal shortcomings that helped destroy federal prospects at the Second Battle of Bull Run.[6]

---

4 Miller, *Words and Deeds*, 30-38.

5 Party affiliation is not always reliable here. Some Democrats were "hard" warriors (for example, Benjamin Butler) and some Republicans were "soft" warriors, especially during the war's first two years. Indeed, until this time (and in some respects thereafter) the leading "soft" war Republican was probably Abraham Lincoln.

6 Peter Cozzens, *General John Pope*, 72-73, 85.

II. The Speech

By special assignment of the President of the United States I have assumed command of this army. I have spent two weeks in learning your whereabouts, your condition, and your wants, in preparing you for active operations, and in placing you in positions from which you can act promptly and to the purpose. These labors are nearly completed, and I am about to join you in the field.

Let us understand each other. I have come to you from the West, where we have always seen the backs of our enemies; from an army whose business it has been to seek the adversary and to beat him when he was found; whose policy has been attack and not defense. In but one instance has the enemy been able to place our Western armies in defensive attitude. I presume that I have been called here to pursue the same system and to lead you against the enemy. It is my purpose to do so, and that speedily. I am sure you long for an opportunity to win the distinction you are capable of achieving. That opportunity I shall endeavor to give you. Meantime I desire you to dismiss from your minds certain phrases, which I am sorry to find so much in vogue amongst you. I hear constantly of "taking strong positions and holding them," of "lines of retreat," and of "bases of supplies." Let us discard such ideas. The strongest position a soldier should desire to occupy is the one from which he can most easily advance against the enemy. Let us study the probable lines of retreat of our opponents, and leave our own to take care of themselves. Let us look before us, and not behind. Success and glory are in the advance, disaster and shame lurk in the rear. Let us act on this understanding, and it is safe to predict that your banners shall be inscribed with many a glorious deed and that your names will be dear to your countrymen forever.

— "To the Officers and Soldiers of the Army of Virginia," Major-General John Pope, July 14, 1862[7]

III. Parsing the Speech

John Pope could have avoided damaging his reputation had he ended his AOC speech after the first paragraph. Few generals suffer in their soldiers' estimation by announcing that they have devoted "two weeks in learning your whereabouts, your condition, and your wants" with the result that "[I am]

---

7 "To the Officers and Soldiers of the Army of Virginia," *OR*, Series I, Volume 12, Part III, 473-474. The day after his June 26 appointment Pope had issued a terse, two-line announcement of the fact; but the July 14 statement was really his AOC speech. "General Orders, No. 1," *OR*, Series I, Volume 12, Part III, 436-437.

placing you in positions from which you can act promptly and to the purpose."
Newspapers had applauded Pope's appointment—"Now that a clear head, a
determined will, and a swift-moving General has the work given him, the public
will not need to wait long for results," the *New York Times* had declared—so
many in the ranks probably welcomed Pope's announcement that "I am about to
join you in the field."[8]

But that hope faded quickly when Pope self-inflicted his first wound. He
began his second paragraph inauspiciously. "Let us understand each other" he
said—adopting a stern, parental tone before he had earned that right.

> I have come to you from the West, where we have always seen the backs of our
> enemies; from an army whose business it has been to seek the adversary and to beat
> him when he was found; whose policy has been attack and not defense.

Instantly, these words widened two fault lines. First, Pope declared that he
was from the "West"—thus implying that the Army of Virginia was from the
East, an assertion that may have left some soldiers wondering exactly how much
"learning" Pope had really done during his two weeks of study: of the Army of
Virginia's 131 units, 26 were from Ohio, Michigan, Indiana, and Wisconsin.[9]

Of far greater importance is the question of what purposes were served by
raising this regional difference. Nothing constructive, for Pope next proceeded
to widen another fault line: an invidious implication that dominated the rest of
the speech and which transgressed what was almost certainly the core unit
historical narrative of his soldier-audience. According to the soldier-audience
narrative, it did not lack courage, but only competent commanders. But now
Pope declared that it was only Western armies that put rebels to flight ("backs of
our enemies"), sought battles, won them, always attacked and never defended.
Pope implied that eastern armies did not intimidate rebels, seek or win battles,
and were always on the defense because they never attacked. This, coupled with
later assertions ("disaster and shame lurk in the rear"), implied Eastern timidity
at least, with fainter yet unmistakable whispers of something worse. In short,

---

8   "Pope Against Jackson—Flank Movement Upon Richmond," *New York Times*, June 27,
1862.

9   Frederick H. Dyer, *A Compendium of the War of the Rebellion* (Des Moines, Iowa:
unknown printer, 1908), reprint, Dayton, Ohio, Press of Morningstar Bookshop, 1978,
"Army of Virginia," 349-352. I culled this list to eliminate those units that joined the Army
of Virginia after Pope's AOC speech.

Pope unwisely questioned how these soldiers understood themselves as soldiers, and perhaps their courage and manliness as well.

And there were other reasons why this implication must have rankled his soldier-audience. While the Valley armies had been generally unsuccessful, they had also paid enormously for the privilege of being badly led: in six battles fought during the first six months of 1862, they had suffered an aggregate of 4,567 casualties; by contrast, Pope's casualties from the capture of New Madrid, Island No. 10 and at Farmington, Mississippi—his largest battle in the advance on Corinth—were 32, 0, and 178 respectively. Indeed, Pope was not even present at the horrific Battle of Shiloh, "the one instance" where "the enemy [has] been able to place our Western armies in [a] defensive attitude." There was no denying Pope's achievement in his relatively bloodless victories at New Madrid and Island No. 10 or his initiative in advancing on Corinth. But these were not the kind of large-scale battles that defined the American Civil War. Nor were Pope's rebel adversaries in the West remotely equal to Thomas "Stonewall" Jackson, the bane of so many units that now composed the Army of Virginia.[10]

The next four sentences were a bridge between Pope's emphasis on fault lines (regional chauvinism and his attack on unit historical narrative); this section was a series of bombasts aimed directly at the still-popular George McClellan and the school of war he represented. Simply put, what the transitional sentences subtracted by their arrogance was not restored by Pope's attempt to genuinely connect with his men.

"I presume that I have been called here to pursue the same system and to lead you against the enemy," Pope declared. Just as Pope was premature in adopting a parental tone, so was this statement excessively formal, opening the speaker to ridicule. *Presume*? Did Pope not know why he was given command? *System*? This must have struck Pope's fully-veteranized soldier-audience as their new commander's real presumption. In fact, while Pope was about to introduce a new "system"—a harsher hand of war beginning with a series of

---

10 "Losses, By Battles—Union Armies," William F. Fox, *Regimental Losses in The American Civil War, 1861-1865* (Albany, New York: Brandow Printing Company, 1898), reprint, Press of Morningside Bookshop, 1985, 543. The six battles are Kernstown, McDowell, Front Royal, Winchester, Cross Keys, and Port Republic. (The Battle of Kernstown (March 23, 1862) was a rare federal victory over Stonewall Jackson); "Statement of the organization and return of casualties in the Army of the Mississippi during the operations against New Madrid, Mo., February 28-March 14, 1862," *OR*, Series I, Volume 8, 91-93; Peter Cozzens, *General John Pope,* 63-64.

"hard war" proclamations—these were not connected with Pope's western successes. Pope did attempt to connect with his men ("I am sure you long for an opportunity to win the distinction you are capable of achieving"), and such a sentiment is entirely appropriate to AOC speeches, as was Pope's follow-on: "That opportunity I shall endeavor to give you." But whatever beneficial effects these sentiments contained had dissipated before they were uttered.[11]

Pope's greatest rhetorical blunders occurred as he moved to finish his speech. Although the two weeks that he had spent "learning" about his command were passed in Washington, Pope somehow felt able to identify three phrases that he was "sorry to find so much in vogue among you." They were:

"taking strong positions and holding them"
"lines of retreat"
"bases of supplies"[12]

Pope urged that his men "dismiss from their minds" these phrases. Of course, these phrases are merely descriptive of most planned military operations, ancient or modern, successful or unsuccessful. Almost every battle plan must look to the possibility of holding strong positions, imagining lines of retreat, and connecting forces to some base of supply, be it a forward cache, rearward depot, or a farmer's barn just up the road. Pope was a West Point graduate and an intelligent man who understood this full well. Why would he urge his new command to "discard such ideas"?[13]

The answer is that in mid-July 1862 these ideas had become politically-charged memes that now conveyed far more meaning than they otherwise might have. The day that Pope delivered his AOC speech, George B.

11 Pope's hard war policies quickly followed his AOC speech. They appear in General Orders No. 5 and 6 (infantry and cavalry shall subsist upon the country); General Order No. 7 (local civilians held responsible for insurgents' acts); General Order No. 11 (arrest of disloyal males within army lines). These orders are compiled in Appendix A in the still-useful account of John Codman Ropes, *The Army Under Pope* (New York: Charles Scribner's Sons, 1881), 173-177. Pope's policies were welcomed by many in the Army of Virginia; Cozzens, *General John Pope*, 87.

12 Cozzens, *General John Pope*, 79-80 (remaining in Washington).

13 How fundamental these concepts were can be seen in Jomini, *Summary of the Art of War* (Philadelphia: J.P. Lippincott & Co., 1871). Jomini was a key text at antebellum West Point and elsewhere. Under "The Fundamental Principles of War" Jomini includes such sections as "Bases of Supply," "Depots of Supply, and their Relations to Operations," and in a later chapter, "Retreats and Pursuits."

McClellan and the Army of the Potomac were still holding one very strong position at Harrison's Landing on Virginia's Peninsula. Just over three weeks earlier, McClellan's army had been within sight of the Confederate capital at Richmond; aggressively attacked by Robert E. Lee, McClellan—incorrectly believing his army was badly outnumbered by rebels—ordered a fighting retreat southeast to Harrison's Landing. This retrograde movement was completely unexpected and shocked the Lincoln administration, the public and even many in the blue ranks.[14]

Unwisely, McClellan tried to influence public perception about what had happened. He called his retreat a "change of base." He began to boast, accurately, that his Harrison's Landing fortification "is very strong & daily becoming more so," thereby implying to many (especially those of the hard-war school) that he had lost sight of his army's offensive purpose on the Peninsula. To the Lincoln administration and many of the press and public, words such as "bases of supplies" and "taking strong positions" had become supporting memes of a neologism: "McClellanism," a word that later historians have variously defined as a "reluctance to fight," "paralysis" and, after the release of the Preliminary Emancipation Proclamation several months later, "opposition to the government's policy of abolition and harsh prosecution of the war."[15]

---

14 Subsequent historiography has been hard on McClellan, and finding objective accounts of McClellan's Peninsula Campaign and its sequel is difficult. Two balanced accounts are Ethan Rafuse, *McClellan's War: The Failure of Moderation in the Struggle for Union* (Bloomington, Indiana: Indiana University Press, 2005) and Brian K. Burton, *Extraordinary Circumstances: The Seven Days Battles* (Bloomington, Indiana: Indiana University Press, 2001).

15 McClellan in a number of post-Peninsula communications approximated the phrases Pope ridiculed. The following examples are drawn from Stephen W. Sears, *The Civil War Papers of George B. McClellan: Selected Correspondence, 1860-1865* (New York: Da Capo Press, 1989): "To Abraham Lincoln," July 4, 1862 ("change of base"), 336-338; "To the Army of the Potomac," July 4, 1862 ("changing your base of operations"), 339; "To Abraham Lincoln," July 7, 1862 ("my position is very strong . . . ."), 341; finally, of probable importance to Pope's AOC speech is McClellan's July 7, 1862, letter to him (probably received before his AOC speech). Here McClellan talked of resuming his army's offensive operations, but that his strong bias was to "maintain my present position as long as possible" (342-343). For various definitions of McClellanism, see Stephen Sears, *George B. McClellan: The Young Napoleon* (New York: Da Capo Press, 1999), 349; Edward H. Bonekemper, III, *McClellan and Failure: A Study of Civil War Fear, Incompetence and Worse* (Jeffersoin, North Carolina: McFarland & Company, 2007), 171; Jeffrey D. Wert, *The Sword of Lincoln: The Army of the Potomac* (New York: Simon & Schuster, 2005), 325. For a contemporary's use of the word, see Allan Nevins and Milton Halsey Thomas,

Pope's "quotation" of these phrases—incidentally, none of them McClellan's exact words—nevertheless served as a thinly-veiled subterfuge, a way of attacking George McClellan and what he "represented" without having to mention his name—which also happened to be the name of the man who still commanded not only the eastern theater's largest army but also the loyalty of many in the soldier-audience Pope now addressed. Many other soldiers, whatever their loyalty, simply found such veiled attacks unseemly.

Pope then expanded the meaning of these phrases in what amounted to his own sneering definition of McClellanism: he would describe its opposites. Rather than "taking strong positions," Pope declared that "[t]he strongest position a soldier should desire to occupy is the one from which he can most easily advance against the enemy;" instead of planning their own lines of retreat, soldiers should "study the probable lines of retreat of our opponents, and leave our own to take care of themselves." What Pope did here was to graft the various military and political criticisms of George B. McClellan's Peninsula Campaign onto another army serving on different topography in a completely different theater of war. The "cat-and-mouse" tactics which had heretofore defined fighting in the Shenandoah Valley required intelligent commanders to be especially aware of "lines of retreat" and "taking strong positions and holding them"—all of which Pope would soon learn to his dismay.

Finally, Pope may have had differences with McClellan's tactics, personality, or command style, but it was inappropriate for him to publicly proclaim these to largely rank-and-file bluecoats, or to hold them personally or their units responsible for, in effect, no more than obeying their commanders' orders. If there was a morale disease called "McClellanism," it principally afflicted higher levels of command. For Pope to have raised these criticisms army-wide simply compounded the blunder of raising them at all. Perhaps this lends credence to Pope's later claim that Stanton and Chase insisted on these passages, for they bear the mockery and scorn of a partisan stump speech—not an effective battle oration.

eds., *The Diary of George Templeton Strong: The Civil War, 1860-1865* (New York: The MacMillan Company, 1952), III: 297, 409.

Immediate Result

Historians are virtually unanimous in their view that Pope's AOC speech was a disaster.[16] Even for some of his soldier-audience's staunch Republicans and abolitionists, it was too much. "Pope criticizes and abuses McClellan with a will, showing in a man in his position no better taste than appeared in his proclamation," declared Harvard-educated gentleman Robert Gould Shaw, future colonel of the Fifty-Fourth Massachusetts Infantry. "He looks like what we have always understood he was,—a great *blow-hard,* with no lack of confidence in his own powers." [Italic original] Corporal Henry Newton Comey, perhaps more sensitive to his own army's narrative than to gentlemanly courtesies, pinpointed the underlying problem in Pope's speech:

> When we were in formation, General Pope made a speech. His remarks indicated that he thought his soldiers in the West were tougher fighters than we eastern soldiers. This is not a good way to inspire us, and we had no need to hear this from him.[17]

Legacy

Pope's AOC speech would probably rank first on any list of unsuccessful American battle speeches. Had he won the Battle of Second Manassas, perhaps his speech would have been remembered as but a minor blunder in an otherwise great career of triumph over Confederate generals Lee, Jackson and James Longstreet.

But Pope not only failed to win, *the way in which he lost* virtually guaranteed that this speech, especially its criticisms of McClellan, would permanently tarnish his career. It was Pope's failure to properly secure both his

16 Ropes, *Army Under Pope*, 9; Shelby Foote, *The Civil War: A Narrative, Fort Sumter to Perryville* (New York: Vintage Books, 1958), I: 529; Allen Nevins, *The War for the Union: War Becomes Revolution, 1862-1863* (New York: Charles Scribner's Sons, 1960), II: 150-152; James M. McPherson, *Battle Cry of Freedom: The Civil War Era* (New York: Ballantine Books, 1988), 524; Edward J. Stackpole, *From Cedar Mountain to Antietam* (Harrisburg, Pennsylvania: Stackpole Books, 1993), 14-15.

17 Robert Gould Shaw to Father, August 3, 1862, *Blue-Eyed Child of Fortune: The Civil War Letters of Colonel Robert Gould Shaw,* ed. Russell Duncan (Athens, Georgia: University of Georgia Press, 1992), 224-225; *A Legacy of Valor: The Memoirs and Letters of Captain Henry Newton Comey, 2nd Massachusetts Infantry,* ed. Lyman Richard Comey (Knoxville: The University of Tennessee Press, 2004), 58.

base and his lines of supply that deprived his hard-fighting army of critical resources during the battle. Moreover, once defeated frontally and then outflanked, it was Pope's utilization of "lines of retreat" that ultimately saved his army. Naturally, these ironies were not lost on Pope's contemporaries or later historians. In the long view, the speech, although given before the battle, represented a neat ironic coda to Pope's performance during the battle itself.

Leadership Principle

One leadership principle that requires perpetual vigilance—even at the cost of ceasing to lead—is protecting what should be *military* judgments from serving nakedly partisan ends. According to Pope's most recent biographer, Secretary of War Stanton, who was by then a passionate McClellan-hater, had "urged such public declarations so strongly that [Pope] felt constrained to go along." Pope's concurrence was not a question of proper subordination to civilian authority. Civilians make policy, soldiers obey, and while the line between policy and partisanship can blur, there are occasions when it is clearly crossed. Commanders, when instructed to do some partisan act that betrays common sense, decency, or the efficacy of their commands, may have a duty to resign—which is precisely what Pope should have threatened to do when Stanton insisted (to take Pope at his word) on dictating obviously partisan, and ultimately self-sabotaging, passages of the AOC speech. To many in the Lincoln administration, McClellan was more than just an unsuccessful general, he was a political threat; and, to some of the administration's more paranoid members, a menace to the Republic's existence. McClellan thus became a partisan issue for "hard warrior" politicians to deal with in partisan ways. That the soldier Pope allowed the politicians Stanton and Chase's partisanship to enter his speech might suggest cravenness, but more likely the fact that the general shared his civilian superiors' dislike of McClellan—and could not restrain himself. Pope, too, was a "McClellan-hater."[18]

Persuasive Strategy

Pope used several time-tested persuasive strategies to introduce the sought-after discontinuities. First was a carrot-and-stick approach that

---

18 Cozzens, *General John Pope*, 85.

alternated shame with incentives. "Let us look before us, and not behind," he urged. "Success and glory are in the advance, disaster and shame lurk in the rear." Indeed, he closed with another time-tested appeal, that of Legacy. Take his instruction, he insisted, and "it is safe to predict that your banners shall be inscribed with many a glorious deed and that your names will be dear to your countrymen forever." These were appropriate declarations.

But the power of these appeals was vitiated by Pope's rhetorical blunders, perhaps best termed *unpersuasive strategies*. Battle speeches require simplicity of message and the soldier-audience's complete engagement with the message's emotional world—for example, appeals to pride, shame, anger, or revenge. Sentiments that complicate the message or detract from emotional engagement—for example, by introducing controversial political themes or other divisive topics—immediately distracts the soldier-audience. The issue then shifts, as it did for the Army of Virginia, from accepting necessary exhortation to the unnecessary salting of wounds.

Pope blundered as well by attacking his soldier-audience's unit historical narrative. However badly demoralized, much of Pope's soldier-audience had fought hard battles, suffered casualties, remained in the field, and had shown great loyalty even to incompetent commanders. Pope needed to acknowledge that past, or, at the very least, avoid criticizing it. Even where a discontinuity of tactics or strategy is necessary—and for federal forces in the Shenandoah Valley, it surely was necessary—battle exhortations must strive for unity, and emphasize shared history, goals, and values. Even battle speeches that strive for discontinuity must always give soldiers their due. Valor, even when displayed under an earlier failed tactic or strategy, remains praiseworthy—and always will be praised by astute battle speechmakers.

Chapter Eleven

Stand or Die: General Walton Walker in Korea

I. Historical Background

On the morning of June 25, 1950, the North Korean Peoples Army (NKPA) crossed the 38th Parallel and attacked south with artillery, infantry, tanks and planes. Within hours frontier-stationed Republic of Korea (ROK) units and their handfuls of American advisors were besieged, overrun, or in full retreat. Cable traffic between Seoul, Tokyo (General Douglas MacArthur's occupation headquarters), Washington DC and United Nations officials in New York spat shock and dismay. This soon turned to indignation. "We are going to fight," a determined President Harry S Truman declared. UN Secretary-General Trygve Lie supposedly said, when informed of the attack, that "[t]his is war against the United Nations."[1]

In fact, President Harry Truman and his advisors had reached a narrower conclusion: Joseph Stalin was testing Western, specifically American, resolve to contain Communism. Twenty-four hours before the attack South Korea had been deemed marginal to United States security; now, it suddenly had become critical.[2]

---

1 Roy E. Appleman, *South to the Naktong, North to the Yalu* (Washington, D.C.: Center of Military History, United States Army, 1992 edition), 21 (NKPA attack), 37 (Lie quoted); Clay Blair, *The Forgotten War,* 67.

2 Appleman, *South to the Naktong,* 38. The "cloak" phrase is T.R. Fehrenbach's, *This Kind of War* (Dulles, Virginia: Potomac Books, 2008), 56.

Feverish diplomacy at the UN followed. On June 27 the Security Council recommended "that the Members of the United Nations furnish such assistance to the Republic of Korea as may be necessary to repel the armed attack and to restore international peace and security in the area." The United States now had the cover it sought in order to proceed: "the U.N. cloak."[3]

The military problem was with what lay beneath the cloak. The American military was no longer the victorious force that had defeated the Axis five years earlier. Drastic post-war budget cuts (rationalized in part by the belief that atomic bombs had reduced the need for a sizeable military) had downgraded the postwar army far below operational requirements; moreover, it was a badly-trained, poorly-disciplined and under-equipped force. Perhaps worse, the soldiers first sent to stem the NKPA tide knew little of the mission (merely "a police action," they were told) and even less about the enemy (who, it was assumed, "would bolt at the sight of American uniforms"). And implied here was another failure that General Matthew Ridgway would later term "truly inexcusable": a gross underestimation of the NKPA's numbers and combat capabilities. Coupled with a gross overestimation of the ROK's fighting effectiveness, the results should have been foreseeable: disaster.[4]

Overall responsibility for Korea was given to the legendary Douglas MacArthur, since 1945 America's viceroy in Japan. His available military assets—naval, air, and infantry—were initially limited to what were already in theater. For infantry, this meant dispatching the Japan-based Eighth Army, which epitomized the general condition of postwar American forces, and then some: softened by years of occupation duty and under-trained for combat, the average GI was in poor physical condition for a war that would be fought in human waste-fertilized rice paddies or on mountains, in summers of triple-digit heat and winters of double digits below zero. Moreover, the Eighth was supplied with World War II-vintage weapons that were either mismatched to NKPA capabilities or degraded from improper storage. Fed piecemeal into the maw of a fiercely-determined NKPA, many Americans and Koreans fought bravely; but

---

3 Appleman, *South to the Naktong*, 38. The "cloak" phrase is T.R. Fehrenbach's, *This Kind of War* (Dulles, Virginia: Potomac Books, 2008), 56.

4 Blair, *The Forgotten War*, 4-29 (Truman's dismantling of the postwar military); 44-45 (weakness of ROK); 55-57 (American overestimation of ROK); 97 ("bolt" statement); Matthew B. Ridgway, *The Korean War* (Garden City, New York: Doubleday & Company, Inc., 1967), 14.

many did not, and a new phrase entered the military's vocabulary: to "bug out" in an unauthorized mass retreat, sometimes panicked, while under fire.[5]

Commanding Eighth Army and reporting directly to MacArthur was sixty-one-year-old Texan and 1912 West Point graduate General Walton H. Walker. During World War II, he had risen in Patton's Third Army to become one its most distinguished Corps leaders. Despite his weight (Patton usually despised "fat" officers), Patton described Walker as "a very fine soldier." Walker seemed to return the praise in its most sincere form: his command style has been described as "Pattonesque," with his polished helmet and a jeep equipped with sirens and a "grab bar" that permitted him to stand as he sped from post to post. More importantly, Walker shared Patton's quality as a determined fighter. In person, however, he cut a far less imposing figure. "He was not an impressive individual," his pilot recalled. "He did not have physical 'command presence.' His chest had slipped; he was pudgy. He didn't talk much. All business. No chitchat." Unfortunately for Walker, one historian described him as "inept at public relations," and as a speechmaker, "melodramatic and absurd."[6]

When Walker gave the first iteration of his "Stand or Die" speech on July 29, 1950, there was no underrating the seriousness of the UN position in Korea: the NKPA owned the initiative, had long since captured Seoul, and continued to force American and ROK troops farther south and east toward the port of Pusan. To anyone whose knowledge of South Korea was limited to a map, it looked as if the NKPA might eventually force UN troops into the Sea of Japan.

But Walker and his soldier-audience knew better. Three days before making his "Stand or Die" speech, Walker's headquarters had issued instructions that the army should prepare to move to more defensible positions, there to regroup for a later offensive. This was sensible, and not just because of the American and ROK forces' many weaknesses: between the UN lines of late July and the Sea of Japan were the Naktong River and other natural barriers that "enclosed" a very large area, including airfields and the logistically indispensable port of Pusan. This line was soon dubbed the Pusan Perimeter, and it was perhaps the most naturally defensible line in South Korea. In fact,

---

5 Blair, *Forgotten War*, 48-50; Fehrenbach, *This Kind of War*, 175 (bug out), 66 (condition and morale of Task Force Smith, the first organized American resistance drawn from Eighth Army).

6 Blair, *Forgotten War*, 34-36 (Walker background); 241 (pilot's description); 168, 650 (Blair's assessment of Walker).

Walker's able defense of that perimeter would prove to be his strongest performance as army commander in Korea.[7]

But that was later. On July 29 Walker was a man under extreme pressure. His often-imperious superior Douglas MacArthur, not fully comprehending the situation on the ground, had flown to Korea two days before to meet with Walker and to insist that there be no further withdrawals. Walker was also unsettled by the poor morale of American forces, epitomized by recent and pervasive "bug outs." So, perhaps momentarily forgetful of what his men actually understood about both South Korean topography and the state of affairs, Walker decided it was time to stiffen spines—time for a battle speech.[8]

II. The Speech

General MacArthur was over here two days ago; he is thoroughly conversant with the situation. He knows where we are and what we have to fight with. He knows our needs and where the enemy is hitting the hardest. General MacArthur is doing everything possible to send reinforcements. A Marine unit and two regiments are expected in the next few days to reinforce us. Additional units are being sent over as quickly as possible.

We are fighting a battle against time. There will be no more retreating, withdrawal, or readjustment of the lines or any other term you choose. There is no line behind us to which we can retreat. Every unit must counterattack to keep the enemy in a state of confusion and off-balance. There will be no Dunkirk, there will be no Bataan, a retreat to Pusan would be one of the greatest butcheries in history. We must fight until the end. Capture by these people is worse than death itself. We will fight as a team. If some of us must die, we will die fighting together. Any man who gives ground may be personally responsible for the deaths of thousands of his comrades.

I want you to put this out to men in the Division. I want everybody to understand that we are going to hold this line. We are going to win.

— Best surviving paraphrase of General Walton H. Walker's "Stand or Die" speech.[9]

---

7   Appleman, *South to the Naktong*, 205-206.

8   Appleman, *South to the Naktong*, 207.

9   Appleman, *South to the Naktong*, 207-208. For clarity, I have created a new paragraph beginning with the words, "We are fighting a battle against time."

III. Parsing the Speech

Walker first attempted to build the confidence of his soldier-audience by trading on the authority and prestige of five-star General of the Army Douglas MacArthur. After all, the very name "MacArthur" long had been established as a worldwide symbol of American military genius and national resolve. Walker hitched these memes to his message by declaring that this living legend was "over here two days ago," was "thoroughly conversant with the situation," knows "where we are and what we have to fight with" as well as "our needs and where the enemy is hitting the hardest." Moreover, there were other reasons for confidence: reinforcements, including "Marines" (a metonym containing yet more confidence-building memes) were "being sent over as quickly as possible." Few could argue with the sheer conventionality of these passages: they amounted to an ordinary Midst-of-Battle speech with its conventions of Sitrep, Inspiring Confidence and Hope.[10]

Walker might have remained on firm ground with his next sentence—"We are fighting a battle against time"—had he put a period after it and left the room. After all, no matter what MacArthur might say (or anyone else intend), UN forces were in effect doing exactly that: purchasing time by reluctantly yielding real estate in the hope that supplies, reinforcements, or a more-defensible position lay in the immediate future. To "fight a battle against time" is a phrase that might lend urgency to whatever message might follow, but few would argue that the UN's situation was not then urgent.

But the statement that Walker did invest with this urgency represented the most serious order that a soldier can ever give or receive, one that should be reserved for circumstances so extreme and apparent as to be instantly grasped by both the leader and the led. With the very next sentence—"There will be no more retreating, withdrawal, or readjustment of the lines or any other term you

---

10 MacArthur was responsible for two of the most important Speechlets of World War II: "I shall return" after evacuating Corregidor in early 1942, and "I have returned" when he returned to Leyte in October 1944. (See Chapter Fifteen.) Images of MacArthur smoking his corncob pipe or wading ashore at Leyte ("I have returned") enhanced his celebrity; Miller, *Words and Deeds*: Sitrep has been discussed above; Inspiring Confidence is defined on 158-159; Hope will be found on 263 and is defined thus: "Unless death or capture is inevitable (and soldiers can be persuaded to accept them), a way out of the predicament must be shown or hinted at. In short, in order to prevent flight or destruction, soldiers must be given some hope that fighting on might produce a better result."

choose"—Walker's speech began to earn its sarcastic nickname: "Stand or Die."[11]

Many soldiers greeted this order with disbelief largely because—as was apparent to men actually engaged in the fighting as well as to those who could read a map—Walker seemed to be calling for the "last full measure" without the grave, reality-based justifications usually behind such orders. Indeed, Walker's exhortation was virtually irrelevant to the topographical reality as well as the overall situation. First, just rearward was the eminently-defensible line of the Naktong River, which would eventually form the most important barrier of the Pusan Perimeter. Second, in view of this fact, absolutely nothing would be gained by making "last stands" on the far-less-defensible terrain in front of the Naktong. Third, such "last stands" were likely to be very short ones: as was known to every combat infantryman in Korea, the surging NKPA method was to isolate and overwhelm units by flooding their flanks; what UN forces needed in order to recover their stride was a continuous, defensible line, behind which they could regroup, be reinforced, and prepare for a later offensive.[12]

Finally, on this last point, Walker had already zeroed the gravity inherent in his "stand or die" command (and sowed considerable confusion besides) because his own headquarters had, before MacArthur's visit, already issued orders for Eighth Army to prepare for a withdrawal. Thus, his declaration that "[a]ny man who gives ground may be personally responsible for the deaths of tens of thousands of his comrades" struck some listeners as contradictory, and caused others to wonder whether the first man to "give ground" was none other than Walker himself.[13]

Walker's earlier declaration—"There is no line behind to which we can retreat"—sealed his speech's failure. Here he baldly asserted a fact that his soldier-audience knew was not true. Indeed, Walker knew that it was not true,

---

11 Appleman, *South to Naktong*, 205-206. Readers will note that the phrase "Stand or Die" does not appear in Walker's speech. One indication of soldier-audience skepticism is the sudden and anonymous circulation of a nickname that is not included in the speech itself. These nicknames should be understood as representing how a soldier-audience would respond to the speaker if it were not otherwise barred from doing so by rule, etiquette, or opportunity.

12 These reasons for questioning Walker's facts and assumptions were extracted from two principal sources: see Blair, *Forgotten War*, 168-170 and Appleman, *South to Naktong*, 205-209.

13 Appleman, *South to Naktong*, 205-206.

and his soldier-audience knew that he knew. But by asserting it Walker appeared to be using the gravest of orders (stand or die) as a mere exhortatory manipulation. Knowing what his audience knew, one could only assume either that Walker could not read a map (and no one believed that), or that he was hyperbolizing at the expense of something that, for soldiers, is a solemn business. Whichever his soldier-audience might believe, Walker's prestige suffered.

And it is here that I wish to focus on Walker's second, related error exemplified by this speech: his flawed use of historical analogies. This is important because the inappropriate use of historical analogies is a common problem in both battle and political speeches. By invoking specific grand, tragic, or decisive past events, the speechmaker runs the risks of unnecessary hyperbole or a failed analogy and thereby invites criticism, disdain, or ridicule. And Walker seemed to invite all three when he declared, "There will be no Dunkirk, there will be no Bataan."

To understand how absurd these analogies struck Walker's listeners, one must recapture something of their immediate, or at least quite recent, experience. Both Dunkirk (1940) and Bataan (1942) had occurred not just within living memory, but within the *adult* experience of many listeners. (Indeed, a few of Walker's own subordinates and probably a number of enlisted personnel were survivors of the Bataan Death March.) Both Dunkirk and Bataan were metonyms for military disaster. The rescue of the British Expeditionary Force (BEF) at Dunkirk by the Royal Navy and an armada of private craft might stand for British grit, but it also stood for near- catastrophe: the British had become trapped on Dunkirk's beaches after failing to stop Hitler's push through the Ardennes. For Americans, Bataan signaled something much worse: when General Jonathan Wainwright yielded Corregidor Island to the Japanese in May 1942, it was the largest surrender of U.S. forces in history. But it was the surrender's awful sequel that Americans had found especially embittering—and frightening for soldiers now facing the specter of a reprise: the Japanese forced some 75,000 surrendered men (almost 12,000 Americans, the rest Filipinos) on a homicidal march over 85 miles to POW camps. This was followed by years of brutal captivity.[14]

---

14   William Edwin Dyess, *Bataan Death March: A Survivor's Account*, intro. Stanley L. Falk (Lincoln, Nebraska: Bison Books, 2002), xi-xii; Blair identifies two commanders as

Why would Walker's men find these historical analogies inappropriate? After all, the UN forces were retreating toward the Sea of Japan. Who could say that they would not find themselves stranded helplessly on a Korean beach? And the NKPA had already amply demonstrated its own homicidal policy toward surrendered men: when UN forces occasionally managed to return to areas once occupied by the NKPA, they often discovered the bodies of GIs, hands bound by wire behind their backs and shot in the head. No one doubted that if the NKPA could force the surrender of all UN and ROK forces, a similar fate might await many. These were all terribly frightening possibilities.[15]

But, for a variety of reasons, these were not probable scenarios. The reasons were simple: 1950 was neither 1940 Europe nor 1942 Philippines. There had been nothing surrounding Dunkirk as strongly defensible as the Naktong River. In 1940 the Germans had held air superiority over Dunkirk, thus precluding British resupply, but in 1950 Korea the UN had near-absolute air superiority. In 1940, no realistic amount of time that the BEF might have gained by battling Germans to the water's edge could have brought relief from Britain to British forces; but in 1950 Korea, as the case proved over the next several months, nations with abundant resources would be sending substantial UN reinforcements steaming toward the theater. Even if an evacuation were necessary, the presence of the U.S. Navy (including the powerful Seventh Fleet) coupled with air power would have assured a relatively smooth evacuation. So much for the Dunkirk analogy.

Walker's use of the Bataan analogy likewise falls apart: first, unlike in 1942, in 1950 the United States had atomic weapons. The same president who had twice ordered their use against another Asian power still occupied the White House. Faced with a catastrophic surrender of the American Eighth Army, would Truman (or any American president) allow a repeat of the Bataan Death March without making credible threats to annihilate those nations (North Korea, Red China, and the Soviet Union) thought to be responsible? And whatever Truman might actually do, would Communist decision makers run the risk of atomic war in exchange for the *en masse* brutalization of UN forces under the scrutiny of a media that was now more global than had been the case in 1942?

---

having survived Bataan: Dennis M. Moore, commander of the 15th Infantry, and Harold Keith Johnson, commander of the 3/8 battalion.

15 Fehrenbach, *This Kind of War*, 87, 95.

These failures of Walker's historical analogies are not only apparent in retrospect, they were evident to many listeners at the time. Thus, they weakened his speech and diminished him personally, because, again, his soldier-audience assumed (probably correctly) that Walker himself knew better.

Immediate Result

Among the troops, Walker's speech was greeted with widespread skepticism. UN forces were being overwhelmed by the NKPA's tactics, which were a repeating sequence of very rapid mini-Cannae-type envelopments, in which units were quickly outflanked and surrounded. Given this reality, obeying Walker's order was virtually impossible. One American commander declared that his troops understood the order as meaning, "Stay and die where you are." Roy Appleman, who recorded this comment while writing the army's official history of the Korean War, added that he had "listened to many similar comments among officers and men of the Eighth Army with respect to this order." Other historians who have reviewed Walker's remarks have been even more unsparing, describing it as "inaccurate or silly" and "pointless."

As might have been predicted, whatever Walker intended, the speech and its embedded order had almost no effect. The withdrawal of UN forces continued—fortunately—until the Pusan Perimeter was established and stabilized. Over the ensuing six weeks, defending the Perimeter against constant NKPA assaults would prove difficult. But Walker's smart tactical management, assisted by superb intelligence, air supremacy, and the advantages of interior lines, held the Perimeter until MacArthur answered the NKPA invasion with one of his own—at Inchon.[16]

---

16 Appleman, *South to the Naktong*, 208, see especially footnote 70. In fairness to Walker, Appleman cites one case of a commander and his unit who experienced "a great sense of relief when the order reached them." Here Walker succeeded in putting some moxie into his troops. But this was clearly a minority view; Blair, *The Forgotten War,*168; however, for a more sympathetic treatment of Walker's speech—not so much how it was received but for Walker's motives in giving it—see Robert Leckie, *Conflict: The History of the Korean War, 1950-1953* (Cambridge, Massachusetts: Da Capo Press, 1996), 95-97.

Legacy

Failed speeches produce few imitations. However, in assessing Walker's "Stand or Die" speech, one must be careful not to confuse the legacy of the speech with that of the speechmaker.

The legacy of Walker's speech was that it was utterly emblematic of the confusion that governed the UN command during its first two months in Korea. Viewed in a wider context, "Stand or Die" can now be understood as taking in everything from MacArthur's limitations in attempting to manage from Tokyo the fast-moving events in Korea to the demoralized condition of both American and ROK forces.

However, Walker's personal legacy would, despite the setback of "Stand or Die," be a very different matter. His best days in Korea lay immediately ahead, as he would prove over the next six weeks in his spirited, decisive defense of the Pusan Perimeter.[17]

Leadership Principle

The "Stand or Die" speech was a direct consequence of Walker's inability to confront MacArthur over military policy (more below). The day before MacArthur's visit on July 27, Walker's headquarters had issued a prepare-to-withdraw order; after MacArthur's visit, everything changed, at least for several days, until the realities on the ground again overwhelmed the UN command. One historian has commented that Walker's Korean War nickname—Bulldog Walker—was deserved except in one respect: "He would not challenge his superior, MacArthur. In that relationship he groveled, lest he lose his job." One direct result of this groveling was the "Stand or Die" speech.[18]

Persuasive Strategy

Walker's speech certainly contained traditional and unobjectionable elements of battle speech persuasion: his use of authority (MacArthur's

---

17 Fehrenbach, *This Kind of War*, 146; Walker's defense of the Perimeter is not without critics; see Blair, *The Forgotten War*, 555. The controversy revolves around whether Walker's successful defense can be attributed to his management or mistakes by the NKPA.

18 Blair, *The Forgotten War*, 554.

prestige) to instill confidence; employing a voice of urgency; and appeals to comradeship ("We will fight as a team"). But at the heart of Walker's persuasive strategy were historical analogies. Most of Walker's hyperbolic declarations flowed directly from his citations of the disaster and near-tragedy of Dunkirk and the unmitigated tragedy of Bataan.

For battle and political speechmakers, the use of historical analogies is seductive. By merely uttering a word the speaker can appear to appeal to historical "fact" while simultaneously charging his argument with powerful emotional associations. At the heart of historical analogies are metonyms that in turn carry memes. Using an obviously absurd example, but one which illustrates the power of historical analogies, consider a speech that Walker might have given, had he had a more poetic bent. It would have been a hyper-concise version of the speech that he did give:

> Dunkirk,
> Bataan,
> Awaits in Pusan. No more withdrawals!

The mere mention of the names "Dunkirk" and "Bataan" become their own propositions in the above quasi-syllogism. The names are enthymematic because Walker had only to utter the words and the audience would supply the meanings. And Walker deployed them in a meaningful sequence. First, the UN forces would be trapped on a Korean beach (Dunkirk); then, a merciless enemy would slaughter them as POWs (Bataan). The underlying emotional appeals were powerful. Bataan was an American humiliation; the survivors' tales had provoked national fury. However, for soldiers facing capture by the NKPA (and a bullet in the head), Bataan could only summon the worst fears of the Death March. At least, it was Walker's hope that his analogies would work that way.

Historical analogies are so common in persuasive argument that both Walker's use of them and several more general aspects deserve further comment.

Walker's use of Dunkirk and Bataan may have been inapplicable to his particular circumstances; but, as I have argued throughout this book, battle speeches are cultural artifacts of their times, and Walton Walker was very much a man of his times. His generation had just passed through the historic events of World War II, and Walker was not alone in picturing the Korean War in a Second World War frame. For example, in Independence, Missouri, Harry

Truman, after being informed of the NKPA invasion, recalled his return to Washington:

> I had time to think aboard the plane. In my generation, this was not the first occasion in which the strong had attacked the weak. I recalled some earlier instances: Manchuria, Ethiopia, Austria. I remembered how each time that the democracies failed to act it had encouraged the aggressors to keep going ahead. Communism was acting in Korea just as Hitler, Mussolini and the Japanese had acted ten, fifteen, and twenty years earlier. [19]

World War II analogies were also used by everyone from Chairman of the Joint Chiefs of Staff General Omar Bradley to editorialists at the *New York Times*. Indeed, just two days before the "Stand or Die" speech, Walker was at lunch with Douglas MacArthur when the latter declared—in a voice loud enough for others to hear—his determination that his mission would not end in "a Korean Dunkerque."[20]

Speechmakers who use tragic or dramatic historical analogies do so at their own peril. Tragic analogies (for example, Bataan) soon become sacrosanct; their incorrect use can trivialize the original event or draw the current comparison into the realm of the ridiculous. Dramatic analogies (for example, Dunkirk) require equally dramatic comparisons. Speechmakers who take a less-than-epochal current event and analogize it with some historical event that was epochally tragic or dramatic risk losing the audience in the same way that Walker lost his: through skepticism and ridicule.

However, in fairness to the practice of using inappropriate historical analogies, one must concede that they are often successfully used, typically in two general circumstances. First, where the audience does not consist of historians, and thus will pay far more attention to the memes carried by the analogy than any factual debate about the analogy's "appropriateness." Second, where the memes carried by historical analogies are so powerful, so charged with emotion, and thus so utterly irresistible to speechmakers—the analogies of "Hitler," "Nazi," or "Gestapo" come to mind—that their pervasive use has

---

19 Harry S Truman, *Memoirs by Harry S Truman, Volume Two: Years of Trial and Hope* (Garden City, N.Y.: Doubleday & Company, Inc., 1956), II: 332-333.

20 Omar Bradley, *A General's Life: An Autobiography*, by General of the Army Omar N. Bradley (New York: Simon and Schuster, 1983), 535; "Warning to the West," *New York Times*, June 26, 1950; Appleman, *South to Naktong*, 207.

actually (and probably for the first time in rhetoric) produced "laws" that attempt to predict *when* these analogies will be used. In 1990, intellectual property lawyer Michael W. Godwin formulated what since has been dubbed Godwin's Law: "As an online discussion grows longer, the probability of a comparison involving Nazis or Hitler approaches one." Thus, by overuse and inappropriate application, the Nazi analogy today verges on being a spent force. (Unless one is dealing with bona fide Nazis.)[21]

21 Mike Godwin, "Meme, Counter-meme," www.wired.com/wired/archive.2.10/godwin.
if.html. Accessed September 24, 2009. Godwin refers to online discussions as opposed to speeches. But the pervasiveness of the "Nazi" meme, coupled with the fact that it has now become the property of all political colorations, means that Nazi analogies, once used gingerly by a generation that actually understood the unique evil of Nazism, now deluge public space. The signage and speeches of mass demonstrations, whether protesting the Iraq War or Obama's health care proposals, bear testimony to this. Moreover, Nazi analogies have begun to appear in speeches or comments by elected representatives dealing with otherwise mundane matters.

Chapter Twelve

Beyond Rhetoric:
Evil and the Failure of Battle Speeches

I. Historical Background

On March 30, 1941, some 250 members of the German High Command, together with Army, Navy, and Air Force commanders and staff, gathered in Berlin's Reich Chancellery. They sat by rank on long rows of chairs for nearly three hours as Adolf Hitler delivered a pre-invasion speech for the planned blitzkrieg on Russia. The attack was almost three months away, but Hitler had decided it was time to impress this "cream of the German officer corps" with his own—and what would become, at least officially, the military's own—ideological rationale for the looming war in the East. It was to be, as Colonel-General Franz Halder's notes of the speech (excerpted below) revealed, "a war of extermination," and those to be exterminated were "Bolshevik commissars and Communist intelligentsia." One participant recalled that "[the audience] sat there before [Hitler] in stubborn silence, a silence broken only twice—when the assembly rose as he entered through a rear door and walked up to the rostrum, and later when he departed the same way. Otherwise, not a hand moved and not a word was spoken but by him."[1]

---

1 Walter Warlimont, *Inside Hitler's Headquarters, 1939-1945*, trans. R. H. Perry (New York: Frederick A. Praeger, 1962), 160-161; "cream of the German officer corps" is Warlimont's phrase. No recording or full transcript of Hitler's speech has been found.

General Walter Warlimont, who would ultimately reduce Hitler's intent to written orders, recalled that for some five weeks after the speech there was a headquarters' "conspiracy of silence" about the speech. What did this silence portend? First, probably fear: not only of Hitler and for one's own career, but also the fears of actually adopting written directives that for the first time would implicate directly the *Wehrmacht* in documentable war crimes. As late as June 1939 the *Wehrmacht's* Army Service Regulations, counterparts of which probably existed in professional militaries around the world, provided that "war was waged only against the armed forces of the enemy" and that "prisoners were not to be mishandled" and could be "killed only if they tried to escape."[2]

First, Hitler's wish to exterminate "Communist intelligentsia" meant murdering Soviet civilians—intelligentsias usually consisting of civilian intellectual and political elites. But killing "Bolshevik commissars" meant murdering Soviet prisoners of war. The Germans never really defined "commissar" beyond the fact that they were uniformed "political leaders in Russian units" whose sleeves bore "a red star with a gold hammer and sickle." There was much that the Germans seemed not to know about how Stalin controlled his army: *commissars* were generally found in battalions or regiments; *politruks* were political officers found in companies and below; while *komsorgs*—komsomols (roughly, Stalin's equivalent to the Hitler Youth)—could be found anywhere. Unfortunately for many in the Red Army, it was the politruks who served as "the central figure for all educational work among soldiers." In fact, although *politruks* spied on and propagandized their units, they were also soldiers. They might teach military skills—riflery or drill—and when hostilities commenced they would shoulder as much of the fighting as any other Soviet soldier. In sum, by international law and custom, they were soldiers, and thus entitled to the protections afforded surrendered men. However, events would prove that German vagueness in defining

---

2 Warlimont, *Inside Hitler's Headquarters*, 163; Eugene Davidson, *The Trial of the Germans: An Account of the Twenty-two Defendants before the International Military Tribunal at Nuremberg* (New York: The MacMillan Company, 1966), 339. Some Germans argued that because the Soviet Union had not signed the 1929 Geneva Convention on Prisoners of War (the prevailing standard for treating POWs humanely), Russians could not benefit from its protections. This argument was demolished in September 1941 when Admiral Wilhelm Canaris' office produced a memorandum of law demonstrating that Soviet POWs were not exempt from protections of the convention. However, the memo was ignored. Davidson, 89-90.

"commissar" helped transform a criminal order into an instrument for mass murder.[3]

On May 6, 1941, Warlimont's hopes that a combination of colleague reluctance and the preoccupations of war would cause the Fuhrer's March 30 speech to be forgotten were suddenly dashed. He received a proposed order entitled *"General Instructions for dealing with political leaders and for the co-ordinated execution of the task allotted on 31 [sic] March 1941."* [Italic original] The draft rule declared that "political authorities and leaders (commissars) constitute a special menace to the security of the troops and the pacification of the conquered territory," and thus

> [i]f such persons are captured by the troops or otherwise apprehended they will be brought before an officer who has disciplinary powers of punishment. The latter will summon two military witnesses (officer or NCO rank) and establish that the person captured or apprehended is a political personality or leader (Commissar). If adequate proof of his political position is forthcoming, the officer will forthwith order his execution and ensure that it is carried out.

As to Commissars in particular:

> It is of particular importance that they should be immediately detected and segregated since they will be the ones primarily responsible for continuing propaganda if sent back to Germany as prisoners of war. They should be liquidated if possible at prisoner-of-war collecting points or at the latest on passage through the transit camps.

This draft order classed both civilian leaders ("political authorities") and commissars ("leaders") together as eligible for immediate execution, subject to a rather perfunctory field formality of "military witnesses." Given the vast geographical scope of the proposed blitzkrieg, such an order could mandate the

---

3 Warlimont, *Inside Hitler's Headquarters*, 163; Chris Bellamy, *Absolute War: Soviet Russia In the Second World War* (New York: Alfred A Knopf, 2007), 26; Bellamy points out that the *politruk* "was merely an adviser and did not have to countersign orders," thus suggesting the far greater authority of Commissars; Catherine Merridale, *Ivan's War: Life and Death in the Red Army, 1939-1945* (New York: Picador, 2006), 63-66.

murder of every village official in occupied Russia, whether or not they were involved in anti-German activities.[4]

In sum—and by design—the draft provided that Soviet politicals of all grades were to be treated as Jews: their status, unappealable, would merit near-instant death. This flowed directly from Hitler's hallucinatory convictions that he had expressed ever since the publication of *Mein Kampf* (1925/26) that Bolsheviks were either Jews or irremediably under their control. Just before his March 30 speech Hitler had ordered his High Command to remember that when drafting guidelines for dealing with soon-to-be conquered eastern territories, "[t]he Jewish-Bolshevik intelligentsia, as the oppressor in the past, must be liquidated."[5]

Warlimont was apparently successful in slightly diluting the Commissar Order, key excerpts of which appear below. Now "only" commissars (at least on paper) found on the battlefield or engaged in acts of resistance were to be "finished immediately;" others, including civilian leadership, were (at least on paper) left outside the Commissar Order's reach. On June 6, 1941, Field Marshal Wilhelm Keitel, Commander-in-Chief of the High Command (whose relationship with Hitler had earned him the whispered nickname *Nickesel*: "a toy donkey that nods his head") affixed his signature to the notorious *Kommissarbefehl*, or Commissar Order. Unbeknownst to Keitel, his signature would also help frame his death warrant at the postwar Nuremberg trials.[6]

---

4   Warlimont, *Inside Hitler's Headquarters*, 163-164.

5   As quoted in Bellamy, *Absolute* War, 24.

6   A complete consideration of the Commissar Order would have to include the equally notorious Maintenance and Discipline Order issued three weeks earlier. This exempted German soldiers from punishment for most crimes they committed (were expected to commit?) against Soviet civilians. It charged officers contemplating prosecution of soldiers to remember that "the collapse of Germany in 1918 [and] the subsequent sufferings of the German people and the fight against National Socialism which cost the blood of innumerable supporters of the movement were caused primarily by Bolshevik influence." Davidson, *Trial of the Germans*, 336-338, 329. Moreover, the Commissar Order with its mention of "Bolshevism" was also intended as an anti-Semitic measure. In "War in the East and the Extermination of the Jews," Andreas Hillgruber noted that "Until the turn of 1938/1939 the slogan of 'Jewish-Bolshevism' remained central in National-Socialist agitation. But then, the temporary tactical need for a rapprochement with the Soviet Union dictated the separation of anti-Semitic propaganda from anti-Bolshevik slogans for two and a half years…." Andreas Hillgruber, "War in the East and the Extermination of the Jews," available at www.1yadvashem.org/untoldstories/documents/studies/andreas_hillgruber.pdf. Accessed September 11, 2009.

II. The Speeches

Clash between two ideologies... Bolshevism equals a social criminality. Communism [is a] *tremendous danger for the future. We must get away from the standpoint of soldierly comradeship. The Communist is no comrade, either before or after. It is a war of extermination... We do not wage war in order to conserve the enemy. . . . The extermination of the Bolshevik commissars and Communist intelligentsia. . . . The battle must be conducted against the poison of decay. It is not a question of military courts. The leaders must know what is involved. They must take the lead in this struggle! The troops must defend themselves with the methods with which they are attacked. Communists and secret service personnel are criminals and must be treated as such. The troops should not get out of control of their leaders. The leader must give the orders in accordance with the feelings of the troops. The leaders must make sacrifices and overcome their scruples.*

—Notes describing Adolf Hitler's March 30, 1941, Pre-Invasion (Soviet Union) Speech, as taken by Colonel-General Franz R. Halder

Staff Command Secret Document	*June 6, 1941*

Staff Command Secret Document   *June 6, 1941*
Chief Only
Only Through Officer
High Command of the Wehrmacht
WFST Div. L (VI/Qu)
No. 44822/41 g.K Chiefs

Guidelines for the Treatment of Political Commissars

In the fight against Bolshevism it is not to be expected that the enemy will act in accordance with the principles of humanity or international law. In particular, the political commissars of all kinds, who are the real bearers of resistance, can be expected to mete out treatment to our prisoners that is full of hate, cruel and inhuman.

The army must be aware of the following:

1. In this battle it would be mistaken to show mercy or respect for international law towards such elements. They constitute a danger to our own security and to the rapid pacification of the occupied territories.

2. The barbaric, Asiatic fighting methods are originated by the political commissars. Action must therefore be taken against them immediately, without

further consideration, and with all severity. Therefore, when they are picked up in
battle or resistance, they are, as a matter of principle, to be finished immediately
with a weapon.

— Extract from Commissar Order[7]

III. Parsing the Speeches

Hitler's March 30 speech to his commanders was a Pre-Invasion Speech, while the Commissar Order was an Instructional Speech. Although these are different genres of battle speech defined by their own sets of conventions, they share an important connection (aside from historical causation—the Order resulted from Hitler's speech): a statement of the *reasons* why men are being asked to invade or obey. One of the Pre-Invasion Speech's most important conventions is that of Historical Review. Here the speechmaker in some way reviews the war's history in an effort to justify the invasion. As the proposed invasion may represent huge risks in blood and treasure, so must the Historical Review given the soldier-audience be equally grand. And Hitler, the master of the historical narrative, did not disappoint. He informed his soldier-audience that the war would be nothing less than a "Clash between two ideologies" that, by his lights, mandated "a war of extermination."[8]

An Instructional Speech—a speech intended to disclose "the *operation* of existing things or how things *should* operate in the future" [Italics original]—is similar to a Pre-Invasion Speech in that it often contains a Rationalization convention, in which reasons are given for the instruction. (The chief difference is that Rationalization does not require historical narrative, although Instructional Speeches often use one.) And the centerpiece of both Hitler's and Warlimont's speeches was their rationalizations for killing commissars. Both relied on the ancient military idea of reciprocity in which POWs are likened to hostages, thus holding them against ill treatment meted out by the enemy's

---

7 Halder notes quoted in Dr. Jurgen Forster, "The Wehrmacht and the War of Extermination against the Soviet Union," available at Yad Vashem website, www1.yadvashem.org/untoldstories/documents/studies/Jurgen_Forster.pdf. Accessed on August 31, 2009. Excerpt from Commissar Order available at Yad Vashem website, www1.yadvashem.org/about_holocaust/documents/part3/doc170.html.   Accessed   on August 31, 2009.

8 Miller, *Words and Deeds*, 105-108, 145-152.

wardens. Therefore Hitler declared, "The [German] troops must defend themselves with the methods with which they are attacked;" and Warlimont rationalized the Order by declaring that

> [i]n the fight against Bolshevism it is not to be expected that the enemy will act in accordance with the principles of humanity or international law. In particular, the political commissars of all kinds, who are the real bearers of resistance, can be expected to mete out treatment to [German] prisoners that is full of hate, cruel and inhuman.

Thus, the shared conclusive direction: for Hitler, it was "extermination;" for Warlimont, to "finish [them] immediately with a weapon." Warlimont's bulky phrase, with its implication of one-execution-at-a-time, is one of several "improvements" he introduced in an effort to limit the scope of Hitler's wishes.

Warlimont had other, more important successes (again, on paper) in delimiting his Fuehrer's policy. To grasp these one must first understand that Hitler's description of the war as a "[c]lash between two ideologies" was (probably—see below) intentionally incomplete. More accurately, Hitler understood the looming conflict as a bio-ideological struggle, that is, that the basis of the ideas on which he planned to extirpate Bolshevism was the product of enemy biology—race. Although, for the important reasons discussed below, in his March 30 speech Hitler declined to emphasize his racial ideology, years of National Socialist propaganda had inseparably joined the words "Jewish" and "Bolshevik."[9]

Thus for those soldiers already inclined to the charms of National Socialism, Hitler would rely on enthymematic argument, the speechmaker's friend: "Bolshevik" meant "Jew." For these soldiers, liquidation was logical. Why force racial enemies into Communist-style "re-education" camps when one could not be "re-educated" out of one's race? Moreover, given Hitler's objective of *Lebensraum* (Living Space), which would necessitate dispossession of the Slavs and some depopulation thereof (by eliminating their leadership classes), POWs were not being held for any other reason than eventual death, enslavement, or some other service to the Reich. Soldiers in sympathy with National Socialism understood these objectives as being enfolded in Hitler's statement that "We do not wage war in order to conserve the

---

9   Hillgruber, "War in the East and the Extermination of the Jews," 113.

enemy." There was no point in "conserving" an enemy whose land would be taken, leadership killed, and lower orders enslaved.[10]

Thus Hitler emphasized the enemy's inherent evil. Bolshevism might be an idea, but it was also a "social criminality." Hitler immediately intensified this inherent evil by employing the same race-allusive medical metaphors that he had used throughout his political career: the enemy as bacilli. In fighting Bolsheviks the Germans fought the "poison of decay." Bolshevism was a bacterial infection, and the battle against infection is zero-sum, for the infected host can only gain from the death of each bacillus.[11]

By contrast, Warlimont's racist rationale was so toned down as to barely meet the definition. First, he characterized the enemy as "inhuman;" next, he referred to the enemy's ethnicity—"Asiatic"—the very mention of which he must have thought was sufficient to summon ideas of "Asiatic hordes" inflicting torture, death, and unimaginable captivity. (Perhaps not trusting to his soldier-audience's imagination, he also described the likely treatment of German POWs as "full of hate, cruel and inhuman.") While Warlimont's orders were rare in modern warfare (but not unprecedented historically, given the occurrence of No Quarter orders), his "racial" rationalizations were utterly conventional within the long history of battle speeches. If Hitler downplayed race for the reasons discussed below, Warlimont sought to reduce it even further.

However, parsing these similarities and differences begs an important question: why would either Hitler or Warlimont dance around the subject of race? Except for Hitler's well-known code words, the March 30 speech is, based on Halder's notes, silent about race; without knowing more, a reader might assume that Hitler referred only to ideology. Why not simply declare, as Hitler had on so many prior occasions, that Bolsheviks were Jews and Bolshevism was Jewish, and that commissars, the avatars of Jewish-Bolshevism, should be killed on that account alone?

---

10 Adolf Hitler, *Mein Kampf*, trans. Ralph Manheim (Boston: Houghton Mifflin Company, 1971), 138, 646, 653-654 (*Lebensraum* doctrine). Hitler's conviction that *Lebensraum* was essential to German survival is even more explicit in his second, unpublished book. – see Gerhard L. Weinberg, ed., *Hitler's Second Book: The Unpublished Sequel to Mein Kampf by Adolf Hitler* (New York: Enigma Books, 2003), 17-24.

11 In Hitler's narrative, metaphors of disease and parasites were often combined: "[The Jew] is and remains the typical parasite, a sponger who like a noxious bacillus keeps spreading as soon as a favorable medium invites him." Hitler, *Mein Kampf*, 305.

Absent the racial motive, the Commissar Order becomes absurd on its face. First, by definition, Soviet POWs would be under exclusive German control. How could Warlimont reasonably argue that surrendered men, segregated by rank, concentrated in presumably isolated and well-guarded POW camps, "constitute a danger to our own security and the rapid pacification of the occupied territories"? Second, while reciprocity of treatment had always been a universal principle of POW policy, at least at the trench level, how could Hitler and Warlimont have ordered reciprocal killing three months before hostilities even began? Significantly, neither speechmaker even bothered with any "if, then" mechanism, as in "if commissars kill our surrendered men, then we will kill them."

The answer here is that Hitler's speech and (to a far lesser degree) Warlimont's order are only explicable by the logic of National Socialist racial theory; the other rationalizations given by Hitler and Warlimont were mere fig leaves. Hitler demanded an exterminatory policy, and of course Warlimont obliged his master, albeit limiting its scope as far as he was able. But why provide any fig leaves?

The reason will be found in a major, although half-submerged assumption, present in both speeches: Hitler's great fear (and perhaps Warlimont's great hope, or so he claimed in his postwar memoirs) was that the army would not execute this order. In fact, when this issue is posed alongside Halder's notes, Hitler's concern with his military's potential reluctance actually consumed more words than his rationale for committing the murders. And no great inference is necessary to understand, by the inclusion of these appeals in Hitler's speech, that the "enemy" was as much his soldier-audience's obsolete notions of chivalry and human rights as it was the commissars themselves:

We must get away from the standpoint of soldierly comradeship;

The Communist is no comrade, either before or after;

We do not wage war to conserve the enemy;

The leaders must know what is involved. They must take the lead in the struggle!

The leaders must make sacrifices and overcome their scruples.

Warlimont incorporated the same idea, but stripped it of drama and reduced it to a sentence: "In this battle it would be mistaken to show mercy or respect for international law towards such elements." The word "exterminate" does not appear in Warlimont's order.

Hitler's comments revealed his insecurity about the *Wehrmacht*. It had not (yet) been transformed into an instrument of National Socialist *ideology*. No matter how strongly implied in his speech, Hitler was not yet prepared, nor would Warlimont specify, what "sacrifices" were required to overcome what "scruples." To dwell on definitions would be bad speechmaking, only serving to remind the soldier-audience that which the speechmakers wanted it to forget. It should be remembered that these speeches were made in the first half of 1941. Russia had not yet been invaded; thus, *Einsatzgruppen* (SS Special Operation Units) had not yet swept behind the German advance, shooting an estimated 1.5 million Jews; nor had *Lebensraum's* brutal anti-Slavic policies been implemented. Although Germany's armed forces had long been compromised *institutionally*—the personal loyalty oath to Hitler, key personnel changes, and Hitler's assumption of supreme command had assured that—*ideologically* it never would march in complete lockstep with National Socialism. The March 30 speech revealed Hitler's belief that some and perhaps many commanders would be reluctant to execute National Socialist bio-ideological directives.[12]

However, by late 1941 the war had changed. The massive German blitzkrieg into Russia had long since begun; and the *Einsatzgruppen* were doing their work just behind the front lines, as most in the *Wehrmacht* looked on, looked away, or actively cooperated. Begun also were the brutal anti-Slav *Lebensraum* policies that would ultimately create vast numbers of partisans seeking to repay German atrocities measure for measure. *Now* Hitler felt comfortable directly conveying to the *Wehrmacht* the essence of what the Commissar Order and related crimes were really about. This declaration was issued on October 2, 1941, in the form of a Midst-of-Battle exhortatory speech to all soldiers in the east:

On the Red Army: "For this enemy does not consist of soldiers, but a majority of beasts."

12 Ian Kershaw, *Hitler, 1936-1945: Nemesis* (New York, W.W. Norton, 2000), 56-60.

On *Lebensraum* and the purpose of the war: "Now, *my comrades*, you have seen with your own eyes 'the paradise of workers and farmers.' In a country that, owing to its vastness and fertility, could feed the whole world, poverty rules to such an extent that we *Germans could not imagine*." [Italics original]

On Bolshevism: "This [poverty] is a result of nearly a twenty-five-year-long Jewish rule that, as bolshevism, is basically similar to the general form of capitalism. The bearers of this system in both cases are the same: Jews and only Jews."[13]

Hitler's misgivings about the *Wehrmacht* were partly correct. Not every member of the soldier-audience would prove a willing tool for Hitler's *rassenkrieg* (see below.) However, as most of the *Wehrmacht's* behavior subsequently demonstrated, the "daylight" between it and National Socialism doctrine had narrowed considerably.

Immediate Result

Hitler's speech and subsequent Commissar Order (even as modified by Warlimont) failed to create a favorable consensus among senior commanders. Prominent generals protested the Commissar Order—through channels—and lobbied for its repeal or amendment. But Hitler rejected these out of hand. Significantly, the objectors included three Field Marshals commanding Army Groups in Russia as well as Admiral Wilhelm Canaris, chief of the *Abwehr*, the military intelligence service. Others objected passively. For example, General Heinz Guderian, commanding *Panzergruppe* 2, wrote that he never received the Commissar Order and speculated that his superiors had intentionally withheld it. Still others resorted to outright fraud: to satisfy headquarters, some field officers simply invented "commissar" body counts.[14]

---

13 "Hitler's Secret Order to His Troops," *New York Times*, October 10, 1941, original order dated October 2, 1941.

14 Correlli Barnett, *Hitler's Generals,* (New York: George Weidenfeld & Nicolson, 1989), 91-92. The Army Group officers were Field Marshals von Leeb, von Rundstedt and von Bock. Gerald Reitlinger, *The House Built on Sand*, (New York: Weidenfeld & Nicolson, 1960), 91-92; Heinz Guderian, *Panzer Leader*, (New York: Da Capo Press, 1996) 152; Eugene Davidson, *Trial of the Germans*, 559.

While occasional resistance to the order is duly noted, it failed to prevent the profound disaster wreaked by Hitler's policy, first for its victims—Soviet POWs—and finally for the *Wehrmacht* itself. While the number of "commissars" murdered pursuant to the order will probably never be known (one estimate puts the number at "several hundred" in the invasion's immediate aftermath), the larger truth renders even this crime cruelly irrelevant. As one historian has observed, "the Commissar Order became an excuse for the wholesale murder of prisoners of war." Some *Wehrmacht* commanders enthusiastically endorsed Hitler's policy, and exhorted their troops on its behalf in terms that "were not easily distinguishable from the high command of the SS in their hatred of Jews and Communists." Only 2,000,000 of an estimated 5,700,000 Soviet POWs survived German captivity. Of the dead, 473,000 were "officially" reported executed. Most others died from disease, exposure and starvation.[15]

German POWs fared little better under Stalin. The Russian tyrant's own propensity for murder certainly rivaled Hitler's. However, when the Commissar Order became known to Russian troops—as it quickly did—no official Soviet policy, whether harsh or benign, likely would have made a difference to Red Army soldiers at the front. Many surrendering Germans were simply shot on sight or dispatched later; many of those who survived capture disappeared in Soviet POW camps. Hitler had quickly achieved the war of extermination that he had sought—but it was mutual extermination.[16]

Legacy

Hitler's March 30 speech did not begin the process by which the *Wehrmacht's* integrity was compromised, but it did, in Warlimont's words, represent "[t]he first occasion on which Hitler openly demanded unlawful conduct." Warlimont may have limited the final order's scope, but he nevertheless abetted murder. Thus, there is no escape from the historical judgment, expressed by historian Dr. Jurgen Forster, that "[a]lthough it was Hitler who wanted to transform *Barbarossa* into a war of extermination against

---

15 Davidson, 567; for an example of a Nazified Wehrmacht commander, see the October 10, 1941, proclamation of Field Marshal Walter von Reichenau, 565, 568 (Soviet POWs); Barnett, 91.

16 Bellamy, *Absolute War*, 27-28.

Bolshevism and Jewry, it was the *Wehrmacht* senior officers and their legal advisors who cast his ideological intentions into legally valid form." The Commissar Order figured prominently at the first trial at Nuremberg and helped send Warlimont's immediate superior, Colonel-General Alfred Jodl, as well as Keitel to the gallows.[17]

However, the Commissar Order, in combination with other abuses of POWs during the Second World War, had another, far-reaching legacy: the world's embrace of the Geneva Convention on Prisoners of War of 1949. The influence of the Commissar Order was clear. For example, among the Convention's many humanitarian requirements, the agreement declared that "[a]lthough one of the Powers in conflict may not be a party to the present Convention, the Parties who are parties thereto shall remain bound by it in their mutual relations"—thus officially dispensing with World War II German claims that because the Soviet Union had not signed the 1929 Geneva Convention, its prisoners were owed nothing.[18]

Leadership Principle

About Hitler's leadership expressed in his speeches, seven decades after the war there is both everything and little enough left to say. But in the context of battle speeches and military history, one should scrutinize the means by which the Commissar Order was translated from Hitler's speech to *Wehrmacht* directive and wonder anew at how the armed forces, Germany's most socially conservative institution, could have allowed itself to become not so much politicized as cowed into accepting a policy that many officers understood at the time would promise nothing but disaster. Not only did the Commissar Order guarantee retaliation from the Red Army (and thus helped kill more *Wehrmacht* soldiers than commissars), it immeasurably strengthened the one thing that Germany needed to weaken in order to win: the Red Army's will to resist.

As discussed in Chapter Ten, John Pope's failure to resist civilian dictation contributed to a personal disaster for him; here, a similar failure to enforce boundaries also spelled disaster, not for one man but for millions.

---

17 Forster, quoted in Correlli Barnett, *Hitler's Generals*, 89.

18 See Part I, Article 2, Geneva Convention Relative to the Treatment of Prisoners of War, 75 U.N.T.S. 135, entered into force October 21, 1950.

Persuasive Strategy

Based on Halder's notes and other recollections of the March 30 speech, Hitler seems to have downplayed National Socialist racial theory in favor of casting the proposed eastern war as a purely ideological struggle: Bolshevism versus Western civilization. No doubt Hitler wanted to suggest that those slated for summary execution were Red Army "commissars" or COMINTERN or NKVD-type politicals who were responsible for international subversion or domestic terror. Hitler, the street politician, understood that his March 30 crowd probably consisted of few die-hard Nazis.[19] German military elites still had chivalric convictions—notably the conviction that POWs were entitled to humane treatment.

Hitler obviously believed that he could overcome these "scruples" by resorting to a rhetorical device used in battle speeches since antiquity: the atrocity story. During the speech, according to General Hans Reinhardt, Hitler detailed atrocities that commissars had inflicted on Finns during their recent war with Russia; Hitler also claimed that he had special intelligence that the Russians intended to similarly abuse captured Germans. (Hitler never explained how he knew this, given that the Soviets were completely ignorant of *Barbarossa*, and Stalin disbelieved what warning intelligence was received.) At one point during the speech, according to Reinhardt's recollections, Hitler came close to acknowledging his problems with this soldier-audience of elite officers: "He did not expect the German Officer Corps to understand his orders but he demanded that they obey them unconditionally." However, it is likely that everyone in that room understood perfectly well the reasons for his orders. Unfortunately, too many were willing to obey them.[20]

19 Warlimont on the March 30 soldier-audience: "[Hitler] was undoubtedly aware that ideologically there was still a great gulf between him and this assembly of the cream of the German officer corps." – Warlimont, *Inside Hitler's Headquarters*, 161.

20 Reitlinger, *House Built on Sand*, 68.

Section Five

Speechlets

Speechlets were defined in the Introduction, so this section resumes that discussion with three questions: first, how did some battle one-liners come to be Speechlets? Next, how did they come to be famous? Finally, why did some Speechlets endure and prove astonishingly durable, "leaping" not from "brain to brain", as Dawkins would have it, but from meme-stream to meme-stream? As an example, think here of "Don't give up the ship!" First uttered (probably) by a mortally wounded ship captain, the words then leaped to newspapers, the general public, back to the U.S. Navy as an unofficial motto, later to football coaches and, at some point, to parents stiffening their children's resolve to finish their homework.

But first, there is no better introduction to all three questions than a famous non-military Speechlet that should be within the memory of many readers. In January 1984 fast food chain Wendy's International aired a commercial featuring three elderly women examining an oversized hamburger bun. One of them lifted the top of the bun only to discover that the meat patty beneath was only slightly larger than the inch-wide sliced pickle sitting on it; the bun dwarfed both the patty and the pickle. "Where's the beef?" then eighty-two-year-old character actress Clara Peller asked, before repeating the question twice more. Meanwhile, a voiceover explained that "[a]t Wendy's, you get more beef and less bun." It was a popular commercial defined by its clever refrain. It was also intended as a Speechlet—a persuasive argument—but one meant to reach no further than fast food customer meme-streams. However, these words did not remain in that meme-stream for long. By February the *New York Times* could entitle an article "Where's the Beef? All Over [T]own," which noted that the phrase had become "grist for humor mills from the playground to the pulpit."[1]

But the Speechlet's status changed forever on March 11, 1984. That evening five Democrat Party candidates for president debated in Atlanta. Moderator John Chancellor asked the group: "[I]f one of you wins the election will there be less involvement [of the federal government in peoples' lives] or will it be a return to the way things were before Reagan?" Candidate Gary Hart's 177-word answer employed the generalities customary in presidential debates. Then Walter Mondale turned towards Hart and replied in fourteen words: "When I hear your new ideas, I'm reminded of that ad: 'Where's the beef?'"[2]

A Speechlet had not been born; but an existing Speechlet had both merged and morphed. It had merged: first, the meme-streams of Madison Avenue had flowed towards fast food patrons; next, this stream widened to include Manhattanhites generally; finally, with a push from Walter Mondale, the Speechlet joined the widest of all meme-streams, the national consciousness. Simultaneously, it had morphed: what had been a Speechlet arguing that competitors' hamburgers did not deserve the name "hamburger" now became one political candidate's argument that a rival's argument was devoid of substance, and thus (by implication) so was the rival. Both applications of "Where's the beef?" were a brilliant bundling of question-authenticity memes, first for hamburgers and then fashioning a hamburgers-as-politics metaphor. Today, "Where's the beef?" is routinely deployed as a lightning strike aimed at any claim that appears thinly evidenced. In all likelihood, this Speechlet will endure for at least several generations.[3]

---

1 The commercial continues to amuse, and may be viewed at www.youtube. com/watch?v=Ug75diEyaA0. Michael Norman, "Where's the Beef? All Over [T]own," *New York Times*, February 11, 1984. Accessed November 3, 2009.

2 "Excerpts From Transcript of 5 Candidates' Debate in Atlanta," *New York Times*, March 12, 1984.

3 The *New York Times* called the phrase a "punch line," but as Walter Mondale demonstrated, "Where's the beef?" was much more than this. Like most rhetorical questions, it is actually a conclusion to an argument: "There is no, or at least, not enough, beef." It is an enthymeme—the premises are missing. These absent premises are as follows:

And so I lay bare this chapter's route of investigation. [4] The history of battle Speechlets—and this is what makes them so interesting—is usually far more complex than a Wendy's advertisement. Of the Speechlets covered in this section, several were used to influence civilian opinion; one surfaced decades after the battle; one is traced as it wended its way through the civilian meme-stream to resurface (again) as a battle speech. But the principles of merge-and-morph are surprisingly similar.

Premise #1: A proper hamburger (or a candidate for president) must have enough beef (or political substance) to completely cover or even exceed a bun's circumference (or run for office); *Premise #2*: McDonalds' and Burger King's (Gary Hart's) patties (views) do not cover the bun (lack substance); Therefore: McDonalds and Burger King (Gary Hart) hamburgers are not proper hamburgers (should not taken seriously as a candidate for president).

4 Readers should note that the template previously used to analyze full-length battle speeches has been modified for this section; the categories of "Immediate Result," "Leadership Principle" and "Persuasive Strategy" have been used (or not) to fit each case.

Chapter Thirteen

Cut and Paste:
The Origin of Two Modern Speechlets

I. Introduction: Cut and Paste

A Cut-and Paste Speechlet is any Speechlet "cut" from a longer communication and "pasted" onto the public consciousness. The snipped words are not just prominent quotations or maxims, intended to convey some general wisdom; they are persuasive arguments usually intended to support or oppose some public issue. For Oliver Hazard Perry and Ulysses S. Grant, that issue was war. Perry's words helped build public support for the War of 1812, a conflict so unpopular that it threatened the Republic with its first major secession crisis. Grant's cut and pasted words were deliberately intended (by others than Grant) to soothe public angst over a military campaign whose extreme bloodletting and uncertain prospects had deeply unsettled the North. Typical of many Speechlets (and almost all of the Cut and Paste variety), the men who originally wrote the words never imagined that they would be used as freestanding arguments, let alone retailed through various meme-streams of public opinion.

How these words evolved from private letters into Speechlets is the subject of this chapter. It must be noted that these Speechlets were not battle Speechlets per se—the words of Perry and Grant first were used to persuade civilians, not soldiers. And it was civilian interests that lifted the words from private military communications in order to make public Speechlets. In Perry and Grant's cases, these civilian interests were different combinations of government, private associations, editors, reporters, retail news distributors, and finally the news-consuming public.

These Speechlets proved to have "legs" as all successful Speechlets must. What are "legs?" The metaphor usually refers to news (and, for our purposes, Speechlets) that are imbued with public interest sufficient to enable them (to extend the metaphor) to "rise" and "walk," splashing their way through wholesale and retail meme-streams. I will explain why "legs" grew under the Speechlets of Perry and Grant. Here I am less concerned with the influence of any particular media than with how these Speechlets precisely reflected their historical moments—in short, why the public was interested. This means examining how these Speechlets satisfactorily answered questions, or explained or rationalized difficult subjects—in short, how they presented arguments—so as to resonate with the consumers of war news. Powerful media cannot guarantee public resonance; but without such resonance legendary Speechlets might otherwise have become ephemeral slogans or crude, forgettable arguments. Instead, these two Speechlets quickly entered the retail meme-streams—and have remained there ever since.

II. The Speechlets: Perry and Grant

Dear General:

We have met the enemy and they are ours; Two Ships, two Brigs, one Schooner, and one Sloop.

Yours with great respect and esteem,
O.H. Perry

—Message sent after the Battle of Lake Erie by Oliver Hazard Perry to General William Henry Harrison, September 10, 1813

I am now sending back to Belle Plain all my wagons for a fresh supply of provisions and ammunition, and propose to fight it out on this line if it takes all summer.

—Thirty-three words of a 271-word letter to General Henry Halleck, sent from "near Spottslvania C.H." at 8:30 A.M., May 11, 1864[1]

---

1   Skaggs, *Oliver Hazard Perry*, 118; U.S. Grant to Maj. Gen. H.W. Halleck, May 11, 1864—8:30 a.m., *OR*, Series I, 36 (2) 627-628.

III. Words to Speechlet: Oliver Hazard Perry and the Simple Cut

"We have met the enemy and they are ours."

Immediately following the Battle of Lake Erie, Oliver Hazard Perry, the victorious commander, using his hat as a table, scratched out 27 words and two initials on an envelope. He handed it to a midshipman with orders to row ashore and deliver the message to General William Henry Harrison. Unlike "Don't Give Up the Ship!" which Perry had recycled from his deceased friend Captain James Lawrence, the words "We have met the enemy and they are ours" were entirely of his own creation. They were not intended as a Speechlet, but as a simple statement of victory, albeit one that embodied the elegant concision of his day. (Besides being the Age of Nelson, it was also the Age of Wordsworth, Byron, Keats, Shelly, and Coleridge.)

However, like most Cut-and-Paste Speechlets, the famous phrase never originally aspired to retail circulation. This can be inferred from two facts. First, as the note's second section makes clear, Perry intended it as part of a whole, an informal after-action report to Harrison: "two Ships, two Brigs, one Schooner and one Sloop." And there is the note itself: it was addressed to Harrison alone, not copied to personal boosters or sympathetic newspapers, politicians, and other war supporters. Had Harrison read the epistle and then tossed it into the fire, Perry might never have thought to resurrect it.[2]

For many Americans, Perry's two Speechlets (the recycled "Don't give up the ship!" being the first) would become indistinguishable from the battle and from Perry himself, soon dubbed the "Hero of Lake Erie." The precise route by which "We have met the enemy" traveled from Harrison to the larger public is unclear (probably by publication of official dispatches), but it quickly made the journey. Soon newspapers and broadsides cut and pasted the words and promoted their author-hero. By the time Perry began his journey from Erie, Pennsylvania, to his home in Newport, Rhode Island (what one biographer has called "a victory procession"), his path was paved with triumphal celebration. Perry was "greeted, toasted, wined and dined; honored with oratory, parades, dinners, dances and military escorts; saluted with flags, bunting, illuminations,

---

2 Skaggs, *Oliver Hazard Perry*, 118; here I have only expanded on a thought that originated with Mr. Skaggs, who notes that the Speechlet "is one of the most graphic, succinct, and accurate after-action reports in history. It rivals Julius Caesar's famous *Veni, vidi, vici.*"

bonfires, clanging church bells and cannon fire. He was given medals, swords, keys-to-cities, and silver services." At Albany's Eagle Tavern a transparency reminded all comers that "We have met the enemy and they are ours." These were words that Perry would hear *ad nauseum*.[3]

Newspaper poems were popular meme-retailing devices of the day, and the Hero of Lake Erie summoned many a versifier's muse. Here is a sample:

Full many a heart of valor bled,
Full many a hero sought the dead;
And victory hung in doubtful gloom,
Till fate and Heaven assigned the doom—
When Perry cried—By all the powers,
We've met the Enemy—they're ours!

This poem is one example of civilian reprocessing of a Speechlet. The poem (and perhaps the poet too) imagines Perry shouting rather than writing the epic words. Moreover, the poem implies that Perry made the shout (presumably to his comrades) not hours after the battle, but at its climax: Perry began to shout at the very moment that "fate and Heaven assigned the [British] doom."[4]

And it is only a slight stretch to perceive in President James Madison's Fifth Annual Message to Congress, delivered that December, faint cadences of Perry's Speechlet. Praising Perry, Madison declared in a less-memorable paraphrase, "On Lake Erie, the squadron under the command of Captain Perry, having met the British squadron of superior force, a sanguinary conflict ended in the capture of the whole."[5]

Thus was Perry's elegant phrase, penciled by a battle-worn commander, cut from a note and pasted onto the body politic. It mattered to its subsequent popularity that the memory of Britain's last major—and, in the United States, celebrated—defeat—the American Revolution—was well within middle-aged memory. However New England Federalists might rail against the War of 1812

---

3   Skaggs, *Oliver Hazard Perry*, 135.

4   Richard Dillon, *We Have Met the Enemy: Oliver Hazard Perry, Wilderness Commodore* (New York: McGraw Hill Book Company, 1978), 183.

5   Skaggs, *Oliver Hazard Perry*, 120; James Madison, "Fifth Annual Message to Congress" (December 7, 1813), Miller Center of Public Affairs, Scripps Library & Multimedia Archive, available at http://millercenter.virginia.edu/scripps/digilibrary/prezspeeches/madison/jma_1813_12007, accessed December 12, 2006.

as "Mr. Jemmy's War," most of the general public welcomed the idea that the British were "ours" once again. The Hero of Lake Erie had serendipitously penciled his way into a pre-existing, popular narrative.[6] (I will consider more War of 1812 memes in my discussion of "Don't give up the ship" in Chapter Fifteen.)

IV: Words to Speechlet: Grant and Propaganda

"I propose to fight it out on this line if it takes all summer."

Perry's case illustrates how the basic process of cutting-and-pasting works. "We have met the enemy and they are ours," once circulated by official dispatches and newspapers, appears to have been embraced spontaneously by various feeders in the existing meme-streams. But other Speechlets are more deliberate creations, with those doing the cutting and pasting having agendas perhaps different from that of the words' author. One example of this type of Speechlet began with Lieutenant General Ulysses S. Grant on the morning of May 11, 1864, four days after his nighttime ride through the Wilderness.

The sixth day preceding May 11th had been among the most remarkable—and bloodiest—in American military history. On May 5 Grant ordered the Army of the Potomac across the Rapidan River; the following day he was attacked in the flank by Robert E. Lee, commencing the Battle of the Wilderness, which raged for two days. Daylight of May 7 brought a brief respite, but, as discussed in Chapter One, that evening Grant moved his headquarters towards Spottsylvania Court House. Grant's hope was to reach Spottsylvania before Lee and stand between the rebels and Richmond. But he arrived at Spottsylvania too late and found the Confederates already entrenching. On May 8 and 9 Grant assaulted various rebel positions as Lee further extended his line. Grant reserved his heaviest blow for May 10, bringing on the Battle of Spottsylvania; a second attack came on May 12. Sandwiched between these awful bloodlettings was the morning that Grant authored a letter containing his soon-to-be-famous Speechlet.[7]

---

6 Dillon, *We Have Met the Enemy*, 183-184.

7 Porter, *Campaigning with Grant*, 97; E.B. Long with Barbara Long, *The Civil War Day By Day: An Almanac, 1861-1865* (New York: Da Capo Press, 1971), 492-499.

Grant would spend most of the 11th reconnoitering enemy lines. But first came his usual breakfast: coffee and beef burned to a crisp. Joining him at the mess table was his long-time friend and sponsor, Elihu B. Washburne, a Republican Congressman from Illinois. Washburne had been a recent fixture at Grant's headquarters; that morning he awaited a cavalry escort for his return to Washington. When Grant moved from the mess table to a camp chair outside his tent to chase breakfast with a cigar, Washburne followed; at 8:15 A.M. the cavalry finally arrived and Washburne rose to leave. "General, I shall go to see the President and the Secretary of War as soon as I reach Washington," he told Grant. "I can imagine their anxiety to know what you think of the prospects of the campaign, and I know they would be greatly gratified if I could carry a message from you giving what encouragement you can as to the situation," he added.[8]

It was an unremarkable request. The Congressman probably wanted to show something tangible beyond a few anecdotes for his considerable exertions in the field. But Grant's response was typically measured. He thought a moment before answering, and then explained that his campaign was "making fair progress" and that "all the fighting had been in our favor." But as Grant well knew, one bane of his many predecessors had been boastfulness that encouraged unrealistic public expectations; Grant was not about to repeat this mistake. "[The] campaign promises to be a long one," he finally explained to Washburne, "and I am particularly anxious not to say anything just now that might hold out false hopes to the people." Yet he agreed to write a brief dispatch.[9]

Cigar still in his mouth, Grant entered his tent and wrote a letter to General Henry Halleck, Army Chief of Staff. It was like most of Grant's writing: clear, brief and to the point. He explained that the fighting was "very hard," although "up to this time it is much in our favor." But Grant spared no detail about the casualties (insofar as he accurately knew them): "eleven general officers killed, wounded and missing, and probably twenty thousand men." Yet he noted that the enemy's losses "must be greater," as the Federals had captured over four thousand Confederate prisoners; he claimed that fewer Federals were captured. Perhaps unintentionally, he hinted at Federal exhaustion, if not low morale:

---

8 Porter, *Campaigning with Grant*, 97-98. Grant's relationship with Washburne is a trope in all Grant biographies. An extensive treatment can be found in William S. McFeely, *Grant: A Biography* (New York: W.W. Norton & Company, 1982), see Index, 591.

9 Porter, *Campaigning with Grant*, 97-98.

reinforcements would be "very encouraging to the men;" of Confederate morale he volunteered that "the enemy are very shaky, and are only kept up to the mark by the greatest exertions on the part of their officers."[10]

Grant was as careful to avoid self-inflation as that of battlefield results. His not-yet-famous line—originally written as, "I am now sending back to Belle Plaines [sic] all my wagons for a fresh supply of provisions, and Ammunition, and propose to fight it out on this line if it takes me all summer"—was revised: he scratched out the word "me." This fight properly belonged to the army, or the nation, or the government, or the Union, but he was determined not to make it about "me."[11]

After Washburne's departure Grant's staff reviewed a copy of the dispatch. "[N]either the general himself nor any one at headquarters realized the epigrammatic character of the striking sentence it contained," recalled headquarters aide Horace Porter, "until the New York papers reached camp a few days afterward with the words displayed in large headlines, and with conspicuous comments upon the force of the expression." Porter summarized perfectly how raw "news" is cycled from the battlefield to politicians and newspaper editors before being returned to the front in final form. (See Legacy, below.) However that may be, Grant's letter is best understood as a necessary but insufficient condition for the Speechlet's birth.[12]

If Grant and his staff failed to recognize the importance of this line, who midwifed it to notoriety? Two parties were responsible. The first was almost certainly Secretary of War Edwin M. Stanton. On May 11 at 11:30 PM the War Department released an official dispatch above Stanton's name. It consisted of selected lines from Grant's letter to Washburne, heavily censored for security reasons and probably truncated for narrative flow. Gone were casualty figures, references to the depot at Belle Plain and any mention of resupply, reinforcements and like matters; curiously, also censored was Grant's belief that the rebels were "shaky." The rewritten version was reduced from 271 to 75 words; by May 13 the "complete" dispatch appeared in the *New York Times* and simultaneously in newspapers across the country. The whole read:

10 *OR*, 36 (2) 627-628.

11 Perret, *Ulysses S. Grant*, 318.

12 Porter, *Campaigning with Grant*, 98.

We have now ended the sixth day of very heavy fighting. The result to this time is much in our favor. Our losses have been heavy, as well as those of the enemy. I think the loss of the enemy must be greater. We have taken over 5,000 prisoners in battle, while he has taken from us but few except stragglers. I propose to fight it out on this line if it takes all Summer.[13]

It is probable that Stanton intentionally rewrote this dispatch to place the famous line as the coda, whose Speechlet potential he must have recognized. But he did more than this. By inserting the word "I" before the word "propose," Stanton transformed "*and propose* to fight it out on this line if it takes all summer" to "*I propose* to fight it out on this line if it takes all summer." [Italics added] The change is significant. By restoring Grant to the first person (remember that the general had crossed out the word "me"), Stanton not only heightened the Speechlet's dramatic effect but also conscripted Grant into the political service to which the line was soon put.

What political purposes was it made to serve? First, Stanton's bulletin provided a conclusion to a story that, for the Lincoln administration, had remained perilously open-ended: the story of Grant's campaign. By May 11, bloody, frustrating combat was, as I discuss below, a fact that could not be concealed from most Northerners. By acknowledging "heavy fighting" Stanton sought to get in front of that part of the story; by noting that the fighting had gone "much in our favor" Stanton sought to reassure the public in the time-honored manner of official war bulletins. But there was much more at stake even than this.

It was now the turn of the Speechlet's second midwife, the press, to retail the meme-bearing Speechlet. "FROM GENERAL GRANT," the *Boston Daily Advertiser* headlined on May 13, "He Proposes to Fight It Out." The *Brooklyn Eagle* added—in all caps, in case anyone should miss the message—"I PROPOSE TO FIGHT IT OUT ON THIS LINE IF IT TAKES ALL SUMMER." Editorials in both newspapers commented on the situation, using the meme as the measure. "The duty of all patriots then is epitomized in the sturdy resolution of the Lieutenant-General, 'to fight it out on this line if it takes all summer'" (*Boston Daily Advertiser*); the *Brooklyn Eagle* agreed that Grant was resolute, but urged its readers to be realistic: "One thing is certain, the

13 Dispatches from the War Office, First Dispatch, Washington, Wednesday, May 11—11:30 P.M.," *New York Times*, May 13, 1864.

fighting 'on this Line' cannot continue 'all summer,'" it opined. "These desperate struggles cannot be long maintained." But it was the *New York Times* that not only caught the spirit of Stanton's now-launched Speechlet but also brilliantly connected it to older Grant memes:

> Grant's First Proposition and His Last—At the opening of Gen. Grant's military career at Fort Donelson, he sent a proposition to Gen. Buckner, who had requested a cessation of hostilities after two days' fighting, in these words: '*I propose* to move immediately upon your works.' We have had but few other propositions from him till now, when he makes another, after six days' fighting: '*I propose*,' says he, 'to fight it out on this line, if it takes all Summer.' Both of these proposals are very cool, but terribly determined. [Italics original][14]

The Speechlet surged through the public meme-streams, one of which included President Lincoln's speeches. On the very evening that Stanton released Grant's reworked dispatch, President Lincoln addressed the Twenty-Seventh Michigan Regiment, en route to the front. "I believe I know (and am especially grateful to know) that Gen. Grant has not been jostled in his purposes," Lincoln declared from the portico of Willard's Hotel, "that he has made all his points, and to-day he is on his line as he purposed before he moved his armies." Four weeks later the Speechlet had become so well known that Lincoln could not only quote it (if inaccurately) but also stretch its meaning for his own purposes. "Speaking of the present campaign," Lincoln declared to the Sanitary Fair in Philadelphia on June 16, 1864,

> General Grant is reported to have said, 'I am going through on this line if it takes all summer.' This war has taken three years; it was begun or accepted upon the line of restoring the national authority over the whole national domain, and for the American people, as far as my knowledge enables me to speak, I say we are going through on this line if it takes three years more.

---

14 "FROM GENERAL GRANT," *Boston Daily Advertiser*, May 13, 1864; "The First Despatch [sic] of Gen. Grant," *Brooklyn Eagle*, May 12, 1864; The *Eagle's* account actually appeared the day before that of the *Times* or the *Advertiser*; the *Eagle's* editorial, "The Great News from Virginia," was printed May 13, 1864; untitled editorial, *Boston Daily Advertiser*, May 13, 1864; "Grant's First Proposition and His Last," *New York Times*, May 13, 1864.

Lincoln had stretched Grant's tactical resolve to include political resolve to win the war.[15] Of course, by then the Speechlet had been born.

V. Why Did "I propose to fight it out" Grow 'Legs'?

Grant's words might have lacked the elegance of Perry's, yet his line was also embraced with popular enthusiasm. Why? The most important answer is that, until Grant's May 11th letter, the Overland Campaign (not yet named such) had been a terrifying story with a beginning but no middle and certainly no end.

Initial reporting about the campaign consisted of "wild and exaggerated rumors." But by May 7 casualty lists had started to appear in the nation's newspapers. They began as short lists: for example, on that day the *Boston Daily Advertiser* could name only 11 casualties; but they were enough to generate immense public anxiety. Large crowds had begun to gather around street news outlets. "The popular pulse beat feverishly, yesterday, and the eagerness to get the news from our armies has only been equaled on a few occasions," the *Advertiser* reported on May 9. "Several times when a report of some grand success appeared, the enthusiasm broke out in repeated cheers." True enough, but the paper was less likely to give the more morbid reason—that the crowd undoubtedly included many friends and relatives awaiting news of loved ones in the army.[16]

The very next day (May 10) the *Advertiser* ran three separate casualty lists, together with an estimate by the Army that "twelve to fifteen hundred [were] killed, eight thousand wounded, the remainder missing." Named casualties totaled 112 men. One day later (May 11) the *Advertiser* reported local despair:

> The natural reaction of feeling came yesterday and the public which had believed hastily that there was a race for Richmond, began to look doubtfully upon reports from Virginia, and to question whether our successes there should be called a victory or an escape. The feeling of distrust was carried to as great an excess as the over-confidence of the day before, and the more sober accounts from trustworthy

---

15 "The President on Gen. Grant's Success," *New York Times*, May 13, 1864; "Speech at a Sanitary Fair in Philadelphia, June 16, 1864," *Abraham Lincoln: His Speeches and Writings*, edited by Roy P. Basler (New York: Da Capo Press, 1990), 751-753.

16 "By Telegraph," *Boston Daily Advertiser*, May 7, 1864 (rumors); "The following deaths in Massachusetts regiments….," May 7; "Local Matters," May 9, 1864.

sources were read by many with a sense of depression, not justified by the facts faithfully narrated.

The *Advertiser* was a pro-war, Republican-establishment sheet, but its slant was slight, and it reported the truth about public anxieties. [17]

Immediate Result

In May and June 1864, this Speechlet created the dominant narrative for the federal war effort. It explained Grant's strategy simply—his trumpet would never sound retreat—and gave civilians, despite being war-weary and grieving, good reasons to continue to support the war. In short, it satisfied the most important requirements of successful wartime propaganda: the narrative encouraged home-front hope, perpetuated a successful commander's "brand" with the public, and of paramount importance, convinced people—for a time—that victory was worth the cost.

Legacy

Although the American Civil War claims certain "firsts"—transporting troops by rail, telegraphy for orders, the foreshadowing of World War I-style trench warfare—these three elements also contributed to another development: the ubiquitous Cut-and-Paste Speechlet. As attested by other examples of Speechlets discussed in this book, the Civil War did not witness the first use of these; but hereafter, they became more common; cultural, military and technological trends had joined to create new avenues of meme wholesaling and retailing. Railroads carried troops, but also newspapers and journalists; the telegraph transmitted military communications, but also news reports; the lengthy periods between battles and the trench warfare that consumed the war's

17 By Telegraph," *Boston Daily Advertiser*, May 10, 1864 (estimates); lists for May 10: "The Army of the Potomac;" "Washington, May 9," and "The following are among the wounded....." The reason multiple lists appeared is best analogized to the streaming chyron familiar to today's cable news television viewers. In 1864, new telegraphed reports would be received even as the next edition's news type was already being set. Rather than merging the new reports with existing news or lists, it was easier to simply add them as separate reports. Thus, experienced readers likely regarded newspapers as time scrolls; unfortunately, the contradictions contained in news (and lists) running in the same edition could only add to public confusion, doubt and anxiety. Untitled comment, May 11,1864. The characterization of the *Boston Daily Advertiser* is my own.

final year (in the east) guaranteed bored soldiers, thus giving already highly literate armies ample opportunities to read newspapers, which they avidly did. Thus information moved in a circular pattern: journalists and soldiers sent stories home via telegraph and mail (facilitated by railroads); there it was processed into news by families and editors; then it was returned to the front via mail and newspapers (again, carried by railroads) and telegraph. The meme-stream here was thus closer to a whirlpool: Speechlets and their embedded memes fit perfectly into the current, foreshadowing the mass propaganda and sound bites of the next century. (The topic of meme recycling will be discussed more extensively in Chapter Fifteen.)

Persuasive Strategy

This Speechlet persuaded on several levels. First was its function as an enthymeme, the specifics of which were products of the public's experience with the Army of the Potomac's previous leadership:

Missing Premise: Only a commander willing to fight can win this campaign.

Given Premise: Grant says, *"I propose to fight it out on this line if it takes all summer."*

Missing (but obvious) Conclusion: General Grant is the necessary man for victory.

But this Speechlet also worked on an entirely different and more profound level. Soaring casualty lists and the unknowns about Grant's progress rocked the public emotionally. Emotional needs cry out for emotional solutions, and this Speechlet's success will be found in how well it answered that call.

On May 12, one day before the newspaper published Grant's reworked dispatch, the *Advertiser* listed even more casualties: a staggering 517. And the story still had no hopeful narrative. For three years the public (like many Army of the Potomac soldiers) had been conditioned to expect the eastern army to withdraw after being out-maneuvered by superior Confederate leadership; that public now wanted to know whether Grant was the newspaper Grant of bulldog determination, or yet another general in the mold of McDowell, McClellan, Burnside, Hooker and Meade, all of whom had withdrawn the army after a setback. For years the war had scythed through tens of thousands of Northern homes; how much blood was another stalemate worth?[18]

But with Grant's Speechlet invented in Stanton's bulletin, the public now had an answer. "I propose to fight it out on this line…." What line did Grant mean? The route from Washington to Richmond and final victory. Grant would not withdraw north of the Rapidan River. Here it was only May, and thus Grant's pledge was good for months. The staggering casualty lists that now publicly circulated told the public that victory would not be bloodless, so if blood had to be spilled, it must be in service to a redemptive narrative, a commitment to victory by those who were taking tax dollars and young men and spending both freely. "To fight it out" meant not to withdraw; "on this line" was a pledge to stay south of the Rapidan and continue the relentless drive toward Richmond; "if it takes all summer" meant, to those already familiar with Grant memes, that he would continue to wield his hammer until it shattered or he was relieved.

"To fight it out on this line if it takes all summer" was simply a way of proclaiming that now, unlike in the past, the price of all this, in a collective sense, would be worth paying.

---

18 The Casualties," "The following wounded Massachusetts soldiers . . . ," "The Twentieth Massachusetts," May 12, 1864. To the great disappointment of the Lincoln administration, the previous November Meade chose to withdraw rather than to attack Lee's fortifications at Mine Run.

Chapter Fourteen

A Long Journey: From Recollection to Legend

I. Introduction

Perry and Grant's Speechlets were well attested, being derived from current documents. But Speechlets find other ways to enter the meme-stream and ultimately attain iconic status. "Don't fire till you see the whites of their eyes!" is one such Speechlet. It joins John Paul Jones' "I have not yet begun to fight!" (final version) and Admiral David Farragut's "Damn the torpedoes, full speed ahead!" (popular but inaccurate version) in having surfaced years after the battle.[1]

"Don't fire," supposedly uttered during the Battle of Bunker Hill (June 17, 1775), made one of its first archival appearances forty-three years afterwards in an 1818 history by historian Samuel Swett:

> General [Israel] Putnam rode through the line, and ordered, that no one should fire until they [the British] arrived at eight rods, nor any one till commanded. 'Powder was scarce and must not be wasted. They should not fire at the enemy till they saw the white of their eyes. . . .

---

1 Thomas, *John Paul Jones*, 192; Jack Friend, *West Wind, Flood Tide: The Battle of Mobile Bay* (Annapolis: Naval Institute Press, 2004), xii. Farragut's Speechlet resurfaced (or surfaced) in an 1877 speech by Naval Academy Superintendent Foxhall Parker.

Seven years later, as part of the 1825 semicentennial of the battle, Swett updated his account with affidavits from surviving veterans. According to several of the affiants, someone—accounts differed as to the speaker's identity—shouted something like the famous Speechlet, although the exact words, like the speaker's identity, also differed among the affiants.[2]

In the last chapter, I discussed how, when a Speechlet was minted, contemporary circumstance could render it immediately useful coin to creators and consumers alike. But "Don't fire" not only surfaced much later, it was but one of several Speechlets that appeared in the 1818 narrative and the 1825 affidavits. In this chapter I am less interested in determining what was actually said (if anything) or who actually said it (if anyone); instead, two main questions present: first, why was iconic status almost immediately conferred on "Don't fire" and not on the other remembered Speechlets? Second, what was it about "Don't fire" that met some *nineteenth-century* historical need but not (apparently) an *eighteenth-century* one? The issue can be framed broadly: the historical moments that create battle Speechlets can occur decades after the last shot was fired and most of the participants are long dead.

"Don't fire" is a good example of a Rule of Engagement (ROE) Speechlet. These are the one-liners by which the commander specifies "the 'if, when, where and how' an enemy can be 'engaged'—that is, avoidance of the enemy or force applied and the enemy damaged or completely destroyed." ROEs are an important source of Speechlets and include such well-known lines as Admiral George Dewey's "You may fire when you are ready, Gridley" and even Nelson's famous ROE advisory before Trafalgar:

[N]o Captain can do very wrong if he places his Ship alongside that of an enemy.[3]

As debunkers fondly note, "Don't fire till you see the whites of their eyes" was probably a military commonplace long before the American Revolution; as

---

2   Colonel David Humphreys, *An Essay on the Life of the Honorourable Major General Israel Putnam, Addressed to the State Society of the Cincinnati in Connecticut, with an Appendix containing an Historical and Topographical Sketch of Bunker Hill Battle by S. Swett* (Boston: Samuel Avery, 1818), 229-230; Samuel Swett, *Notes to His Sketch of* [the] *Bunker Hill Battle* (Boston: Munroe and Francis, 1825), 14-15, 17.

3   Miller, *Words and Deeds*, 134; Admiral George Dewey, *Autobiography of George Dewey, Admiral of the Navy* (Annapolis: Naval Institute Press, 1987), 191; Heinl, *Dictionary of Military and Naval Quotations*, 20.

a ROE it was necessitated by the limited range and accuracy of smoothbore muskets. At the Battle of Dettingen (June 27, 1743), Lieutenant Colonel Sir Andrew Agnew of Lochnaw, 5th Baronet, commanding 21st Foot, gave this command: Dinna fire till ye can see the whites of their e'en. . . . if ye dinna kill them they'll kill you.[4]

Fourteen years later at the Battle of Prague (May 6, 1757) in a "Prussian Order of the Day," Frederick the Great said much the same thing: "By the push of bayonet; no firing, none, at any rate, till you see the whites of their eyes!" And Frederick's utterance was likely well known to some American readers after Thomas Carlyle wrote *der Grosse's* biography in 1865. William Cullen Bryant and Sidney Gay (1879) and Edward Everett Hale (1881) had in two separate works performed the sober, if not always welcome, task of informing their readers that "Don't fire" had been said long before the Battle of Bunker Hill.[5]

It is interesting to note that while "Don't fire" became a hoary American Speechlet, the aforementioned similar ROE in British and German history acquired only footnote status. One obvious explanation is that neither Dettingen nor Prague was as critical to their nations' histories as was Bunker Hill to American history. Thus, a seminal battle may be one condition for Speechlets to attain iconic status; but important battles are by themselves not sufficient to confer iconic status. As readers will discover below, Swett's 1818 account and his 1825 update claimed many interesting ROE that were uttered at the same time as "Don't fire," yet only one achieved iconic status.

II. The Speechlets

Don't fire till you see the whites of their eyes *

4   Major Sir Crispin Agnew of Lochnaw Bt, "Regimental Miscellany: Famous Men of the Regiment, General Sir Andrew Agnew of Lochnaw Bt—28 Years a Fusilier," *The Journal of the Royal Highland Fusiliers*, Winter 2000, Volume XXIV, Number 2.

5   Thomas Carlyle, *History of Frederich II of Prussia, Called Frederick the Great*, (London: Robson and Son, 1865), V: 38; William Cullen Bryant and Sidney Howard Gay, A *Popular History of the United States, from the First Discovery of the Western Hemisphere by the Northmen, to the End of the First Century of the Union of the States* (New York: Charles Scribner's Sons, 1879), III: 408; Edward Everett Hale, "The Siege of Boston," contained in *The Memorial History of Boston*, edited by Justin Winsor (Boston: James R. Osgood and Company, 1881), III: 85. See also footnote 1 on that page where Hale adds that "Prince Charles, when he cut through the Austrian army, in retiring from Jagendorf, gave this order to his infantry: 'Silent, till you see the whites of their eyes." (May 22, 1745).

Fire Low! **
Take aim at the waistbands! **
Aim at the handsome coats! **
Pick off the commanders! **

—Various ROE from the Battle of Bunker Hill (June 17, 1775) attributed to General Israel Putnam or as recalled decades later by veterans.[6]

III. The Recollections

In 1818 historian Samuel Swett described the opening scenes of the fighting at Bunker Hill:

> The [British] lines advanced and soon opened to view. The American marksmen are with difficulty restrained from firing, General Putnam rode through the line, and ordered that no one should fire till they arrived within eight rods, nor any one till commanded.

Swett was born seven years after the Battle of Bunker Hill. His 1818 *Historical and Topographical Sketch of* [the] *Bunker Hill Battle* was his entry in what might be called the Second Battle of Bunker Hill: the dispute waged decades later over who was really in command during the first battle; candidates included Swett's favorite, Israel Putnam, and William Prescott, the competitor for the honor. For battle speech historians the particulars of this second fight are less important than the evidence the dispute generated: perhaps the earliest published appearance of the Speechlet "Don't fire till you see the whites of their eyes"—or words to that effect.[7]

Still, delayed publication should not be confused with later invention; perhaps veteran memories were, on the whole, accurate. In 1825 Swett updated his work to include veteran affidavits; these were critical in introducing the

---

6 Humphreys, *An Essay on the Life of the Honorourable Major General Israel Putnam,* 229-230; Samuel Swett, *Notes to His Sketch of* [the] *Bunker Hill Battle,* (Boston: Munroe and Francis, 1825), 14-15, 17. A single * indicates Speechlet taken from 1825 Swett affidavits. The classic formulation was remembered by Philip Johnson of Newburyport. A double ** indicates Speechlet taken from Humphreys' 1818 narrative, which was also reaffirmed by Swett in 1825.

7 Humphreys, *An Essay on the Life of the Honourable Major General Israel Putnam;* Samuel Swett, *Appendix,* 229-230.

"Don't fire" Speechlet to the wider public. Yet these too were disputed. After all, half a century had passed since Bunker Hill. In an effort to clarify matters, a panel of distinguished historians was convened (chaired by George Ellis, it included distinguished historians George Bancroft and George Ticknor) to consider the evidence. In 1842 Ellis concluded that the veterans' affidavits were extravagant, boastful, inconsistent and utterly untrue; mixtures of old men's

> broken memories and fond imaginings with the love of the marvelous. Some of those who gave in affidavits about the battle could not have been in it, nor even in its neighborhood. They had got so used to telling the story for the wonderment of village listeners as grandfathers' tales, and as petted representatives of the 'the spirit of '76' that they did not distinguish between what they had seen and done and what they read, heard, or dreamed.[8]

Nevertheless, several of the affidavits were consistent in remembering the Speechlet "Don't fire," although they differed as to its precise words and whether it was Putnam or his subordinates who spoke. But other than these recollections, there is no evidence contemporary with the battle suggesting that "Don't fire" was said. Thus, the veterans' affidavits remain the strongest evidence for its utterance.

However, other, more tenuous, evidence favoring the Speechlet might be added: it fit the technology of smoothbore musketry and field tactics; commanders may have already known of it as a military commonplace; Americans were short of powder at Bunker Hill, and some instruction designed to make every shot count would have been logical. In any case, while the affidavits have been criticized for many sound reasons, the fact that several affiants recalled the same ROE (more or less) should count for something. My own opinion is that between June 17, 1775, and Swett's 1818 narrative some combination of memory and oral tradition may have kept the Speechlet alive.[9]

8 Ellis, quoted in Harold Murdock, *Bunker Hill: Notes and Queries on a Famous Battle* (Boston: Riverside Press, 1927), 50.

9 Samuel Swett, *Notes to His Sketch of* [the] *Bunker Hill Battle* (Boston: Munroe and Francis, 1825). In particular, see affidavits of Elijah Jourdan, 14-15, and Philip Johnson, 17.

IV. Recollection to Speechlet

The next question to be considered is *how* "Don't fire" morphed from recollection to Speechlet. In order to answer this question, I will begin by asking what Swett said Putnam (Old Put) said as he rode the American lines on that intensely hot June day in 1775. In his history Swett seems to have merged different accounts of Old Put's instructions, exhortations and ROE into one continuous narration.

First, Swett wanted to suggest that the entire narrative stream was one direct quotation—either Old Put's words, or different veterans quoting Old Put. Based on internal evidence, the following quotation, while in the third person, was clearly reconstructed from some other source(s). Those sources were obviously based on first-person affidavits collected by Swett for his 1825 book. The quotation is as follows:

> Powder was scarce and must not be wasted. They should not fire at the enemy till they saw the white of their eyes, and then fire low, take aim at their waistbands. They were all marksmen, and could kill a squirrel at a hundred yards; reserve their fire, and the enemy were all destroyed. Aim at the handsome coats, pick off the commanders.

In a note of realism, Swett then adds, "The same orders were reiterated by Prescott at the redoubt, by Pomeroy, Stark and all the veteran officers." Readers should feel free to exchange the order of names (or insert new ones) to suit their own theories of who really commanded at Bunker Hill; but this process of commands repeating as they descended the chain of command was a standard feature of line-of-battle warfare.[10] And at least by 1818, one of those commands was, "They should not fire at the enemy till they saw the white of their eyes."

Swett preserved this third person narrative form in his 1825 *Notes to his Sketch of* [the] *Bunker Hill Battle*; but by including the first person affidavits, historians, whatever their doubts about other issues connected with Swett's account and affidavits, were naturally attracted to veteran Philip Johnson's recollection that Old Put had said, "Don't fire till you see the whites of their eyes." This version helped robustly flesh out an already-epic story, was a marvelous coda to the first phase of the battle, and it even may have been true.

---

10 Swett, *Sketch* (1825), 229-230.

Thus, the eternal need for a dynamic narrative (incidentally, one of the most important functions that battle rhetoric serves for journalists) as well as historical truth provided compelling reasons to accept "Don't fire" as part of the story.[11]

Later nineteenth-century historians did not always abide by Swett's attribution of the Speechlet to Old Put—they had other candidates, notably William Prescott—but they did accept the Speechlet as having been said by *somebody*. However, one thing these later historians did change was Swett's narrative stream—they broke it up, in order to isolate what may (or may not) have been a series of freestanding, probably shouted commands. Thus with these later (including some very distinguished) historians, the quotations in the epigraph appear as isolated instructions, exhortations and ROE. To cite the most prominent of several examples, Richard Frothingham, whose 1873 *History of the Siege of Boston* is deservedly one of the most influential and still-useful narratives about the Battle of Bunker Hill, offers as freestanding orders what Swett had offered as a third person narrative stream.

Here, Frothingham avoids the 1818 arguments by dispensing with Old Put as Speechlet-giver in favor of a gaggle identified only as "their officers" who "ordered them to reserve their fire" and demanded that they:

"Fire low"
"Aim at the waistbands"
"Wait until you see the white of their eyes"
"Aim at the handsome coats"
"Pick off the commanders"

Some recent historians have abandoned all of Swett's Speechlets, probably regarding their provenance as too uncertain. But by the early twentieth century, it was too late: "Don't fire" had already achieved iconic status.[12]

---

11 Swett, *Sketch* (1825), 229-230; *Notes*, 17, 33.

12 Richard Frothingham, *History of the Siege of Boston, and of the Battles of Lexington, Concord and Bunker Hill*, 4th ed. (Cranbury, New Jersey: The Scholar's Bookshelf, 2005, originally printed 1873), 140; see also Allen French, *The Siege of Boston* (New York: The Macmillan Company, 1911), 270; also see for example Victor Brooks' excellent *The Boston Campaign: April 1775—March 1776* (Conshohocken, Pennsylvania: Combined Publishing, 1999). By this account, as the British come within range, Putnam simply yelled, "Fire!" Presumably, Brooks avoids the other, more colorful material as of doubtful origin.

V. Speechlet to Icon

The foregoing may help answer *how* "Don't fire" moved from recollection to Speechlet, but not *why* it became iconic, a Battle of Bunker Hill meme, and arguably an important meme for the entire American Revolution. As with Grant's famous set-jaw-and-chomped-cigar letter from Spottsylvania, words alone were insufficient to produce iconicity; there must have been something else, a certain public receptivity to existing memes that instantly coalesced around the Speechlet like scattered iron filings to a magnet. After all, "Don't fire" produced no new knowledge about the battle. But what it did do was buttress existing memes and flatter a national vanity.

And "Don't fire" did become iconic. A full study of how this Speechlet became eponymous with the Battle of Bunker Hill would fill its own book, so my footnote (see below) will cite only the better-known examples. "Don't fire" and the memes it carried must have filled tens of thousands of speeches, newspaper and magazine articles, textbooks, as well as prints and paintings throughout the nineteenth century, in an annual cycle comprised of April 15, July 4, Washington's birthday and, later, Lincoln's—not to mention the great Centennial of 1876 and the hundreds of centennial commemorations that followed in which various Revolutionary War events were marked between 1875 and 1883.[13]

As to *why* this happened: first, "Don't fire" should be considered alongside the other five one-liners Swett attributed to Old Put. They are all ROE, and

13   Here is a selected sampling of nineteenth century textbooks and histories that carried the "Don't fire" Speechlet in its Bunker Hill narrative—in most cases, reproduced from Swett: Charles A. Goodrich, *The Child's History of the United States, designed as a First Book of History for Schools* (Philadelphia: Thomas, Cowperthwait & Co., 1839), 76; J.H. Siddons, *A Familiar History of the United States of America, from the date of the earliest settlements down to the present time* (London: Darton and Hodge, 1865), 136; Jacob Harris Patton, *Patton's Concise History of the American People, From the Discoveries of the Continent to 1876, The Centennial Year of the Nation's Independence* (New York: J.B. Ford & Company, 1876), 331; Hezekiah Butterworth, *Young Folks' History of America* (Boston: Estes and Lauriat, 1882), 258; David Pulsifer, *An Account of the Battle of Bunker Hill, Compiled from Authentic Sources* (Boston: A. Williams and Co., 1872), 37; [Local History] Mrs. E. Vale Smith, *History of Newburyport, From the Earliest Settlement of the Country to the Present Time* (Boston: Damrell and Moore, 1854), 90; [Poetry] "The Battle of Bunker Hill, or The Temple of Liberty; an Historic Poem in Four Cantos, Col. William Emmons," 10th edition, Col. William Emmons (Boston: 1865, first published 1839), Canto III, 82: Still Putnam keeps his sword suspended high—They now so close, he looks them in the eye!—They caught the rising vengeance of his soul... .

propositions of the "If-Then" variety—albeit the "ifs" are unstated: implied before each Speechlet was "*If* you hear my order" or "*if* you see the British within range," *then* you are to: "Fire Low!" and/or "Aim at the waistbands!" and/or "Pick off the commanders!" Only the "Don't fire" Speechlet is entirely self-executing: Don't fire, that is, you will refrain, until the enemy's sclera is in view; then fire. For this Speechlet, there is tactical logic: the commander may be preparing for the possibility that he will be *hors de combat* or outside of earshot (whether because of distance or din) by the time the enemy is within the desired range.

Although these one-liners were offered (1818) and reoffered (1825), why did "Don't fire" receive the glory while the others were ignored? After all, there was at least some meme sizzle to several of them. "Aim at the handsome coats!" or "Pick off the officers!" might have testified to the speaker's penetrating tactical insight and presence of mind as he sought to disrupt British command by targeting officers. Or "Fire Low!" might testify to the speaker's great knowledge of musketry: that the recoil produced by these weapons forced their barrels upwards even before the ball was discharged, thus requiring a slightly lowered aim for accuracy.

But I believe that the reason why "Don't fire" became preeminent was because first, it was simply dramatic, and thus had a powerful literary attraction to those who later wrote or spoke of the battle. But it also embedded meanings that went to the heart of how Americans remembered—and wanted to keep on remembering—their Revolution.

Here, readers should note that "Don't fire" was a civilian and not a military phenomenon. For soldiers at the battle, if the ROE was said at all, it likely had limited influence. Colonel John Stark, commanding the American left, had already marked a kill line by driving a stake some forty yards in his front; when the Brits reached that point, Stark's troops fired with devastating effect. On Stark's right was the redoubt commanded by William Prescott. The surrounding slopes were killing fields covered with an uncut, tall grass. The day was exceptionally hot (at least 95 degrees), humid, and bright, and the American soldiers, although more coolly garbed than their British counterparts, were undoubtedly sweating by the time the battle began after 3:00 PM. This temperature likely produced ground level heat distortions that would have impaired visual acuity even over short ranges. Moreover, Americans seeking to comply with "Don't fire" would likely have interpreted it literally, squinting through sweat-stung eyes for what enemy sclera might be seen. It is far more likely that Putnam's (and/or others', including Prescott's) simple command "Fire!" was the chief cause of pulled triggers.[14]

Thus, the meanings of "Don't fire" are really about civilians, not soldiers. And the place to begin is with the Speechlet itself. Its most arresting image is that of "the whites of their eyes." On first hearing "Don't fire," one imagines the eye's appearance at normal conversational distance or perhaps one's own eye reflected in a mirror. (Only a trained sniper would be able to quickly and accurately estimate the exact distance, in normal atmospheric conditions, at which the human sclera first becomes visible to the unaided eye.) But in that first moment of most listeners' untutored imaginations, neither conversational distance nor the space between a gazer and his mirror is even the full length of a "Brown Bess" (British Land Pattern) musket. In most peoples' imaginations the Speechlet briefly inserts the enemy at the distance of hand-to-hand combat. And it is important to remember here that the full image is not hand-to-hand but rather musket-to-the-enemy's face or chest—point-blank range. Coupled with the word "fire," the resulting image is terrifying in one sense and horrifying in another.

First, nineteenth-century civilians would have been even more terrified at the image of an enemy that close because they knew (or would have learned from popular illustrations) that British muskets at Bunker Hill were tipped with socket bayonets. This was the "cold steel" cliché of eighteenth and nineteenth century combat; this image would have amplified the scene's imaginary terrors. (One only had to gaze at John Trumbull's 1786 painting, *The Death of General Warren at the Battle of Bunker Hill*, or the widely-distributed prints of that scene—and countless Americans did so—to see a British regular whose bayonet was only inches from the prostrate Warren; the background scene depicts a forest of British bayonets and a foreground of conspicuously untipped American muskets.) And dwelling on the common-sense implications of the "Don't fire" scenery leads to other alarming impressions. What if the enemy fires first? After all, if the American can see British sclera, the British grenadier can see American sclera. And the Briton is imagined to be (as he was) a professional soldier, skilled with the bayonet, whereas the Americans are armed with mostly civilian firearms, most without bayonets; thus, in close combat, once the musket was discharged or no longer useful as a club, one either fled,

---

14 Brooks, *The Boston Campaign*, 156; 145 (temperature).

surrendered, or was stabbed to death—which in fact is what happened to many Americans defending the Bunker Hill redoubt.

But these imaginings also summon horror. Long before the mind has worked out that the sclera becomes visible long before normal conversational distance is reached, the Speechlet is likely to give rise to ghastly imaginings about what happens to an enemy should the Americans fire first—and what will happen to Americans when the enemy inevitably returns fire. Here the images of death inflicted upon on the enemy are not anonymous; withholding fire until one sees the sclera, whether at normal conversational distance or even at 132 feet (the approximate equivalent of "8 rods") means shooting another human being with recognizable features. Nor will the injury inflicted resemble anything heroic. Using a Brown Bess .75-caliber musket, with a low-velocity, soft lead ball that tended to flatten upon impact, the wound ballistics might actually rival (or exceed) those caused by today's M-16. Putting the matter bluntly, such a .75-caliber projectile fired at the imagined point-blank range will literally blow out entire brains, create baseball-sized exit wounds, and do such terrible damage to bones that would defy the skill of even modern-day reconstructive surgeons to repair.

But these associations with "Don't fire" led to some important memes about the Battle of Bunker Hill, and perhaps the Revolution generally. Here two questions are raised by "Don't fire." First, what sort of man would have stood firm as the British closed to this intimate distance? Second, what sort of man would inflict this kind of death on other men? One might answer "a British Regular" or, later in the war, "a Hessian mercenary." Both of these enemy groups had repeatedly demonstrated in European battles that they could stand firm and kill other men. Yet American civil society had to find answers to these two questions other than "regular" or "mercenary." The American problem was really an old one: how could one reconcile fathers, husbands and sons, farmers, clerks and merchants, with the killers that these men had temporarily become in the late afternoon of June 17, 1775? (And for some of them, for many years to come.) As these questions were answered, "Don't fire" would become iconic.

Contemporaries of the battle o Bunker Hill also grappled with these questions. Five days after the engagement, readers learned from the *Massachusetts Spy, or American Oracle of Liberty* that, "Though this scene was horrible and altogether new to most of our men, yet many stood and received wounds by swords and bayonets before they quitted the lines. . . . Our men are in high spirits."

Sometime later, in a famous anecdote often repeated over the years, George Washington, then bound for Cambridge to assume army command, lent (what would eventually become) his great prestige to the same meme. When he first learned of Bunker Hill,

> he inquired if the militia had stood the fire of the Regulars? And when told that they had not only stood that fire, but reserved their own till the enemy was within eight rods, and then poured it in with tremendous effect—"then," exclaimed [Washington], "the liberties of the country are safe!"[15]

In a written account that also would circulate later, Benjamin Franklin in Paris reacted to the news by echoing Washington. "Americans will fight," he concluded. Thus, "England has lost her colonies forever." Reinforcing this meme came tributes from enemies. Writing to Lord Dartmouth after the battle, British General Thomas Gage declared that "the rebels are not the despicable rabble too many have supposed them to be…. The conquest of this country is not easy…."[16]

From the beginning the first question—about what sort of man would stand firm as the Brits advanced—was answered: a very *disciplined* man. Despite the fact that this man was a farmer, clerk or merchant, he had proved that he could hold fast with the best of them. He could wait until he saw the "whites of their eyes." Contemporaries thus framed the issue: American "rabble" had indeed faced down British Regulars.

But how had the Americans done this? During the battle the British Regulars also held fast and displayed great discipline. How was the American different? Here an answer evolved to the second question: What kind of man could not only hold his fire, but also pull a trigger to kill other men—and yet not

---

15 Newspaper quoted in Richard Frothingham, *The Centennial: Battle of Bunker Hill* (Boston: Little, Brown, and Company, 1875), Appendix. The reporter was misinformed. Many of the Americans who had fought at Bunker Hill were not only not in high spirits, but were convinced that the British had won a decisive victory due to the treachery of American officers. An investigation was demanded and finally conducted; no treachery was found. But the episode suggests considerable daylight between later judgments of the battle and the attitude of those who were there; Daniel Webster, *An Address Delivered at the Completion of the Bunker Hill Monument, June 17, 1843* (Boston: Tappan and Dennet, 1843), 9.

16 Robert C. Winthrop, "The Unveiling of the Statue of Colonel William Prescott: An Oration Delivered on Bunker Hill, June 17, 1881," *Addresses and Speeches on Various Occasions, from 1878 to 1886* (Boston: Little Brown and Company, 1886), 264-265.

share the presumably lower moral character of Regulars and mercenaries, who had come "three thousand miles and died/to keep the Past upon its throne," or because they were paid, or impressed, or were, as Wellington famously declared, "the scum of the earth" who had no better prospects than the mean profession of soldiering?[17] Daniel Webster answered that question for his generation in 1825 when he delivered his famous speech at the cornerstone-laying for the Bunker Hill Monument:

> War on their own soil and at their own doors, was, indeed, a strange work to the yeomanry of New England; but their consciences were convinced of its necessity, their country called them to it, and they did not withhold themselves from the perilous trial. The ordinary occupations of life were abandoned; the plough was staid in the unfinished furrow; wives gave up their husbands, and mothers gave up their sons, to the battles of a civil war.[18]

In short, these Americans who killed other men were reluctant killers: farmers, not soldiers; sons and husbands defending their homes, not Regulars or Hessians invading the homes of others. Americans killed because compelled by conscience; they killed because they were patriots. To fit Bunker Hill's legacy, such men could only be "yeomanry," and the work of killing had to be "strange;" but because the cause was just, these men would, when British sclera came in view, willingly execute the "fire" instruction in the "Don't fire" Speechlet. For Sir Andrew Agnew, Prince Charles of Lorraine, and Frederick the Great, "Don't fire" was just another ROE, and its role in the histories of Great Britain, Austria and Prussia barely a footnote; but in those battles, the Speechlet, the men and the national memes had not connected. But the memes and images bundled in America's "Don't fire" neatly summarized a vast reservoir of national memory.

---

17 "Lines Suggested by the Graves of Two English Soldiers on Concord Battle-Ground," by James Russell Lowell, *The Poetical Works of James Russell Lowell* (Boston: Houghton, Mifflin and Company, 1890), 97-98. The classic statement of why *they* (in contrast to *we*) fought in the Revolution can be found in the poem's complete stanza: These men were brave enough, and true / To the hired soldier's bull-dog creed / What brought them here they never knew / They fought as suits the English breed / They came three thousand miles, and died / To keep the Past upon its throne / Unheard, beyond the ocean tide / Their English mother made her moan.

18 Daniel Webster, *An Address Delivered at the Laying of the Corner Stone of the Bunker Hill Monument*, 63.

VI. Iconicity

"Don't fire" exercised a powerful hold on American imaginations. How powerful was illustrated sixty-three years after the publication of Swett's first *Sketch*. Precisely at noon on June 17, 1881, cannon from the Charlestown Navy Yard began firing salutes as church bells pealed throughout the town. The weather was magnificent, so a large tent, erected out of respect for New England's unpredictable weather, had become a hindrance. It was meant to seat a thousand people, including the Commonwealth's governor and assorted elites. But an overflow crowd now spilled onto the slopes around the Bunker Hill Monument.

Faces turned toward the raised speaker's platform that the organizers, the eminently respectable Bunker Hill Monument Association, had elevated so that all could see and hear. And near this platform stood the reason for it all: a bronze statute of Revolutionary War hero William Prescott, for the moment draped in the Stars and Stripes. (By now, most historians had decided that it was Prescott who actually had been in command on Bunker Hill.) And the day's speaker was no less a figure than Robert Charles Winthrop, a direct descendent of Massachusetts Bay governor Jonathan Winthrop; this latest Winthrop would say his piece before ordering the much-anticipated sculpture unveiled. [19]

Winthrop stood in many venerable meme-streams beyond his own ancestry. He held, among numerous other posts, the presidency of the Bunker Hill Monument Association. The Massachusetts General Court had chartered the Association in 1823. Two years later, when the monument's cornerstone was laid, the great Daniel Webster had addressed an audience that included many Revolutionary War veterans, among them the Marquis de Lafayette. In 1843, when the capstone was emplaced, Lafayette was gone but Webster remained to speak again.

The seventy-two year-old Winthrop, like Webster, was considered a formidable orator; and, like Webster, he had had a lifetime of practice to hone his oratory. He had held elective offices in state and local government, became Speaker of the U.S. House of Representatives, and had served in the United States Senate. But as politics veered towards the extremes of civil war,

---

19 *Proceedings of the Bunker Hill Monument Association at the Annual Meeting, June 17, 1881, with the Address of The Hon. Robert C. Winthrop at the Inauguration of the Statue of Colonel William Prescott* (Boston: Bunker Hill Monument Association, 1881).

Winthrop's ideas of "the best men" form of conservatism lost favor; after the 1850s he remained politically active but as a private citizen. However, in the three decades since he had also found ready acceptance as an *eminence grise* of matters historical, a worthy replacement for the long-gone Edward Everett, and, like the latter, the necessary man to mark the great anniversaries of Boston and Massachusetts. After all, one or another of the Winthrops had been present from the beginning. However, of importance to the "Don't fire" Speechlet was another of Winthrop's traits: a noted historian in his own right, he was also an intellectually honest man.[20]

He told the audience that he would not review the Battle of Bunker Hill in any great detail. "Where could I turn for any materials which have not already become hackneyed and threadbare, and which are not as familiar as household words to those who surround me?" he plaintively asked his listeners. By 1881 that was certainly true. So Winthrop decided to remind his audience about matters that were perhaps not as familiar: that the battle was first seen as a defeat, and few in its immediate aftermath recognized its significance; that many American soldiers left the field angry, and that "Nobody for years…came forward to claim the honor of having directed this battle." Even General Artemus Ward, the Cambridge-based commander who had ordered the defense of Charlestown, had not bothered to enter that order into his official record. Only with the passage of time, and by the judgments of such famous outsiders such as Washington, Franklin, and General Gage, did the battle's true significance emerge.[21]

In his lifetime Winthrop had witnessed Bunker Hill's narrative enter into the realm of cliché, recounted repeatedly by local, state and national histories. In the moments after the flag was pulled from William Wetmore Story's sculpture of Prescott, Winthrop proceeded to re-imagine for the audience the events of the day of battle, using the statue as his outline. He provided what later generations would call voice-over, although the images described moved only in the imagination. Winthrop summoned Prescott's ghost:

> His eagle gaze is riveted with intense energy on the close-approaching foe. With his left hand he is hushing and holding back the impetuous soldiers under his command, to await his word. With his right hand he is just ready to lift the sword

20 Appleton's *Cyclopaedia*, VI: 576. The judgment on Winthrop's candor is my own.

21 Winthrop, *Addresses*, 258, 262-263, 264-265.

which is to be their signal for action…. That same sword, which, tradition tells us, he waved where he now stands, when seeing at length, 'the buttons on the coats,' or it may have been, 'the whites of the eyes,' of the advancing enemy in the original onslaught, he first gave the order 'Fire!'

Here Winthrop may have tried to break a spell. Since 1818 "Don't fire till you see the whites of their eyes" was the standard entry in countless textbooks, including that of the enormously popular fabulist, Mason ("Parson") Weems' *Life of Washington*, a sure sign of its widespread acceptance. Now Winthrop demoted the Speechlet to "a tradition," and not the only one; perhaps Prescott had urged his men to wait until it was British buttons and not sclera that were visible.[22]

But for that generation and others that followed, it was too late for footnotes. Soon after Winthrop's speech the power of "Don't fire" would be demonstrated anew. When the Bunker Hill Monument Association published its official account of the proceedings, the unknown writer could not let the old story go. In summarizing Winthrop's speech, he wrote that the bronze figure of Prescott "represents the colonel at the moment preceding the attack, and when he is said to have uttered the memorable words, 'Don't fire until I tell you; don't fire until you see the whites of their eyes.'" The anonymous writer made no mention of any buttons.[23]

Legacy

Renewed usage of "Don't fire" would be well attested in later American wars: it was uttered at the Battle of San Jacinto, at Shiloh and during the Spanish-American War. The Speechlet outlived the day of the smoothbore musket. As long as soldiers would need an instant, widely recognized, American meme with strong patriotic associations in order to hold fast and prepare for close action, "Don't fire" would serve the purpose.[24]

---

22 Winthrop, *Addresses,* 274; M. L. Weems, *The Life of George Washington with Curious Anecdotes Equally Honorable to Himself, and Exemplary to His Young Countrymen* (Philadelphia: Joseph Allen, 1833), 75-76.

23 *Proceedings of the Bunker Hill Monument Association,* 10.

24 Examples of these could fill yet another volume. One selected from each war: "Recollections of Sparks," *Texas Historical Association Quarterly,* 70; John S.C. Abbott, *The History of the Civil War in America* (Springfield, Massachusetts, 1866), II: 215; Willis

Yet one has to look beyond this Speechlet's discipline memes to its summoning of some specific imagery about the Battle of Bunker Hill, the American Revolution, and even later wars. Because most American armies have been citizen armies, Revolutionary attitudes about who *we* are, and *why* we fight, as well as about who *they* are and about *why* they are fighting us, have proven remarkably durable. In a some way, we remain the same kind of Americans battling the same kind of enemy that Webster described in 1825: *we* are the undrilled yeomanry, the Minute Men, hastily dropping the plow because impelled by conscience; *they* are either professionals who, as Lowell suggested, fight from some "bull-dog creed," or are misguided masses, conscripts, fanatics fighting on orders, ideology, from indoctrination or ignorance.

The memes of Bunker Hill foreshadowed those of wars to come. Looked at through millennial eyes, the battle was really a reiteration of a far older tale: the story of moral righteousness prevailing over larger numbers of professionally trained soldiers wielding superior weapons. The backstory that illuminated this "history" played well to subsequent generations of Americans, whose understanding of the Revolution incorporated memes of undrilled-but-righteous yeomanry, a cause favored by God, one that triumphed over brave-but-soulless professionals whose cause was not so favored. This story has been told ever since the shepherd David met the soldier Goliath.

John Abbot, *Blue Jackets of '98: A History of the Spanish-American War* (New York: Dodd, Mead and Company, 1899), 201-202.

Chapter Fifteen

The Short Journey of a Modern Speechlet: "Last" Words to Immortal Words

I. Introduction

The last words of the well-known have always held imaginations. Whether esteemed or reviled, a speaker's final utterance will be probed for advice concerning this world or hints about the next. Thus in his final moments did Mattathias appoint his son Judah as Maccabean commander and offer advice on defeating the Syrians; "Stonewall" Jackson's last utterance—"Let us cross over the river, and rest under the shade of the trees"—gave hope to many contemporaries that there was a natural "translation" from earth to heaven; finally, we have the last words of Field Marshal Alfred Graf von Schlieffen, originator of the plan that bore his name: his ghost departed in 1913, but just before doing so left this admonition, presumably to his colleagues on the German General Staff: "See that you make the right wing strong." One year later they would heed his advice.[1]

---

1 Maccabees, 2:49-69, *Harper Collins Study Bible*, (New York: HarperCollins Publishers, 1993), 1653-1654; Frank E. Vandiver, *Mighty Stonewall* (College Station, Texas: Texas A&M University Press, 1957, reprint 1988), 494; J.F.C. Fuller, *A Military History of the Western World, From the Seven Days Battle, 1862, to the Battle of Leyte Gulf, 1944*, (New York: Funk & Wagnalls Company, 1956), III: 196 n. 1.

No matter the speaker, last words do enjoy a natural advantage: since the deceased can no longer clarify his meaning, it falls to the living to supply it. Here history becomes self-interested séance.

Perhaps the most famous Speechlet in United States Naval history was widely believed to have been the speaker's last words: "Don't give up the ship!" uttered by the gravely wounded Captain James Lawrence. It was not the first time in American naval history that these words had been spoken. In 1776 the Continental Navy's Captain James Mugford was mortally wounded during a British assault on his schooner *Franklin*, then in Boston Harbor. His final words were, "Don't give up the ship! You will beat them off!" Somebody took notes; but, unlike the case with Lawrence, in 1776 the meme, the man, and the moment had not yet met.[2]

Were "Don't give up the ship" Lawrence's last words? In the summer of 1813 and for many decades thereafter, few Americans doubted it. On August 23, 1813, no less a personage than Joseph Story, Associate Justice of the United States Supreme Court, delivered the eulogy at Captain James Lawrence's Salem funeral (Lawrence eventually would have three burials; a hero's work is never done). The bespectacled, thirty-four-year-old judge and scholar declared, "He nobly maintained [his honor], and with his dying declaration," Story declared, "'never give up the ship—the flag shall wave, while I live'—he sealed the immortality of his own fame."[3]

It was only seven weeks earlier that Lawrence had been mortally wounded on the deck of the *USS Chesapeake* as that ship battled with its British adversary, the *HMS Shannon*. The *Chesapeake*, its crew and captain were all killed or captured; Lawrence died four days later en route to British detention in Halifax. The first detailed accounts of the battle did not reach the United States until the third week of June.

Eighteen thirteen did not witness any communication revolutions: the telegraph and railroads still lay in the future; steamboats were fledglings; and the great canal systems were mostly proposals. But the fact that Judge Story could recognize "immortality" in "Don't give up the ship!" only seven

---

2 *Dictionary of Military and Naval Quotations*, 29.

3 *An account of the Funeral Honours Bestowed on the remains of Capt. Lawrence and Lieut. Ludlow, with the Eulogy pronounced at Salem, on the occasion, by Hon. Joseph Story* (Boston: Joshua Beicher, 1813), 50.

weeks after its utterance did testify to something new; after all, "Don't fire" had taken decades to travel from the past to the present (or vice-versa, depending on one's view of that Speechlet's authenticity). And less than one month after Story pronounced, Oliver Hazard Perry invested his friend's utterance with even more fame and meaning when he recycled the words onto his banner during the Battle of Lake Erie. In sum, Lawrence's words had made a remarkable round trip in only three months: from the battlefield to newspapers; thence wholesaled through such media as Story's widely reprinted eulogy, the declarations of patriotic associations, and so forth; before returning to the battlefield on Perry's banner. Currents of information, stirred by growing numbers of newspapers, literate readers, and democracy itself, had begun to move faster.

II. The Speechlets

Don't give up the ship!

—One version of the "last words" spoken by the mortally wounded Captain James Lawrence, June 1, 1813

Don't Give Up the Ship

—Speechlet appearing on the fighting flag of Oliver Hazard Perry's ship *USS Lawrence* at the Battle of Lake Erie, September 10, 1813[4]

III. The Words

At noon on June 1, 1813, thirty-two-year-old Captain James Lawrence, a fifteen-year Navy veteran, ordered the frigate *USS Chesapeake* from Boston Harbor to sea. The *HMS Shannon* was then some thirty miles offshore, its sails a taunt to the honorable Lawrence. Unbeknownst to Lawrence, but utterly typical of this Nelsonian age, the Shannon's commander, Captain Philip Broke, had sent a note challenging the *Chesapeake* to a duel—using ships instead of pistols. While Lawrence never received the note, it told him what he

---

4　Donald R. Hickey, *Don't Give Up the Ship!* (Urbana, Illinois: University of Illinois Press, 2007), 111.

probably already knew: the two ships were fairly evenly matched in size, crew, and guns. The honor ethos of the day required Broke to disclose the *Shannon's* fighting capabilities, for the Code Duello demanded that contenders be similarly armed. And, except as to luck, they were: the *Shannon* displaced some 1,066 tons to the *Chesapeake's* 1,244 tons; the former had 300 crewmen and thirty "seamen, boys and passengers" taken from recently captured vessels, the *Chesapeake's* crew was 382; Broke disclosed "twenty four guns upon her broadside, and one light boat gun," the *Chesapeake* had thirty-eight guns.[5]

Lawrence was well suited to his command. He had served off the Barbary Coast for five years, acting as Stephen Decatur's first lieutenant aboard the ketch *Intrepid* during the dangerous but successful mission to burn the captured frigate *USS Philadelphia* in Tripoli Harbor. Lawrence later commanded *Gunboat No. 6*, and served as first lieutenant aboard the *USS Constitution*; in the years before the War of 1812 he had also commanded a series of brig-sloops and then larger ship-sloops, ranging from 185 to 480 tons and boasting between 14 and 18 guns. Three months before meeting the *Shannon*, Lawrence, commanding the ship-sloop *USS Hornet*, had gained fame by sinking the *HMS Peacock* off the coast of present-day Guyana.

There he had also distinguished himself by more than just a naval victory. Widely and favorably noted was Lawrence's magnanimous treatment of British prisoners. "The officers of the *Peacock* were so affected by the treatment they received from Captain Lawrence," Washington Irving wrote later, "that on their arrival at New York they made a grateful acknowledgment in the public papers." Lawrence's public persona was marked by memes of honor. Resolutions had been introduced into the

---

5 Albert Gleaves, *James Lawrence: Captain, United States Navy, Commander of the "Chesapeake"* (New York: G.P. Putnam and Sons, 1904), 153, 209; Harry L. Coles, *The War of 1812* (University of Chicago Press, 1966), Table 1, 73; Lewis Deare, *Biography of James Lawrence, Esq., Late a Captain in the Navy of the United States* (New Brunswick, New Jersey: L. Deare, 1813), 168-172. Deare contains the complete text of Broke's challenge.

Massachusetts Senate tendering him the official thanks of the Commonwealth.[6]

Just before the *Chesapeake* unmoored, Lawrence assembled the crew for a Pre-Battle Speech. (When the Americans hove in view Captain Broke would do likewise for the *Shannon's* crew.) Lawrence's speech was not recorded, but the recollections of survivors offered a paraphrase:

> [Lawrence] told them that a frigate was in sight, and that it was his intention to go out and bring her to action. He pointed to the flag at the peak and exhorted the crew to die, sooner than see the colors dishonored, and closed his remarks by reminding them of the "Hornet's" splendid victory, and urged them when they closed with the Englishman to "'Peacock' her, my lads, 'Peacock' her.'"

It was also at this point that Lawrence raised a white flag bearing the Speechlet by which he sought to exhort the crew: a banner with the words "Free Trade and Sailors' Rights."[7]

The battle commenced at 5:55 PM. From the first exchange of fire until the British hauled down *Chesapeake's* flag perhaps fifteen minutes passed. For the Americans, the affair was a disaster from the start. In the first minutes, the *Shannon's* cannon and topmast snipers killed or wounded most of the *Chesapeake's* senior and many mid-level officers; American leadership was thus decapitated when it would be shortly needed to organize the crew to resist British boarding parties. Worse, as the *Chesapeake* passed the *Shannon*, tangles of shredded sail, dragged rigging and shot-up deck rails somehow hooked the *Shannon's* sheet anchor. Thus the two ships were temporarily joined, with the *Chesapeake's* unfavorable position preventing it from using its guns. In the midst of this combat, a British hand grenade detonated a *Chesapeake* arms chest, engulfing the deck in flame and smoke.[8]

For battle speech historians, two aspects of this fight are worth exploring. First was the sheer violence of close-quarter naval engagements

---

6   Washington Irving, *Biographies and Miscellanies*, edited by Pierre Irving (New York: G.P. Putnam and Son, 1869), 39-40, 43-44; Gleaves, *James Lawrence: Captain,* 57; Harry L. Coles, *The War of 1812,* Table 1, 73.

7   Gleaves, *James Lawrence*, 174; Broke's speech may be found at 185; Irving, *Captain James Lawrence*, 47.

8   Gleaves, *James Lawrence,* "The Battle," 177-202.

during the Age of Sail: blasts from opposing cannon just yards apart created maelstroms of secondary projectiles—notably wood splinters—that were as lethal as metal; blast heat would ignite any combustibles; and blast overpressures could shred human tissue. Even more-distant persons not shredded or burned by the heat and overpressure would face exploding eardrums at a time when balance and maneuver were key—to simply do one's job, organize for defense or attack, or dodge the hail of musket balls raining on deck. Finally there was the reciprocal violence of boarding and repelling boarders, with the special terrors of edged weapons—in such combat a cutlass was likely more useful than a single-shot, muzzle-loaded firearm.

Those lacking imagination should consider Canadian Judge Thomas Chandler Halliburton's visit to the captured *Chesapeake* after it docked in Halifax. No one had bothered to clean the ship since the battle, and it was unlikely that Halliburton, who later gained great literary fame as the humorist "Sam Slick," was in a very good humor afterwards:

> Externally [the *Chesapeake*] had just returned from a short cruise, but internally the scene was one never to be forgotten by a landsman. . . . [The] coils and folds of rope were steeped in gore, as if in a slaughter house. She was a fir-built ship and her splinters had wounded nearly as many as the '*Shannon's*' shot. Pieces of skin with pendant hair were adhering to the sides of the ship, and in one place I noticed portions of fingers protruding, as if thrust through the outer wall of the frigate.

Such gore rivals the aftermath of an IED attack. Given all this, readers can form some idea of *why* survivors' memories might conflict about what precisely it was that Captain James Lawrence had said during the battle.[9]

When the action commenced at 5:55 PM the two ships were "within pistol shot;" the *Shannon's* cannon fired first, and then continued firing at will. This fire was probably decisive: blast, heat and projectiles scoured the *Chesapeake's* spar deck and killed and wounded approximately one hundred of the estimated one hundred and fifty men on the upper deck. Here the Americans lost many officers; it was at this moment when, amidst the storm of larger projectiles, a pistol ball slammed into the back of James Lawrence's

---

9   As quoted in Gleaves, *James Lawrence*, 207.

knee. Meanwhile, the *Chesapeake* returned fire, also wreaking devastation on the *Shannon's* decks; as one historian observed, the ships "were too close for any shots to miss."[10]

Lawrence, in great pain, and bleeding profusely, nonetheless raised himself and, supported by the starboard binnacle, struggled to manage the ship even as successive waves of cannon blast swept the decks. By all accounts his demeanor was calm. As the two ships were about to collide into temporary joinder, Lawrence, white trousers now bloodstained, limped from starboard to port. In "a clear voice" he ordered that boarding parties assemble; however, by then it was too late. The British had begun to board, perhaps as many as seventy men during the first swarm. British cannon ceased firing in an effort to avoid killing their own as the battle now shifted from ship-to-ship to hand-to-hand.

As the crew assembled in response to Lawrence's call, echoed by those officers who had survived the *Shannon's* first attack, Lawrence was gut shot by British marine Lieutenant Low, who had recognized his target. Lawrence collapsed to the deck and Midshipman William S. Cox ran to his side. Lawrence, now gravely wounded but still conscious, began to utter a series of statements. As with the Battle of Bunker Hill, history would have its choice of Speechlets to immortalize.

Prostrate on the deck, Lawrence still tried to direct the action. "Fire away, lads," was one utterance later remembered. To Cox, Lawrence clearly needed immediate medical attention; so, together with four seamen, he began to carry the stricken captain below. At this time, Lawrence was still conscious, had observed the crew fragmenting as the British boarded, and became agitated. His "last words," declared Washington Irving, whose contemporary biography of Lawrence was widely reprinted and was the source from which most Americans learned of the action, was "Don't surrender the ship!" But as Irving tried to make clear, these were Lawrence's "last words" on deck, but not in life.

Once brought to the wardroom, now converted into the charnel house that characterized most nineteenth-century field hospitals, Lawrence continued to converse about various matters, and yet several more of his recollected utterances might have qualified as Speechlets in their own right. Perhaps characteristically, Lawrence turned the surgeons away: "No," he

---

10 Gleaves, *James Lawrence*, 187-188.

objected, "serve those who came before me, Doctor; I can wait my turn." When the noise above deck subsided, Lawrence wanted to know why, and he ordered Surgeon's Mate Dr. John Dix to "Go on deck, and order them to fire faster and to fight the ship till she sinks; never strike; let the colors wave while I live." Dix could not comply because by this time the British controlled the upper deck. Learning this, Lawrence rebuked his subordinates: "Then the officers have not toed the mark," he declared. ""She [the *Shannon*] was whipped when I left the deck." By now, Lawrence was repeating himself, but with greater emphasis. "Doctor, go on deck and tell the Commanding Officer to keep the guns going and fight till she sinks. The flag shall wave while I live," he said to Surgeon Richard Edgar. In the meantime, Lawrence continued to repeat himself, "Don't give up the ship. Blow her up."[11]

So, what were Captain Lawrence's last words? Written almost a century after Lawrence's death, Albert Gleaves' sympathetic yet exhaustive 1904 biography had access to important British and American sources that had been unavailable to Washington Irving and Lewis Deare, whose separate biographies were published during the war. According to Gleaves, after the surrender Lawrence requested a visit from the Shannon's surgeon. Following an examination, Lawrence baited the British doctor with the remark that "I see from it that there is no hope. What is your opinion?" "Sir, I grieve to tell you," Dr. Alexander Jack solemnly replied, "that I cannot entertain a hope of your recovery." Lawrence lingered for four days "in extreme bodily pain" before he died on June 4, most likely from infection. "He made no comment on the battle, nor indeed was he heard to utter a word," Irving wrote, "except to make such simple requests as his necessities required." As Lawrence's life flickered out, his last words, whatever they were, likely followed suit.[12]

---

11 Gleaves, *James Lawrence*, 190-195; Irving, *Biographies*, 49.

12 Gleaves, *James Lawrence*, 205; Irving, *Biographies*, 52. Writer James Fenimore Cooper had once served under Lawrence, was fond of his former commander, and made a determined effort to authoritatively establish what was said. The closest Cooper came was, "Never strike the flag of my ship." Modern historian Donald R. Hickey is probably correct when he observed that "Each of these accounts may well be true, since Lawrence probably expressed his wishes in several different ways." Donald R. Hickey, *Don't Give Up the Ship!*, 111; Appleton's *Cyclopaedia*, I: 726.

IV. Words to Speechlet to Partisan Controversy

Why—and how—did "Don't give up the ship" become instantly popular during the summer of 1813? Indeed, so widely known that at the Battle of Lake Erie Oliver Hazard Perry hoisted his banner bearing these words from his flagship, not coincidentally named the *U.S. Brig Lawrence*? Again: forty-three years had elapsed before "Don't fire" emerged to bear canonical Revolutionary War memes; in contrast, Lawrence's words would be injected into the national meme-stream within thirty days of his death.

The *whys* of this Speechlet's popularity rest with the memes it carried and the reasons many Americans found these persuasive during the War of 1812. This issue is discussed a little later.

First, I want to briefly explore *how* this Speechlet could emerge as an emblem of anything. The answer is best illustrated by comparing the meme retailing networks of 1775 with those of 1813. There was probably no shortage of meme-producers during either age. As I discussed with the minting of Grant's moniker "Unconditional Surrender," meme creation can function either "bottom up" or "top down." On the other hand, the existence of organized meme wholesalers and retailers can powerfully influence both the speed and reach of meme transmission. For battle (or any) Speechlets, in 1775 or 1813 newspapers were the first among equals as meme transmitters; these were probably followed in importance by sermons, government itself (especially the post office), and then various civil associations—patriotic, ethnic, or commercial. But it was the newspaper that often linked these groups, their activities and statements, to the wider public.

A few comparative factoids help make the case. When the Battle of Lexington was fought two months before Bunker Hill, there were thirty-seven newspapers publishing throughout what would become the United States of America; although by war's end there would be forty-three newspapers, perhaps only twelve had been in publication throughout the war. So, for example, if "Don't fire" was actually said, certainly one reason that it never enjoyed the same recognition as "Don't give up the ship" was that "[n]ot one newspaper in the principal cities, Boston, New York, and Philadelphia, continued publication throughout the war." In short, during the Revolutionary War, trees fell aplenty, but there were few to relate what noise they made, and—for our purposes, just as important—few to wholesale reports of the noise.[13]

In contrast, by 1810 there were 366 newspapers publishing in the United States—an increase of tenfold since Bunker Hill. In terms of meme wholesaling and retailing, this represents an order of magnitude far greater than ten. Unlike a ration of beer, bread, or beef, the same newspaper could be consumed many times; moreover, once read, spreading a newspaper's content no longer required the newspaper. Here, the retail character of meme-streams becomes clear: one family member reads a newspaper and discusses its contents with three, five or twenty others who might never see a newspaper; and so on.[14]

How did this work in contemporary "real time" with the Speechlet "Don't give up the ship"? Consider a recollection of Richard Rush. Son of the patriot and Declaration signer Benjamin Rush he served during the war as President Madison's Comptroller of the Treasury. He was in Washington when vague reports were first received that the British had captured the *Chesapeake*:

> I remember, who among us can forget, the first rumor of it. I remember the startling sensation. I remember, at first, the universal incredulity. I remember how the post-offices were thronged, for successive days, by anxious inquiring thousands, under the disheartening reports that successively reached the Capital; and then how collections of people rode out for miles upon the highway, to catch something by anticipation as the mail came in. At last, when hope gave way, and the certainty of [the *Chesapeake's*] capture no longer remained in doubt, I remember the universal gloom. Funeral orations, badges of mourning, testified it. "DON'T GIVE UP THE SHIP!" the dying words of Lawrence, slain by the first broadside, were on every tongue.[15]

Readers can see how civilian reprocessing of Lawrence's Speechlet and the story behind it were already at work.

---

13 Frank W. Scott, "Newspapers, 1775-1860," *The Cambridge History of English and American Literature in 18 Volumes* (1907–21), VOLUME XVI, Early National Literature, Part II; Later National Literature, Part I, Section 1, 1.

14 Frank W. Scott, "Newspapers, 1775-1860," Part I, Section 8, 14.

15 Richard Rush, *Residence at the Court of London,* 3rd ed. (Philadelphia: Lippincott & Co, 1872), 360.

Rush's "disheartening reports" almost certainly included Boston, New York and Philadelphia newspapers, which, because of geographical proximity to the battle and returning crew, would have carried the first reports; the "funeral orations" and "badges of mourning" illustrate one retail meme-stream. And the whole suggests what happens when Speechlets match the *zeitgeist*, and how they create powerful, perpetually transmissible ideas throughout the collective mind.

As I next turn to how the memes embedded in "Don't give up the ship" matched the *zeitgeist*, readers should look at the contemporary evidence I cite—newspapers, magazines, government pronouncements, quickie biographies, and the activities of civic associations—and note that in 1775 some of these media categories had not yet existed, and those that did were more limited than they would be forty years later.

What was the likely significance to contemporaries of Lawrence's Speechlet? One factor in its spread was the fact that just as it was on the cusp of diffusion, the Speechlet's now-deceased speaker was injected into the heart of a bitter controversy—not over what he said or even what he did as the *Chesapeake's* captain, but rather something the Massachusetts Senate did. Readers will recall that after Lawrence's sinking of the *HMS Peacock*, resolutions honoring him were introduced in the Federalist-controlled (and thus vehemently antiwar) Massachusetts Senate. But two weeks *after* the *Chesapeake* was captured (although eight days before reports of Lawrence's death and "last" words were received in Boston), the eminent Federalist leader and state senator Josiah Quincy successfully introduced a measure to *withdraw* the testimonials to Lawrence.

Quincy's resolution also recited the Senate's reasons for denying Lawrence his recognition, thus compounding atrocious timing with language that seemed to diminish the new hero and besmirch his sacrifice. Quincy declared that similar resolutions honoring other officers "have given great discontent to many of the good people of this Commonwealth." If the Massachusetts Senate were to pass this resolution honoring Lawrence, it might be seen "as an encouragement and excitement to the continuance of the present, unfair, unnecessary and iniquitous war;" that war, the resolution continued, was being "waged without just cause, and prosecuted in a manner which indicates that conquest and ambition are its real motives," and that as a result "it is not becoming a moral and religious people to express approbation of military and naval exploits, which are not immediately connected with the defense of our own sea coast and soil." The Massachusetts Senate approved Quincy's resolution.[16]

This action would have been controversial in any case. But as reports of Lawrence's fate and words reached the United States, the resolution ignited a firestorm. Josiah Quincy's son Edmund recalled that the resolution "drew down the most violent denunciations of the war party upon [my father's] head." He was accused of "moral treason" in Washington and around the country. I would argue that this bit of timing helped invest "Don't give up the ship" with powerful, highly partisan, and intensely pro-war memes. More than just honoring a hero was now involved. Thus (for example) the "badges of mourning" that Rush observed were more than funereal; they became statements of patriotism, support for the war, and contempt for the antiwar faction.[17]

Thus were Lawrence's death and words joined with the bitter controversy over "Mr. Jemmy's war." During the summer of 1813 tributes flowed. Washington Irving's sympathetic biography of Lawrence first appeared in the *Analectic Magazine*, one of the most popular American journals of its day. Lewis Deare's likewise-sympathetic collection of documents and essays about Lawrence was published shortly thereafter. In June the newspaper *Palladium* (Boston) declared that Lawrence had "met his fate [with] the first ball. 'Give not up the ship,' he said, and fell. . . . He cared only for victory and his country, never for life." On June 25 the *United States Gazette* used Lawrence's memory to implicitly criticize the Massachusetts Senate. "We hope for the honour of our common species, that there is not one man in the community so dead to the honour of his country as not to feel with us the propriety, and in fact the obligation that there is of testifying that the grave of Lawrence is incapable of hiding him from the gratitude of his country." On July 4 the Marine Artillery of Baltimore offered a lengthy salute which closed, "To the memory of Captain Lawrence, whose last words were, 'Sink the ship, sooner than surrender her.'" Two days later the New York Society of the Cincinnati followed with a similar toast.

---

16 Gleaves, *James Lawrence*, 230, 294-295. The first news of Lawrence's fate was received on June 23.

17   Edmund Quincy, *Life of Josiah Quincy* (Boston: Little Brown and Company, 1874), 324-325.

Poets too were heard from, such as "J.S.M.," whose verses were printed by the *New York Evening Post* on July 26: "'Don't yield the ship!' its only cry/ In din of arms the accents die." And much was made of the fact—at the expense of Federalist New England—that the *British* Navy had accorded Lawrence full honors at his temporary interment at Halifax. Perhaps the highest official acknowledgement came on July 4 from Secretary of State James Monroe. "To the memory of Captain Lawrence," the future president declared, "whose last words were 'Sink the ship, sooner than surrender her.'[18]

V. Iconicity

What was the persuasive strategy behind "Don't Give Up The Ship"? When first uttered (in whatever words), it was clearly the command of a captain whose grave wounds only thickened the fog of war already enveloping his command. Indeed, by the time Lawrence was wounded a second time, the battle was lost. His words were those of a commander no longer aware of the reality on his own decks, and the words were thus a forlorn exhortation, or perhaps even wishful thinking. Considered completely out of its historical context, Lawrence's "last words" might have attested to a perverse tragicomedy of war, or its futility, or (returning some context) even buttressed the Federalists' case that the war was "iniquitous" to have cost a good man his life in support of a bad cause.

But Lawrence's Speechlet stood for none of these things, for older, more powerful historical memes were at work. America was at war for the second time with the world's foremost naval power. And to Americans, that war would not, could not, be decided simply by competing with Britain in ships, tonnages, cannon or crews; by such a standard America must lose. Instead the "final words" of James Lawrence embraced a sentiment that in its very denial of reality concealed a profound truth about war, a truth that for Americans would join with memes from the Revolution: victory favors not only those with superior virtue but also those with superior will. If the memes summoned by "Don't fire" came to mean that average American virtue exceeded that of "perfidious Albion's" professional soldiers, then "Don't give up the Ship" relit that virtue in a frame of defiance and stubbornness against impossible odds. When Perry named his ship

---

18 Irving's article in the *Analectic* is reprinted in *Biographies and Miscellanies*; Deare, *Biography of James Lawrence, Esq.,* 89-90 (*Palladium*); 186 (*United States Gazette*); 217-219 (*New York Evening Post*); Gleaves, *James Lawrence*, 235 (Baltimore Marine Artillery and James Monroe), 236 (New York Society of the Cincinnati).

Lawrence and chose to sail under a banner bearing his "martyred" friend's Speechlet, he quite literally "branded" his victory: as Lawrence had died by British lead and the *Chesapeake* was captured by the Royal Navy, so Perry would blow Great Britain off the Great Lakes, redeem Lawrence's name and honor—but also prove that Lawrence's defiance was unrealistic only as to its timing, not its victorious consummation. Perry's branding of the Battle of Lake Erie was yet another gesture of defiance—only, this time, successful.

American memes of defiance, stubbornness, and virtue would shortly come in handy. The year after Lawrence's Speechlet and Perry's victory the British invaded New York and Maine, and to the south, in a humiliating demonstration of American weakness, they burned Washington. But 1814 would also witness the American "codification" of the same memes embodied by Lawrence's Speechlet "Don't give up the ship." It came in the form of a poem scratched on the back of a letter and entitled "The Defence of Fort McHenry"—better known today as the lyrics to "The Star-Spangled Banner." Each stanza is replete with memes of defiance and virtue. Here the fourth stanza merits special consideration:

O, thus be it ever when freemen shall stand,
Between their lov'd home, and the war's desolation,
Blest with vict'ry and peace, may the heav'n rescued land
Praise the Pow'r that hath made and preserv'd us a nation!
Then conquer we must, when our cause it is just,
And this be our motto— "In God is our trust"
And the star-spangled [banner] in triumph shall wave
O'er the land of the free, and the home of the brave![19]

Legacy

"Don't give up the ship" has, together with a few other battle Speechlets, overflowed its original meme-stream to join the inventory of evergreen phrases. Perhaps this is legacy enough. But there is more to the Lawrence/Perry

---

19 Defence of Fort M'Henry," National Poetry, Supplement to *Niles' Weekly Register, edited by H. Niles, From September 1815 to March 1816* (Baltimore: Franklin Press, n.d.), XI: 83. Astute readers will note that these lines differ in a few details from the national anthem's modern version. It is likely that Americans first became acquainted with Key's lyrics from this publication, and thus, I use the original.

Speechlet than even this. One claims "firsts" at one's peril, and so I will not; but at the least, "Don't give up the ship" is a very early instance of a noticeably tightening circle in which a Speechlet begins on a battlefield, "returns" to the home front for "reprocessing" (that is, a civilian meme-maker consensus forms around what was "really" said and meant), and then returns to the battlefield as a "finished product." Indeed, if one places in chronological order three of the four Speechlets considered in this section—"Don't fire," "Don't give up the ship," and Grant's "I propose to fight"—the circle becomes progressively tighter and the round trip faster.

Seventy-eight years after Grant's Speechlet, General Douglas MacArthur arrived in Australia after being evacuated from the doomed American-Filipino island garrison of Corregidor. In Adelaide, MacArthur issued his first public statement since leaving the Philippines. It was brief and lacked the eloquence from another, more-stylized age that under other circumstances the general could easily summon.

However, MacArthur's statement concluded with seven words (soon shortened to three) that can only be considered the progeny of Putnam (or Prescott), Lawrence, Perry and Grant:

I came through and I shall return.[20]

---

20 Byron Darnton, "General Tells Aim," *The New York Times*, March 21, 1942.

Section Six

Three Speeches by President Barack Obama

This section considers three speeches by President Barack Obama, only one of which was made directly to soldiers.

Why include them in a book on battle speech persuasive strategies? A recent student of the "politics-is-war" metaphor gives one justification: "politics resembles warfare, so military literature can teach us something about political action." This is a perceptive and valuable observation, to which I would add that military speech can teach us something about political speech. Here the historian must ask, "Why is this so?" In part, the answer requires the inevitable consult with Carl von Clausewitz. "War belongs . . . to the province of social life," the Prussian famously observed. Indeed, war is a society's most concentrated form of conflict: more than any other conflict, war requires the greatest collective will, the most efficient organization, and the most developed self-identifications; and it costs more in lives and resources than other social conflicts. As noted in the Introduction, war also invokes dramatic action and profound human emotions.[1]

---

1 Carl von Clausewitz, *On War*, edited by Anatol Rapoport (London: Penguin Books, 1968), 202.

Thus, it stands to reason that down-scale social conflicts, such as civil politics, not only will resemble war (and invoke its narrative-minting metaphors), but that these metaphors will also invest less-dramatic events with war's (sometimes self-inflating) high drama, the better to focus the aggression, deepen the divisions with opponents, and enhance the imagined status of any victory. Those political candidates who create "war rooms" in order to "fight" for "victory" have, in the realm of words, achieved so much more than merely attaining a numerical majority of votes. Thus do small-scale political conflicts become "battles" that "annihilate" opponents, leaving "blood in the streets," but nevertheless conclude in "final victory" and "spoils" to the winner. And these metaphors may be invoked for nothing more than a small-town mayoral election.[2]

There may be other reasons that have more historical resonance for applying battle speech persuasive strategies to political rhetoric. One reason was suggested in the Introduction: the separation of powers enshrined in the United States Constitution is, in world historical terms, a rather recent phenomenon. In theory the "Divine Right of Kings" meant monarchs were never required to plead overmuch with parliaments for funds or soldiers for wars. (The reality was often different.)[3] Thus, for millennia sovereigns wishing to wage war would simply declare the war, impose the tax, and conscript the subjects. Here the royal "we" might be construed to mean "I as your highest civil magistrate" as well as "I as your supreme military commander"—that is, *we* speaking as both king and general. Today most Western-modeled states divide war-making powers among different governing institutions. But old rhetorical habits persist; for example, political leaders whose war-making powers may have been sharply delimited still borrow armed conflict's drama by declaring "wars" on poverty, inflation, drugs, and terrorism.[4]

---

2   John J. Pitney, Jr., *The Art of Political Warfare* (Norman, Oklahoma: University of Oklahoma Press, 2000), 3.

3   When Parliaments or Estates General came into fashion, the road to separation of powers would be long, twisted and bloody; witness the English Civil War or the French Revolution late the following century.

4   For the United States Constitution, see *The Declaration of Independence and the Constitution of the United States of America* (Washington: The Cato Institute, 1998). In listing some relevant sections, I have included all provisions dealing with topics that were once exclusively within the control of absolute rulers, and necessary to make war: Article I, Sections 8, 9, 10 (various powers relating to war vested in legislature), Article II, Section 2

A second historical reason is that few constitutions bar from elective office those who have served in (or were otherwise connected with) a nation's armed forces. The list of examples is long, but any such would include a great military historian, First Lord of the Admiralty and combat journalist who once led Britain (Winston Churchill); a brilliant tank commander and resistance leader who once led France (Charles de Gaulle); and many generals and subalterns who have served as presidents of the United States. It would be unreasonable to expect a man who had spent his entire adult life, or even just his impressionable youth, in uniform not to see himself as "battling opponents," "declaring war" and winning "great victories"—even when the conflicts are with peaceful men and women with whom he expects to have lunch after the legislation is signed.

(Another reason why battle speech rhetoric may frame civil arguments is the distinct possibility that human beings are hard-wired for war; moreover, even in the absence of real war, the rhetoric of conflict remains an important way to organize people. I will not discuss this further as—to use a current military metaphor—the topic is well "above my pay grade.")

As readers know by now, I believe that speeches are reciprocal affairs, negotiations between speakers and audiences in which both sides often come prepared for the event. Thus, in considering Obama's speeches one needs to be mindful of the audience as well. Our current president (like many others) never served in the armed forces, wrote military history, filed a dispatch from the front or had previous service overseeing some military department; yet his political speeches use military metaphors, and make battle-speech type appeals—and his audiences have no problem accepting these as normal presidential discourse.

Why?

The reason is not historical per se, but instead is a function of rhetoric itself, relating to the way that language helps human beings organize information and create narratives. Here I wish to apply the notion of *living metonym* to President Obama; that is, that the figure of the president is by itself an argument. Exactly how is President Obama (and every other modern-day president) the incarnation of a respirating military metonym? Put another way, if metonymy is "using one entity to refer to another that is related to it," what are the entities of Barack Obama? The answer to this question involves not only the hierarchical structure of the Constitution (Article II, Section 2: "The President shall be Commander in

---

(president as commander in chief), Article III, Section 3 (specifying legal requirements for treason conviction).

Chief of the Army and Navy of the United States....") but also the thick crust of historical memes that have accumulated around the presidency itself.[5]

In making this argument, readers probably will not be surprised to discover that my approach is holistic. The following chart attempts to relate the two things that must bear some pre-existing relationship with each other for President Obama to be a living metonym. Obviously, the president (and presidency) is one of those things. The others—the things he "stands in for"—are actually a more extensive net of laws, music, props, gestures, and historical ideas that are closely associated with American presidents and the wars they have waged.

Living Metonym: Things relating to President Barack H. Obama and/or which refer to his office:

Legal: Article II, Section 2, United States Constitution;

Command: the military hierarchy;

Musical: *Hail to the Chief*;

Props: American flags, Marine Corps One (the helicopter), Air Force One (the jet), Marine Corps guards/escorts in White House, president often accompanied by high-ranking, uniformed officers;

Gestures: hand salutes, uniformed audiences sometimes at attention, 21-gun salutes;

Patent Historical Memes: Washington, Harrison, Taylor, Lincoln, Grant, Theodore and Franklin Roosevelt, Wilson, Truman, Eisenhower, all presidents associated with American wars; the Revolution, War of 1812, Mexican War, Civil War, Spanish American War, World Wars I and II, Korean War, Vietnam War, Desert Storm, OEF and OIF;

Latent Historical Leadership—War Memes: *Indomitability* (e.g., Washington at Valley Forge, Grant in the Wilderness); *Compassion* (e.g.,

---

5 George Lakoff and Mark Johnson, *Metaphors We Live By* (Chicago: University of Chicago Press, 1980), 35.

Lincoln in the Telegraph Office, Lincoln's frequent pardoning of condemned soldiers, Wilson doling out food at soldier canteens); *Power* (Cold War presidency memes of red telephone to the Kremlin, "red button" on desk wired to missile silos, 24/7 presence of uniformed officer carrying launch codes); *Firm Hand in a Crisis* (e.g., Kennedy advisors during Cuban Missile Crisis); *Secret Knowledge* (President receiving end-product of intelligence agencies).

Indeed, a president cannot speak on any topic without having some or all of these things invoked. This may occur implicitly (Obama's Inaugural referring to himself as the "44th president" is enough to recall the chain that links him to wartime presidents) or more obviously, as during a speech from the Oval Office for which the room is conspicuously adorned with flags, or busts and paintings of worthy (and usually wartime) predecessors. I would argue that the public mind is so imbued with president-as-metonym that (putting aside motive) most criticism of a president is based on some perceived disconnect between a particular president's actions and the continuities of the established metonym. Thus, the recent controversies about President Obama's bowing to foreign leaders claims a discontinuity between his bowing and "what American Commanders in Chief have [always] done" when greeting foreign potentates, especially royalty.[6]

What is the point of imagining the president as a living metonym, a fleshed-out figure of speech with a heartbeat? Just this: to better understand the mental process of an audience in crediting the arguments of presidents, as well as anyone else representing certain established institutions. *It is a way of understanding situations in which the speaker herself becomes an automatic premise in whatever argument she may be making.*

Political speeches tend to be longer than their military counterparts, often much longer; moreover, not everything in the three speeches considered here is relevant to the points I wish to make about similarities in appeals and structure to battle speeches. Therefore, rather than reproduce each speech in its entirety I have isolated those passages relevant to my themes. I have also changed the template: although these are full-length speeches, I have omitted "Immediate

6   Just in case the controversy is forgotten by the time this book goes to print, see Foster Klug, "Spin Meter: Did Obama Grovel?" Associated Press, reprinted in the *Washington Post*, November 17, 2009.

Results," "Legacy" and "Leadership Principle" from the analysis that had concluded some earlier chapters. My reasons are that, first, as of this writing, President Obama continues to "write the text" of his presidency; thus it is too soon for "Legacy;" together with the recency of these speeches, means that you, the reader, are as competent to judge Immediate Results and Leadership Principles as I am.

Chapter Sixteen

Assumption of Command:
Inaugural Address, January 20, 2009

I. Historical Background

"Forty-four Americans have now taken the presidential oath," Barack Obama declared early in his Inaugural Address; here, the President began to forge his own link in the chain of American presidents. However, as readers might suspect, President Obama's Inaugural Address was, in rhetorical structure and purpose, far older than even the United States: Inaugural Addresses are really Assumption of Command (AOC) Speeches, whose lineage, probably rooted in prehistory, began the first time a new leader introduced himself to the led. And President Obama's Inaugural Address shared the same conventions as most AOC Speeches: Authority, Acknowledge Predecessors, and—the paramount convention—Managing Expectations. Here the President stood on the same ground as Joshua ben Nun did when he first he addressed the Israelites after assuming command from Moses.[1]

---

[1] All quotations from President Barack Obama's Inaugural Address are taken from the official text that may be found at www.whitehouse.gov/blog/inaugural-address. Accessed September 29, 2009; Miller, *Words and Deeds*, 318-321; readers should also refer to Chapter Seven's discussion of General David H. Petraeus' AOC Speech; *Book of Joshua*, 1:10-15, KJV.

In modern, institutionalized speeches (such as presidential inaugural addresses), Authority has ceased to be a problem simply because the process of acquiring it has become so routinized: a public election is held; its outcome is accepted by the loser; the inaugural date is set as fixed by law; an oath is publicly administered by the Chief Justice of the United States; and all this is conducted in the presence of high-profile Platform People who include not only the incoming President's predecessor but also leaders of the continuing government. As for Acknowledging Predecessors, simply appearing with them meets this burden; many modern presidential inaugurals address them in the salutation, while others, like that of Barack Obama, recognize them by name. "I thank President Bush for his service to our nation," Obama declared, "as well as the generosity and cooperation he has shown throughout this transition."[2]

Just like military AOC Speeches, the heart of an inaugural address is found in how it Manages Expectations; and inaugural speech audiences, like their military counterparts, will sift every word, voice tone, and facial gesture for signals about continuity or discontinuity. When faced with the possibility of war or having to wage an existing war, the most-scrutinized portion of a president's inaugural address will be passages relating to armed conflict, hot or cold. Thus did most of Abraham Lincoln's first inaugural address attempt to persuade many southerners that his election represented continuity with established doctrines of constitutional government, especially regarding slavery. John F. Kennedy memorably declared, "Let every nation know, whether it wishes us well or ill, that we shall pay any price, bear any burden, meet any hardship, support any friend, oppose any foe to assure the survival and success of liberty." Here he signaled to adversaries that his incoming Democratic administration would be as zealous in waging the Cold War as had been the outgoing Republican one. President Obama, assuming command of existing conflicts in Iraq and Afghanistan and facing the threat of transnational and state-sponsored terrorism, declared:

---

2 "Routinized" satisfaction of the Authority Convention does not mean that it cannot be destabilized; indeed, there have been several occasions when (for different reasons) it has been: Lincoln's election in 1860 and 1864; the 1876 Hayes-Tilden Controversy, and more recently, the Bush-Gore election of 2000. The president is required to take an oath whose words are specified in Article II, Section 1 of the United States Constitution. A speech is not required, but has become customary.

We will not apologize for our way of life, nor will we waver in its defense. And for those who seek to advance their aims by inducing terror and slaughtering innocents, we say to you know that our spirit is stronger and cannot be broken—you cannot outlast us, and we will defeat you.[3]

While an Inaugural Address is certainly close to the military AOC, the comparison should not be overdone. Presidents are not generals, and their scope of executive responsibility extends far beyond military matters. Moreover, the Inaugural Address has developed several unique tropes and memes that are usually only implied in or entirely omitted from its military cousin. The first of these is the unity trope, most famously expressed by Thomas Jefferson ("We are all Republicans; we are all Federalists"). Next is a trope harder to define but probably present in the expectations of inaugural audiences since the beginning of the Republic: that the president, at least on his inauguration day, is an exceptional man elected by an exceptional people to lead an exceptional government—thus forming an audience expectation that the Inaugural Address will be an exceptional speech, characterized by soaring rhetoric, statesman-like cadences, nobility of spirit, and firmness where required. This expectation has been fulfilled many times, notably by Washington (first inaugural), Jefferson (first inaugural), Jackson twice, Lincoln twice, Franklin D. Roosevelt (first inaugural), and John F. Kennedy. On January 20, 2009, Barack Obama took his turn.

My discussion will focus on only two of the many themes present in Obama's Inaugural Address. The first is his use of military metaphors; the second is how he uses military history, both as a unity theme and as a means of applying "military" lessons to several distinctly non-military subjects. This last point is probably most important in understanding the wider implications of this speech.

In reading the speech excerpts, readers should note:

1. The dual roles of the president—Chief Magistrate and Commander-in-Chief;

---

3 *Abraham Lincoln: His Speeches and Writings*, edited by Roy P. Basler (Cleveland, Ohio: Da Capo Press, Inc., 1946), 579-590; Safire, *Lend Me Your Ears*, 970.

2. How the use of military metaphors and history adds *gravitas* to the speaker as well as drama and urgency to his message

II. The Speech

[NB: In one case below I have joined two paragraphs that were separated in the original transcript.]

My fellow citizens: I stand here today humbled by the task before us, grateful for the trust you've bestowed, mindful of the sacrifices borne by our ancestors.

Forty-four Americans have now taken the presidential oath. The words have been spoken during rising tides of prosperity and the still waters of peace. Yet every so often, the oath is taken amidst gathering clouds and raging storms.

That we are in the midst of a crisis is now well understood. Our nation is at war against a far-reaching network of violence and hatred . . . . [A]nd each day brings further evidence that the ways we use energy strengthen our adversaries and threaten our planet.

For us [our ancestors] fought and died in places like Concord and Gettysburg, Normandy and Khe Sahn.

As for our common defense, we reject as false the choice between our safety and our ideals. Our Founding Fathers, faced with perils that we can scarcely imagine, drafted a charter to assure the rule of law and the rights of man—a charter expanded by the blood of generations. Those ideals still light the world, and we will not give them up for expedience [sic] sake.

Recall that earlier generations faced down fascism and communism not just with missiles and tanks, but with sturdy alliances and enduring convictions. They understood that our power alone cannot protect us nor does it entitle us to do as we please. Instead they knew that our power grows through its prudent use; our security emanates from the justness of our cause, the force of our example, the tempering qualities of humility and restraint. We are the keepers of this legacy. Guided by these principles once more we can meet those new threats that demand even greater effort, even greater cooperation and understanding between nations. We will begin to responsibly leave Iraq to its people and forge a hard-earned peace in Afghanistan.

We will not apologize for our way of life, nor will we waver in its defense. And for those who seek to advance their aims by inducing terror and slaughtering innocents, we say to you now that our spirit is stronger and cannot be broken—you cannot outlast us, and we will defeat you.

As we consider the role that unfolds before us, we remember with humble gratitude those brave Americans who at this very hour patrol far-off deserts and distant mountains. They have something to tell us, just as the fallen heroes who lie in Arlington whisper through the ages. We honor them not only because they are guardians of our liberty, but because they embody the spirit of service—a willingness to find meaning in something greater than themselves. And yet at this moment, a moment that will define a generation, it is precisely this spirit that must inhabit us all. For as much as government can do, and must do, it is ultimately the faith and determination of the American people upon which this nation relies. It is the kindness to take in a stranger when the levees break, the selflessness of workers who would rather cut their hours than see a friend lose their job which sees us through our darkest hours. It is the firefighter's courage to storm a stairway filled with smoke, but also a parent's willingness to nurture a child that finally decides our fate.

So let us mark this day with remembrance of who we are and how far we have traveled. In the year of America's birth, in the coldest of months, a small band of patriots huddled by dying campfires on the shores of an icy river. The capital was abandoned. The enemy was advancing. The snow was stained with blood. At the moment when the outcome of our revolution was most in doubt, the father of our nation ordered these words to be read to the people: "Let it be told to the future world . . . that in the depth of winter, when nothing but hope and virtue could survive . . . that the city and country, alarmed at one common danger, came forth to meet [it]."

America: In the face of our common dangers, in this winter of our hardship, let us remember these timeless words. With hope and virtue, let us brave once more the icy currents, and endure what storms may come. Let it be said by our children's children that when we were tested we refused to let this journey end, that we did not turn back nor did we falter; and with eyes fixed on the horizon and God's grace upon us, we carried forth that great gift of freedom and delivered it safely to future generations.

—Excerpts from President Barack H. Obama's Inaugural Address, January 20, 2009[4]

III. Parsing the Speech

Obama's use of military history includes the mention-via-metonym of six American "hot" wars and a "cold" one: the Revolution ("Concord"), Civil War ("Gettysburg"), World War II "("Normandy"), Vietnam ("Khe Sahn"), several references to Operation Enduring Freedom and Operation Iraqi Freedom, and the Cold War ("earlier generations faced down . . . communism"). The Introduction noted how battle names sometimes function as metonyms. But did President Obama's battle references serve any broader purposes? The answer is yes: the battle/war references were Obama's tribute to the trope of unity, and were reminiscent of the closing lines of Abraham Lincoln's First Inaugural Address:

> The mystic chords of memory, stretching from every battle-field, and patriot grave, to every living heart and hearth-stone, all over this broad land, will yet swell the chorus of the union, when again touched, as surely they will be, by the better angels of our nature.

What Obama did in his Inaugural Address was to update and describe Lincoln's "mystic chords of memory" by specifying not only the "battle-fields" but also the "patriot grave[s]" (As noted below, Obama also referred to the "fallen heroes who lie in Arlington").

Unity is an appeal that is usually rooted in a historical narrative. And in his speech Obama creates a historical narrative that is centered on the nation's military past. Its purpose was to remind his listeners that they share a history of blood, suffering, and unity of purpose, if not always victory. (The Battle of Khe Sahn was fought in a war that the United States lost.) War as a unifying theme was not Obama's only choice, here; indeed, he devotes a few passages to other broadly appealing narratives from American history. In one sentence he speaks to the we-are-a-nation-of-immigrants meme: "For us [our forebears] packed up their worldly possessions and traveled across oceans in search of a new life." He also used the our-forebears-worked-and-sacrificed-for-us-their-posterity meme,

---

4   www.whitehouse.gov/blog/inaugural-address. Accessed September 29, 2009.

another time-honored American narrative: "For us, they toiled in sweatshops, and settled the West, endured the lash of the whip, and plowed the hard earth." These narratives of immigration and work/sacrifice easily could have been moved to the speech's center just by further elaboration.

But President Obama chose war. And his references to war extended beyond the battle metonyms. He linked the inaugural month (January) and its season (winter) with early 2009's various crises (financial market and real estate meltdowns, plunging public confidence) via an inspiring historical anecdote. President Obama returned his audience's minds' eye to the winter of 1777-1778 and George Washington's struggling encampment at Valley Forge, Pennsylvania:

> So let us mark this day with remembrance of who we are and how far we have traveled. [Here Obama confirmed the centrality of the war anecdote by using it to measure both "who we are" and "how far we have traveled."] In the year of America's birth [*sic*, if by "birth" he meant 1776], in the coldest of months, a small band of patriots huddled by dying campfires on the shores of an icy river. The capital [then in Philadelphia] was abandoned. The enemy was advancing [*sic*; the British were not advancing; they remained quartered in Philadelphia]. The snow was stained with blood. At the moment when the outcome of our revolution was most in doubt, the father of our nation ordered these words to be read to the people:

> "Let it be told to the future world . . . that in the depth of winter, when nothing but hope and virtue could survive . . . that the city and the country, alarmed at one common danger, came forth to meet [it]."[5]

American suffering at Valley Forge was a logical war anecdote for Obama to use. First, it belonged to the American Revolution, the conflict of First Principles that ultimately resulted in the Constitution under whose authority Obama had just taken the Oath of Office. Moreover, in a speech seeking unity, the Revolution's legacy is more fitting than that of some other wars because it is

---

5 President Obama did not claim that Washington wrote the words, only that he had them publicly read. The words are from Thomas Paine's *The Crisis*. Here is the full passage: "Let it be told to the future world, that in the depth of winter, when nothing but hope and virtue could survive, that the city and country, alarmed at one common danger, came forth to meet and to repulse it." – *The Life and Writings of Thomas Paine,* edited by Daniel Edwin Wheeler (New York: Vincent Parke and Company, 1908), *The Crisis,* 11. Why the official transcript of the Inaugural Address contains ellipses at the points indicated is not clear.

not controversial; in contrast, mentioning some other wars might raise sensitive or counterproductive issues. For example, the War of 1812 triggered America's first secession crisis; the Mexican War remains a sensitive subject for many Mexicans (and also struck some Americans as unjust); the Spanish American War produced American colonies and thus emits bad odor in a post-colonial world; and mentioning the Korean War might be seen as provocative to North Korea, a nation with which the United States was then in difficult nuclear nonproliferation discussions.[6]

In contrast, the past wars Obama did mention (besides the Revolution), were either obligatory references or served the unity meme without being counterproductive. For example, "Normandy" was fought in the "Good War;" Cold War references involved antagonists that mostly no longer existed; mentioning Iraq and Afghanistan were obligatory; more conjecturally, Khe Sahn also served the unity meme: a liberal president was making honorable mention of a battle from a war that had been deeply opposed by many in his own party. Finally, there was Gettysburg: it would have been surprising if as America's first African-American president, Obama had not made some reference to the Civil War. (In fact, he made two such references.) In mentioning Gettysburg, he chose a battle whose historical memes emphasize both Northern grit and Southern valor (Pickett's Charge), a good balance to strike in a speech striving for national unity. These were all reasons for choosing some wars and excluding others.

But Obama mentioned these wartime anecdotes not for their own sake but to extract meaning from each past military event and apply it to a current, non-military situation: the country's economic crises.

In the first case, what meaning did Obama find at Valley Forge that he thought applied in January 2009? To what events did he seek to apply these meanings?

In the very next paragraph after the Valley Forge reference he answered the first question:

America: In the face of our common dangers, in this winter of our hardship, let us remember these timeless words. With hope and virtue, let us brave once more the

---

6 General Ulysses Grant, who fought with distinction in the Mexican War, famously observed that "[T]o this day I regard the [Mexican] war . . . as one of the most unjust ever waged by a stronger against a weaker nation." Grant, *Personal Memoirs*, I: 53; also see Footnote 9.

icy currents, and endure what storms may come. Let it be said by our children's children that when we were tested we refused to let this journey end, that we did not turn back nor did we falter; and with eyes fixed on the horizon and God's grace upon us, we carried forth that great gift of freedom and delivered it safely to future generations.

From these various metaphors ("winter of hardship . . . . timeless words . . . . icy currents . . . what storms may come") Obama was extracting another metaphor: The Test.

And just as he believed that Valley Forge had tested America's Revolutionary forbears, so the January 2009 crises were testing their descendants. But this penultimate paragraph was also a thinly veiled lecture; Obama confronted his audience, "America," with what was essentially an admonition to "buck up." After all, anyone despairing about unemployment, portfolio losses, overdue credit balances, or the prospect of foreclosure need do is remember their heritage—frozen men dressed in rags, "huddled by dying campfires," who, "at the very moment when the outcome of our revolution was most in doubt," had heeded Thomas Paine's call "to meet," that is, to pass, The Test.

For rhetorical purposes, it matters little that being tested in a war is quite different from, say, facing unemployment or finding oneself suddenly unable to provide for a family; both are genuine crises; but each crisis tests different mettles. All historical analogies eventually break down—the past is not the present—and in his Inaugural Address, President Obama does no worse than anyone else, which is to say everyone else who at one time or another has sought a usable yore. What matters is that Obama uses the evergreen meme/metaphor—War-as-Test—to make his point. And one does not have to return to antiquity to find War-as-Test: Thomas Paine said much the same thing when he declared in *The Crisis* that "These are the times that try men's souls."[7]

Obama's use of military analogies went far beyond buttressing American civilian morale in a difficult present; he also conscripted living and dead American soldiers in an effort to enlist their support for the future. Many have wondered what the dead might say if they could only return; but since antiquity politicians, princes and priests have always seemed to know. Here President

---

7   How I name my metaphors mimic the templates used by Lakoff and Johnson, *Metaphors We Live By*; for example, see "Argument is War," 4; *The Life and Writings of Thomas Paine,* 1.

Obama takes his turn speaking for those who had given the "last full measure" as well as active duty soldiers:

> As we consider the role that unfolds before us, we remember with humble gratitude those brave Americans who at this very hour patrol far-off deserts and distant mountains. They have something to tell us, just as the fallen heroes who lie in Arlington whisper through the ages. We honor them not only because they are guardians of our liberty, but because they embody the spirit of service—a willingness to find meaning in something greater than themselves. And yet at this moment, a moment that will define a generation, it is precisely this spirit that must inhabit us all.

Of course, what President Obama says that "they" have to say is that we must sacrifice on behalf of something greater than ourselves. Alas, on January 20, at least, he was not overly specific about what that something was. In fairness, few Inaugural Addresses are very specific. But in light of his first year in office, President Obama's Inaugural Address offered important hints about his overall approach.

(What hints? Although not excerpted above, recall some other words from President Obama's Inaugural: "Now, there are some who question the scale of our ambitions—who suggest that our system cannot tolerate too many big plans." As I write these words on the first anniversary of the president's inauguration, in light of the stimulus bill, foreign-policy "resets" and the difficulties with cap-and-trade and health care, who can doubt that Obama took his own words seriously?)

Obama devotes more speech-space to Valley Forge, the serving military, and the honored dead than to any other theme. Why use war imagery and not, say, the struggle of newly arrived Americans that first winter in New England, the struggle of African-Americans to survive slavery, or the struggle that most Americans faced during the Great Depression? The answer is that war works as no other metaphor in its ability to employ words and images of the highest drama. Reduced to minimums, war is about life and death and the struggle to survive, and not against ideological abstractions, the "silent killers" of disease, scorned lovers, unemployment, or anonymous conspiracies; instead, war produces real enemies who seek to kill, maim, and humiliate, and too often succeed. Other than sex, war metaphors are primal in ways that other metaphors cannot be. And as the living metonym of the American war-making power, the last link in a long chain of other men who have led the country through wars,

President Obama was uniquely positioned to use this dramatic imagery without appearing overdramatic.

Drama is certainly one purpose served by war imagery; but it is not the most important purpose. President Obama's speech, like other speeches, must be understood as a story, or, to be more correct, a narrative. All narratives have plots, and (as any litterateur will concede) plots, to be interesting, or to "prove" anything, must possess conflict or tension. And as President Obama acknowledged in his speech, at times eloquently, January 20, 2009, was a day in a new year that promised nothing but conflicts. As of this writing, his list remains drearily familiar: war, financial meltdown, escalating home foreclosures, unemployment, business failures, and—the fruit of all of these— poor national morale.

In Obama's War-as-Test metaphor, these doleful conditions were the enemy, and in the president's inaugural story, these enemies were impeding Americans from resuming their "journey" forward, "up the long rugged path towards prosperity and freedom." Obama combined this Progress-as-Journey metaphor together with an Enemy-as-Weather metaphor: after his salutations, Obama immediately spoke of "gathering clouds and raging storms." Later in the speech, the lessons he extracted from Valley Forge were also framed in meteorological language: "in this winter of our hardship . . . . let us brave once more the icy currents and endure what storms may come."

But these metaphors were not enough. As athletic coaches, politicians, business executives, quarreling lovers, and divorce attorneys have discovered, the best metaphors for communicating conflict are those derived from the most intense conflict of them all: war. Here are some prominent examples from Obama's speech of war metaphors; or words that, because of encrusted memes, are closely associated with war (such as the word "sacrifice") or otherwise are redolent of war [italics added]:

"mindful of the *sacrifices* of our ancestors"
"ways that strengthen our *adversaries*"
"*fought and died* in places like *Concord*"
"*struggled and sacrificed* and worked till their hands were raw"
"*calls for action, bold and swift*"
"when imagination is joined in *common purpose*, and *necessity to courage*"
"a charter expanded by the *blood of generations*"

These words are exhortatory, and exhortation is always employed on *behalf* of one thing or *against* another. Indeed, at this point, readers should be able to recast each of the above phrases into a battle speech of their own design. Weather works for a speech's atmospherics, and journeys help move the narrative. But it is usually war and battle words that organize stories into the narratives of conflict that make them interesting—and coherent.

Persuasive Strategy

On January 20, 2009, the most compelling persuasive strategy in Barack Obama's Inaugural Address was Barack Obama, America's first African-American president. His political triumph represented the confluence of many waters, and historians will some day debate the nature of these tributaries; but Obama's personal narrative will likely always have pride of place. He had already introduced himself to the public through two books, *Dreams from My Father: A Story of Race and Inheritance* (2004) and *The Audacity of Hope: Thoughts on Reclaiming the American Dream* (2006). Both books were essentially about himself, *Dreams* an autobiography and *Audacity* a presentation of political beliefs through the medium of his own experiences.[8]

Personal narrative has likewise informed many of his speeches, and the Inaugural Address was no exception. While the meaning of Obama's election will be debated, Obama confidently offered his own interpretation. His inauguration (and thus, his election) represented a gathering of those "who have chosen hope over fear, unity of purpose over conflict and discord." Later, he characterized his inauguration as "a moment that will define a generation." Finally, he measured the "meaning of our liberty" by referring to his own life and the fact that "a man whose father less than 60 years ago might not have been served in a local restaurant can now stand before you to take a most sacred oath."

The importance of personal narrative to Obama raises a question with important implications for this book. Given that Obama never served in, wrote extensively about, reported on, or otherwise had much biographical connection with the armed forces, why would war words and metaphors inform so much of his Inaugural Address? Was Obama's use of these just another endorsement of

---

8 Barack H. Obama, *Dreams from My Father: A Story of Race and Inheritance* (New York: Three Rivers Press, 2004); Barack H. Obama, *The Audacity of Hope: Thoughts on Reclaiming the American Dream* (New York: Crown Publishing Group, 2006).

Dawkins' notion of memes, with Obama having absorbed millennia-sanctioned usage of Conflict-as-War through some mimetic osmosis? If that is true—and I believe that it is—it is equally true that, for exactly the same reasons, civilian audiences accept, find thrilling, and are inspired and informed by Conflict-as-War metaphors. In sum, Obama's use of military metaphors was culturally derivative, something more than a "figure of speech" but less than from personal experience.

The question of Obama's use begs another: why is Conflict-as-War so effective? Is it true, as author Christopher Hedges' book has it, that *War Is a Force that Gives Us Meaning*?[9] Perhaps some meaning; but our species is far too complex to draw "meaning" from any single source, and besides, human love is a much better candidate as a supplier of human meaning. (The proof may be found in the fact that, despite the prevalence of war, the numbers of human beings continue to increase.) However, Conflict-as-War is a potent persuader, and it is appropriate to offer a brief summary of at least three persuasive strategies that are enhanced by its use:

Narrative as Order

Reality can be chaotic, and to many people frighteningly random. Whether this testifies to the limitations of human brains to detect larger patterns or simply reflects the fact that reality *is* chaotic and random is a matter best left to theologians, philosophers and, for the rest of us, to four o'clock in the morning. But certainly when faced with something like globally catastrophic market fluctuations that throw tsunami-sized economic waves in every direction, Conflict-as-War helps to contextualize it—whether or not conflict or war has anything whatever to do with its causes or effects. Many other metaphors beside Conflict-as-War may serve to impose order. But most human beings get Conflict-as-War in a way that they may not "get" Meltdown-as-Kondratieff Wave" or "Mortgage Chaos-as-Mark-to-Market- Accounting-Principles."

President Obama used conflict to explain the country's economic woes. Conflict always poses an "other," the assigning of blame to which is indispensible to the narrative's scheme. Here Obama assigned blame:

9   Chris Hedges, *War Is a Force that Gives Us Meaning* (New York: Anchor, 2003).

Our economy is badly weakened, a consequence of greed and irresponsibility on the part of some, but also our collective failure to make hard choices and prepare the nation for a new age.

Here is the conflict-formula:

A prosperous present and the chance for a prosperous future
vs. Greed and irresponsibility by some
+
Our collective failure to make hard choices
=
The causes of our badly weakened economy

And here are several examples of Obama's solutions, "militarized" through battle words [Italics added]:

The state of our economy calls for *action, bold and swift.*

Now, there are some who question the scale of our ambitions, who suggest that our system cannot tolerate too many big plans. Their memories are short, for they have forgotten what this country has already done, what free men and women can achieve when imagination is *joined to common purpose and necessity to courage.* What the cynics fail to understand is that the ground has shifted beneath them, and the stale political arguments that have consumed us for so long no longer apply.

One reason for making economic crises equivalent to war has already been noted—war metaphors are more easily comprehended. But war crises as a metaphor for economic crises are inapt as a general matter: the command economy that war usually requires, in which central authority directs production and rations output, has (or should have) little relevance in peacetime. But I believe that this—the common economic focus of wartime—was the real meaning that President Obama sought but only clumsily approached with war metaphors. It was not war's violence that Obama wanted his audience to emulate, but war's shared economic purposes and war's historic transformational effects on an economy and a society, which in American history, as often produced strengthened federal authority in its wake.

Thus "the scale of our ambitions" and "many big plans" hinted at the President's plans for large-scale transformation of the domestic economy regarding (for example) economic stimulus, health care, and environmental programs. His application of the efforts of "free men and women" to "common purpose and necessity to courage" was an invitation to reimagine the highly plural and complex net of competing (and cooperating) economic interests of peacetime as the more fully-integrated economics of war. The reason Obama advanced was "What the cynics fail to understand"—that "the ground has shifted beneath them." Although the meltdown of the winter of 2008-2009 was not the Japanese attack on Pearl Harbor, what Obama likely sought to summon was the spirit that drove the American *economy* from late 1941 to 1946.

Economic crises had left many reeling; by his explanation, Obama not only imposed an orderly narrative on events, he also simultaneously posited a conflict. And he offered a way to resolve the conflict: action, bold and swift, joining in common purpose, and displaying courage. Any battlefield commander might use similar exhortations in his own speeches. And so might an economic "czar" when exhorting a Five Year Plan or an earlier president declaring a War on Poverty.

Clarity: Narratives attempt to impose order, but not all narratives are orderly. Narratives that do impose an intelligible order clarify, and there are few narratives as clear as conflict. Recall the example immediately above. There President Obama introduced Conflict-as-Clarity in justifying his call to action.

Using the President's words, one might recast that conflict as follows: First, there is the unnamed opposition. These are questioners who doubt the system's capacity for big plans; these doubters and skeptics also have short memories; they are cynics, who, despite their pretentions to worldly knowledge, have failed to grasp the most fundamental change of all: that the ground has shifted beneath them, and that "we" (us) will no longer find persuasive "their" stale political arguments. Pitted against these are free men and women, joined in common purpose, who will act boldly, swiftly, and courageously.

The President refused to name names, and the opposition only appears in coded speech, a necessary bow to the unity trope of Inaugural speeches; besides, too many specifics here might shorten the "honeymoon" that presidents seek with political foes in order to launch their policy initiatives. Yet, in context, the identity of the opposition to the unspecified "big plans" is not difficult to discern, and a rather large group it is: they are those who voted against Obama, whose very election actualized the biggest plan and fulfillment of the largest ambition of them all—his own. Those befriending the new President—"free men and women"—are those who voted for him. Thus is the Conflict-as-Clarity theme that defines a campaign subtly moved from the stump to inauguration day.[10]

Action: In politics, clarity can mean distinguishing friends from foes; if the enemies can be successfully demonized and the stakes are sufficiently high, the need for action is at the least, strongly implied. "Politics, as a practice, whatever its professions," Henry Adams observed in his *Education*, "had always been the systematic organization of hatreds[.]" The key words are *systematic* and *organization*, because nothing mobilizes for action better than hate, or its civil counterpart, loathing.[11]

All verbs are action words; but the verbs of wars and battles are more dramatically so. President Obama asked his audience to emulate their ancestors who "fought and died," "struggled, and sacrificed;" and the President argued that current conflicts would exact the same from the current generation: "action, bold and swift," "All this we can do, All this we will do," "We are the keepers of this legacy," whose spirit [that of those who died fighting America's wars] "must inhabit us all," and so forth. As readers may recall from the Introduction, hortatory battle speeches are meant less to inform than to influence attitudes or action. And so it has become with most political speeches.[12]

---

10   For an extreme example of another "inauguration speech" that had no qualms about naming names, see Adolf Hitler's February 1, 1933, Proclamation to the German Nation, especially these passages about Communism: "All about us the warning signs of this collapse are apparent. Communism with its method of madness is making a powerful and insidious attack upon our dismayed and shattered nation. It seeks to poison and disrupt in order to hurl us into an epoch of chaos. . . . This negative, destroying spirit spared nothing of all that is highest and most valuable. Beginning with the family, it has undermined the very foundations of morality and faith and scoffs at culture and business, nation and Fatherland, justice and honor. Fourteen years of Marxism have ruined Germany; one year of bolshevism would destroy her. The richest and fairest territories of the world would be turned into a smoking heap of ruins. . . . The thousands of wounded, the hundreds of dead which this inner strife has already cost Germany should be a warning of the storm which would come. . . .

11 Henry Adams, *The Education of Henry Adams* (New York: Oxford University Press, 1999), 12. The principal difference between hate and loathing are their fruits: hate can produce violence; loathing, votes, political contributions, or lawn signs.

12 Exhortation and information are not mutually exclusive. For the model of a political speech that exhorts and informs, see Daniel Webster's Second Reply to Hayne, January 26-27, 1830, *American Speeches: Political Oratory from the Revolution to the Civil War*, edited by Ted Widmer, (New York: Library of America, 2006), 182-254. For a model military speech that does the same, see "To the Officers of the Marine Corps," reprinted in Kenneth W. Estes, *The Marine Officer's Guide* (U.S. Naval Institute Press, 2000), 5-6.

Chapter Seventeen

Midst-of-Battle Speech: Health Care and the Address to Congress, September 9, 2009

I. Historical Background

On September 9, 2009, President Obama stood behind the Speaker's Rostrum in the House of Representatives and spoke for forty-seven minutes about health care. His goal was to persuade the assembled joint session of Congress to adopt some version of health care reform. Although the president had not endorsed any specific legislation, he made clear—or did not make clear, as expedience required—that any legislation produced by Congress should contain certain provisions, such as extending insurance to the uninsured and prohibiting private health insurers from denying coverage because of pre-existing conditions. With the president's own party constituting a majority of both houses, his in-chamber reception ranged from civil to positive, with the exception of one Republican Member of Congress (MC) who shouted, "You lie." However, the applause masked deep internal divisions among Democrats, as opposition from party moderates had thus far prevented the full House from voting on a bill.[1]

---

1 According to the official White House transcript the president's speech began at 8:16 EDT and concluded at 9:03 EDT. The transcript of the speech can be found at www.whitehouse.gov/the_press_office/Remarkes-by-the-president-a-joint-session-of-congress-on-health-care/. All references to this speech are derived from this transcript.

Health care reform was arguably the most complex and far-reaching legislation that Congress had considered in decades. Contentious issues were many and included concerns about cost, deficit neutrality, coverage for abortion and illegal immigrants, as well as philosophical arguments about government's role in providing health services. Republican MCs, bolstered by increasing public opposition to the House version of health care reform, were unanimously opposed to the Democratic bill, HR 3200. Democrats with conservative bents and some with uncertain re-election prospects shared some Republican objections.[2]

Nothing in this chapter will advance any reader's understanding of the substance of health care reform; instead I address other questions. Did President Obama's speech use rhetorical conventions similar to those found in battle speeches? I believe that it did, and argue that, structurally, elements of Midst-of-Battle and Pre-Battle Speech conventions are present in this speech. Battle speech comparisons work because the circumstances in which this speech was delivered surely resembled a political version of a battle. Not only had moderate Democratic MCs prevented a vote before Congress' August 2009 recess, but public opposition was also rising. Angry opponents of health care reform had confronted some MCs at August town hall meetings. As images of anger filled television screens that month, polls confirmed further slippage in public support for the President's initiative.

Faced with the possibility that his signature initiative might perish, Obama's speech was meant to "renew the battle" and "rally support." (Or, if one prefers other military metaphors, the President sought to "stiffen his battle lines," "counterattack" against his opponents, or be seen personally "directing the action" from the "trenches.") Although I will not plumb tactical manuals in search of more obscure military analogies, I will parse a few excerpts from Obama's health care speech to try to identify several major persuasive strategies that he used to carry his message.

2 For the period of August/September 2009 see, for example, Rasmussen Reports, www.rasmussenreports.com/public_content/politics/current_events/healthcare/september _2009/healthcare_reform . For the same time period, most major opinion polls reflected rising public opposition to the House version of health care reform. Accessed December 1, 2009.

Fighting for a Bill vs. Fighting an Enemy

First, however, I must note one important difference between Obama's health care speech and battle speeches generally. Politicians, even living metonyms atop the National Command Authority, are not really uniformed commanders, and certainly not when they appear in the House to speak on behalf of health care reform. (This might be opposed to when they speak about war, as when President Franklin D. Roosevelt stood behind the Speaker's Rostrum to ask for a Declaration of War against Japan.) Nor are MCs, Senators, or the public-at-large "soldiers," except in the realm of metaphor. In short, while metaphors might help explain limited aspects of reality, they should never be confused with reality. (A fact that audiences also need to remember about historical analogies.)

Some differences between political and battle speeches already have already been noted—in particular, length and the environments in which the two speeches are often made. But there is another difference even more important than these: battle speeches can credibly employ the Comrade Convention; political speeches generally cannot. (Readers will recall from Alexander's speech at the Hyphasis and General Petraeus' Midst-of-Battle Speech that the Comrade Convention entails having the speaker step out of his command role to address his soldiers as equals.) Politicians may feint towards the Comrade Convention (the salutation "My fellow Americans" being an example); but other than one another, politicians have few peers. *What they do have is constituencies*. For the purposes of analyzing rhetorical appeals, this makes all the difference; the real dissimilarities between battle and political speeches cannot be understood by comparing politicians and soldiers, but rather by comparing their *audiences*.[3]

Peers are equal; constituencies are not equal: some constituencies are favored, others disfavored; some must be lied to, others leveled with; elision and silence are employed to mollify some constituencies, and to lull or distract others. Of course, the military is as political as any other organization whose membership exceeds one person. But military peers generally share not only broad interests but also shared stakes in outcome: phrases such as "for the good of the service" or the "best interests of the country" may be debated, but only to a point; after that point, orders are issued and compliance is expected, if not

---

3 Miller, *Words and Deeds*, 234-235.

always received. Moreover, a host of social identifications between fellow soldiers (generals as well as privates) are far stronger than those between fellow citizens or even political peers. Soldiers face the exactions of self-executing codes—Duty, Honor, Country, as West Point idealizes it; politicians face voters or only exacting prosecutors doing eviscerations.[4]

In the political realm there is no consensus about outcomes; there never will be agreement about the meaning of such words as "in the public interest," "constitutional," "freedom" or "fairness." And disagreement about outcomes can be less important than another, often unpleasant reality: to get things done, politicians must confront constituencies with different ideological and economic interests; moreover, these constituencies may also consist of those who dislike or distrust the politician for a host of non-ideological reasons, such as race, gender, region, sexual orientation, religion, and ethnicity. It is the politician's need to enlist support, suppress opposition, deceive the wary, frighten the vulnerable, or stoke the loathing of these different constituencies that goes far in explaining the rhetorical structure of political speeches.

This constituency-juggling is really what politicians mean when they conceive of themselves as "battling" for certain outcomes or "fighting" for certain programs. The "strategy" and "tactics" they adopt to secure "victories" for themselves on the hustings or with bills in the chamber are actually negotiations that amount to schemes that divide, neutralize, or suppress opposing constituencies while persuading, uniting, and motivating friendly constituencies.

In the persuading or unpersuading of different constituencies, battle speech formats that are produced by one form of conflict (armed) are adapted to another form of conflict (civil). Of course, adapted is not adopted. In probing the similarities and limitations of President Barack Obama's adaptation, I will focus on several battle speech conventions: Staging and Props, SitRep, and the great constituency motivators—Stakes and Rewards. In politics, the last two are paramount. Using the same speech to simultaneously persuade opposing constituencies to support similar measures is political high craft, best expressed by an old saw from the retail clothing business: "If a man wants a blue suit, turn on the blue light."

---

4   Although West Point was founded in 1802, the motto "Duty, Honor Country" was not officially adopted until 1898.

II. The Speech

Madame Speaker, Vice President Biden, Members of Congress, and the American people:

When I spoke here last winter, this nation was facing the worst economic crisis since the Great Depression. We were losing an average of 700,000 jobs per month. Credit was frozen. And our financial system was on the verge of collapse. . . .

I am not the first President to take up this cause, but I am determined to be the last. It has now been nearly a century since Theodore Roosevelt first called for health care reform. And ever since, nearly every President and Congress, whether Democrat or Republican, has attempted to meet this challenge in some way. A bill for comprehensive health reform was first introduced by John Dingell Sr. in 1943. Sixty-five years later, his son continues to introduce that same bill at the beginning of each session....

. . . . More and more Americans pay their premiums, only to discover that their insurance company has dropped their coverage when they get sick, or won't pay the full cost of care. It happens every day. . . .

One man from Illinois lost his coverage in the middle of chemotherapy because his insurer found that he hadn't reported gallstones that he didn't even know about. They delayed his treatment, and he died because of it. Another woman from Texas was about to get a double mastectomy when her insurance company canceled her policy because she forgot to declare a case of acne. By the time she had her insurance reinstated, her breast cancer had more than doubled in size. That is heart-breaking, it is wrong, and no one should be treated that way in the United States of America. . . .

Here are the details that every American needs to know about this plan. First, if you are among the hundreds of millions of Americans who already have health insurance through your job, or Medicare, or Medicaid, or the VA, nothing in this plan will require you or your employer to change the coverage or the doctor you have. Let me repeat this: Nothing in our plan requires you to change what you have.

What this plan will do is make the insurance you have work better for you. Under this plan, it will be against the law for insurance companies to deny you coverage because of a preexisting condition. As soon as I sign this bill, it will be against the law for insurance companies to drop your coverage when you get sick or water it down when you need it most. They will no longer be able to place some arbitrary cap on the amount of coverage you can receive in a given year or in a lifetime. We will place a limit on how much you can be charged for out-of-pocket expenses, because in the United States of America, no one should go broke because they get sick. And insurance companies will be required to cover, with no extra charge, routine checkups and preventative care, like mammograms and colonoscopies because there's no reason we shouldn't be catching diseases like breast cancer and colon cancer before they get worse. That makes sense, it saves money, and it saves lives.

Now, that's what Americans who have health insurance can expect from this plan—more security and more stability.

Now if you're one of the tens of millions of Americans who don't currently have health insurance, the second part of this plan will finally offer you quality, affordable choices. If you lose your job or you change your job, you'll be able to get coverage. If you strike out on your own and start a small business, you'll be able to get coverage. . . .

Now, for those individuals and small businesses who still can't afford the lower-priced insurance available...we'll provide tax credits... In the meantime, for those Americans who can't get insurance today because they have preexisting medical conditions, we will immediately offer low-cost coverage that will protect you against financial ruin if you become seriously ill. . . .

Now, even if we provide these affordable options, there may be those—especially the young and the healthy—who still want to take the risk and go without coverage. There may still be companies that refuse to do right by their workers by giving them coverage. The problem is, such irresponsible behavior costs all the rest of us money....

. . . . There will be a hardship waiver for those individuals who still can't afford coverage, and 95 percent of all businesses, because of their size and narrow profit margin, would be exempt from these requirements. . . .

My guiding principle is, and always has been, that consumers do better when there is choice and competition. That's how the market works. Unfortunately, in 34 states, 75 percent of the insurance market is controlled by five or fewer companies. In Alabama, almost 90 percent is controlled by just one company. And without competition, the price of insurance goes up and quality goes down. And it makes it easier for insurance companies to treat their customers badly—picking the healthiest individuals and trying to drop the sickest, by overcharging small businesses who have no leverage, and by jacking up rates.

III. Parsing the Speech

Staging and Props

Staging and Props have long informed Midst-of-Battle speeches. One has only to look at this book's cover, depicting Jacques Louis David's fantasy *Napoleon Crossing the Saint-Bernard Pass* (1801). Bonaparte is depicted mounted on his rearing white horse (prop) wearing his general's uniform (prop) with soldiers manhandling artillery up the mountain passes (props) against the background of mountains (staging). In case anyone missed the historical narrative, David painted the names of Hannibal and Charlemagne (both famous Alps-crossers) on rocks in the foreground. In real-life battles, too, staging and props (for example, the flag-raising at Iwo Jima) have often furnished scenes worthy of an artist, photographer, or television crew—had any been around to record the moment.[5]

In choosing to deliver his speech to a Joint Session of Congress, President Obama reaffirmed the ancient wisdom that persuasive strategies are not limited to words alone. Among the most influential non-verbal persuaders are Staging and Props. In both cases, the speaker seeks to piggyback existing historical memes of locales and objects onto his message. An extreme example of this was the February 20, 1939, German-American Bund rally at Madison Square Garden. Prominently displayed behind the dais was a gigantic, hagiographical picture of a standing George Washington (whose well-known tolerance for Jews went unmentioned) flanked by two columns of long, suspended drapes of the American flag. The point was obvious—Nazism, a twentieth-century phenomenon, sought to piggyback certain memes of "Americanism," a concept that it located in the eighteenth century. In sum, the props argued that Nazism was entirely consistent with Americanism—and (had it only existed at the time) always would have been.[6]

Of course, this was not Obama's point in choosing to speak to a joint session of Congress. Rather, he sought to graft onto his message the memes associated with the stage and props accompanying a speech to a joint session of Congress: to enhance the importance of the speech and speaker, and to place both in the long chain of history that had been established by two centuries of speakers who had addressed such sessions. These began with George Washington and eventually included all presidents who personally delivered the constitutionally mandated State of the Union address (once called "Annual Messages"). Joint sessions have been convened to declare war, and to lend ears to and confer honor upon foreign leaders as well as national heroes. Within living memory, joint

5 Several versions of this painting exist. The book cover uses perhaps the most widely reproduced version of Jacques Louis David, *Napoleon Crossing the Saint-Bernard Pass* (1801), located at Chateau Malmaison, Rueil-Malmaison, France.

6 This image may be viewed at www.ushmm.org/wlc/media_ph.php?lang=en& moduleid-1005684&mediaid=2745, accessed November 15 2009.

sessions (or the almost indistinguishable "joint meetings") have hosted every president, foreign dignitaries such as Winston Churchill, Douglas MacArthur, various astronauts, Anwar El Sadat, Yitzhak Rabin, Margaret Thatcher, Francois Mitterand, Nelson Mandela and Boris Yeltsin, to name only a few. Thus, "to address a joint session of Congress" stages the message by elevating its importance to constitutional, even global significance.[7]

With joint sessions come important props, also encrusted with historically significant memes. These are chiefly images, of which two dominate: the first is that of the speaker standing behind the podium (prop), a large American flag (prop) filling the background, and two of the country's most important Platform People (props); in President Obama's case, to the audience's left was Vice President (and President of the Senate) Joseph Biden, and to the right Speaker of the House Nancy Pelosi. Although the podium is on a lower level than that of these Platform People, because the speaker stands (and is in the foreground) the effect is quite literally "picture perfect," summoning memes, some quite dramatic, of democracy, patriotism, constitutional succession, war and peace, and so forth.

The second image, closely tied to the first, is the cutaway shot showing the speaker addressing legislators semi-circularly seated in the "People's House." Almost daily presidents are imaged addressing a variety of audiences. But this cutaway image—televised today, though only photographed in the past—is intended to distinguish the joint session from, say, a political convention or the annual meeting of the National Association of Manufacturers. Here is the political elite assembled, not to contend but to listen, usually politely or even enthusiastically.

The point to Staging and Props is to support an historical narrative that promotes the speaker's message. They contribute to the narrative simply by being visible throughout the speech.

Of course, George Washington and the like will only go so far; at some point, the speaker and his message, having maxed out the historical credits of props and stage, must launch his own historical narrative. And President Obama's health care speech worked towards his departure at three junctures, gradually widening his own historical narrative on behalf of health care reform.

---

7 http://clerk.house.gov/art_history/house_history/Joint_Meetings/jointAll.html. Accessed on September 15, 2009.

First, his salutation was such as could only be given at a joint session; thus, using the history inherent in the props and the stage, he "located" his speech's importance: "Madame Speaker, Vice President Biden, members of Congress, and the American people." Thus was everyone (especially those watching at home) figuratively placed in the same historically significant room.

In the next paragraph President Obama extended his historical narrative. He referred to the last time he had spoken before a joint session:

> When I spoke here last winter, this nation was facing the worst economic crisis since the Great Depression. We were losing an average of 700,000 jobs per month. Credit was frozen. And our financial system was on the verge of collapse.

The "here last winter" may have referred to Obama's inauguration ceremony or his speech given on February 24, 2009, also at a joint session of Congress; either way, the President reaffirmed the seriousness of his speaking to joint sessions: he had done so only in the face of tough, national crises (recession then, urgent health care reform now).

Finally, Obama subsumed the history of his location (stage and props) and his "personal" history with joint sessions within the larger history of health care reform whose coda he would declare that evening:

> I am not the first President to take up this cause, but I am determined to be the last. It has now been nearly a century since Theodore Roosevelt first called for health care reform. And ever since, nearly every President and Congress, whether Democrat or Republican, has attempted to meet this challenge in some way. A bill for comprehensive health reform was first introduced by John Dingell Sr. in 1943. Sixty-five years later, his son continues to introduce that same bill at the beginning of each session.

With the above paragraph, Obama wrote the text of his historical narrative; the rest, to paraphrase Rabbi Hillel, is commentary. Built on the usually sturdy foundation of Staging and Props inherent in the joint session imagery, the president's narrative would now have to grow its own "legs" to walk with some constituencies and step on some others.[8]

---

8 Rabbi Hillel, *Babylonian Talmud,* Shabbat 31a.

SitRep

"The spoken word is the greatest of steadying forces in any time of crisis," S.L.A. Marshall wrote in his landmark study, *Men Against Fire*. But what exactly should one say? Marshall answered this question for one type of Midst-of-Battle Speech—the retreat. "When a retrograde movement becomes necessary in combat," he observed, "it is an invitation to disaster to move before men are told why they are moving." Of course, this is not the "why" of "Why We Fight." In combat few dwell on long ago motivations from some faraway recruitment office. The "why" to which Marshall refers is included in or immediately follows a SitRep or situation report. In battle speeches, the SitRep is "information about the tactical situation shared with the soldier-audience."[9]

Of course, the trumpet President Obama blew in this speech was charge, not retreat. But charges must also be explained and SitReps pervade President Obama's speech; they cite morality, urgency, and cost efficiency as reasons for health care reform. Like all political SitReps, they rationalize; they purport to be fact-based, and in a few arguments may be straightforward reasons justifying the conclusion. In effect, the SitRep declares, "Here is the current situation...;" the conclusion should then follow the evidence. But SitReps, especially the political variety, often aim for exhortation as well as truth—or something of both. When commanders seek combat SitReps from subordinates, truth is preferable; slanted or misleading SitReps can be lethal. But in exhortatory political or Midst-of-Battle speeches, "the facts" are often marshaled in a way so as to make the speaker's conclusion inevitable (he hopes). Such marshaling must be implicit; to work best, a SitRep should appear as fact-based.

President Obama's speech is exhortatory, and his frequent use of SitReps is of a piece. He uses two types of SitReps, which are also found in battle speeches: individual anecdotes (putting faces on facts) and the masked SitRep (which offers "facts" but leaves only argument). Both types of SitRep will be illustrated by addressing how the President dealt with the subject of private medical insurance.

Individual anecdotes are political evergreens that probably have been used since the first politician recognized someone in the audience with a usable woe.

---

9   Marshall, *Men Against Fire: The Problem of Battle Command in Future War,* 1947, (reprint, Gloucester, Mass., Peter Smith Publications, 1973), 140; Miller, *Words and Deeds*, 232.

Using this convention, President Obama cited two unnamed individuals who, although no longer able to attend the speech, did have—or, to be precise, once had—useful troubles. Both of the "speaking dead" also shared another important feature: their life-threatening illness had been compounded by private insurance company malpractice. The claimed circumstances were egregious, and Obama probably hoped to provoke something of an "Emmanuel Goldstein moment" with the television audience.[10]

"More and more Americans pay their premiums, only to discover that their insurance company has dropped their coverage when they get sick, or won't pay the full cost of care. It happens every day," the President declared. Having pilloried the insurance industry, Obama now invited the audience to throw some rotten fruit:

> One man from Illinois lost his coverage in the middle of chemotherapy because his insurer found that he hadn't reported gallstones that he didn't even know about. They delayed his treatment, and he died because of it. Another woman from Texas was about to get a double mastectomy when her insurance company canceled her policy because she forgot to declare a case of acne. By the time she had her insurance reinstated, her breast cancer had more than doubled in size. That is heart-breaking, it is wrong, and no one should be treated that way in the United States of America.

In life, these citizens paid their taxes, fed city parking meters and refrained from jaywalking. Now, using another timeless convention, the President channeled the dead to speak, or, to be more exact, complain about the misdeeds of private health insurance companies. As with fallen soldiers, these civilians rendered a posthumous service to their country, at least by President Obama's lights. And the situation they reported was bleak, at least regarding private medical insurance.

The President had not finished with private insurance companies. But his subsequent SitReps about them illustrate the masked variety, that is, factual presentations that really conceal an argument. This practice is normal for any hortatory speech; after all, the speaker is making a case, not weighing evidence.

---

10 Remember, all narratives have tension; in Orwell's dystopian novel *1984,* the government of Oceania sustained its own narrative by periodically flashing the image of party turncoat Emmanuel Goldstein, which in turn produced tension among the viewing audience—and also safely governed the release of tension. The audiences would jeer the image, that is, would blame Goldstein for the crisis *du jour.*

And President Obama continued to make his case about the limitations of private insurance:

> My guiding principle is, and always has been, that consumers do better when there is choice and competition. That's how the market works. Unfortunately, in 34 states, 75 percent of the insurance market is controlled by five or fewer companies. In Alabama, almost 90 percent is controlled by just one company. And without competition, the price of insurance goes up and quality goes down. And it makes it easier for insurance companies to treat their customers badly—picking the healthiest individuals and trying to drop the sickest, by overcharging small businesses who have no leverage, and by jacking up rates.

Thus for a second time is the situation reported regarding health insurance companies. Adorned by statistical "facts"—assuming they are such—the masked argument looks like a SitRep but is really an argument, which might be reduced to the following syllogism:

> Consumers always do better when there is choice and competition
> Private insurance fails to provide choice or competition;
> Therefore, consumers will do better if. . . .

In order for the audience to complete this sentence, Obama inexplicably waits for two paragraphs. The answer finally arrives: "But an additional step we can take to keep insurance companies honest," the president declared, "is by making a not-for-profit public option available in the insurance exchange." Yet, despite this rhetorical delay, readers (or listeners)—even those who knew nothing of the months or years of debate surrounding health care policy—would still have been "on the ready" for the President to propose some alternative to private insurance; that expectation would have been nurtured by his recitation of the "facts" in the above SitRep.

The reason for this reasonable expectation is that the "facts" cannot be understood without reference to the narrative in which they are couched; and Obama's narrative concealed several deeply submerged appeals. For some these appeals were meant to summon outrage. One appeal is to fairness and is meant for audience members who believe that life should be fair, or at least fairer, and become angry when learning that life is not fair; there is also an appeal to guilt of those "haves" wondering why they are so; this is closely paralleled by an appeal to compassion, for those who believe in meliorating the condition of "have-nots;" and finally there is another appeal to the fairy tale within most listeners: that evil should be punished, good rewarded, and injustice rectified. These are oft-told tales, to be sure; but success in hortatory speeches (political or battle) depends on appealing to what audiences already know or believe, and not by informing them of what they do not know or do not believe.

As these appeals illustrate, the hortatory SitRep appeals to moral passion. (Fear and greed are discussed below.) After all, without the morality, the factoids mean nothing. One might ask, so what if health insurance companies treat their customers badly? So do many institutions, government and private. And, by definition, insurers will always favor less risky individuals over riskier people, or charge small businesses more than large cooperatives. Moreover, businesses "jack up" rates all the time, whether because of inflation, squeezed profit margins, or plain greed. It is Obama's version of morality that gives his hortatory SitRep coherence.

Needless to say, the President's version of morality is not the only possible version. But to analyze this (or any other) speech, readers must begin by first isolating the speaker's moral vision (and one is always present) before they can decide whether, or to what extent, they concur. In this case, President Obama's moral vision was straightforward although, like any other moral vision, debatable: health care is a right, not a commodity; it is a right that inheres in American citizenship (and perhaps even residency); and that the guarantor and provider of that right is the federal government. This is the linking narrative, sometimes visible, sometimes obscured beneath the "facts" and arguments; but without this moral argument, Obama's speech would have been incoherent.

Stakes and Rewards

President Obama may not have believed that health care is a commodity; but he certainly believed that benefits used to persuade constituencies were commodities. Few politicians or the publics they represent believe in the efficacy of moral suasion alone; thus, Stakes and Rewards.

In general, to induce audience action or inaction, or to change or retain some audience attitude, speakers must appeal to existing interests or invent new ones. In battle speeches, these appeals are called Stakes, as in, "What's *my* stake in the outcome of this war, invasion, or battle?" Often found in Pre-Battle Speeches, Stakes generally include four categories of appeals: fear, hate, hope (glory/God/historical legacy/survival) and desire/greed (plunder, rapine, land, power). Readers will recall various Stakes from earlier chapters: Alexander promised great riches to those who followed him across the Hyphasis; Pope Urban II promised remission and the hope of everlasting life to those who perished on the way to Jerusalem; Hitler (through Warlimont) used hate and fear to justify the murder of commissars, based on what they were believed likely to do to German POWs. To these examples must be added the Stake of glory and its emblem, the medal. When Napoleon created the Legion of Honour, he commented,

> Do you suppose you can persuade men to fight by a process of analysis? Never; that process is valid only for the man of science in his study. The soldier demands glory, distinction, rewards.[11]

Political appeals in rule-of-law democracies also offer audiences Stakes, although generally in the form of checks and not medals. President Obama's villainization of private insurers gave his audience something to fear—"If I get sick, what if my insurance company drops me?"—and something to hate—after he made the dead speak, Obama declared, "That is heart-breaking, it is wrong, and no one should be treated that way in the United States of America." (A neat use of metonymy, that.) But the politics of health care required him to promise one very important subset of Stakes: Rewards. On his audience's behalf, he answered the ancient question: What's in it for me?

Thus were the President's dire SitReps balanced by his soothing Rewards. Both in political speeches and on playgrounds, bad actors are usually quarantined from the audience or the "good" children, as the case applies. The challenge for political speakers is to vest every "good" constituency with a Reward in exchange for its support. The heart of President Obama's health care speech consisted of explicating these Rewards in separate appeals to different constituencies.

The first constituency consisted of those who had health care, liked their coverage, and feared reform for the changes it might bring to them. To these doubters, Obama traded the fear of change for a reaffirmation of the status quo: "Nothing in our plan requires you to change what [health insurance] you have." But this was not all. Holdouts in the audience would not only have fears assuaged but Rewards granted in exchange for their support, as people who

---

11 *In the Words of Napoleon*, 121, May 14, 1802 (comment on creation of Legion of Honour).

retained their current plans, would, after the passage of health care reform, find them much improved: "What [my] plan will do is make the insurance you have work better for you." With Rewards, there is by definition no change except for good change. "Now, that's what Americans who have health insurance can expect from this plan," the president concluded, "more security and more stability."

Second, the president addressed those constituencies who had no health insurance. He identified at least eight of these, several of which required a different Reward. He began by noting that there were "tens of millions of Americans who don't currently have health insurance," but then differentiated them by type and Reward (the following chart quoting from the speech may be helpful):

Constituency/Reward: "tens of millions without health insurance"/ "quality, affordable coverage";

Constituency/Reward: "If you lose your job coverage"/ "quality, affordable coverage";

Constituency/Reward: "If you change your job coverage"/"you'll get . . . coverage";

Constituency/Reward: "If you…start a small business"/"you'll get . . . coverage";

Constituency/Reward: "Individuals who . . . Can't . . . afford"/ "we'll provide tax credits";

Constituency/Reward: "Small businesses [that] can't afford" / "we'll provide tax credits";

Constituency/Reward: "Preexisting medical conditions" / "low cost coverage";

Constituency/Reward: "Individuals who still can't afford"/"hardship waiver";

Constituency/Reward: "95% of small businesses"/"exempt from requirements."

These last two constituencies—those who still cannot afford insurance and 95% of all small businesses—require a brief additional comment. It is almost certain that during the writing of this speech, someone noticed that significant benefits were being promised to an audience that had become increasingly skeptical about how these rewards would be funded. In political speeches, there is an interesting moral tension in answering the question of "Who pays?"

Speakers not only ask payers to part with resources, they also slight them—those who take away (the government) and those who receive (the favored constituencies) must provide a moral rationale for the taking and getting. Remembering Henry Adams' comment that politics are about the "systematic organization of hatreds," the rationale that comes easiest is that which appeals to the universal fairy tale: payers "deserve" to pay because something about them or their behavior merits a rebuke; which government, acting in its role as tribune, administers by taking.

The President identified the two classes of such payers: "the young and the healthy—who still want to take the risk and go without [health insurance] coverage" and "companies that refuse to do right by their workers by giving them coverage." As most analysts know, the reason for requiring these two groups to pay was actuarial arithmetic: the larger the pool of insureds, the more efficient (in theory) the system and the greater (in theory) the reduction in premiums. But few great speeches in history have had arithmetic as their subject; villains, not statistics, are the more reliable persuaders.

According to President Obama's moral vision, the decision by some young, healthy people and businesses to forgo paying for health insurance was no longer a choice or a right; he now declared that "such irresponsible behavior costs all the rest of us money." Thus, not only are these two classes of payers villainized ("irresponsible"), but the balance of good burghers paying into the system are given a material stake in making them pay ("costs all the rest of us money").

At first it might seem that the moral balance between the responsible ("the rest of us") and feckless and freeloading is redressed; but the President had two more Rewards to dole out: of the two groups just condemned, 95% of businesses and young people unable to pay would be exempt. Thus with a confused message are the offending constituencies (which includes many voters) reduced to the most taxed species in American life: "the other guy." Such confused messages—in which groups were simultaneously rewarded and penalized—added to public skepticism that health reform could simultaneously save money while extending coverage.

Persuasive Strategy

Every persuasive strategy used by President Obama had the same foundation: the moral appeal. The President acknowledged this toward the end of his speech by once more channeling the dead. (I have not excerpted this quotation from the speech.) It was an effortless séance because this particular deceased, Senator Edward M. Kennedy, had given the President the next best thing to a video from beyond the grave: a personal letter to President Obama that he had written four months earlier, "shortly after he was told that his illness was terminal." "He asked," the President solemnly averred, "that it be delivered upon his death."

In fact, President Obama did not use Kennedy's letter so much for a séance as to tap the familiar trope discussed in Chapter Fifteen, "the last words" of a great man. The President's paraphrase of the letter effectively gathered his audience around the Senator's imaginary deathbed so that all might hear his final thoughts. True, Kennedy's letter was rather lengthy for the last words genre; but the scenes invoked by the President were deeply sentimental in a way that would have been instantly familiar to Victorian readers whose literature teemed with characters whose life's work was incomplete unless they could impart some final wisdom moments before being translated to Heaven. While the President did disclose that the letter had been written in May, his paraphrasing was sufficiently ambiguous (italics added below) so as to summon the perspective of a man whose remaining time was measured in minutes, not months (Kennedy would die on August 25):

> In it, he spoke about what a happy time *his last months were*, thanks to the love and support of family and friends, his wife Vicki, his amazing children, who are all here tonight. And he expressed confidence that this would be the year that health care reform—'that great unfinished business of our society,' he called it—would finally pass. [Italics added.]

As the audience lowered its collective ear to hear this faintly rasped message of bliss and contentment, seasoned with a pinch of prophecy, the President next quoted the "last words," or at least the last words that he intended to quote from this letter: "What we face is above all a moral issue," Kennedy wrote, "at stake are not just the details of policy but fundamental principles of social justice and the character of our country."

Readers should feel free to join the five millennia-old conversation about what the "fundamental principles of social justice" are; but whatever their theory, this was the letter's only sentence on which the President would elaborate. Having uttered the words "social justice," an important meme of his (and the late Senator's) liberal left constituency, Obama then proceeded to tack right by focusing on another of Kennedy's words—"character"—arguing that

America had "character;" that "character" was "our ability to stand in other people's shoes;" that Ted Kennedy had this same "character," and thus what some believed was his ideological rigidity ("an affront to American liberty") was really just "large-heartedness—that concern and regard for the plight of others." And large-heartedness "too, is part of the American character." Thus the Senator Kennedy who in life was thought to be a left-edged liberal was in death relocated to the mainstream.

The Kennedy séance was arguably the speech's climax, what TV comedy writers call "the moment of sentiment" (when the plot resolves its tensions with a moment of honesty or reconciliation among the characters.) Obama may have had his fill of John Rawls as a student at Columbia and Harvard, but this moment did not rest on any theory of social justice or even the expedience-driven revision of Kennedy's politics; rather it drew from the raw sentiment contained in another trope: what might be called, "Do It For the Dead Guy."

There is a modern precedent for this section of the speech: the 1940 film, *Knute Rockne All American*. The film includes the story of Notre Dame's great football star and All-American, George Gipp, played by future president Ronald Reagan. With Coach Rockne by his side, the historical Gipp died of pneumonia in 1920 while still in his athletic prime. In a modern version of biblical apocrypha, Gipp's dying spawned a "last word" legend that was accepted by the film and later became a Cut-and-Paste Speechlet for the 1988 George H.W. Bush presidential campaign. In his last moments, Reagan-Gipp (also adding a pinch of prophesy) declared to Rockne that:

> I've got to go, Rock. It's all right. I'm not afraid. Some time, Rock, when the team is up against it, when things are wrong and the breaks are beating the boys, ask them to go in there with all they've got and win just one for the Gipper. I don't know where I'll be then, Rock. But I'll know about it, and I'll be happy.

Indeed, eight years later, facing a formidable Army team, Rockne would, as Gipp accurately foresaw, urge his players to win one "for the Gipper," a man that the film Rockne conceded that his 1928 football players did not know. [12]

The moral appeal of this, as well as Obama's parallel call to (in effect) "win one for Ted Kennedy," will not be found in Deuteronomy, the Sermon on the Mount or even John Rawls. Rather, its appeal resides in something more basic

---

12 *Knute Rockne All American* (1940).

and far older than even biblical antecedents: it lives in the heart of anyone who has lost a comrade, parent, child, spouse, leader or mentor—which is to say virtually every adult of voting age. It consists of a bundle of emotions that include reverence for the dead, guilt, a denial that death terminates the deceased's life purposes, social strictures against irreverence, and an assertion of immortality through attachment to causes thought to transcend human mortality. It faintly echoes the Comrade Convention; but like most good persuasive strategies, it pierced the heart first.[13]

Coda: January 20, 2010

In an earlier writing, I noted the Midst-of-Battle speech genre included

a vast number of words and deeds that, though they arise in different tactical circumstances, all share the attribute of occurring during a battle. They might occur during an attack, a defense, or a retreat.[14]

Based on public opinion polls and anecdotal evidence (August's widespread demonstrations and town hall meetings), by September 9 the president's health care reform policy was clearly embattled; soon it became besieged. In his speech President Obama chose to attack by aggressively pressing "his" health care reform measure forward.

Does this speech indicate that the president was aware that his health care reform policy was imperiled? I think not; and as I write these words, his disconnection has produced, for both his presidency and his party, bitter fruits: Republican gubernatorial victories in Virginia and New Jersey and on January 19, 2010, a Republican Senator from Massachusetts. This last event terminates the Democrats' filibuster-proof 60-vote Senate majority and with that, the prospects for health care reform, at least one that includes the so-called "public option." While President Obama has not "lost" his battle for health care reform, he has clearly lost the public argument.

Henceforth, if he is to succeed, it will be by some combination of parliamentary legerdemain, one party rule, and the ability to divide budgetary

---

13 References are to the Book of Deuteronomy, 16:20, KJV; Gospel of St. Matthew, 5-7, KJV; John Rawls, *A Theory of Justice* (New York: Oxford University Press, 1999).

14 Miller, *Words and Deeds*, 232.

spoils among congressional dissenters (or those who appear to dissent) from his vision of health care reform. The persuasion of power is quite different than the power of persuasion; the latter's achievements tend to endure while the former's may last only through some future election cycle. But more germane to *Fighting Words* is the question of what lessons about persuasive strategies might be extracted from President Obama's apparent failure to carry public opinion.

The place to begin is with Chapter One and Grant's nighttime ride. That episode demonstrated that with enough *moral* capital (the real basis of so-called *political* capital) few words are necessary to accomplish an end; what matters in battle or political speech is the audience's perception of the speaker's moral character (the golden goose of moral capital) that precedes his call to action.

Thus, when speeches fail, one should first look to the speaker, not the speech, and always keep in view how *Fighting Words* defines moral character. While that definition may (or may not) include standards of bourgeois morality, it is never limited to such; it includes such attributes as energy, competence, professional judgment, fear, luck, and some sense that the speaker has special insight about his subject matter—greater experience, a record of success, prophetic gifts, or accurately reflects the *zeitgeist*.

Using public opinion polls as a rough surrogate for audience perceptions of moral capital (as related to health care), it is clear that President Obama's moral capital on the subject of health care was depleting quickly by the time he delivered his speech. As of this writing, according to one poll, 58% of the public opposed reform with only 40% in favor; almost seven months earlier 50% had favored reform with 45% opposed. If anything reveals something surprising about moral character as a concept, it is this: despite declining support for health care, Obama's job approval averaged 51% in the three months preceding the Massachusetts election, and his "Favorable Rating" (which measures the esteem in which the public holds the president) was 56% in December 2009. In short, the first lesson to be learned is about the true contours of a speaker's moral character. It may (or may not) include job approval and personal popularity; but the moral character required for leadership—for the negotiation that takes place between the leader and the led—requires more than likeability. Indeed, like-ability is not only not required, under some circumstances it may be a liability.[15]

15 Health care polling data taken from www.rasumssenreports.com/public_content/politics/toplines/pt_survey_toplines/january_2010/toplines_health_care_january_16_17_2010. Job approval polling data taken from www.gallup.com/poll/125096/obama-averages-approval-first-year-office.aspx. "Favorability Rating" may be found at

What then is required? I suspect that the president probably would have been better off remembering Vegetius's shade rather than summoning Ted Kennedy's. Readers will recall from Chapter One Vegetius's recommendation that

> It is necessary to know the sentiments of the soldiers on the day of an engagement. Their confidence or apprehensions are easily discovered by their looks, their words, their actions and their motions.

The politician's equivalent of this would be to try and genuinely understand how the electorate really thinks and feels about issues (a strong dose of natural empathy can help.) It was Obama's lack of these that suggest the second great lesson of his failure to persuade the public: Obama not only failed to learn the people's "sentiments," he also confused the audience gathered in the House chamber with his real audience—the tens of millions of people listening to the speech on television. The speech is crowded with talk of constituencies and rewards; while vastly oversimplified for public retail, these topics still remain the chitchat of bill negotiators and lobbyists. The speech also brims with rage inducers: greedy insurance companies, who, by their avarice and stupidity, actually kill people; other citizens are freeloaders, gaming the system, while the president further peoples his narrative with unnamed but nameable opponents who live to obstruct, delay, and defy the forces of history.

For truly great changes in policy, in which leaders persuade the public, Americans expect political unity, firm reassurance from their speakers, and a sense of rock steady leadership. Indeed, these expectations were inherent in the Staging and Props that the president used. In my view, the health care reform speech not only failed to meet the historical benchmarks of successful speeches proposing great policy changes, it did not even meet the historical expectations inherent in the president's own choice of setting.

In short, this speech might be compared with that of Alexander the Great at the Hyphasis. Like the Macedonian, the president was disconnected from his audience. After nine months in office, the audience had gotten to know him; but it was (and remains) a question of how much the president knew about them.

---

www.gallup.com/poll/124736/Palin-Favorable-Up-Slightly-Obama-Holds-Steady.aspx. Accessed on January 20, 2010.

Chapter Eighteen

The Military Eulogy: Commemorating the Slain of Fort Hood, November 10, 2009

I. Historical Background

On November 10, 2009, President Barack Obama was at Fort Hood to deliver a eulogy for the victims of a massacre that had occurred just five days earlier. Army Major and psychiatrist Nidal Malik Hasan had reportedly shouted "*Allahu Akbar!*" before opening fire inside Hood's Soldier Readiness Center. When the melee was over thirteen lay dead or dying and thirty were wounded.[1]

When the President spoke he entered a meme-stream that almost certainly originated in prehistory and remains a part of daily life: the eulogy. It vies with the AOC as the most frequently encountered genre of speech, military or civilian. It is the one speech that, at some sad point in life, most readers may reluctantly find themselves having to deliver—and it is a dead certainty that, at some later point, readers themselves will become a subject. The Hebrew Bible refers to Abraham eulogizing the death of Sarah (Genesis 23:2, KJV), and more famously gives David's eulogy for King Saul and his son Jonathan, David's best

---

1 Robert D. McFadden, "Army Doctor Held in Ft. Hood Rampage," *New York Times*, November 5, 2009. The dead also included one unborn child.

friend (2 Samuel, 1:17-27, KJV). Homer's Achilles eulogizes Patroclus, and Pericles the Athenian war dead.[2]

By Aristotle's time the tropes and memes of eulogies were well established. In *Rhetoric* he defined eulogies as a species of epideictic oration, and distinguished them from other types of praise such as panegyrics. His observations about eulogies remain sound advice to this day:

> Eulogy is a speech setting forth magnitude of virtue. It is the business then of an orator in eulogy to demonstrate that the actions of his hero are virtuous.... [We] should eulogize a person even without his actual performance of the deeds, if we believed him capable of performing them. . . . Exaggeration naturally finds a place in eulogies; for it is a means of establishing superiority [that] is one kind of nobleness. It follows that, even if you cannot compare your hero with persons of reputation, yet it is best to compare him with some other persons, as superiority is taken to indicate some virtue.[3]

But anyone who has read the Gettysburg Address, arguably the greatest eulogy since Pericles', understands that in matters military it is rarely individuals who are praised, but rather collectives—the "fallen." One reason is practical: warfare ancient and modern usually harvests too many dead for individual recognition. And the fallen as an abstraction simplifies matters for eulogists, because it is much easier to attribute virtue to abstractions than to individuals. As I will discuss below, because the Fort Hood dead numbered (relative to historical battles) "only" thirteen people, President Obama was able to eulogize both individuals and the collective.

The specific virtues that eulogists find among the fallen—qualities of bravery, courage, comradeship, and the espousal of just and good causes—are products of the historical moment and artifacts of a speaker's culture. Of interest here are the rhetorical vehicles used to articulate these virtues; these seem to transcend history and culture. And here there are two relevant battle speech analogues: the Post-Battle Speech and the Victory Speech. The core of both is the explanatory narrative, and what they often rationalize are the deaths and maiming produced by the battle or war; thus both genres of battle speech often

---

2 Homer, *The Iliad*, 23.12-34; *The Landmark Thucydides: A Comprehensive Guide to the Peloponnesian War*, edited by Robert B. Strassler (New York: Touchstone, 1996), 2.34-46.

3 *The Rhetoric of Aristotle*, translated with analysis and critical notes by J.E.C. Welldon (New York: MacMillan and Company, 1886), 67-70.

explicitly reference the fallen. This is so common as to merit its own convention, which I have called Remembering the Fallen. In short, the Post-Battle and Victory Speeches sometimes contain collective eulogies.[4]

To illustrate how this operated historically (and to likewise link President Obama's speech to this long chain), here are two examples of Remembering the Fallen. They are separated by two millennia and the cultural values are different, but the need to rationalize combat death by narrative is identical. First is a Post-Battle Speech from Plutarch's *Lives*:

> And Stesimbrotus tells us that, in his encomium on those who fell in battle at Samos, he said they were become immortal, as the gods were. 'For,' said he, 'we do not see them themselves, but only by the honours we pay them, and by the benefits they do us, attribute to them immortality; and the like attributes belong also to those that die in the service of their country.'[5]

Here the cultural values of religion and "nationalism" are melded, insofar as the latter attribute may be said to apply to the Greek city-state of the fifth century BCE.

The second example is from a Victory Speech delivered by Lieutenant General Ulysses S. Grant to the Army of the Potomac at the end of the Civil War. Typical of battle speeches made on behalf of secular, modern-era states, it values nationalism, and substitutes posterity ("a grateful nation [that] will ever cherish") for a religion-based immortality:

> To achieve these glorious triumphs, and secure to yourselves, your fellow-countrymen, and posterity the blessings of free institutions tens of thousands of your gallant comrades have fallen and sealed the priceless legacy with their lives. The graves of these a grateful nation bedews with tears, honors their memories, and will ever cherish and support their stricken families.[6]

As an American president, Barack Obama was heir to more than just the ancient eulogy meme-stream; a more immediate and arguably more influential

---

4   Miller, *Words and Deeds*, 283-288 (Remembering the Fallen); 349-355 (Final Victory).

5   *Plutarch's Lives*, I: 208.

6   *OR*, Series I, Volume 46, Part III, p. 1248, General Orders No. 108. War Dept., Adj. General's Office, Washington, D.C., June 2, 1865.

ancestor was Lincoln's Gettysburg Address. Its presence in American collective memory would influence the audience's expectations and invite comparisons between Obama's effort and that of the 16th president.

What were the Fort Hood's audience's expectations? Perhaps several: brevity, concision, and elegiac eloquence to be sure; but above all, it was expected that Obama would create a master narrative that would achieve collective consolation by transforming a killer's random infliction of suffering and death into something transcendent yet accessible to mourners. In parsing his remarks, my chief interest is in identifying both the master narrative and its transformative effort. In fairness to the President, it must be said that Fort Hood was not Gettysburg. Not surprisingly, the magnitude of the historical event being narrated will always contribute to the "greatness" of the narration. Unlike Gettysburg, the deaths and wounds at Fort Hood were not in the tens of thousands, nor did the shootings follow years of pitched battles that had claimed hundreds of thousands of American lives. There were causes to be vindicated at Fort Hood, but the Republic's immediate survival was not among them.[7]

President Obama spoke to a "sea of mourners" estimated at several thousand. The day's visuals inadvertently emphasized the mixed imagery of fighting a war on terror in which conventional concepts of "frontline" and "rear" often blur. In front of the President were the familiar props of modern military memorial services, including "13 sets of boots, rifles, helmets and photographs." Off to the side, "[m]ore than 100 massive shipping containers were stacked to form a wall around part of the field, while sharpshooters were positioned on the roof of the III Corps building behind the lectern." For those familiar with similar ceremonies from the current theaters of war, the scene recalled the same memorials from inside the wire at distant garrisons in Iraq and Afghanistan. In the past, the archipelagos of operating bases in Iraq and Afghanistan, have served as such venues; this time it was Texas.[8]

---

7   In order to transform Gettysburg into something greater, Lincoln used a series of verbs whose meanings signified transformation; that is, the application of one thing (a death or a battle) to something "larger," through metaphor, For example, a new "birth" of freedom. "Dedicate" and "dedicated" were used six times, "consecrate" and "consecrated" twice, and "hallow" once. Lincoln, Gettysburg Address, in Safire, *Lend Me Your Ears*, 60-61.

8   Peter Slevin, "Obama speaks at Fort Hood memorial service," *The Washington Post*, November 10, 2009; Peter Baker and Clifford Krauss, "President, at Service, Hails Fort Hood's Fallen," *New York Times*, November 11, 2009.

II. The Speech

. . . . We come together filled with sorrow for the 13 Americans that we have lost, with gratitude for the lives that they led; and with a determination to honor them through the work we carry on.

This is a time of war. Yet these Americans did not die on a foreign field of battle. They were killed here, on American soil, in the heart of this great state and the heart of this great American community. . . .

For those families who have lost a loved one, no words can fill the void that's been left. . . .

. . . . Your loved ones endure through the life of our nation. . . . Their life's work is our security, and the freedom that we all too often take for granted. Every evening that the sun sets on a tranquil town; every dawn that a flag is unfurled; every moment that an American enjoys life, liberty and the pursuit of happiness—that is their legacy.

Neither this country—nor the values upon which we were founded—could exist without men and women like these 13 Americans. And that is why we must pay tribute to their stories.

Chief Warrant Officer Michael Cahill had served in the National Guard and worked as a physician's assistant for decades. A husband and a father of three, he was so committed to his patients that on the day he died, he was back at work just weeks after having a heart attack.

Major Libardo Eduardo Caraveo spoke little English when he came to America as a teenager. But he put himself through college, earned a PhD, and was helping combat units cope with the stress of deployment. He's survived by his wife, sons and step-daughters.

Staff Sergeant Justin DeCrow joined the Army right after high school, married his high school sweetheart, and had served as a light wheeled mechanic and satellite communications operator. He was known as an optimist, a mentor, and a loving husband and loving father.

After retiring from the Army as a major, John Gaffaney cared for society's most vulnerable during two decades as a psychiatric nurse. He spent three years trying to return to active duty in this time of war, and he was preparing to deploy to Iraq as a captain. He leaves behind a wife and son.

Specialist Frederick Greene was a Tennessean who wanted to join the Army for a long time, and did so in 2008, with the support of his family. As a combat engineer he was a natural leader, and he is survived by his wife and two daughters.

Specialist Jason Hunt was also recently married, with three children to care for. He joined the Army after high school. He did a tour in Iraq, and it was there that he reenlisted for six more years on his 21st birthday so that he could continue to serve.

Staff Sergeant Amy Krueger was an athlete in high school, joined the Army shortly after 9/11, and had since returned home to speak to students about her experience. When her mother told her she couldn't take on Osama bin Laden by herself, Amy replied, "Watch me."

Private First Class Aaron Nemelka was an Eagle Scout who just recently signed up to do one of the most dangerous jobs in the service—defuse bombs—so that he could help save lives. He was proudly carrying on a tradition of military service that runs deep within his family.

Private First Class Michael Pearson loved his family and loved his music, and his goal was to be a music teacher. He excelled at playing the guitar, and could create songs on the spot and show others how to play. He joined the military a year ago, and was preparing for his first deployment.

Captain Russell Seager worked as a nurse for the VA, helping veterans with Post Traumatic Stress. He had extraordinary respect for the military, and signed up to serve so that he could help soldiers cope with the stress of combat and return to civilian life. He leaves behind a wife and son.

Private Francheska Velez, daughter of a father from Colombia and a Puerto Rican mother, had recently served in Korea and Iraq, and was pursuing a career in the Army. When she was killed she was pregnant with her first child, and was excited about becoming a mother.

Lieutenant Colonel Juanita Warman was the daughter and granddaughter of Army veterans. She was a single mom who put herself through college and graduate school, and served as a nurse practitioner while raising her two daughters. She also left behind a loving husband.

Private First Class Kham Xiong came to America from Thailand as a small child. He was a husband and father who followed his brother into the military because his family had a strong history of service. He was preparing for his first deployment to Afghanistan.

These men and women came from all parts of the country. Some had long careers in the military. Some had signed up to serve in the shadow of 9/11. Some had known intense combat in Iraq and Afghanistan, and some cared for those [who] did. Their lives speak to the strength, the dignity, the decency of those who serve, and that's how they will be remembered.

For that same spirit is embodied in the community here at Fort Hood, and in the many wounded who are still recovering. As was already mentioned, in those terrible minutes during the attack, soldiers made makeshift tourniquets out of their clothes. They braved gunfire to reach the wounded, and ferried them to safety in the backs of cars and a pickup truck. . . .

These are trying times for our country. In Afghanistan and Pakistan, the same extremists who killed nearly 3,000 Americans continue to endanger America, our allies, and innocent Afghans and Pakistanis. . . .

As we face these challenges, the stories of those at Fort Hood reaffirm the core values that we are fighting for, and the strength that we must draw upon. Theirs are the tales of American men and women in answering an extraordinary call—the call to serve their comrades, their communities, and their country. In an age of selfishness, they embody responsibility. In an era of division, they call upon us to come together. In a time of cynicism, they remind of us of who we are as Americans.

We are a nation that endures because of the courage of those who defend it. We saw that valor in those who braved bullets here at Fort Hood, just as surely as we see it in those who signed up knowing that they would serve in harm's way. . . .

We're a nation that is dedicated to the proposition that all men and women are created equal. We live that truth within our military, and see it in the varied backgrounds of those we lay to rest today. We defend that truth at home and abroad, and we know that Americans will always be found on the side of liberty and equality. That's who we are as a people. . . .

We need not look to the past for greatness, because it is before our very eyes. This generation of soldiers, sailors, airmen, Marines and Coast Guardsmen have volunteered in the time of certain danger. They are part of the finest fighting force that the world has ever known. They have served tour after tour of duty in distant, different and difficult fighting places. They have stood watch in blinding deserts and on snowy mountains. They have extended the opportunity of self-government to peoples that had suffered tyranny and war. They are men and women; white, black and brown; of all faiths and all stations—all Americans, serving together to protect our people, while giving others half a world away the chance to lead a better life.

In today's wars, there's not always a simple ceremony that signals our troops' success—no surrender papers to be signed, or capital to be claimed. But the measure of the impact of these young men and women is no less great. In a world of threats that no know [sic] borders, their legacy will be marked in the safety of our cities and towns, and the security and opportunity that's extended abroad. . . .
Here, at Fort Hood, we pay tribute to 13 men and women who were not able to escape the horror of war, even in the comfort of home. . . .

Long after they are laid to rest—when the fighting has finished, and our nation has endured; when today's servicemen and women are veterans, and their children have grown—it will be said that this generation believed under the most trying of tests; believed in perseverance—not just when it was easy, but when it was hard; that they paid the price and bore the burden to secure this nation, and stood up for the values that live in the hearts of all free peoples. . . .

III. Parsing the Speech

President Obama's eulogy illustrates the relationship between rhetorical *structure*—how certain themes are "timed" within a speech—and the *rhetoric* used to impute transcendent meanings to the dead. For purposes of this analysis, I will divide the speech into three parts. In Part I Obama introduces his themes of transformation leading to transcendence. Here he reintroduces to the living the Fort Hood dead as a group. They are no longer just the innocent victims of a murderer (an idea reinforced by news reports) but have, through Obama's narrative of their lives and deaths, been transformed from personhood to embody 'higher' values. In Part II Obama introduces the victims themselves, offering a several sentence proto-eulogy for each. This is his eulogy's core: the dead are introduced as individuals before being merged again into "the dead." In Part III, Obama imputes specific values to "the dead" and then connects them to a series of larger abstractions—the military, the Fort Hood community, America, and finally a generation.

As in any speech, military or civilian, readers should be mindful of both continuities and discontinuities. For eulogies, continuities reside in such things as biographical narrative and the extraction from these lives of larger meanings for which the dead either lived or died. These are then presented to the audience as lives and values to be emulated. Eulogies sometimes seek to project these larger meanings onto survivors, communities or institutions, especially those connected with the dead; examples might include children of the deceased, the army, the state, a charity, or a church, all of which may serve as vehicles to perpetuate the meaning. In short, today's eulogies use lives for the same purposes claimed two millennia ago by Plutarch in his *Lives*: "But virtue, by the bare statement of its actions, can so affect men's minds as to create at once both admiration of things done and desire to imitate the doers of them."

But readers should also note the discontinuities: the virtues themselves. Eulogies may be a constant of human civilization; the specific virtues that eulogies extol are not necessarily so.[9]

Part I: The Transformation

President Obama had no sooner finished his salutation than he began the work of investing both the victims as well as the massacre itself with transcendent meaning. "We have come together filled with sorrow for the 13 Americans that we have lost," he declared, "with gratitude for the lives that they

---

9 Plutarch, *Plutarch's Lives*, I: 202. Perhaps not coincidentally, Plutarch made this declaration in his life of Pericles, the great eulogist.

led and with a determination to honor them through the work we carry on." This sentence pays obeisance to the pieties of any eulogy: it immediately acknowledged both dead and the community that grieves them.

But these words conclude with an important signal: first, it constructs the abstraction of "them"—the victims—as well as "we"—the survivors and mourners; then it begins transforming both audience and the victims by imputing relationships between the two abstractions: we grieve ("sorrow") and we are grateful for having known them ("gratitude"). But of supreme importance is what "we" will do about "them": "we" will not just mourn, or become angry or vengeful, but instead we will "honor them through the work we carry on." Exactly how we will honor them and through what kind of work is addressed in Part III of the eulogy; for now, after expanding on the formal pieties ("For those families who have lost loved ones. . . ."), the President resumed the work of transformation.

As noted earlier, except for formulaic references to God, official speeches made on behalf of secular states tend to avoid overt religious themes; nevertheless, the eulogy as a genre invites and usually compels religious themes, and President Obama made two such references. In the first reference, he described the murderer's fate: "[W]e know that the killer will be met with justice—in this world, and the next." This implied a belief in an afterlife, certainly a religious conviction.

The second religious reference was placed after a reminder to the audience that the killer would be given "due process" and that "We're a nation that guarantees the freedom to worship as one chooses." This was followed by a paraphrase of Lincoln in which the audience is admonished not to "claim...God for our side" but rather to "always pray to be on the side of God." Both references were probably intended as a means of social control; perhaps the President assumed that his immediate (or larger) audience was at risk for violence against Muslims, and thus felt the need to channel the imagined rage. Such channeling of emotion is a eulogistic trope, especially when death resulted from another's unjust acts.

But there were important limits to the President's use of religion. He made no attempt to transform the victims into martyrs or apotheosize them into any other religious end state, nor did he ask that the audience adopt a religious attitude towards the incident (for example, a call to "jihad," or an appeal to righteous anger); instead, the persuasive appeals by which Obama transformed the dead consisted of sentiments that were presumably deeply held in an audience of public service-minded, patriotic Americans:

Your loved ones endure through the life of our nation.... Their life's work is our security, and the freedom that we all too often take for granted. Every evening that the sun sets on a tranquil town; every dawn that a flag is unfurled; every moment that an American enjoys life, liberty and the pursuit of happiness—that is their legacy.

(Overt religious appeals may be absent; but astute readers will note that there is in fact a powerful religious meme in the foregoing, albeit one that is submerged: eternal life.)

President Obama then transitioned to Part II of his speech by reaffirming the secular legacy of the victims. "Neither this country—nor the values upon which we were founded," he declared, "could exist without men and women like these 13 Americans. And that is why we must pay tribute to their stories." In short, the lives of the dead support "this country" and not some religious value. Yet Part II, which gave clipped biographical details about each of the dead, clearly sought more ambitious goals than simply to affirm that the dead died for their country.

Part II: Abstracting the Dead

Part II is the core of the eulogy. In choosing to mention names President Obama put faces on the dead, thereby restoring a human dimension to the events of five days earlier. Eulogies are a form of biography, and by naming individuals President Obama incurred rhetorical advantages as well as disadvantages. On one hand, he was able to personalize the speech, especially for immediate mourners, in ways not available to speakers who eulogize the deaths of hundreds or millions. On the other hand, the use of individuals introduces a complication: a speaker who seeks to draw transformative meaning from mass death has an easier time with larger numbers; mass equals abstraction, and abstraction is a speaker's blank Teleprompter.

For that reason how Obama individualized the dead was important. He used a deliberately crafted template: victims were listed alphabetically, and introduced by rank and name; this was followed by one or several personal references (13 of 13 bios), and then a job description (12 of 13 bios); where applicable, each entry concluded with a reference to immediate survivors.

Of course, this figurative tolling of the bell satisfied two of the eulogy's important pieties: honoring the dead via personal recognition (where possible), and if possible, doing so in a way intended to soothe the grief of their immediate families. But the President addressed an audience that extended far beyond these families. For this wider audience, to whom the dead were personally unknown, the speech must enter the mental territory of the dead-as-abstraction. With skillful shaping, even one named deceased can be transformed into an abstraction; *many* named dead become still easier to abstract. The information about the dead that Obama chose to use amounted to a composite deceased that had the abstract qualities that he needed to create. The traits mentioned by the President included:

Ethnic origin: 3 of 13 bios;
Gender: 13 of 13;
Reference to a personal struggle: 4 of 13 bios;
Family reference: 11 of 13 bios;
Caregivers: 4 of 13 bios;
Tradition of Service/Combatant reference: 5 of 13 bios.

Based on this and the other biographical factoids, President Obama began to craft the abstraction that he would connect with other abstractions, and thereby derive larger meanings.

First, how did Obama abstract the dead? Consider the paragraph that immediately followed the list of bios:

These men and women came from all parts of the country. Some had long careers in the military. Some had signed up to serve in the shadow of 9/11. Some had known intense combat in Iraq and Afghanistan, and some cared for those [that] did. Their lives speak to the strength, the dignity, the decency of those who serve, and that's how they will be remembered.

Here the President began to transform the individuals into small groups— stepping stones of abstractions on his way to still larger meanings. He divided "These men and women" into a series of "Some." In his final sentence, he added the various "somes" into "These," "Their," and "they;" having unified the dead through abstraction, he now connected them to his first large abstraction: the character of the military, or, as the President phrased it, "the strength, the dignity, [and] the decency of those who serve."

This introduces the formula for Part III of the eulogy, in which the abstract dead are connected to various communities. With each connection, President Obama sought to extract a series of larger meanings.

Part III: Larger Meanings

Part III of the eulogy is essentially a two-step: connect the abstracted dead (as well as survivors who "braved bullets" to assist wounded and dying comrades) with other abstractions; these included "the military," the "nation," and "This generation of soldiers." The larger meanings Obama sought to vindicate through the casualties were (in order of apparent importance) ethnic and racial diversity, communal sacrifice, religious tolerance, and rule of law. The virtues of religious tolerance and rule of law, discussed above, used "nation," a community to which the dead obviously belonged, as the vehicle for conveying the desired attributes. Now I will return to the "military" and also consider "generation" as rhetorical freighters for the President's message.

The information that Obama disclosed about the victims met two different (but not mutually exclusive) objectives. First, as wives and husbands, fathers and mothers, daughters and sons, and also as inheritors of family traditions, guitar players, athletes, single mothers, and young people paying their way through school, the group resembled a composite of all Americans without regard to race or ethnicity. But Obama also mentioned race and ethnicity, thereby meeting the second goal: that these lives of different races and ethnicities also spoke to "the strength, dignity, [and] the decency of those who serve."

There are probably few American politicians who, having decided to recite a list of the dead, would have refrained from mentioning the foreign nativities or ethnic connections implied by some victims' surnames. The benefit President Obama sought was to use the dead to vindicate the value of ethnic and racial diversity in American life. Merely reciting the list would have made this point; but adding additional details about the dead or their parents' countries of origin provided more evidence for the virtue of diversity. President Obama then used the abstraction of "the military" to carry this message.

"We're a nation that is dedicated to the proposition that all men and women are created equal," the President declared in an obviously derivative passage. "We live that truth within our military, and see it in the varied backgrounds of those we lay to rest today." Indeed, to Obama diversity was so important that he declared it to be a goal of both foreign as well as domestic policy: "We defend that truth at home and abroad, and we know that Americans will always be found on the side of liberty and equality. That's who we are as a people." And this topic rated another mention. Obama declared that the military was "man and woman; white, black and brown; of all faiths and all stations—all Americans, serving together to protect our people, while giving others half a world away the chance to lead a better life."

President Obama made this second mention of diversity in the context of the next vehicle for which the dead were emblems: the virtue of their generation. In fact, for the President "this generation"—by which he presumably meant service members in their late teens and twenties—became second in importance only to the military as a vehicle for conveying his larger meanings. A "generation" is an imprecise term that, when defined (twenty years? thirty years? all those born in a given year?), certainly has actuarial significance. However, attempting to attribute moral characteristics to "generations" quickly puts one in the realm of pure invention—another blank Teleprompter.

But Obama had no actuarial interest here; rather, he attempted to shoehorn into his eulogy an existing civilian/warrior meme: "The Greatest Generation." Popularized by former news announcer Tom Brokaw in a series of best-selling books, the Greatest Generation was quickly adopted by others to refer to the age cohort(s) that had survived the Great Depression and fought World War II; part of its mimetic "DNA" was to introduce the idea that wars are fought by discrete "generations." Repeatedly using the word "generation" (sans "Greatest;" the President would attach other superlatives) in connection with Fort Hood soldiers allowed Obama to derive the meme without appearing derivative. Consistent with this, President Obama first "located" the generation of the Fort Hood dead in recent history:

> For history is filled with heroes. You may remember the stories of a grandfather who marched across Europe; an uncle who fought in Vietnam; a sister who served in the Gulf. But as we honor the many generations who have served all of us—every single American—we must acknowledge that this generation has more than proved itself the equal of those who've come before.
>
> We need not look to the past for greatness, because it is before our eyes.

Here the virtue of the dead that is being praised is communal service—the term "generation" neatly includes both living and dead soldiers. The same paragraph that used "generation" as a vehicle for the second mention of diversity also included praise for communal service: "This generation of soldiers, sailors, airmen, Marines and Coast Guardsmen have volunteered in time of certain danger…. They have served tour after tour of duty in distant, different, and difficult places." The third and final use of "generation" to praise the dead appeared in the eulogy's penultimate paragraph, which also sealed the generational narrative. How and when will we know that this generation was worthy? The President answers:

> Long after they are laid to rest—when the fighting has finished, and our nation has endured; when today's servicemen and women are veterans, and their children have grown—it will be said that this generation believed under the most trying of tests; believed in perseverance—not just when it was easy, but when it was hard; that they paid the price and bore the burden to secure this nation, and stood up for the values that live in the hearts of all free peoples.

This long sentence is partly derivative (John F. Kennedy's First Inaugural: "pay any price, bear any burden") and partly cliché ("live in the heats of all free peoples"); but its underlying appeal is to the ancient invention of "posterity," an appeal to an imagined future that the speaker avers will honor both the dead and the veteran. And as the followers of apocalyptic cults might confirm, posterity is the blankest Teleprompter of them all.[10]

Persuasive Strategy

Like the Post-Battle and Victory Speeches that often Remember the Fallen, eulogies require a narrative: as biographies, they must tell a story of a life; or, in this case, many lives. Several of those stories were discussed above; here, I would like to identify two other persuasive narratives that President Obama used in his eulogy, each of which illustrates a different point in speech construction generally and eulogies in particular.

Speech narratives are rarely original, nor should they be; if the speaker wants to leverage his message by using what the audience already knows, the less original the narrative the better. (There are few genuinely original narratives in any event—remember Ecclesiastes.)

The first narrative discussed below illustrates how an entire speech can be constructed around one meme—in President Obama's case, one might imagine it as the motto that appears on every United States' coin, E Pluribus Unum. The second persuasive strategy might be called the Foreshadowing Narrative. It is common, but has special resonance in military eulogies. This narrative argues that the event that caused the deaths just foreshadows (or, to use other

10 John F. Kennedy, First Inaugural Address, in Safire, *Lend Me Your Ears*, 970-973.

metaphors, provides a sample, a foretaste, a warning) of what might happen to the audience later, on a larger scale. Here the president used the audience's self-concern (fear, anxiety) in order to demand attention or to promote another agenda.

But in the case of eulogies, whether one draws narrative from a cliché or a metaphor, the stories run parallel towards the same objective: to persuade the audience about some other matter while praising the dead.

E Pluribus Unum—Out of Many, One

E Pluribus Unum, besides being the first motto of the United States (and thus among the first national memes), also served as one of this eulogy's important persuasive strategies. To understand how, Obama's eulogy should be re-imagined as consisting of two parts. Part I was devoted to describing the Pluribus, the Many. This was diversity, or—to use another hoary American metaphor (and meme)—the "ingredients" of the famed "melting pot." The President fleshed out Pluribus by listing the names of the dead and giving biographical factoids for each, as well as in such passages as "man and woman, white, black, and brown, of all faiths and all stations."[11]

Part II was the transformation of Pluribus into Unum. He accomplished this by referencing a variety of mediating institutions—the military, the nation, the Fort Hood community, as well as an imagined demographic entity, "this generation." These institutions were only subsets of the larger Unum: America, or, as President Obama phrased it, "all Americans serving together to protect our people." Thus, the story President Obama told was that of a group of diverse individuals, joined in an Army, a community, and a generation, that combined in order to face a common, if wholly unexpected, challenge: combating jihadists like Major Hasan.

In using an E Pluribus Unum-type meme as his eulogy's mainspring, President Obama had two purposes. The first was to praise the dead, for it is a virtue to join in common cause to accomplish some great thing; and defending one's community and country is a great thing. But there was a second purpose, not necessarily related to praising the dead. By defining the Pluribus as well as

---

11 Congress adopted E Pluribus Unum as the national motto in 1782; although the motto was changed in 1864 to "In God We Trust," E Pluribus Unum remains on U.S. coinage, along with "In God We Trust."

the Unum, the President also defined his audience, at least those members who accepted his definitions (probably most audience members). And a speaker who successfully defines the audience may also control it, or at least what the audience may be thinking. This is not necessarily nefarious (it depends on the speaker's intentions); the speaker has merely identified some common denominator of the audience, which in turn eases his task of persuasion.

The President's point here was to praise the dead and invest the living with the same virtues. "[The] stories of those at Fort Hood," he declared, "reaffirm the core values that we are fighting for, and the strength we must draw upon." Later in his eulogy, the President defined what those core values were: "commitment to justice," "due process," the "proposition that all men and women are created equal," and so forth.

Thus "the stories" (Pluribus) reaffirmed "the core values," which in turn were a property of "all Americans, serving together"—the Unum. The President did not have to mention the motto in order to exploit its meaning; that meaning has long been part of the mimetic DNA of what it "means" to be an American. Thus the Fort Hood eulogy also served as a persuasive argument for unity.

Foreshadowing Narrative

The Foreshadowing Narrative declares in effect, "What happened to *them* is only a sample of what could happen to *you*." Obama began his eulogy with an embedded Murders-As-Combat-Casualties meme:

> This is a time of war. Yet these Americans did not die on a foreign field of battle. They were killed here, on American soil, in the heart of this great state and the heart of this great American community.

This implies a Foreshadowing Narrative: because most Americans live on "American soil," live in a "state" or "community" they may regard as "great," it takes no great leap of audience narcissism to import the tragedy of Fort Hood onto their own particular Main Streets. Of course, the same argument can be applied to many types of death, and occasionally is: for example, speakers fundraising to battle a certain disease might ask the audience to contribute because the illness can strike *them* (or a loved one) at any time. That argument is an appeal to self-interest: "Give to kill the disease, or risk being killed by the disease."

But Obama's particular Foreshadowing Narrative does not appeal to self-interest. Rather it serves to seize audience attention, suggesting that "What I am about to say matters because what happened here could happen to you." Obama has brought the battlefield to Texas from some dusty Afghan plain; the audience members will take the next step: transferring the Texas battlefield to their own neighborhoods. And yet more is implied here. Each audience member is a potential victim, or, if one prefers, combatant; and, although the President's eulogy promoted religious tolerance as a virtue of the living and the dead, the implication is unavoidable that it is Muslim fundamentalists who are everyone's potential enemies.

But what I wish to emphasize is that President Obama also used the Foreshadowing Narrative to make a *political* argument. Readers will recall from the Introduction General Ridgway's speech in which he declared that the Korean War was worth waging because it "has become . . . a fight for our own freedom." President Obama was a commander in chief of a nation at war, and he employed the same narrative as did Ridgway, albeit with greater subtlety. Just after reciting an anecdote about a wounded caregiver, Obama declared that "[t]hese are trying times for our country," and continued,

> In Afghanistan and Pakistan, the same extremists who killed nearly 3,000 Americans continue to endanger Americans, our allies, and innocent Afghans and Pakistanis. . . .
>
> As we face these challenges, the stories of those at Fort Hood reaffirm the core values that we are fighting for, and the strength that we must draw upon. Theirs are the tales of American men and women answering an extraordinary call—the call to serve their comrades, their communities and their country.

Here was a political argument. The President was connecting Fort Hood and 9/11 with a continuing danger from extremists "in Afghanistan and Pakistan." Of course, the Fort Hood killer might have been a jihadist, but he was also an American citizen, who, as of this writing, is not known to have ever visited Afghanistan or Pakistan. But by aggregating these connections, Obama was able to *imply* causation without having to *state* causation.

Why would he do this? Here one must depart the eulogy's confines and ask what other relevant matters were confronting Obama at the time he spoke. One likely answer is that in the weeks before, during and after the Fort Hood killings the President had been engaged in a long and very public "group grope" on what to do about Afghanistan: to send or withdraw forces, or effect some other change in strategy. Less than a month after the eulogy, the President would announce an escalation; but interestingly, he may have begun to argue his case the month before in Texas. To the President's credit, he did not make the argument overtly that the shootings at Fort Hood justified an escalation of forces in Afghanistan; to have done so in a eulogy would only have invited suspicion and even contempt.

In late August 1862, Abraham Lincoln wrote to *New York Tribune* editor Horace Greeley that he would emancipate slaves if necessary to save the Union (thus helping to prepare opinion for the issuance of the Preliminary Emancipation Proclamation exactly one month later); I believe that President Obama used the Fort Hood eulogy in a similar way—to help prepare public opinion for his forthcoming decision to send 30,000 additional troops to Afghanistan.[12]

12 Abraham Lincoln to Horace Greeley, August 22, 1862, *Collected Works of Abraham Lincoln*, Roy P. Basler, editor, (New Brunswick, New Jersey: Rutgers University Press, 1953), Volume 5, 389.

Conclusion

'What!' cried Cyrus, 'can one solitary speech fill the hearer's soul on the selfsame day with honour and uprightness, guard him from all that is base, spur him to undergo, as he ought for the sake of glory every toil and every danger, implant in him the faith that it is better to die sword in hand than to escape by flight?'

— Xenophon, *Cyropaedia*

The Spartans meanwhile, man to man, and with their war songs in the ranks, exhorted each brave comrade to remember what he had learnt before; well aware that the long training of action was of more use for saving lives than any brief verbal exhortation, though ever so well delivered.

—Thucydides, *The Peloponnesian War*, observation before the battle of Mantinea, 419 BCE[1]

One astute critic of my last tome on battle speeches asked an important question: "Is there any evidence that all this hot air in some way affected the outcome of events?" This is the quintessential historian's query. It asks whether, and if so how, words influenced deeds. After all, events that cause nothing of historical significance are deemed unimportant, and, unless useful to somehow adorn a narrative, may be safely omitted from it. For example, historians of America and World War II are presumably interested in, first, the fact that the United States was attacked by Japan on December 7, 1941; second, that the next day President Roosevelt requested from Congress a Declaration of War; and to a far lesser extent, if at all, in what Roosevelt had for breakfast that morning.[2]

---

1 Xenophon, *Cyropaedia*, translated by H.G. Dakyans (Whitefish, Montana: Kessinger Publishing, n.d.), III.51; *Landmark Thucydides*, 5.69.2.

2 Gary P. Cox, Book Review, *The Journal of Military History*, Volume 73, Number 3, July 2009, 934-936.

The influence that a battle speech had on a battle can rarely be shown with precision, and usually not at all. This impossibility may be purely evidentiary. For example, one cannot be sure that the battle speeches of antiquity were even made, or, if they were, then what exactly was said. And for other speeches, the impossibility rests in the absurdity of the question. For example, few would argue that, but for General Eisenhower's "Great Crusade" exhortation, D-Day would have failed or cost even more casualties.

So does that make battle speeches the equivalent of breakfast, or are they something more consequential? In some cases battle speeches are arguably very consequential. The Hitler-via-Warlimont Instructional Speech (the Commissar Order) contributed to the murder of thousands of Soviet POWs and helped shape attitudes that killed many more people. But even here one could argue that no Commissar Order was necessary: that by 1941 Nazi bio-ideological memes had been so thoroughly embedded in German national consciousness that the brutalization of Soviet POWs was inevitable. In short, one could argue that the Commissar Order was only a symptom of an already-well advanced German politico-criminal pathology, not its cause.

Other types of battle speeches had objectives that would have been difficult to quantify. Whereas the Germans required that field commanders file reports of executed commissars (thus giving later historians a metric), how would one measure the success of George Patton's The Speech? Its objectives were to introduce himself to his soldiers and communicate something about the war that they had to fight. Even if soldiers were scientifically polled (to my knowledge, never done in Third Army) it would have been extremely difficult to measure Patton's success here. For example, there is the question of timing—how meaningful could a respondent's answer be before actual combat? The Speech was destined to be remembered in any event; it is my guess that it probably provoked one set of attitudes at first, perhaps a different set after Third Army's baptism of fire, and another set after final victory.

These kinds of doubts are easily transferred to the political realm. Public support for health care was declining before President Obama's speech to the Joint Session of Congress; following a slight bump in the polls after the speech, this support soon resumed its decline. Was Obama's speech a failure? Or, put another way, given the public's growing antipathy toward the proposed health care reform, could any hortatory speech have made a difference? And if public opinion had trended upwards after the speech, what weight would one assign to the President's words as opposed to other factors, such as television ads by pro-reform interest groups, endorsements from the pulpit, or valentines from pro-reform media? Even in politics, the question stands: are these speeches merely breakfast?[3]

As the epigraphed quotations suggest, the battle-speech-as-breakfast case was made several millennia ago by no lesser authorities than Xenophon and Thucydides. Both men were historians who also had extensive combat experience. Xenophon's speeches remain classics of military history. Although Thucydides was a less successful soldier (he was exiled from Athens for twenty years after failing to prevent the capture of Amphipolis by the Spartan Brasidas), he established his historian bona fides in part by claiming that he had personally heard some of the battle speeches that he included in his narrative.[4]

Both men declare the limits of oratory: Thucydides, through the Spartans, observes that combat training is far more important than speeches; Xenophon, through his fictive Cyrus, argues that if on the day of battle a soldier doesn't have "it"—ideals, honor, a willingness to exchange his life for his cause—no speech can give it to him. These were compelling observations by those who presumably had excellent reasons to know.

But does this make battle speeches breakfast? Not quite. Despite discounting the practice, Xenophon himself, his invented Cyrus, and even Thucydides' Spartans are all depicted as making many types of battle speeches. So what gives? Just this: while in many, if not most, cases we cannot really trace causation from word to audience to deed, we do know that there are people to whom such speeches are supremely important: the scribblers (such as Xenophon, Thucydides, and their successors) who center battle and political speeches in their historical narratives, OpEd pieces, textbooks, and newspaper articles; important, too, are these speeches to television pundits, YouTube viewers, documentarians, and screenwriters.

This should matter to readers for three reasons. First, the aforementioned groups are important meme creators and pumping stations in meme distribution; in other words, they are engaged in knowledge production. For example, one important group of knowledge producers—historians—will often use speeches as symbols to help explain highly consequential historical events. One might

---

3 Rasmussen Reports traces the ebbs and flows of public support for healthcare. Findings may be accessed at: www.rasmussenreports.com/public_content/politics/current_events/healthcare/september_2009/health_care_reform. Accessed December 1 2009.

4 Xenophon's speeches may be found in his *Anabasis*, one good translation of which may be had in the ever-reliable Penguin editions: Xenophon, *The Persian Expedition*, translated by Rex Warner (London: Penguin Books, 1972); *Landmark Thucydides*, 5.26.5, 1.22.1.

ask: if historians had not definitively centered the Gettysburg Address, with its "new birth of freedom" concept, in Civil War narrative, would Americans understand that conflict in quite the same way? Possibly, but it would be a much longer homework assignment. The same might be said of President Roosevelt's speech asking for war against Japan: "day of infamy" worked for the public then and has worked for historians since as a brilliantly concise summary of the American *casus belli* as well as a long-traveling popular meme.

Second, battle speeches and their political counterparts, being time-bound, are priceless historical artifacts; no matter how lying, deceptive, or inaccurate, such speeches, if properly unwound (as I have attempted to do in *Fighting Words*), can offer profound historical insights into the worlds of the speaker who produced them and the audience whose characteristics, expectations and mere presence influenced their production. Put simply, some very important things that we know about historically consequential actors—Alexander the Great and George Patton, to name two—are based on the speeches that they gave. More inferentially, the context in which speeches appear also can tell us something about the audiences of yore.

But while the impact of battle speeches and their political counterparts may be difficult to trace, there is a third reason why they are worth studying, and one which is a major point of *Fighting Words*. This is the impact that they have, not on distant armies or faceless voters, but on us. No matter how analytical the ear, separating oneself from the immediate experience of hearing a speech is difficult, although necessary for better understanding. To merely grasp the memes, feel the pathos, comprehend the ethos, and share the hopes of smartly crafted, well-delivered speeches is to instantly become part of its design. Analysis requires distance, and whenever possible speeches of interest ought to be read as well as heard.

This is so because to merely hear and not read for oneself a major speech is to be reliant on the mediums whose business it is to channel spot interpretations of what was said. There are benefits here: speeches are often prismatic, and few listeners can see every side. Reading blogs and columns, especially those from distant bands on the ideological spectrum, may challenge one's own beliefs and, with more frequency than might be imagined, offer new insights. And what others say may be indispensable to monitoring the meme *du jour* that comes floating down various media ideological meme-streams.

(And for those who are—like me—easily amused, nothing better revivifies otherwise dead time than watching how the same memes rip through the meme-streams with nary a peep about plagiarism, let alone originality. For example, at certain junctures in debates about wars and peace, "Munich," "appeasement" and "Neville Chamberlain" suddenly become ubiquitous in some circles, while "Vietnam," "quagmire" and "exit strategy" appear in other circles like a fast-onset pox.)

Enter—and, quite soon, exit—*Fighting Words*. While there are many books that counsel speakers on how to speak, far fewer exist to help audiences listen critically to *what* they are being told. I wrote this book with audiences in mind, and, as readers know by now, history is very important to my analysis. I encourage readers to think of the examples of speeches used in this book as *historical paradigms* rather than *historical analogies*. A paradigm is a model that exists on its own terms, time and place; as such, one may try to emulate it or borrow its components freely for adaptation to other times and places. In contrast, historical analogies are far more dangerous because they are premised on some principle of fundamental repetition, that is, the "lessons" of history; when in fact most "lessons of history" are really moral propositions clothed in factoids.

If there is any hope in this process, it dwells in the land of negative propositions—hard to prove in a chain of causation, but still important. Perhaps as important as whether or not "all the hot air" meant something to final outcomes are those cases in which it meant nothing at all. Although their numbers were sadly minuscule, not every German who heard Hitler's speech and received the Commissar Order accepted it uncritically; a few understood it for what it was and, directly or by subterfuge, refused to comply. A vast majority of American Third Army soldiers who listened to George "Blood and Guts" Patton inveigh against the enemy understood that his histrionic speeches were exhortatory and hyperbolic, and were not meant to and could not exempt them from the Geneva Conventions.

We are surrounded by bad ideas, often attractively packaged and seductively spoken; that more such ideas do not become mainstream is a tribute to audiences. *Fighting Words* will have succeeded to the extent that it has added to this never-large-enough-for-my-taste pool of discerning listeners.

Appendix

An Interview with Author Richard F. Miller

SB: Your first work was in Civil War studies—you co-authored Nantucket: The Civil War Experience, *and of course the award-winning* Harvard's Civil War: The History of the Twentieth Massachusetts Volunteer Infantry. *How did you get from there to battle speeches?*

RFM: I came to see that the same thing connected the Nantucket book and the regimental history of the Twentieth Massachusetts—the problem of leadership. The Nantucket tome explored the question of local civilian and state military leadership—percentage-wise, that island sent more men to war than any other community in Massachusetts. The Twentieth Massachusetts was largely officered by a clique of upper class Boston Brahmins; they led a regiment composed of Germans, Irish, and largely working class men. Prejudice was rife, yet somehow when the bullets flew, the Brahmins led and these very different ranks followed. So I wondered: How did the Twentieth's officers do it?

SB: How did they do it?

RFM: As I was pondering that very question, the United States invaded Iraq. Fate would have it that in 2003, although without previous experience as a journalist, I was offered an embed slot aboard the *USS Kitty Hawk*. I went and observed the drumbeat to war that culminated in the *Kitty Hawk's* important role in Shock and Awe. Following that experience, I returned to Iraq two more times, once with the Marines in Fallujah and once with the army near Buqubah. Later, I embedded with the 101st Airborne in eastern Afghanistan. Through the lens of these experiences the problem of leadership began to resolve.

SB: How so?

RFM: I discovered that historian S.L.A. Marshall had it right: one of the most important factors in small unit tactics is how leaders—officers, NCOs, even privates when they are called upon to lead—spoke to their units. It's not the only factor, of course. There's setting the right example, showing courage under fire, fairness in dealing with subordinates, and bottomless care for the men and women in one's command. But at the end of the day, what was said, how it was said, and the moral authority of the speaker mattered a lot. Thus, in Iraq and Afghanistan I began to see battle speeches as a critical part of the leadership mix.

SB: Can you give some examples?

RFM: Sure. The *Kitty Hawk's* crew held the captain in very high esteem. In the run-up to Shock and Awe, his daily summaries over the ship's PA system became the focal point for a lot of sailors. The captain would provide a situation report about the international politics behind the gathering storm, and would exhort the crew on the importance of teamwork and that their country stood behind their efforts. There were lots of sailors who hung on his every word. On another occasion, I was with a Marine patrol in some very difficult circumstances. The officer, a lieutenant, set just the right note in both reassuring his men and issuing clear instructions about what they needed to do. He was a rock—they became rocks.

SB: You devote the entire first chapter of Fighting Words *to what you call the "wordless speech" of General Grant. Can you give an example of a "wordless speech" from your embed experiences?*

RFM: Actually, I can. Once in Afghanistan during a rocket attack, a senior US officer and his aides had taken cover in an already crowded bombproof. The officer noticed that several Afghan civilian workers had been left standing outside, looking frozen with fear. Without hesitating, he ordered us out of the bombproof and gave our spots to the civilians. His men witnessed this, and later, several commented privately about how this officer routinely displayed courage and was devoted to improving life for Afghanis. The deed became the speech, in fact, the equivalent of a hundred speeches.

SB: Did you ever experience battle speeches that didn't work?

RFM: Oh, yes. Once I was with an army patrol outside of Balad. Everything was routine until they were ordered to do a house search of some local tribal leader who was suspected of helping insurgents. Before going in, the patrol leader—a senior army NCO—briefed his men about the orders. But the briefing was terrible. He didn't describe the house, the grounds, what his men should do, what they were really looking for, or much about why they were supposed to raid the place. When the men hit the house, it was chaos—civilians screaming and running everywhere, soldiers not knowing what they were supposed to do or even where they should be. But we (and especially those civilians) were lucky—had there been organized opposition in that house, it would have been a disaster for everyone.

SB: Who were the greatest battle speechmakers in history?

RFM: All history or modern history?

SB: Either.

RFM: Ok, well, first, you have to remember my rule—battle speeches are those that are made to soldier-audiences. This excludes some powerful wartime speakers, such as Abraham Lincoln and Winston Churchill. They were politicians and their speeches were really aimed at civilians. But to answer your question, I would say Alexander the Great (with an asterisk), Napoleon, Lord Nelson, George B. McClellan, Robert E. Lee, and George Patton.

SB: Why the asterisk with Alexander?

RFM: Because scholars can't be sure that many ancient battle speeches, especially Alexander's, were actually given, or if they were, whether the words handed down to us resemble what was actually said.

SB: George B. McClellan isn't usually associated with military excellence.

RFM: That judgment is partially mistaken. Arguably, he was mostly unsuited for combat command, but as an organizer of armies, a morale builder, and an exhorter of men, he was unmatched in American history. His soldiers would be known to weep for joy when he spoke and they certainly wept in sadness when he was fired.

SB: Who is the greatest living battle speechmaker?

RFM: That's easy, at least for Americans: General David H. Petreaus. Reading his battle speeches, mostly distributed to troops in written form, one is struck by how "Grant-like" they are—plain English, clear, concise, honest and never condescending. He also possesses, albeit in a far lower key, something that George Patton stressed: "visible personality." Petraeus is everywhere, and wherever he is, his messages are remarkably consistent with his demeanor. Listen to his 2006 confirmation testimony before Congress and then read his Assumption of Command Speech in February of 2007. The message discipline and consistency is remarkable. In fact, the manual *Counterinsurgency* that he wrote with General Mattis is one long persuasive argument in favor of message consistency and discipline!

SB: What would you say is Petreaus' greatest speech?

RFM: Probably one of his least known. In May 2007, he delivered a Midst-of-Battle speech directly confronting the connection between combat stress and soldier abuse of detainees and civilians, ala Abu Grahib. His speech was perfectly tuned to the modern *zeitgeist*. It was part Oprah, part U.S. Grant, compassionate and personal, but without sacrificing his authority. Patreaus officially dismissed Patton's ghost—the one that slapped soldiers for malingering—and introduced the idea that courage sometimes means taking oneself out of the fight if psychological pressure might produce behavior that could jeopardize the mission.

SB: You mentioned George Patton as among the greatest battle speechmakers. You've read a lot of battle speeches. Are there any Pattons out there?

RFM: No, and for good reason. Post-World War II Geneva Conventions impose serious liability on military leaders for any crimes that flow from their words. Few commanders wish to run the risk of having their hyperbolic exhortations (ala Patton) induce unbalanced subordinates into committing war crimes. Not even Patton could run that risk today. In 1943, some of his men were tried for the murder of seventy Axis POWs, and they claimed that Patton had authorized it in a battle speech. Patton was investigated and eventually cleared.

SB: Fighting Words *also analyzes three speeches delivered by President Barack Obama. Why did you include them?*

RFM: Although I take pains to differentiate political and battle speeches, the larger truth is that persuasive strategies are seamless. For example, in his healthcare speech, Obama uses the same Appeals to Guilt and Shame that have been stock features of battle speeches for millennia. His Fort Hood eulogy embraces the conventions of eulogies in general, although despite certain supporters' claims, it wasn't quite the Gettysburg Address. Nevertheless, the war metaphors permeate politics and I was interested in exploring just how far that went in political speech.

SB: Some of your analysis is critical of Obama. Why?

RFM: Well, some of my analysis is critical of every speechmaker I examine, and Obama is no exception. Look, whatever criticism I have is not based on policy, but on issues of rhetorical structure and persuasive strategies. In fact, the only battle speechmaker's *policy* that *Fighting Words* criticizes is Adolf Hitler and his notorious Commissar Order.

SB: President Obama has been celebrated as one of the great speechmakers since Ronald Reagan. Do you agree?

RFM: I do not. Remember, for me the paramount issue is rhetorical structure rather than delivery. Through this lens, Obama's speeches are largely mediocrities. First, what differentiates them from say, those of John F. Kennedy is his inexplicably poor wordsmithing. Obama's speeches contain few memorable phrases, and mint few new memes. Also, his speeches are seriously overlong. Worse, as I discuss in his healthcare speech, his message structure is often confused, and badly "timed" within the speech itself. And if you think this is just academic hairsplitting, think again—the particular message inconsistencies that I found in his healthcare speech were emblematic of the reasons why he has failed to carry public opinion on the issue.

SB: Has the president made any speeches that you like?

RFM: Yes, and I wrote so at the time on a Fox News blog of all places. His Inauguration Speech was good. Not great by historical measures—after all, he's competing with Jefferson's first inaugural, Jackson's first inaugural, Lincoln's two inaugurals, FDR and JFK's first inaugurals—tough competition, to say the least. Nevertheless, the president turned in a workmanlike product.

SB: Any final advice for the president?

RFM: Yeah—listen more to General Petraeus, and not just about military matters.

SB: Your first book on battle speeches was In Words and Deeds: Battle Speeches in History. *How does* Fighting Words *differ from that book?*

RFM: *In Words and Deeds* was really a book about classifying the battle speech as its own genre of rhetoric—to use the $25 word it was a taxonomic treatment. *Fighting Words* uses those findings but in service to a larger objective—an attempt to answer the questions of *why* and *how* battle speeches persuade. After all, men will march to their deaths on a say-so. *Fighting Words* then applies those military persuasive strategies to political speeches. There are remarkable similarities here. And this makes sense. After all, the notion of "civilian" government and "separation of powers" is, in historical terms, a fairly recent development. For millennia, the king, emperor, czar, Pope or Caesar embodied the civil and military functions of state.

SB: So is Fighting Words *a book for speakers or wannabe speakers?*

RFM: Neither! The market is flooded with "how to" books for speakers, and has been since Aristotle's *Art of Rhetoric*! Rather, *Fighting Words* is a book for *audiences* although the problem is the same as that which beleaguered Aristotle: what to do about bad arguments. We are besotted with them, and the problem has grown worse with image saturation, which adds an emotive force to persuasive strategies that an Aristotle could never have imagined. The wonder of humankind is not that bad arguments work—they do and together with the historical forces that birth them, were (and are) responsible for some of the worst acts in human history; indeed, the wonder is that bad arguments don't work more often. My hope is that I've written a book that adds not to slick speakers (there will never be a shortage of these) but to the size of informed audiences.

SB: The subtitle of your book is "Persuasive Strategies for War and Politics." I think we have covered the first part, so let's turn to the second. What advice does Fighting Words *have for politicians giving a speech?*

RFM: Know your historical moment, know your audience, and know yourself.

SB: Can you break that down for us?

RFM: Sure. First is the importance of history. *Fighting Words* attempts to pin each speech to its precise moment in time. What was the historical context in which a speech was made? What did this history contribute to its success? Failure? Mixed result? What you will find is that successful speeches match the speaker, the audience, the moment, the memes, and the *zeitgeist*. This has nothing to do with modern, political class narcissism about *making* history; but it has everything to do with speakers *understanding* their historical moments.

SB: Do you have an example in mind?

RFM: Let's talk about speech memes, especially those transmitted in famous "catch phrases," to use Richard Dawkins' words.

SB: For the sake of clarity, define "meme."

RFM: For the sake of simplicity, a "meme" is a notion, idea, or storyline. There is some discussion how to pronounce it—either like the "mem" in memory, or like "meem," which rhymes with "cream."

SB: Ok, thanks. Back to the example about know your historical moment, your audience, and yourself.

RFM: Take the generations that experienced the Great Depression, won World War II, and drove US prosperity during the 1950s. They served under Eisenhower twice—once in Europe and later as president. In JFK's First Inaugural, when he declared, "the torch has been passed to a new generation of Americans—born in this century, tempered by war, disciplined by a hard and bitter peace," and so forth . . .

SB: He knew his audience and appreciated the historical moment.

RFM: Precisely. Kennedy was speaking directly to my parents' generation. He was the first American president born in the twentieth century and he (or his speechwriters) nailed his historical moment. Re-read his Inaugural—it's replete with accurate reflections of his generational *zeitgeist*. Kennedy's voters had been "paying prices, bearing burdens, and meeting hardships" since the 1930s.

SB: How do President Lincoln's inaugurals stack up by comparison?

RFM: At the time of Lincoln's First Inaugural, Fort Sumter hadn't been attacked and most Northerners still had hope that sectional differences could be adjusted without war. When Lincoln declared in his First Inaugural, "We are not enemies, but friends. We must not be enemies. Though passion may have strained it must not break our bonds of affection," and so forth, he perfectly summarized the Northern mindset *de jour*. Four years later in the Second Inaugural, after so much blood and suffering, his religious interpretation of the war's devastation clearly resonated with his Northern audience. Again, and like JFK, Lincoln nailed his historical moment. I particularly believe this because, for a separate study I read more than one hundred Civil War eulogies, and could detect distinct adumbrations of most of the Second Inaugural's themes. And here's the secret sauce . . .

SB: Secret sauce?

RFM: Yes. Those speeches were in, in a very real way, "made" by the audiences!

SB: You lost me.

RFM: A successful speech resides in its audience. Such speeches cannot be compared with, say, Albert Einstein reading his paper on the *General Theory of Relativity* for the first time. There's no "new" information in a successful speech. Everything that the speaker says is already known to the audience. Most Northerners wanted peace without war; later they mourned their dead sons and husbands in churches throughout the loyal states. Kennedy's audience already understood itself as being different, as having been shaped in the crucible of war—several wars—and economic hardship. But what Lincoln and Kennedy did was to brilliantly and eloquently crystallize what their audiences *already knew and believed*. Their genius was the special genius of human empathy.

SB: Let's put all this in modern political terms. What would you advise a politician to do today? Is there a one-size-fits-all piece of advice for political speechmakers? Or is all politics local?

RFM: All politics being local was Massachusetts' Congressman Tip O'Neill's observation, and for his time it was valid. Someday it may be valid again—but it's not valid right now.

SB: Why not?

RFM: In several words—the Internet, 24/7 cable news, Facebook, Twitter, and YouTube. These media have nationalized political memes. True or not, such ideas as party corruption, creeping socialism, abuse of power, spiraling deficits, and so forth have become the filter through which even small acts of obscure politicians must pass. In sum, the "small picture" has disappeared. Now, whether a politician is a philanderer, spends too much money on haircuts, or won't answer questions directly has become national business—because these things fit into pre-existing national political storylines.

SB: Can you provide a couple examples?

RFM: Sure. The fact that politicians don't read the bills they vote on, egregiously misquote the Constitution, and make backroom deals that are awful to look at, has probably characterized American politics since the Revolution. But today, the narrative in which these factoids reside has acquired new significance, driven by instantly nationalized memes that take on a life of their own.

SB: So Congressman Smith says "I don't care about the Constitution," and within two hours that sound bite and Youtube video has gone viral, and suddenly he is branded as an "out of control" legislator . . .

RFM: That's it. What's interesting is that the "new" storylines or memes are historically consistent with the "old" storylines or memes. Americans have distrusted distant government since we threw out King George III. Generation after generation has passed the same meme-torch, albeit with a different colored flame—they (we) have always distrusted governing elites. Daniel Shay rebelled, his children fought the Second National Bank, their Northern children believed that the Slave Power controlled Washington, their children believed that the Robber Barons were monopolizing commerce and power, and their children suspected the influence of corrupt urban political "machines," ala Tammany Hall—I could go on but you get the picture.

SB: So many of today's politicians seem so ignorant of this history . . .

RFM: They are indeed, and it plays into this phenomenon. The difference between today and the Age of Jackson is velocity—memes are instantaneously nationalized.

SB: Where do the memes come from?

RFM: *Fighting Words* identifies two sources of memes— "bottom up," that is, memes that originate spontaneously and often anonymously among the people, and "top down," that is, ideas or memes that originate from editorialists, op-ed writers, academics, and political consultants. What has the governing classes rattled today is that the current set of political memes are being generated "bottom up"—and the elites have no idea what to do about it. And they thought that "mastering the Internet Age" was raising campaign contributions online!

SB: I have heard the term "meme-stream." Can you define that?

RFM: Networks that disseminate information, in particular those that convey memes. Here, think newspapers, certain magazines and journals, comedy shows, and talking heads. But today you must also include blogs, comment sections on blogs, list servers, emailed jokes and factoids, chain letters, Facebook postings, Tweets, etc. New meme-streams are being created all the time, and some of them have enormous influence.

SB: Such as?

RFM: Probably the most prominent recent example is the Tea Party movement. Since the president's healthcare proposal began to generate serious opposition, the Tea Party has grown and now includes meme-streams that most incumbent politicians, having unwisely made malicious or false statements about, can no longer access. Indeed, I would argue that the Tea Partiers now have almost unchallenged control over political meme creation, at least in terms of domestic affairs.

SB: Why do you think that?

RFM: All you need to do is read the columns and listen to the speeches of those who oppose the Tea Party movement. Most of them are obsessed with discrediting Tea Party ideas and storylines. That's one strong piece of evidence of their power. Elites by nature are self-reifying entities, heavily reliant on social boundaries. The boundaries not only separate elites from the governed, they also function as walls to conceal the mechanisms elite control. Any movement that corrodes these boundaries will generate intense elite opposition. And nothing corrodes boundaries more than demands for transparency.

SB: So the elites are running scared.

RFM: To death. "Bottom-up" movements have always frightened those in power. And this one has the velocity tools to take ideas viral in hours, coast to coast. We have never experienced anything like this in political or social history. The elites can no longer control the storyline, largely because *how* they control the process as well as their true attitudes towards the governed have been laid bare.

SB: Translate this into some advice for political speakers.

RFM: A current dominant idea or storyline created and solidified by repetition and example involves rule by unaccountable or arrogant elites. Politicians today can and must offer counter-memes that stress independence in thought and origins, and associations that are distant or opposed to those attributed to the governing elite.

SB: Like . . .

RFM: Like "I did not attend a major blue state university and I am proud of it." Or, "I am not a wire-pulling high-end consultant or lobbyist or associated with dead-tree media." It is quite the paradox today—and some outside-the-Beltway political candidates are finally realizing this—that the associations and credentials so valued by the governing classes are now distinct liabilities.

SB: So a candidate today, whether delivering a speech out on the stump or posting it on Youtube, must take into account the history of the moment, the experiences and feelings of the audience, and unite them into a dominant idea or meme that instantly resonates.

RFM: If they want to win in today's environment, that is exactly what they must do. Audiences today know most of the politicians in Washington have never met a private sector payroll or worn a uniform. People instinctively know this is not a good thing for politicians who pass laws regulating and taxing businesses, and who are constitutionally obligated to defend our nation. The reason is simple, and has been discussed by Republican pollster Frank Luntz: the public is now demanding accountability for the ills being heaped upon us. That's one thing that a small businessperson and a soldier have in common: they are accountable to others.

SB: What about the form of the speech? Has that changed?

RFM: It has indeed. Stylistically, my advice is that speeches today need to be short and very direct in the sense of providing answers to the questions posed. Life is always complicated, but whether or not a politician will vote for healthcare, cap and trade, or immigration reform usually comes down to a simple "yes" or "no." At least for political speechmakers, I would encourage adherence to either version of the KISS principle: Keep It Short and Sweet, or Keep it Simple, Stupid.

SB: A good modern-day example?

RFM: The three speeches made by General David Petraeus highlight my advice—the Surge and confronting mental health issues within the military were problems of enormous complexity. His speeches helped work toward solutions by explaining things clearly and without condescension. Genius resides in few words, not in many.

SB: Are you suggesting that we've entered some period of anti-intellectualism?

RFM: Don't confuse my advice with anti-intellectualism. Remember that the politicians, financiers, and academics who brought us the collapse of the Internet Bubble in 2000-2001, the Meltdown of 2008-2009, and have thus far failed to convince the public that they have a plan for recovery generally boast the best intellectual pedigrees our society offers.

SB: And audiences have changed.

RFM: They have and most politicians forget that the audiences "make" the speech. The Internet is forever—every stupid comment or miscue is an inexhaustible inheritance for opposition research. So here's the first rule, *pace* Socrates: Know Thyself, or at least, have a realistic grasp of one's own reputational memes.

SB: Would a recent example of this be Senator Kerry's run for the presidency in 2004?

RFM: In fact, that is one of my favorite examples—the so-called "swiftboating" of John Kerry. The Swiftboaters only played to powerful, pre-existing public memes or storylines that Kerry himself had established in the early 1970s. Trying to change the subject didn't work for him because of the Internet's elephantine memory. Kerry had more than three decades to heal his sore relations with veterans or assert his persona as an aggressive defender of US security interests. I don't think that he grasped his historical moment, that is, that the Internet could now not only resurrect the dead, but spread the gospel at light speed. Because Kerry never understood this, he never took corrective action (which he should have done long before his presidential candidacy). He never understood his audience, but his detractors did. And for that, Kerry paid a very high price.

SB: So once a politician has an honest understanding about what people really believe about him, and how the audience really understands themselves and their moment in time, then he's ready to give an effective political speech.

RFM: And that is because, as I have indicated, the audience "makes" the speech.

SB: How do a politician's principles enter into this?

RFM: Let me use a business model to explain how, in speeches and in life, politicians need to understand the correct role of "principles." Politicians should be thinking of themselves as fiduciaries, like a trustee of somebody else's money, say a pension fund. That trustee might passionately believe that buying pork belly futures is the road to riches, but if she's competent, she won't be buying pork belly futures for any trust account that she manages.

SB: Why not?

RFM: Because the First Principle, the one that outweighs what I may happen to believe, is *prudence.* You know the opposite of prudence? Any system that values public abstractions over private experience. Abstractions also go by the name of "ideology" and as John Adams once remarked, "ideology is the science of idiocy." In America, it still is.

SB: Who was the greatest political speechmaker in American history?

RFM: So many candidates, so little time! Abraham Lincoln will always have pride of place. But also consider his contemporaries, the lions of the nineteenth century Senate—especially Daniel Webster's Second Reply to Hayne, or Henry Clay's Compromise Speech and that of John Calhoun in 1850. In the eighteenth century, John Adams' summation to the jury in his defense of British soldiers accused of the Boston Massacre may well be the greatest courtroom performance in American history. Washington's Newburgh Address and Farewell Address rate more than just "honorable mention." In the last century, FDR's First Inaugural and Declaration of War speech, Eisenhower's Great Crusade speech and his Farewell Address, JFK's Inaugural, and Ronald Reagan's "Tear down this wall" speech will probably endure for centuries. But you forgot to ask me one question.

SB: And that is?

RFM: What were the *worst* American speeches!?

SB: And the winners are . . .

RFM: Alexander Stephens' "slavery is the cornerstone" speech, which did about as much to damage the Confederacy as Grant's capture of Richmond. General John Pope's Assumption of Command speech was a military-rhetorical disaster of the first order. Also, today's incumbents could learn a lot by understanding the reasons why Jimmy Carter's "Malaise Speech" helped tank him and elect Ronald Reagan. Boldfaced lying (as opposed to routine dissembling) never helps, and Richard Nixon's "I am not a crook" speech ranks with Bill Clinton's "I did not have sex with that woman."

SB: Is it fair to say you are trying to get members of an audience to think about what they're being told and isolate the persuasion *from the* persuasive strategy?

RFM: Exactly right. Then, and only then, can people step back and consider whether the next time some talking head or politician blows a whistle and yells, "Over the top!" they're going to march headlong into machine gun fire, or instead, ask themselves, *cui bono*? Afterwards if they still want to charge, at least they go knowingly. Whether you're voting, buying, paying taxes, or dying, it's always better to go in eyes open.

SB: Thank you.

RFM: The pleasure is all mine, thank you.

Bibliography

Abbott, John S.C., *The History of the Civil War in America* (Springfield, Massachusetts, 1866), 2 volumes.

Abbot, Willis John, *Blue Jackets of '98: A History of the Spanish-American War* (New York: Dodd, Mead and Company, 1899).

Adams, Henry, *The Education of Henry Adams* (New York: Oxford University Press, 1999).

Adams, Henry, *History of the United States of America During the Administrations of James Madison* (New York: Library of America, 1989).

Adams, Michael C.C., *Our Masters the Rebels: A Speculation on Union Military Failure in the East, 1861-1865* (Cambridge, Massachusetts: Harvard University Press, 1978).

Allen, Colonel Robert S., *Lucky Forward: The History of Patton's Third U.S. Army* (New York: Vanguard Press, 1947).

Applegate, Major Rex, *Kill or Get Killed: A Manual of Hand to Hand Fighting* (Harrisburg, Pennsylvania: Military Service Publishing Co., 1943).

Appleman, Roy E., *South to the Naktong, North to the Yalu* (Washington, D.C.: Center of Military History, United States Army, 1992 edition).

Appletons' *Cyclopaedia of American Biography*, edited by James Grant Wilson and John Fiske (New York: D. Appleton and Company, 1887), six volumes.

Aristotle, *Art of Rhetoric*, translated by John Henry Freese (Cambridge, Massachusetts: Harvard University Press, 2000).

Aristotle, *The Rhetoric of Aristotle*, translated with analysis and critical notes by J.E.C. Welldon (New York: MacMillan and Company, 1886).

Arrian (Lucius Flavius Arrianus 'Xenophon'), *Anabasis of Alexander, Books V-VII*, with an English translation by P.A. Brunt (Cambridge, Massachusetts: Harvard University Press, 1999).

Austin, A.B., *We Landed at Dawn: The Story of the Dieppe Raid* (New York: Harcourt, Brace and Company, 1943).

Bancroft, George, *History of the Formation of the Constitution of the United States of America* (New York: D. Appleton and Company, 1889), 2 volumes.

Barnett, Correlli, *Hitler's Generals* (New York: George Weidenfeld & Nicolson, 1989).

Basler, Roy P. ed., *Abraham Lincoln: His Speeches and Writings* (Cleveland, Ohio: Da Capo Press, Inc., 1946).

Basler, Roy P. ed.,*Collected Works of Abraham Lincoln* (New Brunswick, New Jersey: Rutgers University Press, 1953), 10 Volumes.

Basler, Roy P. ed., *Abraham Lincoln: His Speeches and Writings* (New York: Da Capo Press, 1990).

Bellamy, Chris, *Absolute War: Soviet Russia In the Second World War* (New York: Alfred A Knopf, 2007).

Bierce, Ambrose, *The Unabridged Devil's Dictionary*, edited by David E. Schultz and S.J. Joshi (Athens, Georgia: University of Georgia Press, 2001).

Billings, John D., *The History of the Tenth Massachusetts Battery of Light Artillery in the War of Rebellion, 1862-1865* (Boston: 1909).

Blair, Clay, *The Forgotten War: America in Korea, 1950-1953* (Annapolis: Naval Institute Press, 1987).

Blue-Eyed Child of Fortune: The Civil War Letters of Colonel Robert Gould Shaw, ed. Russell Duncan (Athens, Georgia: University of Georgia Press, 1992).

Blumenson, Martin, *Patton: The Man Behind the Legend, 1885-1945* (New York: Quill Press, 1985).

Blumenson, Martin, *The Patton Papers, 1940-1945* (Boston: Houghton Mifflin Company, 1974), 2 volumes.

Bonekemper, Edward H., III, *McClellan and Failure: A Study of Civil War Fear, Incompetence and Worse* (Jefferson, North Carolina: McFarland & Company, 2007).

Bradley, Omar, *A General's Life: An Autobiography*, by General of the Army Omar N. Bradley (New York: Simon and Schuster, 1983).

Britton, Anne Hartwell, and Reed, Thomas J., eds., *To My Beloved Wife and Boy at Home: The Letters and Diaries of Orderly Sergeant John F. L. Hartwell* (Cranbury, New Jersey: Associated University Presses, 1997).

Brooks, Victor, *The Boston Campaign: April 1775—March 1776* (Conshohocken, Pennsylvania: Combined Publishing, 1999).

Bryant, William Cullen, and Sidney Howard Gay, A *Popular History of the United States, from the First Discovery of the Western Hemisphere by the Northmen, to the End of the First Century of the Union of the States* (New York: Charles Scribner's Sons, 1879), 4 volumes.

Bunker Hill Monument Association, *Proceedings of the Bunker Hill Monument Association at the Annual Meeting, June 17, 1881, with the Address of The Hon. Robert C. Winthrop at the Inauguration of the Statue of Colonel William Prescott* (Boston: Bunker Hill Monument Association, 1881).

Burton, Brian K., *Extraordinary Circumstances: The Seven Days Battles* (Bloomington, Indiana: Indiana University Press, 2001).

Bush, George W., George W. Bush, "President's Address to the Nation, 10 January 2007," http://georgewbush-whitehouse.archives.gov/news/releases/2007 /01/print/20070110-7.html. Accessed June 23, 2009.

Butterworth, Hezekiah, *Young Folks' History of America* (Boston: Estes and Lauriat, 1882).

Caesar, Gaius Julius, *The Conquest of Gaul,* translated by S.A. Handford, revised with a new introduction by Jane F. Gardner (London: Penguin Books, 1982).

Field Manual No. 3-24, *Counterinsurgency* (Washington: Headquarters, Department of the Army, 2006).

Carlyle, Thomas, *History of Frederich II of Prussia, Called Frederick the Great* (London: Robson and Son, 1865), 8 volumes.

Carter, Robert Goldwaite, ed., *Four Brothers in Blue: A Story of the Great Civil War from Bull Run to Appomattox* (Norman, Oklahoma: University of Oklahoma Press, 1999).

Catton, Bruce, *Grant Moves South* (Boston: Little, Brown and Company, 1988).

Catton, Bruce, *A Stillness at Appomattox* (New York: Washington Square Press, 1958).

Centcom, Information about CENTCOM may found at http://www.centcom. mil/en/countries/aor/. Accessed August 16, 2009.

Clausewitz, Carl von, *On War*, edited by Anatol Rapoport (London: Penguin Books, 1968).

Coles, Harry L., *The War of 1812* (University of Chicago Press, 1966).

Comey, Lyman Richard, ed., *A Legacy of Valor: The Memoirs and Letters of Captain Henry Newton Comey, 2nd Massachusetts Infantry* (Knoxville: The University of Tennessee Press, 2004).

Commissar Order, http://www1.yadvashem.org/about_holocaust/documents/ part3/doc170.html. Accessed August 31, 2009.

Cooling, Benjamin Franklin, *Forts Henry and Donelson: The Key to the Confederate Heartland* (Knoxville, TN: The University of Tennessee Press, 1989)

Cozzens, Peter, *General John Pope: A Life for the Nation* (Chicago: University of Illinois Press, 2000).

Curtius, Quintus, *Quintus Curtius,* with an English translation by John C. Rolfe (Cambridge, Massachusetts: Harvard University Press, 1946), contained in *History of Alexander,* 2 volumes.

Davidson, Eugene, *The Trial of the Germans: An Account of the Twenty-two Defendants before the International Military Tribunal at Nuremberg* (New York: The MacMillan Company, 1966).

Dawkins, Richard, *The Selfish Gene* (New York: Oxford University Press, 2006).

Day, James M. compiler, *Texas Almanac, 1857-1873, A Compendium of Texas History* (Waco: Texian Press, 1967).

Dean, Eric T., Jr., *Shook Over Hell: Post-Traumatic Stress, Vietnam, and the Civil War* (Cambridge, Massachusetts: Harvard University Press, 1997).

Deare, Lewis, *Biography of James Lawrence, Esq., Late a Captain in the Navy of the United States* (New Brunswick, New Jersey: L. Deare, 1813).

The Declaration of Independence and the Constitution of the United States of America (Washington: The Cato Institute, 1998).

D'Este, Carlos, *Patton: A Genius for War* (New York: Harper Perennial, 1995).

Dewey, Admiral George, *Autobiography of George Dewey, Admiral of the Navy* (Annapolis: Naval Institute Press, 1987).

Dictionary of Military and Naval Quotations, ed. Robert Debs Heinl, Jr. (Annapolis: Naval Institute Press, 1966).

Dillon, Richard, *We Have Met the Enemy: Oliver Hazard Perry, Wilderness Commodore* (New York: McGraw Hill Book Company, 1978).

Diodorus of Sicily, with an English translation by C. Bradford Welles (Cambridge, Massachusetts: Harvard University Press, 1963).

Diogenes Laertius, *The Lives and Opinions of Eminent Philosophers*, translated by C.D. Yonge (London: George Bell and Sons, 1901).

Donnelly, James, "Written by James Donnelly, Late Corporal Co. D, 20th Massachusetts, to Capt. Robbins, from N.Y.C., August 10, 1897," MOLLUS Collection, Houghton Library, Harvard University.

Dustin, Kate, *The Selfish Meme: A Critical Assessment* (New York: Cambridge University Press, 2005).

Dyer, Frederick H., *A Compendium of the War of the Rebellion* (Des Moines, Iowa: unknown printer, 1908), reprint, Dayton, Ohio, Press of Morningstar Bookshop, 1978.

Dyess, William Edwin, *Bataan Death March: A Survivor's Account*, intro. Stanley L. Falk (Lincoln, Nebraska: Bison Books, 2002).

Eisenhower, Dwight D., "Soldiers, Sailors and Airmen of the Allied Expeditionary Force!" Http://www.eisenhower.archives.gov/research/Digital_ Documents/DDay/New%20PDFs/Order_of_the_Day.pdf. Accessed December 2, 2009.

Estes, Kenneth W., *The Marine Officer's Guide, 6th ed.* (Annapolis: U.S. Naval Institute Press, 2000).

Eliot, T.S., *Poems: 1909-1925* (London: The Faber Library No. 4, 2007).

Emmons, Col. William, *The Battle of Bunker Hill, or The Temple of Liberty; an Historic Poem in Four Cantos*, 10th edition, Col. William Emmons (Boston, 1865, first published 1839).

Fehrenbach, T.R., *This Kind of War* (Dulles, Virginia: Potomac Books, 2008).

Foote, Shelby, *The Civil War: A Narrative, Fort Sumter to Perryville* (New York: Vintage Books, 1958), 3 volumes.

Fox, Robin Lane, *Alexander the Great* (New York: Penguin Books, 2004).

Fox, William F., *Regimental Losses in The American Civil War, 1861-1865* (Albany, New York: Brandow Printing Company, 1898, reprint, Press of Morningside Bookshop, 1985).

Frederick the Great, "The Instruction of Frederick the Great for His Generals, 1747," translated by Brig. Gen. Thomas R. Phillips, contained in *Roots of Strategy.*

French, Allen, *The Siege of Boston* (New York: The Macmillan Company, 1911).

Friend, Jack, *West Wind, Flood Tide: The Battle of Mobile Bay* (Annapolis: Naval Institute Press, 2004).

Frothingham, Richard, *The Centennial: Battle of Bunker Hill* (Boston: Little, Brown, and Company, 1875).

Frothingham, Richard, *History of the Siege of Boston, and of the Battles of Lexington, Concord and Bunker Hill*, 4th ed. (Cranbury, New Jersey: The Scholar's Bookshelf, 2005, originally printed 1873).

Fuller, J.F.C., *A Military History of the Western World, From the Seven Days Battle, 1862, to the Battle of Leyte Gulf, 1944* (New York: Funk & Wagnalls Company, 1956), 3 volumes.

Geneva Conventions, Part I, Article 2, Geneva Convention Relative to the Treatment of Prisoners of War, 75 U.N.T.S. 135, entered into force October 21, 1950.

German American Bund Imagery, http://www.ushmm.org/wlc/media_ph.php? lang=en&ModuleId=10005684&MediaId=2745. Accessed November 15, 2009.

Gleaves, Albert, *James Lawrence: Captain, United States Navy, Commander of the "Chesapeake"* (New York: G.P. Putnam and Sons, 1904).

Goodrich, Charles A., *The Child's History of the United States, designed as a First Book of History for Schools* (Philadelphia: Thomas, Cowperthwait & Co., 1839).

Grant, U.S., *Personal Memoirs of U.S. Grant* (New York: Da Capo Press, Inc, 1982).

Grant, U.S., *Personal Memoirs of U.S. Grant, In Two Volumes* (New York: Charles L. Webster & Company, 1885), 2 volumes.

Green, Peter, *Alexander of Macedon, 356-323 B.C: A Historical Biography* (Los Angeles: University of California Press, 1991).

Guderian, Heinz, *Panzer Leader* (New York: Da Capo Press, 1996).

Hale, Edward Everett, "The Siege of Boston," contained in *The Memorial History of Boston*, edited by Justin Winsor (Boston: James R. Osgood and Company, 1881), 4 volumes.

Haley, James L., *Sam Houston* (Norman, Oklahoma: University of Oklahoma Press, 2002).

Hanson, Victor Davis, *The Western Way of War: Infantry Battle in Classical Greece* (Berkeley: University of California Press, 1989).

Hardin, Stephen L., *Texian Iliad: A Military History of the Texas Revolution, 1835-1836* (Austin: University of Texas Press, 1996).

Hatch, Louis Clinton, *The Administration of the American Revolutionary Army* (New York: Longmans, Green, and Co., 1904).

Hedges, Chris, *War Is a Force that Gives Us Meaning* (New York: Anchor Books, 2003).

Hickey, Donald R., *Don't Give Up the Ship!* (Urbana, Illinois: University of Illinois Press, 2007).

Hitler, Adolf, *Mein Kampf*, trans. Ralph Manheim (Boston: Houghton Mifflin Company, 1971).

Hitler, Adolf, *Hitler's Second Book: The Unpublished Sequel to Mein Kampf by Adolf Hitler*, Gerhard L. Weinberg, ed. (New York: Enigma Books, 2003).

Homer, *The Iliad*, trans. E.V. Rieu, rev. Peter Jones and D.C.H. Rieu (London: Penguin Books, 2003).

House of Representatives, http://clerk.house.gov/art_history/house_history/Joint_Meetings/jointAll.html. Accessed September 15, 2009.

Houston, Samuel, *The Writings of Sam Houston, 1813-1863,* edited by Amelia W. Williams and Eugene C. Barker *(*Austin, Texas: University of Texas Press, 1940), 8 volumes.

Humphreys, Colonel David, *An Essay on the Life of the Honorourable Major General Israel Putnam, Addressed to the State Society of the Cincinnati in*

Connecticut, with an Appendix containing an Historical and Topographical Sketch of Bunker Hill Battle by S. Swett (Boston: Samuel Avery, 1818).

Humphreys, Frank Landon, *The Life and Times of David Humphreys, Soldier—Statesman—Poet* (New York: G.P. Putnam's Sons, 1917), 2 volumes.

Huston, Cleburne, *Deaf Smith: Incredible Texas Spy* (Waco, Texas: Texian Press, 1973).

Iraq Study Group Report*: A Way Forward—A New Approach* (New York: Vintage Press, 2006).

Irving, Washington, *Biographies and Miscellanies*, edited by Pierre Irving (New York: G.P. Putnam and Son, 1869).

Jenkins, John H. ed., *The Papers of the Texas Revolution* (Austin, Texas: Presidial Press, 1973), 10 volumes.

Jomini, Henry, *Summary of the Art of War* (Philadelphia: J.P. Lippincott & Co., 1871).

Johnson, R. M., ed., *In the Words of Napoleon: The Emperor Day by Day*, ed. Johnston, with new material by Philip (London: Greenhill Books, 2002).

Jones, Melvin, ed., *Give God the Glory: Memoirs of a Civil War Soldier* (Grand Rapids, Michigan: Paris Press, 1979).

Kemp, Dixon and Louis Wiltz, *The Heroes of San Jacinto* (Houston, Texas: The Anson Jones Press, 1932).

Kershaw, Ian, *Hitler, 1936-1945: Nemesis* (New York, W.W. Norton, 2000).

King James Bible: Books of Deuteronomy, Joshua, Ecclesiastes, Gospel of St. Matthew.

Knox Papers, Microfilm Reel 6A, New York Historical Society.

Kohn, Richard H., *Eagle and Sword: The Federalists and the Creation of the Military Establishment in America, 1783-1802* (New York: The Free Press, 1975).

Krey, August C., *The First Crusade: The Accounts of Eyewitnesses and Participants* (Princeton, New Jersey: Princeton University Press, 1921).

Lack, Paul D., *The Texas Revolutionary Experience: A Political and Social History, 1835-1836* (College Station: Texas A&M University Press, 1992).

Lakoff, George, and Mark Johnson, *Metaphors We Live By* (Chicago: University of Chicago Press, 1980).

Lanham, Richard A., *A Handlist of Rhetorical Terms, Second Edition* (Berkeley: University of California Press, 1991).

Lavery, Brian, *Nelson's Navy: The Ships, Men, and Organization, 1793-1815* (Annapolis: Naval Institute Press, 1989).

Leckie, Robert, *Conflict: The History of the Korean War, 1950-1953* (Cambridge, Massachusetts: Da Capo Press, 1996).

Lend Me Your Ears: Great Speeches in History, selected and introduced by William Safire (New York: W.W. Norton & Company, 2004).

Lendon, J.E., *Soldiers & Ghosts: A History of Battle in Classical Antiquity* (New Haven: Yale University Press, 2005).

Livingston, Gary, *Fallujah, With Honor: First Battalion, Eighth Marine's Role in Operation Phantom Fury* (Topsail Beach, North Carolina: Caisson Press, 2006).

Livy, Titus, *The War with Hannibal, Books XXI-XXX of The History of Rome from its Foundation,* trans. Aubrey De Selincourt, ed. and intro. Betty Radice (London: Penguin Books, 1972).

Long, E.B., with Barbara Long, *The Civil War Day By Day: An Almanac, 1861-1865* (New York: Da Capo Press, 1971).

Lowell, James Russell, *The Poetical Works of James Russell Lowell* (Boston: Houghton, Mifflin and Company, 1890).

Maccabbees, Book Two, 2:49-69, *Harper Collins Study Bible* (New York: HarperCollins Publishers, 1993).

Madison, James, "Fifth Annual Message to Congress" (December 7, 1813), Miller Center of Public Affairs, Scripps Library & Multimedia Archive, available at http://millercenter.virginia.edu/scripps/digilibrary/prezspeeches/madison/jma_181 3_12007. Accessed January 3, 2008.

Marshall, S.L.A., *Men Against Fire: The Problem of Battle Command in Future War* (Gloucester, Massachusetts, Peter Smith, 1978).

McClellan, George B., Stephen W. Sears, *The Civil War Papers of George B. McClellan: Selected Correspondence, 1860-1865* (New York: Da Capo Press, 1989).

McFeely, William S., *Grant: A Biography* (New York: W.W. Norton & Company, 1982).

The MacMillan Dictionary of Political Quotations, ed. Louis D. Eigen and Jonathan Paul Seigal (New York: MacMillan, 1993).

McPherson, James, *Battle Cry of Freedom: The Civil War Era* (New York: Ballantine Books, 1989).

Mental Health Advisory Team, Final Report (MHAT) IV, Operation Iraqi Freedom 05-07, Office of the Surgeon Genera, Multinational Force-Iraq and Office of The Surgeon General, United States Army Medical Command, November 17, 2006.

Merridale, Catherine, *Ivan's War: Life and Death in the Red Army, 1939-1945* (New York: Picador, 2006).

Miller, Richard F., *In Words and Deeds: Battle Speeches in History* (Lebanon, New Hampshire: University Press of New England, 2008).

Moore, Frank, ed., *The Rebellion Record: A Diary of American Events* (New York: Arno Press, reprint 1977), 12 volumes.

Moore, Stephen L., *Eighteen Minutes: The Battle of San Jacinto and the Texas Independence Campaign* (New York: Republic of Texas Press, 2004).

Morgan, James A. III, *A Little Short of Boats: The Fights at Ball's Bluff and Edwards Ferry, October 21-22, 1861: A History and Tour Guide* (Ft. Mitchell, Kentucky: Ironclad Publishing, 2004).

Murdock, Harold, *Bunker Hill: Notes and Queries on a Famous Battle* (Boston: Riverside Press, 1927).

The Mind of Napoleon: A Selection from His Written and Spoken Words, ed. and trans. J. Christopher Herold (New York: Columbia University Press, 1955).

Nelson, Harold Hayden, *The Battle of Megiddo, A Dissertation Submitted to the Faculty of the Graduate School of Arts and Literature in Candidacy for the Degree of the Doctor of Philosophy* (Chicago: Private Edition, Distributed by the University of Chicago Libraries, 1913).

Nevins, Alan, *The War for the Union* (New York: Charles Scribner's Sons, 1960), 5 volumes.

Nicolson, Adam, *Seize the Fire: Heroism, Duty, and the Battle of Trafalgar* (New York: Harper Collins Publishers, 2005).

Niles, H., ed., *Niles' Weekly Register, From September 1815 to March 1816* (Baltimore: Franklin Press, n.d.), XI.

Nye, Roger H., *The Patton Mind: The Professional Development of an Extraordinary Leader* (Garden City Park, New York: Avery Publishing, 1993).

Obama, Barack, *Dreams from My Father: A Story of Race and Inheritance* (New York: Three Rivers Press, 2004).

Obama, Barack, *The Audacity of Hope: Thoughts on Reclaiming the American Dream* (New York: Crown Publishing Group, 2006).

Onasander, in *Aeneas Tacitus/Asclepiodotus/Onasander*, with an English translation of The Illinois Greek Club (Cambridge, MA: Harvard University Press, 1923).

Paine, Thomas, *The Life and Writings of Thomas Paine,* edited by Daniel Edwin Wheeler (New York: Vincent Parke and Company, 1908).

Patton, George S. Jr., "Speech of General George S. Patton, Jr. to His Third Army on the eve of The Normandy Invasion," edited by C.E. Dornbusch (Cornwall, N.Y.: Hope Farm Press, 1963).

"A General Talks To His Army," the Patton File, archives, Virginia Military Institute in Lexington Virginia.

Patton, George S. Jr., *War As I Knew It* (Boston: Houghton Mifflin Company, 1995) .

Patton, Jacob Harris, *Patton's Concise History of the American People, From the Discoveries of the Continent to 1876, The Centennial Year of the Nation's Independence* (New York: J.B. Ford & Company, 1876).

Patton, Robert H., *The Pattons (*Washington, DC: Brassey's Inc., 2004).

Peters, Thomas J. and Robert H. Waterman, in the book *In Search of Excellence: Lessons from America's Best-Run Companies* (New York: Harper Collins Business Essentials, 2004, reprint of 1982).

Pitney, John J. Jr., *The Art of Political Warfare* (Norman, Oklahoma: University of Oklahoma Press, 2000).

Plutarch, *Plutarch's Lives*, edited, notes and preface by Arthur Hugh Clough (New York: The Modern Library, 2001).

Pohl, James W., *The Battle of San Jacinto* (U.S.A.: Texas State Historical Association, 1989).

Porter, General Horace, *Campaigning with Grant* (New York: Da Capo Press, Inc., 1986).

Pritchett, W.K., *Ancient Greek Battle Speeches and a Palfrey* (Amsterdam: J.C. Gieben, 2002).

Pritchett, W.K., "The General's Exhortation in Greek Warfare," *Essays in Greek History* (Amsterdam: J.C. Gieben, 1994).

Province, Charles M., *The Unknown Patton* (New York: Bonanza Books, 1983)

Pulsifer, David, *An Account of the Battle of Bunker Hill, Compiled from Authentic Sources* (Boston: A. Williams and Co., 1872).

Quincy, Edmund, *Life of Josiah Quincy* (Boston: Little Brown and Company, 1874).

Rafuse, Ethan, *McClellan's War: The Failure of Moderation in the Struggle for Union* (Bloomington, Indiana: Indiana University Press, 2005).

Rawls, John, *A Theory of Justice* (New York: Oxford University Press, 1999).

Reitlinger, Gerald, *The House Built on Sand* (New York: Weidenfeld & Nicolson, 1960).

Rhea, Gordon C., *The Battles for Spotsylvania Court House and the Road to Yellow Tavern, May 7-12, 1864* (Baton Rouge: Louisiana State University Press, 1997).

Robert Hunt Rhodes, ed., *All for the Union: The Civil War Diary and Letters of Elisha Hunt Rhodes* (New York: Orion Books, 1985).

Ricks, Thomas E., *Fiasco: The American Military Adventure in Iraq* (New York: The Penguin Press, 2006).

Ricks, Thomas E., *The Gamble*: *General David Petraeus and the American Mlitary Adventure in Iraq, 2006-2008* (New York: The Penguin Press, 2009).

Ridgway, Matthew B., *The Korean War* (Garden City, New York: Doubleday & Company, Inc., 1967).

Ridgway, Matthew, "Korea, 1951, LtGen Matthew Ridgway: 'Why We Are Here,'" http://www.milhist.net/global/whywearehere.html. Accessed September 15, 2009.

Robinson, Linda, *Tell Me How This Ends: General David Petraeus and the Search for a Way Out of Iraq (*New York: Public Affairs, 2008).

Ropes, John Codman, *The Army Under Pope* (New York: Charles Scribner's Sons, 1881).

Rosenblatt, Emil & Ruth, ed., *Hard Marching Every Day: The Civil War Letters of Private Wilbur Fisk, 1861-1865* (Lawrence, Kansas: University Press of Kansas, 1992).

Runciman, Sir Steven, *A History of the Crusades* (Great Britain: The Folio Society, 1994), 3 volumes.

Rush, Richard, *Residence at the Court of London,* 3rd ed. (Philadelphia: Lippincott & Co, 1872).

Scott, Frank W., "Newspapers, 1775-1860," *The Cambridge History of English and American Literature in 18 Volumes* (1907–21), VOLUME XVI, Early National Literature, Part II; Later National Literature, Part I, Section 1, 1, 18 volumes.

Scott, Robert Garth, ed., *Fallen Leaves: The Civil War Letters of Major Henry Livermore Abbott* (Kent, Ohio: Kent State University Press, 1991).

Sears, Stephen, *George B. McClellan: The Young Napoleon* (New York: Da Capo Press, 1999).

Siddons, J. H., *A Familiar History of the United States of America, from the date of the earliest settlements down to the present time* (London: Darton and Hodge, 1865).

Shakespeare, William, "King Henry V," edited by Andrew Gurr, *The New Cambridge Shakespeare* (Cambridge, Great Britain: Cambridge University Press, 1995).

Shaw, Samuel, *The Journals of Major Samuel Shaw, The First American Consul at Canton,* edited by Josiah Quincy (Boston: Wm. Crosby and H.P. Nichols, 1847).

Skaggs, David Curtis, *Oliver Hazard Perry: Honor, Courage, and Patriotism in the Early U.S. Navy* (Annapolis: Naval Institute Press, 2006).

Smith, Mrs. E. Vale, *History of Newburyport, From the Earliest Settlement of the Country to the Present Time* (Boston: Damrell and Moore, 1854).

Solomon, Norman, ed., *The Talmud: A Selection* (New York: Penguin Classics, 2009).

Stackpole, Edward J., *From Cedar Mountain to Antietam* (Harrisburg, Pennsylvania: Stackpole Books, 1993).

Stone, Jon R., *Latin for the Illiterarti: Excorcising the Ghosts of a Dead Language (*New York: Routledge, 1996).

Story, Joseph, *An account of the Funeral Honours Bestowed on the remains of Capt. Lawrence and Lieut. Ludlow, with the Eulogy pronounced at Salem, on the occasion, by Hon. Joseph Story* (Boston: Joshua Beicher, 1813).

Strong, George Templeton, Allan Nevins and Milton Halsey Thomas, eds., *The Diary of George Templeton Strong: The Civil War, 1860-1865* (New York: The MacMillan Company, 1952), 4 volumes.

Sun Tzu, *The Art of War*, translated by Lionel Giles (El Paso, Texas: El Paso Norte Press, 2005).

Sweetenham, Carol, ed. and trans., *Robert the Monk's History of the First Crusade* (*Historia Iherosolimitana*), (Burlington, Vermont: Ashgate Publishing, 2005).

Swett, Samuel, *Historical and Topographical Sketch of Bunker Hill Battle*, contained in Colonel David Humphreys, *An Essay on the Life of the Honorable Major General Israel Putnam* (Boston: Samuel Avery, 1818).

Swett, Samuel, *Notes to His Sketch of* [the] *Bunker Hill Battle* (Boston: Munroe and Francis, 1825).

Thomas, Evan, *John Paul Jones: Sailor, Hero, Father of the American Navy* (New York: Simon & Schuster, 2003).

Thucydides, *The Landmark Thucydides: A Comprehensive Guide to the Peloponnesian War*, edited by Robert B. Strassler (New York: Touchstone, 1996).

Tolbert, Frank X., *The Day of San Jacinto* (New York: The Pemberton Press, 1959).

Truman, Harry S, *Memoirs by Harry S Truman* (Garden City, N.Y.: Doubleday & Company, Inc., 1956), 2 volumes.

United States Marine Corps, http://parents.marines.com/page/Personal-Growth.jsp. Accessed July 19, 2009.

Vandiver, Frank E., *Mighty Stonewall* (College Station, Texas: Texas A&M University Press, 1957, reprint 1988).

Vegetius (Publius Flavius Vegetius Renatus), *The Military Institutions of the Romans* (*De Re Militari*), by Flavius Vegetius Renatus, translated from the Latin by Lieutenant John Clark, *Roots of Strategy: The 5 Greatest Military Classics of All*

Time, ed. Brig. Gen. Thomas R. Phillips, U.S. Army (Mechanicsburg, Pennsylvania: Stackpole Books, 1985).

Vulgate Bible (*Douay-Rheims Bible: Translated from the Latin Vulgate, Diligently Compared with the Hebrew, Greek and other Editions in Diverse Languages*, Oil City Pennsylvania: Baronius Press, 2003).

Wace, Master, *Master Wace, His Chronicle of the Norman Conquest, From the Roman de Rou,* trans. Edgar Taylor (London: William Pickering, 1837).

Warlimont, Walter, *Inside Hitler's Headquarters, 1939-1945*, trans. R.H. Perry (New York: Frederick A. Praeger, Publishers, 1962).

Warner, Ezra, *Generals in Blue: Lives of the Union Commanders* (Baton Rouge: Louisiana State University Press, 1999).

Washington, George, *George Washington's Newburgh Address: A Massachusetts Historical Society Picture Book*, Foreword by Bernhard Knollenberg (Massachusetts Historical Society, 1966).

War of the Rebellion: Official Records of the Union and Confederate Armies in the War of Rebellion (Washington D.C: Government Printing Office, 1894-1922), 128 volumes.

Webster, Daniel, *An Address Delivered at the Completion of the Bunker Hill Monument, June 17, 1843* (Boston: Tappan and Dennet, 1843).

Webster, Daniel, An Address Delivered at the Laying of the Corner Stone of the Bunker Hill Monument, June 17, 1825 (Boston: Tappan & Dennet, 1843).

Weems, M. L., *The Life of George Washington with Curious Anecdotes Equally Honorable to Himself, and Exemplary to His Young Countrymen* (Philadelphia: Joseph Allen, 1833).

Weintraub, Stanley, *George Washington's Christmas Farewell: A Mount Vernon Homecoming* (New York: Free Press, 2003).

Welles, Gideon, *Diary of Gideon Welles, Secretary of the Navy Under Lincoln and Johnson, with an Introduction by John T. Morse, Jr., Volume I: 1861—March 30, 1864* (Boston: Houston Mifflin Company, 1911), 3 volumes.

Wendy's, Where's the Beef? Commercial, http://www.youtube.com/watch?v=Ug75diEyiA0. Accessed November 3, 2009.

Wert, Jeffrey D., *The Sword of Lincoln: The Army of the Potomac* (New York: Simon & Schuster, 2005).

Widmer, Ted, ed., *American Speeches: Political Oratory from the Revolution to the Civil War* (New York: Library of America, 2006).

Wills, Garry, *Lincoln at Gettysburg: The Words That Remade America* (New York: Simon & Schuster, 1992).

Williams, Alfred M., *Sam Houston and the War of Independence in Texas* (Boston: Houghton Mifflin, 1893).

Winthrop, Robert C., "The Unveiling of the Statue of Colonel William Prescott: An Oration Delivered on Bunker Hill, June 17, 1881," *Addresses and Speeches on Various Occasions, from 1878 to 1886* (Boston: Little Brown and Company, 1886).

Wisehart, M.K., *Sam Houston: American Giant* (Washington: Robert B. Luce, 1962).

Xenophon, *Cyropaedia*, translated by H.G. Dakyans (Whitefish, Montana: Kessinger Publishing, n.d.).

Xenophon, *The Persian Expedition*, translated by Rex Warner (London: Penguin Books, 1972).

Websites

Obama, Barack:

"Inaugural Address," January 20, 2009, http://www.whitehouse.gov/blog/inaugural-address/. Accessed September 29, 2009.

""A New Beginning," June 4, 2009, http://www.whitehouse.gov/the_press_office/Remarks-by-the-President-at-Cairo-University-6-04-09/. Accessed September 29, 2009.

"Remarks by the President to a Joint Session of Congress on Health Care," September 9, 2009, http://www.whitehouse.gov/the_press_office/Remarks-by-the-President-to-a-Joint-Session-of-Congress-on-Health-Care/.

"Remarks by the President at Memorial Service at Fort Hood, November 10, 2009, www.whitehouse.gov/the-press-office/remarks-president-memorial- service-fort-hood. Accessed November 12, 2009.

Petraeus, David., Gen.:

Petraeus, David, H., "Petraeus Addresses Coalition, Iraqi Partners," February 10, 2007, MNF-Iraq.com. The official document is available from http://www.mnf-iraq.com/index.php?option=com_content&task=view&id=9830&itemid=128. Accessed on June 22, 2009.

"General Petraeus' Testimony to the Senate Armed Service Committee," April 8-9 2008, http://www.mnf-iraq.com/images/stories/Press_briefings/2008/April/080408_petraeus_testimony.pdf. Accessed July 10, 2009.

General David H. Petraeus, http://www.mnf-iraq.com/images/CGs_ Messages/ 080915_gen_petraeus_final_letter_to_troops.pdf. Accessed August 20, 2009.

"Charts to accompany the testimony of GEN David H. Petraeus, April 8-9, 2008, http://www.mnf-Iraq.com/images/stories/Press_briefings/2008/april/080408_petra eus_handout.pdf. Accessed July 10, 2009.

"Charts to accompany the testimony of GEN David H. Petraeus," *Report to Congress on the Situation in Iraq, by Commander David H. Petraeus, 10-11 September 2007.* http://foreignaffairs.house.gov/110/pet091007.pdf. Accessed August 20, 2009.

Petraeus Biography, http://www.centcom.mil/en/fact-sheets/biography-gen.-david-h.-petraeus.html.

Polls

Gallup:

http://www.gallup.com/poll/124736/Palin-Favorable-Up-Slightly-Obama-Hol ds-Steady.aspx. Accessed January 20, 2010.

http://www.gallup.com/poll/125096/Obama-Averages-Approval-First-Year-O ffice.aspx. Accessed January 20, 2010.

Rasmussen Reports:

http://www.rasmussenreports.com/public_content/politics/current_events/heal thcare/september_2009/health_care_reform. Accessed December 1 2009

http://www.rasmussenreports.com/public_content/politics/toplines/pt_survey _toplines/january_2010/toplines_health_care_january_16_17_2010.   Accessed January 20, 2010.

Washington, George

"Papers of George Washington," http://gwpapers.virginia.edu/documents/ revolution/farewell.

Films, Television, Paintings

Avenge December 7 (1942)

City Confidential, television series, 103 episodes, 1999-2006.

The Death of General Warren at Battle of Bunker Hill (1786), located at the Boston Museum of Fine Arts, Boston, Massachusetts (painting), John Trumbull

December 7 (1943)

Gladiator (2000)

Knute Rockne, All American (1940)

The Man Who Shot Liberty Valance (1962)

Napoleon Crossing the Saint-Bernard Pass (1801), located at Chateau Malmaison, Rueil-Malmaison, France (painting), Jacques Louis David

Patton (1970)

Pearl Harbor: Now It Can Be Shown (1942)

Journal Articles

Agnew, Major Sir Crispin of Lochnaw Bt, "Regimental Miscellany: Famous Men of the Regiment, General Sir Andrew Agnew of Lochnaw Bt—28 Years a Fusilier," *The Journal of the Royal Highland Fusiliers*, Winter 2000, Volume XXIV, Number 2.

Barker, Eugene C., "The San Jacinto Campaign," *The Quarterly of the Texas Historical Association*, Volume IV, No. 4, April 1901.

Barthes, Roland, *Aspen,* Numbers 5+6, Fall-Winter 1967, Roaring Fork Press.

Bliese, John R.E., "Rhetoric and Morale: A Study of Battle Orations from the Central Middle Ages," *Journal of Medieval History* 15 (1989).

Clark, Michael, "Did Thucydides Invent the Battle Exhortation?" *Historia: Journal of Ancient History* 44 (1995), Heft 3.

Cox, Gary P., Book Review, *The Journal of Military History*, Volume 73, Number 3, July 2009.

Erhardt, C.T.H.R., "Speeches before Battle?" *Historia: Journal of Ancient History* 44 (1995), Heft 1.

Forster, Dr. Jurgen, "The Wehrmacht and the War of Extermination against the Soviet Union," available at Yad Vashem website, www1.yadvashem.org/untoldstories/documents/studies/Jurgen_Forster.pdf.

Godwin, Mike, "Meme, Counter-meme," http://www.wired.com/wired/archive/2.10/godwin.if.html. Accessed September 24, 2009.

Halsey, Ashley, "Ancestral Gray Cloud Over Patton," *American History Illustrated*, March 1984.

Hillgruber, Andreas, "War in the East and the Extermination of the Jews," available at, www.1yadvashem.org/untoldstories/documents/studies/Andreas_ Hillgruber.pdf. Accessed September 11, 2009.

Journals of the Continental Congress, 1774-1789, Worthington Ford, et al, Volume XXIV: 1783, January 1-August 29 (1922: GPO), 34 volumes.

Kohn, Richard H., "The Inside History of the Newburgh Conspiracy: America and the Coup d'Etat," *The William and Mary Quarterly: A Magazine of Early American History,* Third Series, Number 2, Vol. XXVII.

Kuykendall, "Recollections of the Campaign," *The Quarterly of the Texas State Historical Association*, Volume IV, Number 4, April 1901.

Hansen, Mogens Herman, "The Battle Exhortation in Ancient Historiography: Fact or Fiction?" *Historia: Journal of Ancient History* 42 (1993), Heft 2.

Petraeus, David H., "Learning Counterinsurgency: Observations from Soldiering in Iraq," *Military Review*, January-February 2006.

Petreaus, David H., "Iraq: Building on Progress," *Army*, October 2008.

Sparks, S.F., "Recollections of S.F. Sparks," *The Quarterly of the Texas State Historical Association*, Volume XII, Number 1, July 1908.

Weingartner, James J., "Massacre at Biscari: An American War Crime," *The Historian: A Journal of History*, Vol. LII, No. 1, November 1989.

Index

(For the convenience of the reader, speakers and speeches that are quoted at length are boldfaced.)

probable failure to carry public opinion, 257-257; compared with Grant's nighttime ride: moral capital and political capital, 258; polls, 258-259; failure to empathize, 259; **Fort Hood Eulogy**, 260-277; transforming the dead, 267-269; abstracting the dead: by particulars, 269-270; attributing larger meaning: diversity, community, a generation, 271-273; Greatest Generation meme, 272; posterity, 273; E Pluribus Unum persuasive strategy, 273; 274-275; Foreshadowing Narrative, 273, 275-277; Murders-As-Combat-Casualties Meme, 275; brings war from Afghanistan to Texas, 276; politics of speech, compared with Ridgway, 276-277; connecting Fort Hood with Afghan War, 276-277; connecting speech with larger policy deliberations, 276-277

Odierno, General Ray, 100, 118, 123

OEF (Operation Enduring Freedom), 220, 228

Ohio, 130

OIF (Operation Iraqi Freedom), 220, 228

Old Glory, 23

Old Guard (Macedonian), 77

Onasander, xx

101st Airborne Division (Air Assault), 90, 109, 113

Opis, xix, xxii

Oval Office (as meme), 221

Overland Campaign, 181

Paine, Thomas (*The Crisis*), 231

Pakistan, 115, 265

Panzergruppe 2, 164

Paris (France), 196

Parmenio, 72-73

Patroclus, 261

*Patton (*film), xix, 41

Patton, General George Jr., xi, xxxiv, 1, 10, 109-112, 128, 143; "Blood-and-Guts," 282; **The Speech**, xix, **xliv, xlv; 41-55 (analyzed);** compared with Petraeus' AOC, 87; 88, 99, 110, 279; Assumption of Command Speech, 44; Acknowledging Predecessors, 44; Authority, 44; Denial, 45; Managing Expectations, 44; Staging, 44; slapping incidents (as memes), 48-49, 109; *Life Magazine*, July 7, 1941,50; opposite temperament of U.S. Grant, 52; "visible personality," 53

Patton, Robert, 53

Pearl Harbor, 50

Pearson, Private First Class Michael, 265

Peller, Clara, 169-171

Pelosi, Speaker of the House Nancy, 246

Peninsula Campaign, 4, 130, 137

Pericles, xl-xli, 261

Perry, Major James, 60214-215

Perry, Oliver Hazard, xvi, xxxiv, xxxvii, xlv, 172-176, 181, 185, 204, 210, 216; **"We have met the enemy and they are ours,"** 173-176

"Don't Give Up The Ship!," 204

Persian Gulf, 74, 77

Persian, modes of dress, 82; invasion of Greece, 82

Peter the Hermit, 21

Petraeus, General David H., xxiii, xxxiv, 85-126, three speeches analyzed; *Newsweek* cover, 88; reputation memes, 89-90; January 2007 Senate confirmation hearings, 90, 94; Senate confirms him as CENTCOM chief, 115; **Assump-**